THE AGE BETWEEN

Adolescence and Therapy

Derek Miller, M.D.

THE AGE BETWEEN
Adolescence and Therapy

Jason Aronson Inc.

Northvale, New Jersey
London

10 9 8 7 6 5 4 3 2 1

New Printing 1986

Library of Congress Cataloging In Publication Data

Miller, Derek.
  The Age Between: Adolescence and Therapy

  Rev. ed. of: Adolescence, 1974.
  Includes bibliographies and index.
  1. Adolescent psychiatry. 2. Adolescent psychology.
I. Title. [DNLM: 1. Adolescent psychiatry. 2. Adoles-
cent psychology. WS 462 M647a]
RJ503.M55 1983   616.89   83-3893
ISBN 0-87668-639-0

For my wife — who has been both loving and patient

Preface

The development of personality in adolescents is modified by the world in which they live; the reverse is also true. Unfortunately this may not be well understood by helping adults, who include not only professionals in the social and behavioral sciences, but also the nuclear family, the extended family, and extraparental adults.

Professionals often do not avail themselves of what is known about brain function, mental processes, and the biochemistry of mood changes. They may not be aware of the biological, sexual, social, and psychological roots of behavior in the young, or in themselves, as they interact with their charges. In order to understand and to solve the problems adolescents have within our society, professionals—including family practitioners, parents, and teachers—need to understand something of child-rearing and maturational processes, and how these are influenced by social systems and personal interactions.

For satisfactory personality development in childhood and early adolescence, the nuclear family is most important. In Western society, in middle and late adolescence, the peer group and extraparental adults are at least as significant. The school is often the most influential social system impacting on the young.

The most common complaints of adolescents are of loss, helplessness, and emptiness. Adolescents often project their despair, see only the corruption of society and the foolhardiness of its leaders, and seek a solution in drugs, in alcohol, or in delinquency. Those who become somewhat alienated may do well, but never achieve their full potential as human beings.

Traditional values of integrity and respect for human needs are threatened when the nuclear family is fragmented by divorce, separation, or death. In our society families are often isolated from each other, and peer groups and extraparental adult relationships are disrupted by progression through a school system that fosters a yearly making and breaking of personal relationships.

Individuals are often reared with little sense as to where they come from. The media, and especially television, foster instant solutions which are often violent, or at best superficial; children become products of fast time and no place. Nuclear war, or its threat, is the ultimate rapid solution.

Prevention of maladjustment has always been an appropriate mental health goal. The intention of this book is to offer to parents and professionals alike the help they need to guide individuals into maturity. In writing this book, I have attempted to keep jargon at a minimum so that all readers, regardless of background, will be able to take what they need, and hopefully apply it, with love and understanding.

The students of Northwestern University Medical School helped in the production of the second edition of this book by an exchange of ideas in many seminars. My secretary, Ellen Karp, struggled with my writing. The children and the young people I talked with on two continents in three decades are the real authors.

Contents

Part III DISTURBANCES AND THERAPY

PART I

NORMAL DEVELOPMENT IN ADOLESCENCE

Chapter 1

Early Adolescence

DEFINITION OF ADOLESCENCE

It is convenient to think of adolescence in terms of an age range, and it is generally assumed that adolescence starts at age eleven or twelve and is completed at age nineteen or twenty. Nevertheless, such rigid age limits are not a satisfactory way of delineating this developmental period.

The physiological changes of puberty invariably produce psychological reactions, which are essentially independent of the culture and include experiences that, although gratifying, also lead to feelings of helplessness and a consequent hypersensitivity to comments by adults. Such comments are easily seen as hypercritical. If, for any reason, biological puberty is not experienced, adolescence is a hollow psychosocial event. Views of adolescence vary from culture to culture, of course, and from class to class in the same culture. Adolescence is, initially, a biosociopsychological process that has been defined as "a process of adaptation to puberty" (Blos, 1962). An additional problem for parents, teachers, and society, in general, is that late developers, although they are physically and emotionally underdeveloped, often behave as if they were adolescents and even consider themselves to be adolescents. So, to define adolescence as "adaptation to puberty" is not necessarily accurate. The nature of adolescence is best understood if the world in which young people live, their own or their family's life-style, and the physical changes of growth are all considered. The personality of any adolescent boy or girl also depends on earlier life experiences: a healthy adolescence depends to a large extent on a healthy infancy and childhood. Without the physical changes of puberty, however, true adolescence does not occur. Thus, adolescence is the last great staging post on the way to maturity.

EXPERIENCE OF ADOLESCENCE

The life experience of individual adolescents depends on how they see and feel the world. The social environment of an adolescent is important, and includes where and how the family lives, whether the family is intact, what the father, and often the mother, does to earn a living, and the school the adolescent attends. City, small town, or country living all make some difference, as does the size of a family's house or apartment and the number of bedrooms. Family life-style obviously affects the behavior and experience of adolescents. Parents who have brought up their children with a peaceful, loving authority may be reproached for being dull, old-fashioned, or "not with it," but their children will not noisily complain that they are uncaring. Highly permissive parents are often felt to be disinterested, even if their children talk of them positively. Children react to how family members relate to each other; an adolescent from an "impulsive," turbulent, shouting family is likely to express anxieties in turbulence and noise; an adolescent from an inhibited "controlling" family may have difficulty expressing feelings (Miller, 1980). Young people who are aware of where they come from, who have not moved so often that they have no sense of place, are generally more secure than those whose families are highly mobile. The commonly made demand for instant satisfaction also distorts adolescent development.

MATURATIONAL OR CHRONOLOGICAL AGE?

If the stages of adolescence could be grouped by age, it would be very convenient. In many ways, society attempts to do this, particularly in school, where age tends to be linked with the expectation of certain types of behavior and academic achievement. This preoccupation with age continues, despite the fact that parents who have several children know perfectly well that age, as an arbiter of capacities in adolescence, is not reliable. At age fifteen or sixteen, one adolescent may be quite mature, whereas another may be physically and emotionally immature. From an emotional, educational, and social viewpoint, maturational age is more significant than chronological age, despite the socially induced preoccupation with the latter that is often held by young people.

Because they compare themselves to one another, adolescents tend to be preoccupied with the issue of fairness. In managing the lives of young people, concerned adults are often preoccupied with a similar issue: Will their actions appear fair to their offspring? Of course, what is truly fair depends on what is best for the adolescent's well-being, and all men are not equal, least of all because they are of similar age. So, in addition to going along with the adolescent's concept of fairness, adults also tend to go along with the age sensitivity of the adolescent. As part of their maturation to adulthood, adolescents also compare themselves on the basis of age, but society does not need to reinforce this. A thirteen-year-old boy, for example, compares himself to others of the same age to see whose physique is more developed, who is socially more successful, physically able, or academically advanced. Since, in our society, adolescents compare their educational progress, which varies with maturational age, schools in which performance is based on age norms may make it even more difficult for many adolescents to progress without unnecessary stress and strain. Although academic ability varies, depending on the individual, a comparison made on the basis of age is certainly not a valid comparison of potential (Mussen and Jones, 1958).

Some of the confusion about typical adolescent behavior can be resolved if the total developmental period is described in three stages. These stages overlap to a certain extent; the divisions can be seen more clearly in some social classes and cultures than in others. Each stage covers about three years. Furthermore, some qualities that are typical of both individual psychology and parent/adolescent interaction in adolescence, are present in childhood, as well as in adulthood, at least in some relationships. Similarly, some qualities highlighted in the early part of the age period are also present later on. Those young people who ultimately go on to some form of further training after the age of seventeen or eighteen show all these stages more clearly. The stages are, however, less clearly defined in young people who leave school early and who are thus exposed to the pressures of a complex society that demands a more adult behavior.

Adolescent turmoil, about which there has been much argument (Offer, 1969), typically is seen in early adolescence, the period of puberty, which lasts three years or more, from age eleven or twelve to age fourteen or fifteen. Mid-adolescence, the period of identification (This is what I am) and self-realization, lasts from age fourteen or fifteen to age seventeen or eighteen; during this period oedipal conflicts should be resolved. Late adolescence, the period of coping, lasts from age seventeen or eighteen to age nineteen or twenty. This last period is associated with advanced training for specific roles in society, but for young people who leave school and attempt to earn a living at sixteen, late adolescence is largely condensed into the mid-adolescent period. Both middle and late adolescence may appear superficially as periods of relative calm, especially in those who are conformists (Lederer, 1964).

In societies in which the nuclear family is fragmented, due to death or divorce—in which children experience, at best, an absence of shared parenting, especially when an extended stable network of involved adults and peers is not available—some attitudes of early adolescence persist into adulthood. This is highly significant when a preoccupation with the perceived attitudes of others continues. Self-esteem comes to depend on a mysterious "they"; unknown others must be fantasized to approve individual attitudes and behavior.

PHYSICAL DEVELOPMENT

Puberty in the male has been variously defined as the time of the first ejaculation, when fertilization becomes possible, or as the second stage of pubic hair development (Kestenberg, 1968). If behavioral change is significant, it is more helpful to regard it as a period starting from the beginning growth of testicles in boys to the time when there is active production of spermatazoa. In females, puberty lasts from the onset of an increase in pubic hair, followed by the budding of breasts, the beginning of vaginal secretion and the enlargement of breasts, to the time when menstruation begins.

In both sexes, these physical changes are associated with a rapid rise of follicle-stimulating hormone (FSH) and lutenizing hormone (LH) and seventeen ketosteroids. There is a greater production of estrogens in girls than in boys, and a greater production of androgens in boys than in girls (Nathanson et al., 1941).

Puberty usually begins at about the age of eleven plus in boys, ten plus in girls. Along with physical changes in secondary sex characteristics, it is also associated with a rapid increase in rate of growth. As pubertal changes occur, girls are suddenly likely to find themselves taller than boys of the same age. Because in childhood boys are bigger and heavier than girls, this change adds to the general feeling of confusion both boys and girls experience. Between the ages of eleven and thirteen, and for the subsequent two years, the average girl is taller than the average boy of the same age for the only time in her life. After the age of fifteen to sixteen, most girls have reached their adult height. Boys have their maximum growth spurt about two years later than girls, from age thirteen to fifteen, and they may continue to add to their height until their early twenties (Tanner, 1962).

Girls usually tend to gain weight between the ages of ten and fifteen. Obsession with dieting may then occur and is often associated with the development of self-starvation syndromes, especially anorexia nervosa. Normally, girls reach their adult weight after the age of eighteen. Boys put on weight rapidly in early adolescence and make small gains until age nineteen or twenty; muscular development depends on more adult androgen levels and thus does not become a predominant issue until well into middle adolescence. Weight training should not be permitted before this time. Most girls are well into the pubertal stage of development by the age of thirteen, most boys by fourteen, although there is a significant number of slow maturers—who more often are boys. Later maturation is often hereditary.

A girl's first periods are frequently irregular, and regular monthly ovulation often does not occur for about two to three years after the onset of regular periods. This explains why many sexually active early-adolescent girls do not become pregnant. First periods tend to be spaced further apart and last about a day longer, on the average, than would be expected in a mature woman. They are usually associated with premenstrual tension. Regular periods are usual about a year after menstruation has begun (Montagu, 1946), when girls acquire the feeling that it is a natural and controllable event (Deutsch, 1944). The change in the shape of the larynx, which leads to boys' voices beginning to get lower in pitch and to break, occurs at the end of the pubertal period. In boys, as in girls, the body gradually changes shape: girls' hips get wider relative to the rest of their bodies; boys' hips get narrower. As boys become more heavily muscled, hair appears on their face, initially in the moustache area and at the hairline at the side of their face, and then over the chin and neck.

During puberty, the sweat glands of both sexes become more active, as do the glands that supply oil to the skin and hair. These sebaceous glands are sometimes overactive during early adolescence, which may be one of the causes of acne. There is no clinical evidence that acne is related to diet (junk foods, soft drinks, or candy), and it is unjustified to pressure adolescents with acne to abstain from certain foods and drinks. All this does is inflict guilt.

BEHAVIORAL CHANGES AT THE ONSET OF PUBERTY

The first warnings of the onset of adolescence are usually family-related. Parents may notice a change in the behavior of a child toward them. Boys of ten, for example, often appear to become preoccupied with the sexuality of their mothers. A boy may comment on how pretty his mother is; he may contrive to touch her breasts as she passes by; he may comment that he, in some way, wishes to be his mother's "boyfriend." Similarly, girls become more feminine for and more seductive toward their fathers. These behavioral changes begin to be apparent before there is very much evidence of breast development in girls; there is, similarly, little in the way of obvious physical change in boys. There are few adequate studies of the relationship between physical change and this type of behavior. Only a general statement can be made: Just before the dramatic onset of puberty, children begin to rehearse their ultimate roles, as sexually aware men and women, within the safety of their family. This process is less possible in single parent families and in those in which significant emotional disturbance or child abuse is present. These emotional signs of coming adolescence usually are seen just prior to the growth of the testicles and an increase in penis size in boys, when there is a low concentration of gonadotrophic and testicular androgen in the urine; in girls, the bony pelvis begins to grow and the nipples to bud, but the estrogen concentration in the urine is still low (Wilkins, 1965).

When children are besieged by the emotions associated with the rapid changes of puberty, there is a further change in their attitude toward their parents. There is some clinical evidence that early adolescents are as preoccupied with the sexuality of their parents as are younger children, but this awareness is denied, and it is not evident from their behavior. Early adolescents may strenuously deny that their parents have sex, and it is often emotionally painful for them if their parents have more children. Their intense embarrassment may border on the shame that their parents are not visible to the world as sexually "dead."

Early adolescence is associated with the wish to be free of dependent feelings on parents that are viewed as childish. Peers are used as support in this "struggle" for freedom against perceived parental domination and possessiveness. For example, when arguments about bedtime occur, allegations are made about the hours to which other children are allowed to stay up. When going out with friends at night becomes an issue, parents are told about how late other children are allowed out. Similar problems include spending money, helping at home, doing homework, and having freedom to choose clothing. Part-time work is often sought, and some children may be babysitting or running a paper route before they are sufficiently mature to handle the demands of such jobs.

Children compare themselves with friends of the same age to try to obtain more freedom and independence; then they assess themselves by the amount of freedom and independence they have managed to obtain compared to that of their friends. So it is inevitable that parents usually will not be told about their children's friends who have less freedom. Parents also are rarely told about parties at which adults are present as chaperons. Instead, the adolescent may imply that all self-respecting fathers and mothers go out on such occasions and that their friends will see them as weak and inferior, if their parents stay around.

The adolescent concept of fairness is often used as an attempt, consciously or unconsciously, to manipulate parents. Everyone likes to feel that they are being fair and just; many parents find it easier to say "yes" than to say "no." Nevertheless, each family unit has its own standards. Parents want their children to get along with their peers, but significant adolescent relationships are not lost if clothes do not exactly match or if one youngster has to be home earlier than the others. Paradoxically, it may be a matter of some pride to boys and girls that their parents insist on certain standards. In the absence of such standards, children may impose them as rigorously as their parents. The more confused is the adolescent's background the more rigid is the demand for conformity with peers—most clearly demonstrated in the clothing of punk rockers, gang members, and the like.

Parents are used by their adolescent children as sounding boards against which to test feelings of independence. There is no expectation that every request will be granted. Adolescents, particularly during early adolescence, tend to ask for more than they really expect to get; thus, they behave like government agencies when they ask the Treasury Department for money. Some fourteen-year-old boys will talk of asking their fathers for things just to see how they will reply.

For both sexes, early adolescence is a stage at which development of control over sexual and aggressive feelings begins to be particularly important. It is also the stage at which an adolescent's ability to feel like a man or a woman and to feel independent of a parent is expressed. In childhood there is always some sense of separateness, which shows in such declarations as "No, I don't want to come in to eat." In the teens this demand becomes more explicit: "Leave me alone."

In both boys and girls, early adolescence involves the development of a sense of mastery over themselves and their environment, while they continue to develop a sense of personal autonomy.

MASCULINE VERSUS FEMININE EXPERIENCE

Boys tend to be more physically uncomfortable about the changes in body size and shape than do girls, although many girls also experience a period of shy embarrassment. The need to gain control over their own bodies and impulses, as they are developing feelings of separateness from their families, creates a particular problem for early adolescents. This is a time of rapid growth, often involving the experience of being out of control. With their dramatic increase in height, boys are no longer sure of where their own bodies are in space, and many become clumsy. Their voices change at just about the same time; although ultimately, the voice will deepen, there is at first a startling variation in loudness and pitch, which increases with emotional stress. An additional problem for boys is that as their penis and testes grow larger, they become quite intensely aware of genital excitement, which is felt to be quite out of their control. Boys can gain active mastery over this state by masturbation: girls have no alternative but to accept the menarche. This event, short of self-starvation, is uncontrollable by an individual. Knowledge makes it less anxiety-provoking and more desirable, but it does not control the uncontrollable. Boys can understand in part what is happening to their bodies, since they have erections; girls may be sexually aroused, but not quite understand what is going on inside them.

Many adolescent boys cope with these changes by an apparent emotional withdrawal from the real world. During this time, both boys and girls may chatter, but they do not appear to be really interested in communicating their thoughts, feelings, or ideas to others, and particularly to adults. Nor are they very interested in hearing what adults have to say. "Are you deaf?" is a common cry from parents. Teachers who see a child over a period of two to three years lament that the youngster who previously paid attention in class goes through a period of six months or so as a restless, difficult daydreamer. In addition to this emotional withdrawal, early adolescents also have a need to retreat, physically, from the adult world, which includes their families. This carries implications for the design of homes and schools. Houses and apartments with no space or physical privacy for adolescents may drive them out on the streets.

THE NEEDS AND BEHAVIOR OF BOYS

It is usual for boys to go through a period of incoordination, during which they are clumsy, and always fall over themselves. Often in association with a period of rapid growth, they are lazy and disinterested in their appearance. At puberty, boys may want to stay in bed in the morning for hours. Along with this apparent laziness, boys may be hyperactive from time to time. Particularly at bedtime, they may deny any feelings of fatigue in a way that is reminiscent of a much younger child. Although pubertal boys may be generally disinclined to wash, they may suddenly appear looking devastatingly clean and well groomed. The typical early-adolescent boy is highly aware of fashion and copies the dress of older adolescents. Sleeping and personal hygiene are major battle grounds over which the dependence/independence struggle is often fought. A boy insists he can make decisions, but may forget or refuse to wash his hair, teeth, neck, and ears. The conflicts of early-adolescent boys with parents may be more or less obvious. In boys who develop a healthy drive for autonomy, there are conflicts, even when they are hidden in an apparent conformity. The biologically derived experience of helplessness becomes part of the struggle for autonomy. Childhood dependence is easier to shake off if parents are temporarily experienced as bad, an experience that is reinforced because biologically induced helplessness carries with it an easily induced sense of being tormented. The early-adolescent boy, although behaving like an irresponsible child, feels as if he should be treated like a responsible adult; thus, an appropriate parental response is likely to be received badly. When parents react, and make the logical, looking-after remarks and gestures, the boy will be angry, offended, or rebellious. Such a boy appears not to expect logical, caring parental responses, but he is really more angry if he does not get them than if he does. For example, if parents suggest to a boy who has difficulty getting up in the morning that he go to bed early, this may be felt to be an unreasonable, interfering suggestion. If, on the one hand, he is wakened in the morning, he may react as though his parents are sadistic monsters—demanding and obtuse. On the other hand, if his parents fail to get him out of bed, they are likely to be seen as uncaring and neglectful. The helplessness and fatigue of early adolescence seem to be a part of the dependency struggle. If, however, there contradictions in behavior and expected response to it continue through later years, they indicate a measure of psychosocial conflict and failure to develop a sense of self.

MALE STRIVING FOR INDEPENDENCE

The inner experience of helplessness and the forbidden yearning to be nurtured make early-adolescent boys particularly intolerant of control exercised by women, in particular, their mothers. Since there is an unconscious attraction to being mothered, the strivings for independence of the male are never quite as clear and definite as they appear on the surface. This is often apparent when a boy is ill. Some boys cannot bear the dependence involved in being sick. As a result, early adolescents are often bad patients—they disobey the doctor's orders, they get up too soon, and they do not eat appropriately. Others appear to welcome the chance to be babied; they may become picky about their food and demand attention of various sorts from their mothers, or, if they are in a hospital, from nurses, nurse's aides, and doctors. The less secure a boy is in his manliness, the more he rejects mothering, but, conversely, the more he provokes his mother into telling him what to do; he then feels ordered about by a woman and becomes defiant.

These two factors, the wish to be mothered and masculine uncertainty, may make a pubertal boy as difficult as a negativistic two-year-old. A pubertal boy often seems to prefer to have a blazing row with his mother over minor trivialities, such as tidying up his room, than to simply pick up a few bits and pieces. Some mothers are hurt by this type of behavior, but it is really not a rejection of her, but rather is a rejection of her mothering behavior.

If there has been shared parenting (a decreasing possibility in a society with a high divorce rate), and if the father's role, as both husband and father, is valued by himself and his spouse, then the early-adolescent boy is more easily disciplined by his father than by his mother, although he may need to compete, sometimes in pitched battles, with his father. Ultimately, the father/son struggle is a struggle over masculine assertiveness. Both parents, in their relationship to their son—particularly, when direct clashes are involved—should be aware that if they win a point and their son loses face and pride in himself, their victory is hollow.

Inevitably, the young adolescent mixes up being independent and being rebellious; in striving to be the one, he almost necessarily becomes the other. Yet, in rebelling, the young often appear to copy what is done rather than what is said: The implicit message is obeyed, the explicit message is disobeyed. A shouted injunction not to shout is not heeded, since the parents are themselves shouting; an action that gives implicit permission for such behavior.

The early adolescent boy experiencing a sense of being tormented may feel more in control of himself and the environment if he can make his parents behave badly. Then, presumably, there is a feeling of understanding the situation—it is actual rather than fantasied.

Parental attempts to control a difficult, recalcitrant, early-adolescent boy may require the use of different techniques from those used in earlier childhood. Mothers may get more cooperation from their sons by appealing to their sense of chivalry; unfortunately, they may also get it by blackmailing them with tears. Similarly, fathers get further by taking a genuine interest in their sons' activities and by being prepared to let them make their own decisions. The father who emerges from behind a newspaper to bark out an order is likely to be less than successful in getting his son's assistance in household tasks or in helping him through a difficult period. In early adolescence, a father can still expect from time to time that his son will enjoy doing things with or for him, unless the father is felt to be overprotective or overdemanding or both. There is no question that parents of early adolescents are likely to respond, from time to time, in a less than ideal way. This, however, is hardly likely to destroy relationships that have generally been sound.

Pubertal boys have obvious problems with self-control. When frustrated, they may become so angry that they are near to tears; their perception of their own lack of control makes them blame their parents for their helplessness. It is not unusual for adolescent boys, under parental pressure, to rush to their room with a dramatic slamming of the door.

Preoccupied with their own bodies, early-adolescent boys need to gain control of their sexual urges, differentiate sexual feelings and aggressive feelings, and make sexuality an emotionally meaningful part of themselves; thus, trying to reassure themselves that they are men and able to ejaculate, boys of this age naturally masturbate (Winnicott, 1971). Some substitute early self-referent sexual intercourse for masturbation (Miller, 1983), but those who never masturbate find it much more difficult to develop a feeling of genuine self-awareness and do not easily come to terms with their own sexuality. They find it difficult to move beyond childhood to the combination of sexual excitement and the expression of loving feelings that is the foundation of adult heterosexual relationships.

During early adolescence, boys assess their masculinity primarily in relationship to other boys; girls are not a significant factor at this time except in fantasy. Boys compare themselves to each other in ways that are acceptable to adults; for example, they compare height, muscular development, ability to work, and competence in sports. They also make comparisons that are less acceptable to the grown-up world. They compare their capacity to spit, to urinate, and to ejaculate, as well as the size of their genitals. Similarly unacceptable to adults may be their spinning of prurient tales and their loud-mouthed uncouthness.

At this stage, boys may need to be emotionally involved with other boys in groups, which may become gangs of a transient or a more permanent nature. Adolescent members of a group thus gain the emotional support and sense of security that often prevent a return to the dependent feelings of childhood. Early-adolescent boys under extreme psychological stress may depend on a gang to help them resolve it. Dependence on their families is unacceptable to boys, both psychologically and culturally (i.e., in peer-group reaction), as a solution to anxiety. Thus, early-adolescent boys under too much psychological stress may have no alternative but to group together more formally and work out their anxieties on society through unduly aggressive behavior.

Most of the time, young people who feel loved and valued are pleasant, alive, interested, creative, and generous. Healthy early adolescents are, nevertheless, difficult from time to time. Those who are always well-behaved, and so conformist that they never give any trouble to parents or teachers, may be troubled or seriously depressed. Such young people may not be able to allow themselves to strive independently, even when their parents and their society wish to grant them more freedom and responsibility; when freedom is thrust upon them, they often are ill equipped to handle it. Tolerant parents, however, may let their children free themselves from their childish wishes so well that there may be little external sign of conflict and turbulence. The complexity of today's society in large cities makes it improbable that this can always be a smooth process, but such a transition is possible for the son of well-balanced, loving parents who have been able to take the stresses and strains of child-rearing calmly.

If parents are felt to be too understanding, their son may never get the opportunity to feel that he has won any significant battles. Good parents may thus experience a situation in which their sons relate to them as if they were harsh and tyrannical; thus, a boy will get the satisfaction of feeling that he obtains something, despite the real absence of parental opposition; he may produce it in fantasy, if it is not there in fact.

THE NEEDS AND BEHAVIOR OF GIRLS

If, as is usual, the growth spurt of girls is less dramatic than that of boys, they usually do not go through a period of poor coordination. Depending on cultural pressures, girls may become preoccupied with their physical appearance very early in puberty. Often, as with boys, their rooms are inappropriately untidy, the external chaos being a measure of internal confusion. Personal cleanliness is often not as much of an issue as with the early-adolescent boy. Girls, at this age, may still like to be cuddled by their mothers, and infantile needs for nurture can be met directly, rather than indirectly, as with early-adolescent boys.

The onset of menstruation is, for nearly any girl, an event that makes her feel truly feminine and grown up. But it also confronts her with a physiological event that is beyond her control. This is often dealt with by a preoccupation with feminine hygiene, partly through a fear of being perceived as menstruating. Because of this biological experience of helplessness, early-adolescent girls may feel vulnerable to what is perceived as criticism by others. A boy can control genital excitement by masturbation; only through pathological self-starvation, as in anorexia nervosa, can a girl control her periods. She can, however, reduce tension through masturbation, although this starts later in girls than in boys.

FEMALE STRIVING FOR INDEPENDENCE

The development of a sense of autonomy in both sexes requires the successful completion of certain life tasks, which begin to be highly significant at adolescence: the ability to tolerate frustration without giving hostages to fortune in the future; the capacity to be empathic and loving; the ability to be appropriately self-assertive; and the successful completion of academic or vocational training. Failure in any one of these areas leads to failure to attain true psychosocial adulthood. These tasks begin in childhood; at early adolescence, they are of primary importance to the individual. Within this context, the independent strivings of girls differ from those of boys. Girls wish to free themselves from their childish dependent feelings, but they need to keep a different type of dependent relationship, if they can, with their parents, particularly with their mothers. Girls find it more tolerable to lean on their mothers for advice, even after they have set up homes of their own. The problem here is that girls may retain a childlike dependence. Thus, a girl may be unable to reach a more mature level of autonomy in which, as an adult, she is able to turn to her parents for an appropriate degree of emotional support.

The battle for independence with boys is fought, first, within the family, and then outside it, whereas girls have more intra-family struggles over a longer period of time. A boy proves his masculinity away from home, primarily with male friends, with girlfriends, and finally with economic self-sufficiency; his family gets the backwash of the struggle. Girls, if they do not become autonomous, may transfer their excessive dependence on their families to overdependence on their lovers or husbands. A girl seeks economic self-sufficiency, but she is still likely to view this objective as secondary to becoming a wife and mother.

A girl's struggle is more dramatic in relationship to her mother than to her father. Girls borrow their mother's clothes and then criticize their mother's taste. At one time, they feel their mothers are dowdy; at another, their mothers are felt to be too seductive with the family's male friends. Shopping for clothes with an early-adolescent daughter can be a hideous experience for her mother. Either daughters spend hours cogitating over a dress, or, much less tolerably, they want clothes that their mothers feel to be in poor taste.

Sometimes daughters willingly help their mother; at other times they are reluctant to help. Because they do not have as dramatic a growth spurt and use physical activity less as a tension release than boys, girls do not usually stay in bed as much as their adolescent brothers. However, narcissism is the constant preoccupation of adolescence; as with boys, girls spend many hours fussing over their appearance. Like their brothers, girls are easily angered and easily reduced to tears. They actively try out mothering roles and enjoy looking after small creatures, whether babies, puppies, mice, or hamsters. This mothering wish can also be seen in early-adolescent boys, who will disguise their enjoyment of looking after babies by complaining about being forced to babysit.

Very often, girls just before and just into the pubertal period are chronic complainers, nothing is ever right. Whatever her parents do is wrong. Although chronically complaining, particularly about her mother, the early-adolescent girl may often appear very seductive, particularly with her father.

Just before the onset of puberty, the girl may want to sit on her father's knee. In puberty, she may wish to see films with him, and join in secrets with him, excluding her mother, if possible. This behavior can be understood as part of the girl's struggle to adopt a culturally acceptable feminine identity. Girls may appear to get along quite well with a slightly older brother; yet, with a group of girlfriends, she may join in giggling and hostile teasing that is calculated to enrage him. Smaller brothers and sisters may at times be carefully looked after, at other times casually disregarded; pseudomaternal care alternates with neglect.

Many early-adolescent girls are preoccupied with the feeling that they are insufficiently attractive, and they compare themselves with a popular model or actress. This may not be realistic, but they are convinced that their legs are too fat; their hair is too curly; their skin is broken out. The current association of thinness and beauty tempts girls to diet excessively. An extreme sensitivity about their self-perceived shortcomings may make girls reluctant to engage in physical activity in which they expose their bodies to their peers. Many early-adolescent girls refuse to swim or to exercise.

Girls who insist they are ugly can accept the reassurance that the adult understands that they are comparing themselves to an ideal; but they cannot accept the statement that they are attractive. When such a hypersensitive girl is forced into what she considers to be excessive exposure, she may refuse or become hypochondriacal or develop a variety of emotional disabilities to avoid it.

The early-adolescent girl is often moody and tense; she daydreams or flings herself into activities. This is the age when having friends stay overnight is just as important as when she was eight or nine; and gossiping for hours is common.

Like her brother, the early-adolescent girl has a need for limits to be set.

Girls in early adolescence can allow themselves to feel dependent on their parents when they feel anxious. Thus, they do not need their own age group for support as much as boys. Girls form one-to-one relationships, rather than larger groups. When, as in Europe, adolescents are in a playground, both boys and girls may appear to be in large groups at first glance, but the girls' group is often a cluster of one-to-one relationships.

DEVELOPMENT OF A SENSE OF FEMININITY

The initial sense of femininity begins in infancy, when girls directly identify with their mothers' nurturing and homemaking roles. In adolescence, peer relationships with other girls are not as important in reinforcing this as same-sex relationships are to the boy in reinforcing his sense of masculinity.

Girls do compare themselves with one another, emphasizing breast size and the time their periods began, but boys are most important to them in assessing, testing, and realizing their femininity. A girl is most truly convinced of her femininity if she has a father who accepts her as attractive and lovable, and if she has in her life men who care about her, who are not members of her immediate family, and who are not trying to exploit her sexually. Older men are often satisfactory in this respect; they include uncles, family friends, and young male teachers. Girls in early adolescence may have a hero about whom they can fantasize an ideal love affair to reinforce their feminine feelings. Early-adolescent girls, and those whose emotional growth is slow beyond this stage, are often preoccupied with pop stars. The socially acceptable mass hysteria toward such cult leaders gives them the opportunity to release sexual tensions and anger toward male authorities. But pop singers are used by girls in a variety of ways, as is shown by the following example:

> Ruth was an eighteen-year-old office worker. Her mother was widowed when Ruth was a child, and so, in her early years she had no man in her life, no father. Although her mother remarried, she was never able to get really close to her stepfather. Until early adolescence and the onset of puberty, Ruth was a tomboy. Soon after, she fell for a well-known pop singer she had never met. By the time she was sixteen, she was a leader of his fan club and had his pictures plastered over her bedroom walls and ceiling. She tried almost weekly to get a job in his manager's office so she might be near enough to talk to him.

Often the overvalued member of the pop group is used by such girls to express contempt for the boys who are available and to protect themselves from real sex:

> Whenever Ruth went out with a boyfriend to a place where she might see or hear her singer, she would get wildly excited; by contrast she was at least cool to the boy she was with at the time. When her boyfriend attempted to kiss her, she would tell him that she did not think he could do it as well as her singer "friend."

Boys, sensing the sort of man girls see as attractive, may respond by copying the heroes in dress and general appearance.

Early-adolescent boys and girls often have the same male pin-ups, boys taking the male pop hero as a model. An admiration of such male pin-ups is one of the first signs of a boy's desire to make himself sexually attractive to girls. Although, at this stage, such admiration does not usually indicate overt homosexual interest, boys' sexual interests have not yet taken their final direction; they can still be drawn to a dashing male figure.

Sometimes boys respond to girls' worship of these heroes violently. When, in certain countries, hysterical feminine screams were encouraged in theaters to boost the stars' reputations, boys who were present with their girlfriends would sometimes wait at the stage door afterwards to attack the singers as they left. These assaults could have been the result of homosexual anxiety as well as heterosexual jealousy.

ADOLESCENTS: WHAT THEY NEED FROM THE WORLD

Boys and girls, in early adolescence, whether they are altruistic or selfish, ascetic or self-indulgent, have two principal needs from adults (Freud, 1958). They need, first, interest and emotional involvement and, second, external control of their behavior by adults, founded on mutual respect rather than fear.

Early adolescents require from school a feeling that their environment is stable and secure. A teacher should be able to offer them external controls whenever they find controlling themselves difficult. Like all children, they are upset by constant changes of teacher: When new or substitute teachers appear, pupils must test the limits of their control.

The turbulent atmosphere of the junior high school in the United States is, in part, due to the fact that a change of teachers every two semesters and exposure to five to eight groups of peers daily do not give pubertal adolescents the continuity they need. Teacher/pupil confrontations are often the result.

Finally, early adolescents need to experiment with a variety of intellectual, emotional, and physical activities. If such opportunities are not provided in early adolescence, it may be too late for them to learn flexibility and tolerance later.

THE INTELLECTUAL AND IMAGINATIVE GROWTH OF BOYS AND GIRLS

Because early adolescents are preoccupied with their bodies, their internal world, and their need to develop inner controls, they do not do as well with work that involves rote learning as they did earlier or will do later. If children are taught in the traditional way, and fail to make much progress before puberty, a reasonable hypothesis is that they will be unlikely to do much better during the turmoil of early adolescence. Insistence may inhibit the development of their imagination. If such demands are made, young people are likely to feel that they are unable to cope with the frustrations in-involved.

Most early adolescents are still concrete thinkers, who think primarily about things (Piaget and Inhelder, 1958); the capacity to make abstractions (Jersild, 1963), to think formally (Dulit, 1972), may or may not develop in mid-adolescence.

Intellectual and imaginative growth rates differ for boys and girls; until the end of adolescence, girls are always about two years ahead of the same-age boy insofar as their imagination, capacity to abstract, ability to perceive the feelings of others, and capacity to tolerate frustration are concerned (Symonds, and Jensen, 1961). This means that if boys and girls are compared to each other in a school system, the boys may actively stop working, if only to assure themselves that they could have beaten the girls if they had so wished.

PROBLEMS OF MATURATIONAL AGE VARIATION

Particular difficulties in early adolescence arise from normal variations in physical development (Schoenfeld, 1964). Boys may experience the extreme embarrassment of having a transient enlargement of their breasts (Schoenfeld, 1962). Girls may develop a faint growth of hair across the upper lip. Both of these usually disappear as adolescence progresses. A developmental variation that causes particularly emotional difficulties is late maturation. Although this is sometimes associated with retarded growth, late developers are often very tall as adults. This is because they continue to grow at the average childhood rate of about two inches a year through puberty; then they have a sudden spurt after others have stopped growing. Late development is more common in boys than in girls.

Late maturation in boys may not be ultimately harmful psychologically; such a late maturer may become a sensitive, perceptive man, more in touch with his inner world than his normatively developed peers (Jones, 1957; Peskin, 1967). During adolescence, boys may have problems when they feel they are physically weak compared to agemates of their own sex; when maturation finally occurs, they, nevertheless, do not feel inhibited and unattractive to girls. Their height may then make them feel that they have the edge over their competitors, and their longer period of maturational childhood may make it easier for them to cope with the physiological changes of puberty. Thus, ultimately, they may have an emotional edge over other eighteen- to twenty-year-olds. But a late-maturing adult may occasionally feel (irrationally) that his penis is too small. This is a consequence of adolescent observation of others in dressing rooms; the earlier experience is internalized and carried into adulthood.

Girls who develop late may feel that they are unattractive and odd as people, because girls of their own age are interested in boys when they are not. They also feel, if they are tall, that it will be difficult to find a boyfriend; tall women are often uncomfortable about their femininity, in later years.

Late-maturing adolescents do not really believe that maturation will occur until it does. Boys, who experience this delay more often than girls, are liable to be teased for being "fags." They may feel that since they do not rate in comparisons their contemporaries make, they have to assert themselves in other ways. Sometimes they work very hard, as if to prove themselves intellectually superior; sometimes they become assertive and rude. Late developers often become gang leaders.

In a rigid educational system, these young people are often wasted if they are as slow to mature emotionally as physically. If they do not do as well academically as their peer group, they may be labeled as failures, and act accordingly. Special efforts may have to be made to rescue them, though this is most difficult in an institution that reflects society's obsession with the need for qualifications:

> Seventeen-year-old Alec failed to graduate from high school not because he was dull but because he was late in developing. He suffered greatly when his friends graduated without him. With counseling, he later completed his work, and attended a community college, where his grades were excellent.

The difficulties of puberty usually fade around the age of fifteen. Then there can be a real flowering of talent. Those who cannot cope with the problems of early-adolescent years, especially when they receive no help, are likely to remain restless, turbulent, and insecure throughout adolescence, and perhaps even into adulthood.

REFERENCES

Blos, P. (1962), *On Adolescence*. Glencoe, Ill.: The Free Press.

Deutsch, H. (1944). *The Psychology of Women*, Vol. I. New York: Grune & Stratton.

Dulit, E. (1972), Adolescent thinking à la Piaget: The formal stage. *J. Youth Adoles.*, 1 (4): 281–301.

Freud, A. (1958), Adolescence. In *Psychoanalytic Study of the Child*, 13: 255–277. New York: International Universities Press.

Jersild, A. T. (1963), *The Psychology of Adolescence*. New York: Macmillan.

Jones, M. (1957), The later careers of boys who were early or late maturing. *Child Dev.*, 28: 113.

Kestenberg, J. S. (1968), Phases of adolescence. Part IV. Puberty growth, differentiation and consolidation, *Am. Acad. Child Psychiatr.*, 7: 108–151.

Lederer, W. (1964), Dragons, delinquents and destiny. *Psychol. Issues*, 4: 3.

Miller, D. (1980), Family maladaptation reflected in drug abuse and delinquency. In *Responding to Adolescent Needs*, ed. M. Sugar, 1–16. New York: Spectrum.

Miller, D. (1983), *Behavior Disorders. Etiology and Treatment*. In press.

Montagu, M. F. A. (1946), *Adolescent Sterility*. Springfield, Ill.: Charles C Thomas.

Mussen, P. H., and Jones, M. C. (1958), Self-conceptions, motivations and interpersonal attitudes of early and late maturing boys. *Child Dev.*, 29: 61–67.

Nathanson, I. T., *et al.* (1941), Normal excretion of sex hormones in childhood. *Endocrinology*, 28: 851–865.

Offer, D. (1969), *The Psychological World of the Teenager*. New York: Basic Books.

Peskin, H. (1967), Pubertal onset and ego functioning. *J. Abnorm. Psychol.*, 72: 1.

Piaget, J., and Inhelder, B. (1958), *The Growth of Logical Thinking from Childhood to Adolescence*. New York: Basic Books.

Schoenfeld, W. A. (1962), Gynaecomastia in adolescents: Effect on body image and personality adaption. *Psychosom. Med.* 24: 379–389.

———— (1964), Body image disturbances in adolescents with inappropriate sexual development. *Am. J. Orthopsychiatr.* 35: 493–502.

Symonds, P. M., and Jensen, A. R. (1961), *From Adolescence to Adult*. New York: Columbia University Press.

Tanner, J. M. (1962), *Growth at Adolescence*. Oxford: Blackwell.

Wilkins, L. (1965), *The Diagnosis and Treatment of Endocrine Disorders in Childhood and Adolescence*. Springfield, Ill.: Charles C Thomas.

Winnicott, D. W. (1971), Adolesence, struggling through the doldrums. In *Adolescent Psychiatry*, Vol. 1, ed. S. C. Feinstein, A. Miller, and P. Giovacchini, 40–51. New York: Basic Books.

Chapter 2

The Life Space of Early Adolescents

MALE AND FEMALE ROLES

In most societies, the male role is to master the environment (Gutmann and Krohn, 1972); the female, to carry the sensitive, imaginative maturity of the society. Since adolescence is a period of preparation for adult roles, it is to be expected that these roles would be tried out then. Thus, early-adolescent boys spend more of their time away from home with groups of their friends roaming around neighborhoods; girls spend time with one or two girlfriends around the house of one or another of them. Both sexes may frequent a local teenage hangout; alternatively, the house or yard of a popular peer may be a favorite meeting place. The large number of mothers who are now working has not changed this type of behavior. All it has done is ensure that ever-increasing numbers of young adolescents are without needed adult supervision for large parts of the day.

THE NEED FOR PRIVACY

Both boys and girls have an intense, if intermittent need for complete privacy (Winnicott, 1971), and a need to keep secrets both from their parents and, to some extent, from other adults. Their fantasy lives and sexual lives are now kept secret from mothers and fathers, and insistence by parents that adolescents not be secretive can become a psychological assault. Adolescents however, sometimes hang around their parents, saying very little, yet appearing most interested in what their parents and their parents' friends are saying. In part, this may be mere curiosity, in part a need for companionship or a search for role-models. Adolescents want and need privacy (Winnicott, 1971), but they are not always prepared to grant it to their parents.

In some families, children are deliberately taught that physical privacy is unimportant. At about the age of two, boys have a healthy interest in the toilet habits of their fathers, and urinating in a standing position is a first step toward a separate masculine identity. However, if parents go out of their way to be naked, in a manner that is socioculturally unusual, parental nakedness may be felt by children to be provocative and possibly worrying; in adolescence, this may inhibit their sexual feeling. Some parents walk around naked under the mistaken impression that they are helping their youngster overcome feelings of shame about the body and body functions. In some progressive nursery schools, children are encouraged to feel free, and go naked. In cultures in which nakedness is the norm, for example, in which children sleep in the same room with their parents and observe parental intercourse, the children are "allowed" to be sexual with each other in a whole variety of games. In cultures that do not tolerate this, parental nakedness then appears as an implicit disregard for the children's budding sexuality. Boys and girls may thus lose touch with important aspects of their emotional, inner worlds. Just as the manliness of boys, when respected, makes parental control somewhat easier, so too does the femininity of daughters.

ADOLESCENTS AND THE EXPRESSION OF ANXIETY

An essential difference in the intrafamilial behavior of boys and girls, is that the healthy adolescent girl feels she can turn to her father or mother for help in times of crisis without sacrificing her independence or losing face; she is allowed to demonstrate her distress by obvious sadness and misery. The early-adolescent girl, but not the early-adolescent boy, can deal with tension by bursting into tears. Thus, girls are more easily able to keep in touch with their feelings and their emotional lives. The early-adolescent boy is still, both culturally and psychologically, encouraged to control any outward expression of distress, although this varies among different ethnic groups. Second- and third-generation ethnics still show differences in the way they handle their feelings; some fathers of Polish origin may spank their fifteen-year-old daughters for disobedience. Since the daughter knows that other girls are treated the same way, this potentially traumatic experience is less damaging psychologically than it would be if a WASP father spanked his daughter.

Because of the pressure to control anxiety in a way the culture, or subcultures, sees as manly, boys are more likely than girls to act out their distress by antisocial behavior at school or in the neighborhood. The girl in equivalent misery is likely to stay home. Thus, girls are better understood by parents, and girls also often seem more appreciative and obviously aware that help is being given. If a girl shows her anxiety by crying, parents are less likely to be controlling or punitive than they might be with a boy who is showing his anxiety by being aggressive.

An early adolescent who behaves antisocially in the community at large and is caught by the police, may be labeled "delinquent." This is much more usual with boys than with girls, and when it occurs some type of intervention takes place. This becomes significantly punitive depending on the social class of the offender, the severity and frequency of the offense and the attitude of the police and the judge, as well as the prevailing attitude in the community. When girls commit serious crimes, the behavior is seen by the community as more extraordinary than when boys do, although this is changing in large cities, and in upper-class neighborhoods. In the latter, minor crime may be a response to boredom.

Since lower-class black girls are allowed, in their subculture, to externalize aggression in both words and actions, their behavior may be seen as incomprehensible by middle-class people from almost all ethnic groups.

Socially acceptable outlets for aggression are more easily found by boys than by girls; sports, for example, are more available to boys, although the admission of girls to junior-league baseball teams is slowly changing this. In later adolescence, both boys and girls may jog.

If appropriate physical outlets for aggression are not available, the early-adolescent boy is likely to demonstrate anxiety by involving himself in a series of misdemeanors at school or by failing to do his homework. Adults then have to deal with the misbehavior, as well as its possible causes. It is easy to see how preoccupation with the former may lead to neglect of the latter. By the time girls become delinquent, if this is not socioculturally allowable, they are likely to be more disturbed than the equivalently misbehaving boy. Parents may find it acceptable when an overanxious girl remains too dependent upon them; the danger is that she may then be unable to make independent decisions as she grows toward adulthood. Boys, on the other hand, who are denied necessary emotional support from parents, may build a pseudo-independence by joining a gang, or by committing minor crimes.

If they have been unable to ask for help in resolving their conflicts verbally, a usual situation, and if their "action" requests are misunderstood, both boys and girls may feel too insecure to develop a satisfactory sense of their own autonomy. A common "solution" in both sexes is by drug abuse which appears as usual with girls, as with boys.

ADOLESCENT VANITY AND SUCCESSFUL PARENTS

Until the last decade, the early-adolescent girl was allowed to be more obviously preoccupied with her body than was the early-adolescent boy. Boys may now show their interest in their own bodies by being openly concerned about clothes, hairstyle, and general appearance. This change in attitude toward male adornment does not apply just to adolescents. Society has now changed its attitude toward the adult male's narcissism. He may now more obviously wear hairpieces and have hair transplants; the use of cosmetics by both adolescent boys and their fathers is growing. In the United States, body building is a common preoccupation of young males, and weights and mirrors are in common use.

An interest in their own feminine attractiveness has historically always been encouraged in girls. One problem for early-adolescent girls may be that their parents or society demand that they become sexually attractive before the are emotionally ready for this step. An extreme case can be summarized here:

> A mother brought her thirteen-year-old daughter to a neurological clinic in a large city, to determine the cause of her fainting spells. A complete neurological examination was negative in all respects. The mother then asked the examining doctor if he could recommend a doctor who would give her daughter hormone shots so that the girl's breasts would be the size of the breasts of many, but not all of the daughter's peers. Psychological counseling of both mother and daughter cured the daughter of her fainting spells.

A girl may or may not feel intensely feminine from childhood onward. Apart from the promptings of overeager adults, this has little significance insofar as an actual relationship with boys is concerned. An early-adolescent girl's interest in her appearance is associated with a more conscious awareness of herself as feminine; it does not mean she is ready to be sexually or emotionally involved with boys.

Because girls more directly model themselves on their mothers than do boys, on either parent, the girls' task in developing a sense of autonomy is in some ways more complex than is that of boys. Although girls are ordinarily not as intolerant of control from mothers as are early-adolescent boys, in order to establish a separate sense of self, they may, for a time, be intensively and directly negative and defiant (Block, 1957). Mothers often get the feeling that nothing they do for their daughters is right, and life is a grim battle. Maternal control, however, is not likely to be felt as a threat to a girl's growing sense of womanhood, unless she feels that her mother is really trying to make a baby out of her.

Adolescent girls are likely to have particular difficulty if they have beautiful and youthful-appearing mothers, especially if, as is often the case, they are at a particularly qawky stage of adolescence. Competition from a beautiful mother for the love and attention of men, in general, and the father, in particular, is a battle they feel they can never win. It is not uncommon for girls in such a situation to be in utter despair: They will never be beautiful; they will always be dumb and stupid; no one will ever want them. The daughter of a very beautiful woman may be in a position similar to the potentially academic or creative son of a very brilliant man. Success in the mastering of life tasks in such youngsters depends, to some considerable extent, on the attitudes of their mothers and the child's perception of her role in the marriage. If children perceive the spouse of a particularly creative individual as sacrificing him- or herself to the talent and creativity of that individual, then the spouse is not seen as valuable. The creative "important" parent thus loves someone who is "incompetent." The child may identify with the devalued parent and thus gain the attention that is craved, even if this is negative. This concept helps explain why the sons of famous fathers are so often relative failures. Sometimes, children need to feel they can be successful in areas of life in which their parents are not involved. They feel they cannot compete with the parents of the same sex, while they are alive, at any rate; children do not compete when they know they cannot win. So a girl will find it hard to be successfully feminine if she sees her mother as too attractive; similarly, a boy may not strive in those areas in which his father is felt to be very successful.

GIRLS AND FATHERS

When a father feels it necessary to correct his daughter, she needs to feel that she is cared for and cared about. Overcritical fathers can be particu-

larly wounding to their early-adolescent daughters. Sometimes the comments are felt as persecutory, even though such was not the intention,
both because a girl is doubtful herself as to how attractive she might be, and
because of normal helplessness. Makeup, a hairstyle, or a certain type of
clothing may be tried with the basic idea of being more feminine and
attractive; being told by father that something else was liked better is painful,
but not as bad as being told to "take that muck off your eyes." An early-
adolescent girl's sensitivity may lead her to distort the intention and meaning
of remarks from adults; and her oversensitivity may create a situation in
which the adults feel emotionally black-mailed. The pretense that something
is liked, when it is not, may then be made. Sometimes a daughter may
provoke her father to gain his attention in the struggle to feel appropriately
loved, especially in competition with her mother or her brothers or sisters.

MALE AND FEMALE TASKS

As in more primitive societies, some tasks in Western culture are seen as
masculine, others as feminine, despite the fact that some women work in
traditional male areas. In general, the masculine areas are those that
require physical effort, the feminine include homemaking and caring-for
tasks. The distinction is crude, but it can be highly meaningful to the young
who perceive some activities as appropriate to boys and other activities to
girls. A pervasive concept among the intellectual middle classes, that men
and women should occupy similar roles in all aspects, is not likely to be held
by early-adolescent boys and girls. Insofar as household tasks are concerned,
anxiety about roles may be reinforced when sons and daughters are expected
to accept chores irrespective of the masculinity or femininity of the job.
Early adolescents may be reluctant to help their parents, because their sense
of autonomy is threatened, but it is often more acceptable to boys to engage
in activities that they see as clearly masculine: obtaining fuel, mowing the
lawn, washing the car, taking out the garbage. Girls may more comfortably
assist in making beds, washing dishes, and helping clean house.

Boys are more likely to be oversensitive about the masculinity or femininity of jobs than girls, because at an equivalent age they are probably less
sure of themselves. What is felt as manly varies from family to family, but to
some extent the masculinity or femininity of any piece of work is associated
with class attitudes. A middle-class adolescent boy does not usually feel that
washing dishes makes him effeminate; some working-class young people do
feel this. In such situations, perceptive parents should not ask their sons to
perform such household chores.

Adults may, however, be confused about the sexuality of certain tasks and become overanxious, lest they be seen as inappropriate. It may not be recognized that, in secure masculinity, there is the capacity to be feminine and motherly; in femininity, a capacity to take charge and master the external world. So boys commonly enjoy cooking, and it may take time for some adults to accept that this does not necessarily lead to sexual confusion.

> The staff running a psychiatric adolescent service became very concerned when it was suggested that cooking be a vocational activity for boys as well as girls. They thought that an implicit message about role confusion might be given. One year after this project started, they realized that the boys did not feel less masculine and enjoyed this activity.

Similarly, in high schools, cooking as an activity may be very popular with many boys, particularly those whose aggressive behavior is the masculine equivalent of "methinks the lady doth protest too much."

A major worry for parents is often how to get their early-adolescent children to take their fair share of household tasks. It often appears that young people prefer to mow the neighbor's lawn rather than their own. Similarly, they will commit themselves to babysit for others, rather than for members of their own family. The reluctance to help parents may be due, in part, to the possible financial gain in working for others, in part because it helps young people feel more independent if they have jobs outside their homes.

ADOLESCENTS AND MONEY

Sometimes parents attempt to resolve their adolescent's wish to be independent, while still having to help around the house, by paying their children for such help. This may create in children an expectation that they will never have to do something for nothing. A balance needs to be struck. Pocket money for early adolescents may be provided for partly by the amount they are able to earn, partly by an allowance from their parents. Early adolescents can often earn substantial sums—golf caddying, lawn mowing, and babysitting—yet they may have no real sense of the value of money; since it is earned, it can be squandered. Thus, many parents feel the need to control the spending of their children, but the early adolescent's substantial earnings may make it hard to justify such control. In societies in which it is difficult for adolescents to earn money, by the time they are able to work they may know better how to spend their income. After the age of fifteen or sixteen, an allowance may no longer be necessary, because sufficient money can be earned; younger adolescents may thus be given a larger allowance than their older brothers and sisters, although this can sometimes cause sibling conflict.

ADOLESCENT CONFORMITY

Many adolescents conform completely to expected social and family norms by the time the middle stages of adolescence are reached. But the more insecure a youngster, the more likely it is that this conformity will be to implicit attitudes rather than explicit ones, which tend to be inconsistent (Miller, 1980). If explicit ways of life are inconsistent with those that are implicit, then mid-adolescence will probably appear as highly turbulent in the psychologically vulnerable.

The less sure a boy or girl is of his or her autonomy, the harder it is for them to help parents. Similarly, the less support obtained from a network of involved peers and extraparental adults, the more difficult are intra-familial relationships.

If an early adolescent is overanxious about a sense of self, it is as though such independence as is felt will be lost if parental wishes are followed. On the other hand, children with no sense of independence may be highly conformist. An early adolescent who never complains and is never felt to be a problem by adults is probably in emotional difficulties. All adolescents are highly conformist to familiar stereotypes (Taba, 1953), but depending on family pressure and individual passivity, some are more obedient than others. Boys may clean house for domineering mothers; girls may wash cars for seductive fathers. When adolescents feel unfairly used, however, the task may be performed, but ways of showing resentment may emerge. The job may be badly done; parents may feel the need to nag; opportunities for success may appear to be almost deliberately lost. Adolescents can be experts at crucifying themselves to show the world of adults its inadequacy.

The untidiness of early-adolescent boys and girls, their reluctance to wash, to brush teeth, to keep clothes clean, may mean that adults who care about the appearance, surroundings, and hygiene of their children are in for a two- to three-year struggle. The external chaos with which early adolescents are often surrounded is a measure of their overinvolvement with themselves, an inability to abandon the role of a child and, because of internal pre-occupation, a disinclination to be bothered with the real world. Sometimes external disorganization is, additionally, a measure of internal confusion. Untidiness may be one more manifestation of the struggle to be independent against the unconscious wish to remain dependent. Implicitly the adolescent wishes to be looked after, but caring actions are resented. Thus, a struggle over mothering is fought (Levy and Monroe, 1938).

ADOLESCENTS AND COMMUNITY ORGANIZATIONS— THE FUNCTION OF GANGS

Relationships of early adolescents in the community help or hinder their developing sense of masculinity or femininity. Extraparental adults are important for the natural development of personality, but in early adolescence, boys and girls of the same age group are particularly significant. Peer-group relationships are consciously felt to be more essential to security than relationships with extraparental adults (Fainberg, 1953). If either relationship is missing, personality growth through adolescence will be difficult. For the early adolescent, an adult provides a social structure of acceptable and unacceptable behavior; surrounds the individual with a world that cares; and offers ideas and feelings, while recognizing that only part of what is said will be immediately absorbed into the personality. If adolescents live in a social system that obviously fails to meet their growing needs, the adults who run the system are often felt to be inhuman. Early adolescents doubt the strength of their own inner controls. Consciously aware of restlessness and tension, early adolescents unconsciously look for control, support, and understanding, not only from parents and other adults whom they know and like, but also from their peers. As a general rule, boys will seek groups of friends of about the same age, with up to six months to a one year difference. They will tend to form "in" and "out" groups, in which people whom they know and like are felt to be superior to others. Although early adolescents tend to have a packlike relationship with each other, usually playing and chasing about in groups of six to eight, gangs, in a formally structured sense, with leaders and followers, are likely to be formed only in two situations. First, they may meet a temporary need related to the reality in which the youngsters find themselves and their state of psychological development. Gangs may be formed over real or imagined slights by an out-group, and in such cases, the gang normally has a very short life. Second, a gang may develop from the possession of a club room, either in the home of one of the boys or if they can find it, in a disused shack or something similar. These gangs are not usually highly organized except sometimes for a specific task. Although daredevil defiance of the rules of society with mildly sporadic antisocial behavior, such as petty theft, is common at the beginning of puberty, only if the emotional climate is difficult do boys behave antisocially.

Again, this behavior is likely to be transient. However, if adolescent boys grow up in neighborhoods or communities that lack the facilities to meet their needs, more structured gangs with a longer life are common (Miller, 1958).

Most gangs are found in emotionally and physically underprivileged neighborhoods, ghetto schools, or prisons. They give their members an opportunity to direct their anger, which is associated with emotional and economic deprivation, onto others. Out-groups are dehumanized (Ottenburg, 1968), both other gangs and the population at large, and thus they can be hunted and attacked by gang members (Miller and Looney 1976) without remorse. Gangs may sometimes be found temporarily in more affluent districts in which there is little or no relationship between adults and children and few local outlets for adolescent creativity, imaginativeness, or aggression. Affluent neighborhoods, however, usually tend to be spared persistent gang activity, as they are less physically constricting than ghetto areas. Since there is more space to move about, tension can be relieved by diffuse physical activity. It is also easier for more affluent adolescents to relieve inner boredom and emptiness by change.

In many parts of the United States, the gang tradition is strong. In the black ghettos and in other deprived communities, gangs are common, and they map out their own neighborhood areas—their turf—in which they jealously guard their rights.

Girls may form groups and attach themselves in a more or less formal way to boys' gangs. In neighborhoods in which developmental needs are not met, especially in the absence of asexual male love from fathers and others—early-adolescent girls may also form gangs (Crane, 1958). Often the appearance of these has a particular plaguelike quality. They may be constructed for a particular task: blackmailing and robbing weaker members of the junior high school, swamping a department store area with children, to make it easier to shoplift, and so on. This type of gang usually does not have a long life. Girls' gangs are often particularly cruel to their members who break the gang codes. Not uncommonly, such girls are made to become the victims of gang rape by a neighborhood boys' gang.

When the quality of neighborhood social life is such that formal gangs are created, after a preliminary probationary period that may date from childhood, adolescents may stay in them for a number of years. Membership may stretch well into early adulthood (Block and Neiderhoffer, 1958). With youngsters whose developmental needs are generally met, by the time puberty is over the need for gang activity has disappeared, although men are always interested in friendships of a fairly superficial kind with groups of their own sex. In some particularly bad ghetto areas, boys join gangs for protection.

It is fairly clear that one function of a gang with boys is to give them external support to help make emotional maturation possible. Gang controls are often very strict. Boys who will defy any limits imposed by their parents will accept highly formal rules in their gangs. They may disobey their parents, but be more obedient to the strictures of their gang. Early adolescents may, similarly, be highly reluctant to wear clothes or adopt hairstyles that please their parents, but may be eager and willing to obey the fashion demands of their own age group. School dress codes are violated; gang emblems are cheerfully worn.

Even when adolescents do not form gangs and are not playing in groups, they often like to wander about in groups. These groups tend to hang out in the same neighborhoods, the same street corner, or the same back alley. The groups may move restlessly to and fro, but they do not generally move very far from their home area, except from time to time when a group of boys will suddenly move for a night to a new neighborhood. This may become a group tradition, and there is a regular foray to a club, cafe, or teenage hangout at the other side of town. This phenomenon is more usual in the middle years of adolescence, when adolescents can drive cars, although it may occur in younger age groups. It is sometimes associated with older boys looking for girls, whom they fantasize will be sexually available—rather like the fantasy late adolescents might have when they travel to a foreign country.

Early-adolescent boys and girls need space. They need the opportunity to play competitive games that are organized by adults and also to take part in activities they organize themselves. Boys, in particular, need the opportunity for unstructured play that allows physical contact with each other. Early adolescence is particularly the age in which boys engage in play fights with each other, and friendly punches are traded. If the environment fails them, or if they are in poor control of themselves, these can escalate into real aggression (Opie and Opie, 1969).

Apart from the need for physical contact sports and games, boys, as well as girls, need outlets for their imagination and sense of creativity. If these are present in a neighborhood or a school, along with the opportunity to be safely adventurous and to withdraw from adults, it is unlikely that any formally structured gangs will be created. If they are not present, then gangs will almost certainly be formed and begin to have a life of their own.

RELATIONSHIP WITH ADULTS

Although early-adolescent boys and girls may willingly accept adult company, they tend to be wary in their relationships with grown-ups. Because they distrust themselves, they tend to distrust others. This wariness means that, usually by unacceptable behavior, adults are tested to see what they are like: Do they lose their tempers? Are they kind, firm, weak, or overpermissive? Do they have the capacity to convey to a boy or girl that feelings are respected and understood? Young adolescents are ready and prepared to accept direction from people they respect and admire, but this admiration usually has to be earned. Involved adults have to show that they have qualities that early adolescents can understand.

Preferably, those adults who form relationships with early adolescents are involved in helping them gain control of themselves, and they should continue to be a part of the child's life through the middle stage of adolescence. This means that adults who have been tested and found worthwhile can then be used as individuals upon whom young people can model themselves, to some extent (Miller, 1969).

Young adult males are necessary to a boy to help him develop and reinforce feelings of masculinity; to a girl, to reinforce feelings of femininity. If adolescents are lucky, they will find a teacher, relative, or friend they can respect, admire, and like. If they are not lucky, they will not. They then become more involved, emotionally, than would otherwise be the case with the folk heroes of the present generation: a pop star, a blues or rock singer. Rarely, nowadays, a revolutionary hero, usually a foreigner about whom less is known, and therefore, fantasy is easier, can be worshipped. For both boys and girls, older women may symbolize safe mothering, and both sexes are needed to help the adolescent develop to mature adulthood. Tenderness, traditionally associated with femininity, is necessary for successful male identity; environmental mastery, traditionally part of the male role, is necessary for women.

MUSIC

Along with, and sometimes without, the preoccupation with singers and musicians, early adolescents are preoccupied with music itself. This preoccupation is due, in part, to the efforts of the communications industry to sell records, in part, to meet adolescent needs. Passive entertainment is only one aspect; music is particularly enjoyed because of the exciting quality of its sound and the rhythm that leads to the movement that is necessary in early adolescence to relieve tension. Early adolescents do not play music loudly because their hearing is less sensitive than that of adults (damage to the hearing apparatus due to excessive noise is now common in the young). Partly loud music is a cultural habit, partly it is played with an awareness that loudness is an irritant to adults, partly it is a way to blot out thoughts and fantasies that the young may wish to avoid. Often the preoccupation with music becomes so intense, prolonged, and isolating that it prevents further emotional development. This is particularly likely in those adolescents who find it very difficult to develop a sense of themselves. Music can occupy the same role that previously was occupied by pinball machines, and is now occupied by video-games. Most video-game parlors also play rock music. These activities can become a sterile dead end to personality growth.

SEXUAL RELATIONSHIPS

Early-adolescent boys are not genuinely or actively interested in girls, who tend to be seen as worthless and are criticized for being weak and soft. The attitudes about girls that were present in the eight-year-old boy are still present, because feelings of being inadequate are always just on the edge of consciousness. Young adolescents always fear they will be unable to control themselves, for boys in early adolescence are interested in sex mostly as it affects their own bodies. Clinical examples demonstrate this problem. Sometimes older sisters of fifteen or sixteen may tease and provoke their younger pubertal brothers. It is as though the girl needs to see just how far she can go in provoking an outburst from a rivalrous male. On occasion, this may lead to tragedy. One seventeen-year-old girl, in a family where verbal communication was minimal and parental interest distant, was knifed by her brother in the following circumstances:

> Kenny, a fourteen-and-one-half-year-old boy, was about two years into early adolescence. He and his friends were preoccupied with such magazines as "Playboy" and "Penthouse" and often his sister would get them for him. She would also ask him if he had a real girlfriend yet. Furthermore, she would engage in wrestling matches with him. Many boys, threatened by such behavior might have lost their tempers; Kenny never did. One night as he was watching television, his sister began to shave her legs in the adjoining room, in full sight of Kenny. The boy went and got a kitchen knife, wrapped the handle in a towel, and entering her room began to attack his sister with it. As they struggled, the telephone rang and the boy stopped his attack to answer it.
>
> He was horrified to discover how badly he had wounded his sister and was almost completely unaware of what had happened.

Kenny's dissociative murderous episode had obviously been precipitated by his sister's consistently provocative behavior. In this pubertal boy there was an intense mixture of aggressive and sexual impulses; usually these were isolated from consciousness and not translated into behavior. When the provocation became too great, violence ensued. The clinical problem was to decide how dangerous Kenny might be, but as is so often the case, the behavior of a disturbed adolescent demonstrates some of the problems of normal growth.

It is obvious from the behavior of early-adolescent boys and girls that they use a variety of techniques to gain control over their sexual feelings. In their groups, early adolescents tend to tell each other dirty stories and, toward the end of early adolescence, they may pass around dirty pictures or watch pornographic films on home video. Pornography is particularly the preoccupation of the pubertal boy just before the middle stage of adolescence is reached, although interest in it may continue into adulthood.

Adolescent jokes are designed to shock adults and, preferably, are on subjects of which adults disapprove (Freud, 1905). In those parts of society where ordinary sexual matters are no longer a subject for adult shock, jokes told by early adolescents include such topics as lesbianism and homosexuality.

Sexual jokes told by boys are also associated with behavior that demonstrates their preoccupation with their genitals and those of other boys. It is common for boys to attempt to "debag" each other in scuffles; this is a preoccupation with exposure and nonexposure.

MASTURBATION

Jokes, physical play, and masturbation are all used by early-adolescent boys as part of the process of gaining control over their own bodies, and particularly control over feelings of sexual excitement. Toward the end of early adolescence, boys very easily experience genital tension. They go through a stage in which they experience an erection with little or nothing in the way of external stimulation. When sexual feelings were thought to be properly hidden, many boys found this a shameful and embarassing occurrence. The shame and embarrassment, however, are now more related to feelings of lack of control, rather than to a feeling of shame of sexuality.

It is a psychological task of early adolescence in boys to separate sexual from aggressive feelings and to begin to connect the feeling of sexual excitement with the physical changes that take place when an erection occurs. Boys who tell dirty stories to each other are trying out their own control of their feelings. They stimulate their sexual fantasies, but, when these occur in a group, they control their bodily expression. Pornography allows sexual excitement partly because it is stimulated from outside the self; thus, fantasies are other people's responsibility, are socially acceptable and need not be felt as incestuous. The relationship between social acceptability and incestuous anxiety is demonstrated by the following clinical example.

> A fourteen-year-old Irish immigrant boy had his first emission when he was thirteen. At that time he was living in a primitive part of Ireland and shared a bed with his two sisters, one older, one younger. Both his

parents were in bed in the same room. Subsequently, the family moved out of Ireland, but this life-style continued in their new urban environment and six months after the move Don began to have "seizures." These were investigated for physical causes and only when all investigations had proved negative was referral made to a psychiatrist. No one in the neurological investigation had checked the boy's sleeping arrangements.

During therapy it was discovered that the move to the city had meant that the boy moved to a school in which sexuality was freely discussed, a situation that did not exist in Ireland. Don now had social permission to be sexual and here was confronted with his incestuous situation. Unable to masturbate as did others, he had "seizures" instead. A change of sleeping arrangements and brief therapy focused on the "normality" of his conflict led to a rapid resolution.

It becomes important to boys toward the end of early adolescence to know that they can ejaculate. They discover this either by masturbating, a natural activity of this age period, or by nocturnal emissions. Masturbation is associated with the discovery that ejaculation can take place. Its importance to boys is obvious in the slang words they give it. *Spunk*, one English swear word used to describe ejaculatory fluid, used to mean bravery. *To come*, another way of describing the act of ejaculation, also means to arrive.

Masturbation itself is described by words that also say a good deal about attitudes in terms of budding manhood. A middle-class, British private school description is to *flog off*. A flogging in Britain means a physical beating. *Beating* is used as a slang word for the act in the United States. In America, *jerk off* is a typical adolescent slang expression for masturbation, and it can be no accident that *jerk* is a slang term describing someone who is inadequate. An English, working-class descriptive word is *wanking*, a word that appears to have a variety of derogatory connotations. In World War I, a wonk or wank was a useless seaman or an inexperienced naval cadet. The pun on the word seaman (ejaculatory fluid = semen) is striking. In East Anglic, "wanky" means feeble, and at Felstead School, in England, in 1892, "wanker" was the school word for a stinker. Since lower-class boys tend to be more contemptuous of masturbation than middle-class boys, as is obvious from the derivation of the slang word, so lower-class adolescents tend to abandon masturbation before their middle-class agemates. Such boys may have heterosexual relationships, though intercourse is highly self-referent and has an obvious masturbatory quality. This type of behavior is illustrated by the greater incidence of illegitimate pregnancy in this social class (G.A.P. report, 1984).

Adults and older adolescents sometimes contemptuously recognize the childish quality of the masturbatory act as something associated with growing up; they talk of boys playing with themselves.

Masturbation is an act that is clearly self-centered. It is a way in which boys appease feelings of loneliness and isolation and a technique by which they gain control, by physical means, over their own state of sexual excitement. It is also an attempt to connect psychological feelings with physical experience, sexual fantasies with the experience of tumescence and detumescence. Finally, it is used to relieve conscious feelings of sexual frustration. There is a quality of aggressiveness in the act in older boys, as it implies that the purpose of women is only to satisfy men.

It is not uncommon in some societies for early-adolescent boys to engage in mutually masturbatory acts with each other. Sometimes this is a part of a group activity; sometimes two boys may masturbate each other. This type of activity does not necessarily indicate the ultimate development of a homosexual involvement. When boys masturbate themselves in front of other boys, the exhibitionism is a way to confirm that sexual feelings can be held in common; it is a primitive way of confirming manhood. This is reinforced because such an activity is disapproved of socially; it becomes a way of defying the standards of the adult world.

Mutual masturbation between two boys in early adolescence is rarely associated with feelings of love and affection. Often when the boys in question like each other before such an act, they are unlikely to be friendly afterwards. This is because such an activity, although often a transient part of development, is felt by the boys who take part in it as meaning that they are going to be exclusively homosexual. Boys whose primary orientation is heterosexual do not want to put together in the world of their feelings, love, affection, and sexual excitement in relation to a member of their own sex. Either group masturbatory activity or mutual masturbation more usually occurs when boys are under stress; it is particularly likely if their environment fails to meet their needs. This is a common situation in neighborhoods that have few outlets for constructive activity for adolescents and in schools or prisons that are too rigid or too permissive. In neither situation, one of which offers too little, the other too much freedom, are adolescents given the amount of responsibility they can handle, a prerequisite for satisfactory emotional growth.

Despite the wide dissemination of knowledge about the normality of the act in the last twenty-five years, masturbation is still a subject of concern and anxiety both to some boys and their parents. It is often believed to weaken boys and to lead to their being unsatisfactory lovers and husbands. Some boys who do not easily make friends and do not get the opportunity to compare personal experiences with other boys, think that they are odd if they masturbate. Others believe that it is harmless, providing it is not done excessively. The definition of excessive varies from individual to individual; some feel it is excessive to masturbate daily, others once a week.

It is inconceivable that any boy can physically harm himself in normal masturbation, and it is impossible to define excessive frequency from a physical standpoint. But the anxiety that can be produced because of the fantasies associated with masturbation can be intense. A boy wrote the following letter:

> Frankly speaking, because I got into the habit of masturbating so often (usually two or three times a day even at home), it is obviously less easy to "come off" each time. To counteract this I find I have to think along more and more perverse (for want of a better word) lines. . . . By the way, sucking and kissing of boy's pricks and balls also enters my thoughts, which is what is most distressing, after I have "come off."

The loneliness and isolation of this boy was intense. He had few friends and was going through the painful experience of having a father who was ill of cancer. He could not tell his parents anything of the anxiety he suffered; they did not even know of his loneliness. To have told them even this would have been to abandon his tenuous sense of autonomy.

Just as the male of the species can have intercourse with a frequency that varies with his sexual drive, the willingness of his partner, and his general state of fatigue or tension, so the frequency of masturbation relates to the first and last of these. The physically active young male cannot become weak and debilitated by masturbating, nor is it possible to deduce that a boy masturbates because in some way he is socially inadequate.

Psychologically withdrawn, isolated, lonely boys who spend too much time alone may be masturbating during these periods. This means that for them masturbation becomes a poor substitute for genuine human relationships; it is no accident that adolescents who take LSD often continue to masturbate during the drug experience. With a failure to make meaningful emotional relationships, the act of masturbation becomes the equivalent of thumbsucking in the lonely infant.

A common sight in classrooms is for some of the early adolescent boys to be manipulating their genitals at the back of the room. This is a measure both of general physical tension and boredom. Sometimes young adolescents tend to sit with their hands covering their penis; these are anxious boys who are unconsciously ready to ward off an attack.

Masturbation in early-adolescent girls is less common than with boys, and masturbation does not become a significant act in girls until the end of mid-adolescence. This is partially because feelings of focused sexual tension do not develop, in those girls who do not have early intercourse, until physical growth has ceased (Kinsey et al., 1953). A girl's need for sexual bodily contact is first experienced as a need to be hugged and cuddled. Sexual arousal in a girl is a slower process than in a boy. Although fantasies give some satisfaction, women have to learn from experience that genital manipulation followed by vaginal penetration is emotionally gratifying. Some girls never have this experience and have intercourse only as payment for being held and cuddled. Other women can enjoy external manipulation of their genitals, but get no satisfaction either from penetration by the male penis or from the awareness that they have given their sexual partners a significant emotional experience.

Tense, overanxious pubertal girls often experience a diffuse physical discomfort that they discover can be relieved by genital play. Sometimes this extends to the use of an artificial penislike object; a tampon may be used, but this is relatively rare. Girls who masturbate, in the past, had more shame about this act than boys, who now mostly accept it as normal, at any rate consciously. Girls may feel that they are behaving in an unsatisfactory, perhaps emotionally sick way. In early-adolescent girls, masturbation is often a response to stressful situations; it is not necessary for mature sexual development.

REFERENCES

Block, H., and Neiderhoffer, A. (1958), *The Gang*. New York: Philosophical Library.

Block, V. L. (1957), Conflicts of adolescents with their mothers. *J. Abnorm. Soc. Psychol.*, 32: 193–206.

Crane, R. A. (1958), The development of moral values in children. *Br. J. Educ. Psychol.*, 28: 201–208.

Fainberg, M. R. (1953), Relationships of background experience to social acceptance. *J. Abnorm. Soc. Psychol.*, 48: 206–214.

Freud, S. (1950), Jokes and their relation to unconscious. In *The Standard Edition of the Complete Psychological Works of Sigmund Freud*. Vol. 8. London: Hogarth Press, 1960.

G.A.P. Report (1984). *Adolescents and Illegitimate Pregnancy*. To be published, 1984.

Gutmann, D., and Krohn, A. (1972), Changes in mastery style with age: A study of Navajo dreams. *Psychiatry*, 34 (3): 289–301.

Kinsey, A. C., *et al.* (1953), *Sexual Behavior in the Human Female*. Philadelphia: W. B. Saunders.

Levy, J., and Monroe, R. (1938), *The Happy Family*. New York: Knopf.

Miller, D. (1969), *The Age Between*. London: Hutchinson.

Miller, D., and Looney, J. (1976), Determinants of homicide in adolescents. *Adoles. Psychiatr.*, IV; 231–254.

Miller, D. (1980), Treatment of Seriously Disturbed Adolescents. *Adoles. Psychiatr.*, VIII: 469–481.

Miller, W. (1958), Lower class culture as a generating milieu of gang delinquency. *J. Soc. Issues*, 14: 5–19.

Opie, I., and Opie, P. (1969), *Children's Games in Street and Playground.* New York: Oxford University Press.

Ottenburg, P. (1968), Dehumanization in social planning and community psychiatry. *Am. J. Psychothera.* 22 (4): 585–591.

Taba, H. (1953), The moral beliefs of sixteen-year-olds. In *The Adolescent: A Book of Readings,* ed. J. Seidman, 592–596. New York: Dryden Press.

Winnicott, D. W. (1971), *Therapeutic Consultations in Child Psychiatry.* New York: Basic Books.

Chapter 3

The Middle Stage

PHYSICAL CHANGES

In the middle stage of adolescence, physiological and anatomical changes in connection with growth are still taking place. Boys show a marked rise in testosterone levels, mature spermatozoa are produced, and facial hair continues to increase in amount (Talbot, *et al.*, 1952). The hairline of boys begins to develop a slight peak. Acne is common. In boys, the years fifteen, sixteen, and seventeen are most commonly associated with this stage; in girls, years fourteen, fifteen, and sixteen. Girls show a great increase in estrogen and seventeen ketosteroid excretion. A girl's periods are regular, and ovulation occurs regularly, between them. Pubic and axillary hair increase in amount. Her body fills out, baby fat is lost, and her hips become wider and her breasts fuller. Full growth may be obtained at this age. A girl's voice changes its timbre, the change not being as dramatic as with boys, and she, too, may develop acne. Severe acne should be treated, in boys as well as in girls, since mid-adolescents are very conscious of how they appear to others.

CONFIRMATION OF IDENTITY

In relating to the world-at-large, middle-stage adolescents often start by demanding to know the reason for the rules set by society, and why such rules should be obeyed. There can be a short period of time, lasting six months or so, when authority appears to be almost totally rejected. The end of early adolescence is thus marked by an extreme psychic turbulence that points to the onset of the development of a firm feeling of identity: "This is what I am." Identity can be defined as a conscious sense of individual uniqueness (Erikson, 1963). When they are sure of their own identity, adolescents can finally free themselves from their childish dependence on their parents and begin to establish a new relationship with them, as grown-up sons and daughters. They remain open to new experiences and a changing self-concept from then onwards, even as adults. Identity foreclosure, the development of a rigid sense of self, to an extent, is the failure to develop an adequate sense of inner freedom. Although such a rigid sense of self can serve the individual well in everyday life, the price in terms of personal rigidity may be high.

From infancy onward, children model themselves on their parents and, to some extent, on other adults; during mid-adolescence, this need for other adults as role-models reaches a peak. The mid-adolescent boy has a particular need for an adult male with whom to identify, although he may also incorporate into his personality some of the tender caring qualities seen in more mature women. Identification is the process by which the individual takes into his personality the qualities of people as he sees them, and the way they seem to get along with each other. To make this possible, it is necessary for adults other than parents to show boys that they are interested in them over a period of years. It is also important that these adults be seen as valuable to the boy and to society-at-large. There is, for example, some evidence (Gold, 1963) that delinquents are more successfully helped by adults who society obviously regards highly than they are by people who society apparently does not value. Girls identify with their mothers more directly than boys with either parent. Not only do girls identify with extra-parental adults, but the nonsexual affection of adult males reinforces their sense of worth as women as well.

TYPES OF IDENTIFICATION

Identification may be either a conscious or an unconscious process (Erikson, 1968). Since the first models with which children identify are their parents, it is not surprising that other people used as models by adolescents often have qualities remarkably like the parents, although adolescents may not be aware of this. The new adult becomes a "mediator" for identification with parents, allowing adolescents to be like their parents, but also to feel independent of them. For example:

> Kenneth, a sixteen-year-old boy, came to see a psychiatrist because of school failure, social isolation, and obvious depression. His parents were divorced, his father being a highly successful self-made man who had married again—this time to an extremely beautiful woman. Kenneth felt his father was a fraud because "no-one can make money like him honestly"; a lecher because his wife was ten years younger than her husband and, finally, a hypocrite because even if he was unstable at home, he was very pleasant to visitors. Therapy was finally not possible, but a recommendation was made to the boys' school, which was relatively small, that a young able teacher be interested in Kenneth. The French teacher changed, and the boy perceived the new teacher as an outgoing, charming, uninhibited person. He came to the conscious decision that he would very much like to have a personality similar to that of the new teacher.

Kenneth imagined that his teacher was, like all Frenchmen, extremely successful with women; he admired his ability and felt that he had a particularly pleasing personality. Kenneth was unaware, when he described this, that the qualities he saw in the teacher were remarkably similar to those he thought his father had. He could not identify with his father directly, because to do so would have meant that he could not see himself as separate from him: he could not then be independent. So he needed the teacher as a male role-model, which made identification with his father possible. His depression disappeared.

Adolescents may consciously decide that there are qualities in other people they wish to have, ones which differ from those of their parents. One boy found himself attached to certain mannerisms of his geography teacher. He decided that this way of relating to people would be a comfortable and agreeable one for him. He consciously copied these mannerisms; at a later stage in his development, they became so much a part of his personality that he was no longer aware of their source.

> An American boy of sixteen met another boy whom he saw relating to people with a "European" ease. He himself was rather shy, and he decided that this way of relating was a highly appropriate one. Therefore, he set out to copy it. By the time he was nineteen, people started to notice how "European" he was. Suddenly another American boy, who was unsure whether he wanted to go to college in the United States or Great Britain, unconsciously had a British accent while talking of England, and an American one while discussing his U.S. home. It was as if he had attempted to retain a partial identification with his parents, through his American accent.

Very often boys and girls who are emotionally involved with adults, especially physicians or social workers (i.e., "helpers"), may unconsciously behave like them without being at all aware of it, and begin to walk or to move as they do.

When the model with whom the adolescent is identifying is unlike the parents, the process of identification may enrich the personality, but it can also cause many problems. This is particularly likely if the model comes from a cultural background that is different from that of the adolescent, a probable experience for children living with their parents in foreign countries and attending local schools. When there is a common language, the problem can be quite subtle: for example, American children in London during their mid-adolescent years may attend English schools, and after three or four years, they tend to develop the identity of English boys and girls.

Not all identifications are positive; if the most significant aspects of the environment are felt as brutal and aggressive, then these qualities are taken into the personality. Adolescents who were in concentration camps may, as adults, have many of the aggressive qualities of their guards. The adolescent victims of brutality are rarely able to adopt a more tender attitude toward humanity. If girls are brutalized, they are often unable to be loving wives and mothers. Boys are more likely to be in some type of penal setting than girls during mid-adolescence; exposed to the depersonalized degradation of such a setting, they are likely to become adults who are cold, distant, and harsh and who degrade both their own humanity and that of others.

The attitudes and feelings adolescents sense in others and adopt for themselves vary among ethnic groups. In families of Finnish descent in the Upper Peninsula of Michigan, commonly the adult male does not express open tenderness. Traditionally, the man is silent in his home and not very communicative; he does not display warmth. His conflicts are resolved, and his impulses released by an open-air life of hunting and fishing or by an intense preoccupation with high school sports; alcohol may be used in excessive amounts. The adolescent son of such a man almost invariably follows in his footsteps. When the boy does not, he may have real identity problems, if he has not found an acceptable role-model elsewhere.

SEXUALITY

The illegitimacy rate among minority adolescents with a socially deprived background has not significantly increased, although increased illegitimacy is particularly evident in white, middle-class adolescents. Nevertheless, most high school students probably do not engage in full sexual relationships, and most academic adolescents still inhibit genital sexuality (Deutsch, 1967).

While needing the adult male as a model, the mid-adolescent boy is ready to try out his sexual identity. Initially, boys daydream about girls they do not know, often older women (Offer, 1969); and as they move through the age period they may begin to experiment sexually with girls, thus assessing their own sexual ability. At the end of early adolescence, the girl feels ready to try out her own femininity, to assume the role of an adult woman. The mid-adolescent girl is looking for a boy to love. To the boy of seventeen, however, the sixteen-year-old girl who loves him is all too often a trophy to be proudly displayed to his contemporaries. During the middle stage of adolescence, other boys are still more important in the assessment of individual masculinity than are girlfriends.

> Tom, a sixteen-year-old in the eleventh grade, was referred to a psychiatrist by his somewhat puritanical, middle-class father because, during a furious row with him he had admitted to having intercourse with his girlfriend of fourteen. The boy said, "He doesn't understand that everyone in my group has fucked a girl—he is trying to make me soft or something."

Apart from those who are responding to sociocultural pressures, and even among that group, girls need to try out loveless sexuality activity *only* if they are psychologically under so much stress that they are unable to tolerate feeling frustrated and unloved. This state may be produced by serious conflict and deprivation during adolescence or by the absence of supportive adults, particularly men. The father may have been the only man in a girl's life, or developmental immaturity may have been produced by an unhappy childhood. Girls brought up in one-parent families without father substitutes, girls with fathers who have abandoned all semblance of an understandably masculine role differing from that of mother, or girls who are members of an isolated family group are particularly at risk. They are likely to be tempted to try out and to reassure themselves of their femininity by becoming sexually involved with a boy in much the same way a boy commonly is sexually involved with girls. It is also likely that they will need to discuss this competitively with other girls—a discussion that is quite different from talking about a love affair to an intimate girlfriend.

Boys in an all-male environment, providing that their integrity is respected, are much less psychologically threatened than girls in an equivalent situation. Masculinity during mid-adolescence can still be assessed if girls are not present, whereas girls cannot perceive themselves as becoming acceptably feminine in the absence of boys or interested adult males about whom fantasy is possible.

Although middle-class attitudes have begun to permeate the lower-class, social-class differences in attitudes toward intercourse are still apparent during mid-adolescence. The double standard is still common in lower-class groups of various ethnic backgrounds. Boys with a certain ethnic background may say that if one is in love with a girl, she should not be spoiled by premarital intercourse; if she agrees to a love affair, she becomes worthless. It is as if she ceases to be good after the boy has had sex with her, a striking comment on his own sexuality. Open aggression toward girls is often acceptable in such groups. Many boys see nothing wrong in slapping a girl's face if they dislike her behavior; not to do this, is not to be man enough.

The findings of two decades ago, that middle-class youth cannot allow themselves as much early heterosexual experimentation as lower-class boys and that they tend to have intercourse two years later than the latter (Schofield, 1965), remain true. Reports of active heterosexual involvement among middle-class youth are now, however, more common. Masturbation remains more acceptable to middle-class youths than to lower-class youths; this is true into young adulthood. A twenty-two-year-old, white, middle-class, medical student will freely admit to masturbation at times when he has no sexual partner; this admission appears intolerable to either a black, upwardly mobile student or to a young white automobile factory worker. Middle-class boys often assess their masculinity, when they finally have intercourse, by their ability to give their girlfriends an orgasm, and they like to feel that they are emotionally involved with their partners. Others regard the sexual possession of a girl as satisfactory proof of masculinity.

More and more, middle-class boys no longer appear to feel that their wives should be virgins. Boys generally seem convinced that a virgin who has intercourse with a boy will inevitably need another lover when the affair breaks up. This idea has been around for decades, and from a great many case histories, it appears to hold true.

Middle-class adolescents appear to be more likely to use contraceptives than lower-class youths. Many insecure boys, especially, find it intolerable if their girlfriends use either a contraceptive pill or a intrauterine device. Secure men find it inconceivable that intercourse might be preferable with anxiety over a possible pregnancy. In the male psyche, however, fertility is equated with potency; boys like to know how much seminal fluid they can produce and how forcefully it can be ejaculated. Boys who are unsure of themselves may prefer to have sex with no contraceptive at all, and may insist that intercourse feels better when their girlfriend does not use the pill. In some such cases, the boy may become impotent if he finds out that his girlfriend is using this contraceptive technique.

Those couples who relate only to each other during middle-stage adolescence, isolating themselves from other young people, are using the relationship as a way of feeling more secure as they attempt to become psychologically independent of their parents. Frequent sexual intercourse is not as common between these youngsters as might be thought, although if the boy needs to impregnate a girl to prove to himself that he is masculine and potent, pregnancy becomes highly likely.

> One sixteen-year-old boy spent all his time with his fifteen-year-old girlfriend. He had regular, unprotected intercourse with her. Despite the fact that he knew when girls were more likely to be fertile, and he claimed that he did not wish her to have a baby, he was more sexually active with her during these times. He said "I don't want her to be pregnant because I don't know what we would do, but I guess I would really like to feel that she is."

The attitude of relating masculinity and potency to pregnancy, is particularly common in Hispanic males. They may refuse to limit family size, and may leave a wife who has a hysterectomy.

Anxiety about homosexuality remains common among all social classes. Some boys who perceive themselves as homosexual are now much more willing to admit this to physicians, although they rarely tell their parents. Comments made in treatment settings nowadays would have been almost inconceivable a decade ago.

> One sixteen-year-old boy said "I used pot a year or two ago because I did not want to admit to myself that I was gay. I know I am because I am not interested in girls and I like to look at young men. I don't know how to find someone; it's much easier to make a pass at a girl, I guess. My friend (a girl) says she thinks I have the sort of body that appeals to gay people. I know this is true because some men look at me on the train."

This youngster made it clear that he had no intention of being picked up because he felt that there was more to life than casual relationships. Tolerance about homosexuality may, however, not be present when it applies to the self. One young student said, "I hate myself because I think of men when I masturbate—if I ever do it I'll kill myself."

VOCATIONAL CHOICE

Young people in their mid-adolescent years begin to develop their first real sense of the future. They begin to ask: "What sort of person am I?" During mid-adolescence there begins to be a definite idea of career choice, although this may not be more than a preliminary sifting (Porter, 1954). For the first time, the mid-adolescent is capable of saying with a degree of certainty: "This is what I like." The choice is less likely to change during mid-adolescence than in the early-adolescent years. A career choice made before the age of fourteen or fifteen is almost always unrealistic. Only those early adolescents with special talents—artists, musicians, and mathematicians, for example—appear capable of making an early choice with any certainty that this will be their vocation, although they often are quite bored in the usual high school situation. Furthermore, they risk rejection by their peers because they are considered odd and unusual (Hollingsworth, 1926), although this is less of a problem in cosmopolitan areas, where exposure to many people with different careers is usual.

The increase in unemployment among youth causes great anxiety to middle-stage adolescents. Those who can no longer find part-time employment angrily (and accurately) feel that their parents are unreasonably pressing them to find jobs; for middle-class youth the need for a continued allowance may be resented. Those who leave school at sixteen and attempt to enter the labor market may make their way with chronic antisocial behavior. Theft becomes more acceptable as a way both of acquiring things and to relieve boredom.

NEED FOR STABLE RELATIONSHIPS

All developing human beings need a stable environment, but the mid-adolescent often appears to have less stability than any other age group. This may be because society has been fooled by the superficial appearance of physical maturity in many adolescents and assumes that they are as mature as they look. Society does not seem to understand that mid-adolescents need to have a three- to four-year period of stable relationships with adults. If no helpful adults are available, they then find it very difficult to make secure identifications. Juvenile court statistics often show that there is a peak of delinquent behavior at the change point from junior high school to high school in those school districts that isolate early adolescents from the rest of the school system. Anxiety about leaving a known environment is one possible reason for this, but antisocial behavior may also occur because the junior high schools, except for those children engaging in athletics, drama, or the school orchestra, commonly do not provide children with stable extraparental adult relationships. With great difficulty, because of the structure of the school, a stable peer group may be found, but another change of school soon threatens this stability. Delinquent behavior may become a form of protest against the loss of developmental security.

The response of girls to the loss of significant anchor points in society was clearly described by a young schoolteacher in Britain. Talking of the behavior of girls in their last year at school, at age fourteen-and-one-half, she said that for the first six months of their last year they seemed extremely interested in what they were doing in the classroom and highly involved with each other and with her. In the last six months, it was as if they had changed completely. They were concerned only with acquiring material possessions and boyfriends; obtaining a boyfriend, at any cost, was crucial. The teacher had wondered whether this change in behavior was due to a failure on her part.

The evidence from clinical work is that this overpreoccupation with materialism and boyfriends comes from despair. If an adult is felt by adolescents to be a worthwhile person and then seems to reject them, the good attitudes that the youngster feels the adult possesses may also have to be discarded. The girls in this teacher's class saw the possession of things as an answer to the anxiety aroused by losing someone they respected and admired. In the United States, equivalent situations occur when young adults develop an apparent interest in the young via "rap sessions" in a school, stay for one semester, and then casually go on to other things.

The pain caused to mid-adolescents by the loss of a significant adult too early appears in many ways. When the mid-adolescent realizes that he is being thrust into the outside world long before he is ready to face it, he may turn to drugs. In typical high schools, adolescents who have experienced repeated changes of teachers often seem by this age to despair of adults as having anything worthwhile to offer. On the other hand, the resilience of youth can be striking, and adolescents never seem to give up hope. In one high school riddled with apparent racial tensions, the adolescents wrote on the hall walls: "Will no teacher ever talk to us?" In another school, with many instances of racial confrontation, both black and white students made the same demands, for interest and involvement, of the staff.

The stages of adolescence overlap, and the delineation is not as definite as these paragraphs suggest. Adolescents who stay at school show a marked stage of early adolescence. In those who are still pupils from age fourteen to eighteen, and who are perhaps bound for college, the middle stage is also marked. In those who go to work after sixteen, and who receive no further education, middle and late adolescence overlap and the individual is psychosocially a young adult at age seventeen to eighteen. The failure to receive adequate psychosocial support during the early and middle stages of adolescence, either because it is not available or because other factors, such as broken families or indifferent teachers, intervene, leads to a failure to become finally autonomous and develop a firm sense of self. Young people may then remain other-directed adults whose self-esteem depends excessively on their perception of what others think of them. They are thus vulnerable to depression, suicide, and drug abuse and often are fearful of using their abilities because the envy of others is intolerable (Miller, 1982). If good jobs are not available, they may turn to a life of crime to satisfy their materialistic yearnings in good clothes, jewelry, and cars. Society thus pays a high price for its failure to provide adequate psychosocial support to its young.

REFERENCES

Deutsch, H. (1967), *Selected Problems of Adolescence*. New York: International Universities Press.

Erikson, E. H. (1963), *Childhood and Society*. New York: Norton.

—— (1968), *The Young Man Luther*. New York: Norton.

Gold, M. (1963), *Status Forces in Delinquent Boys*. Ann Arbor: Institute for Social Research, University of Michigan.

Hollingworth, L. S. (1926), *Gifted Children, Their Nature and Nurture*. New York: Macmillan.

Miller, D. (1982), Adolescent suicide. Etiology and treatment. *Adoles. Psychiatr.*, IX: 327–363.

Offer, D. (1969), *The Psychological World of the Teenager*. New York: Basic Books.

Porter, J. R. (1954), Predicting vocational plans of high school senior boys. *Pers. Guid.* 33: 215–218.

Schofield, M. (1965), *The Sexual Behavior of Young People*. London: Longmans.

Talbot, N. B., *et al.* (1952), *Fundamental Endocrinology from Birth through Adolescence*. Cambridge: Harvard University Press.

Chapter 4

The Life Space of
Middle-Stage Adolescents

At the end of early adolescence, boys and girls are beginning to feel themselves, in an emotionally meaningful way, to be autonomous individuals. They are obviously involved with friendship networks of their own, and begin to demand freedom from parental control. Parents tend to become concerned as to whether they are giving their children too much freedom and responsibility; fathers of girls of fifteen or so may become anxiously aware of the real or fantasized sexually predatory nature of young males. Adolescents enjoy shocking their parents in the conflict areas of society—drugs, language, and sexuality. In mid-adolescence, there is more self-control; boys and girls do what they think is appropriate in a given situation. Often, the newly acquired values of youth are unconsciously similar to those parents have been trying to instill (Bath and Lewis, 1962), and by this stage of development, a significant number of adolescents conform to adult norms (Offer, 1974). Nevertheless, both boys and girls feel that the concepts and ideas they have are original. A sense of self, along with a growing awareness of the needs of others, are perceived by adolescents as coming from the wellsprings of their own personality.

Mid-adolescence is the period when the young should develop a final sense of their own identity. In the middle years of adolescence, many begin to know what they would like to do with their lives, although firm decisions may not be made before young adulthood. A delay in decision-making is more likely with the academic adolescent. When jobs are easily available, the sixteen-year-old school dropout and the high school graduate may try several jobs before finally settling on a permanent occupation.

INITIAL TURMOIL

If turbulence is apparent, the first months of mid-adolescence are commonly a time when it is most obvious, particularly in boys. It is almost as if some wish to determine, as they gain more freedom and responsibility, that external controls will provide that dependent needs can be met. At the same time, as part of the struggle toward independence, authority figures are provoked: A boy of sixteen may agree that he will be home at eleven o'clock; when he arrives home at two in the morning, he may refuse to say where he has been. Apart from the failure to keep the time commitment, the boy's behavior may have been responsible; a lack of parental comment may be interpreted as lack of caring, and more irresponsible behavior may occur. A verbal protest may be seen as fairly meaningless; a withdrawal of privilege, although perhaps appropriate, is likely to leave the boy feeling misjudged and mistreated. It is as if these adolescents need to test people in their environment before they can use them as models. Adults are put under a good deal of stress; boys may be intensely negativistic, difficult, argumentative, destructive, sometimes antisocial, and at times, deceitful. Particularly with first-born children, this behavior may make parents anxious because they lack the experience as to what the young are like.

This phase of negativism is often the period of the omission lie: the truth, but not the whole truth, is told; information is not freely volunteered. The impression is often gained that defiance has become an end in itself. This defiance may be crucial for development; it is a further attempt to assert autonomy.

Adolescents brought up by overpermissive parents may now lack all controls; overrepressive parents may produce passive, compliant young people. Some families abandon all attempts at control, either because they overestimate their child's ability to do the right thing or because they cannot tolerate openly expressed anger. Support, as with young adolescents, is more tolerable when it comes from fathers. Mothering still represents a threat to autonomy because dependent needs still exist. Sometimes boys may cope with changed feelings by withdrawing from adults: sometimes they may plunge into activities. Youth clubs, or political organizations on the extreme left or right, may be joined. Some may involve themselves in sports for the first time or may begin to work very hard at school to obtain emotional support from their teachers. At this time, some adolescents become involved with drugs or other types of antisocial behavior, often to see themselves as members of a special group, rather than for the satisfaction obtained from the activity itself.

Girls may not appear as negative as boys, and their transition to the middle stage of adolescence may not produce a crisis with adults. It is much more likely for a girl of fifteen to feel anxious that she is unacceptable to boys. All her friends are considered to be more successful in finding and keeping a boyfriend. The issue is not to have a number of dates with different boys, but rather to find one boyfriend. There are often elaborate rituals for this; a girl asks her girlfriend to tell her boyfriend that she finds another boy attractive and would like to "go out." A girl's problems are more likely to be personally felt, less likely to be acted out in the community. The perception of social failure often leads to brief acute feelings of despair; even if there is no evidence that this is other than chance, it seems as if the youngster prefers to accept responsibility; misery seems better than helplessness.

Boys are now commonly preoccupied with their physical appearance, and skin blemishes are a cause of great concern. Body building is fashionable, and hairstyling important. Both boys and girls are concerned with being attractive before they really want sexual involvement. Girls may be more involved with securing parental approval about their appearance than boys, and may continue to argue with their mothers over issues of taste, the length of a skirt, the amount of cosmetics. Beneath this there may be, unconsciously, a struggle about sexual exhibitionism. Generally, an alliance between mother and daughter will begin. Daughters are more helpful and more likely to respond to implicit family expectations than are boys.

EMOTIONAL ATTACHMENTS OF GIRLS

Not only do the family relationships of mid-adolescent girls differ from those of boys, their external relationships are also different. Boys, as men, are always comfortable in large groups. They like being on teams, they are comfortable with many diffuse friendships, and they are happy if they have one or two very close friends. When no stable peer group is available, male personality development is hindered. If boys do not have special friends, this is not a major stumbling block on the way to adult maturity. A particular buddy is a desirable bonus that is given to a boy by life (Jersild, 1963). Girls need one-to-one relationships more than boys. Without these, the capacity to form heterosexual relationships is impaired. Large groups do not provide an acceptable substitute.

Whether or not a girl is at ease with herself depends not only on her life experience as an infant and child within her family, but also on experiences during puberty. Girls need their fathers as asexual lovers and to modulate their maternal attachments. At first, early-adolescent girls are competitive with mother, seductive and charming with father. By middle adolescence, girls need to have known men and boys who are not members of the immediate family, who will not be interested in overt sexual behavior, but who will care about them.

In early adolescence, many girls develop almost a passion for horses; they not only ride, they also groom and feed them and clean out the stable. Pubertal girls are also intensely interested in the mother/offspring relationships of small creatures: mice, hamsters, rabbits, dogs, and cats. In mid-adolescence, they become much more interested in small babies.

Girls, at the beginning of mid-adolescence, may also develop "crushes" on slightly older girls or women (Cole and Hall, 1964). If these are grossly exaggerated, the indication is that a girl is under educational or social pressure or that she has received insufficient mothering. These crushes at the beginning of the middle stage occur partly because girls are not yet ready for emotional involvement with boys, partly because of a fear or anxiety about being unattractive to the opposite sex. Sometimes crushes are directed toward obviously different people, almost as if the other girl has desirable qualities that emotional contact will help the individual acquire. An older girl often tries out mothering roles in such situations, which, for those with confused feelings about sexual roles, may cause anxiety about being lesbian or lead to a homosexual involvement.

Mid-adolescent girls may become involved with formalizing emotional experiences. They are great keepers of diaries, in which they may pour out, for their eyes only, their intense hopes, fears, loves, and hates (Jersild, 1963). Both the crush and the diary are only the background music to a girl's assessment of her femininity. In fantasy in early adolescence, in reality by the middle stage, the assessment of desirable womanhood is played out in relationship to men and boys.

PARENTS AND CHILDREN

Parents, fathers in particular, now need to convey to their daughters that their feelings and ideas as young women matter. Boys can hold forth in groups and, to an extent, compensate for what they see as adult and paternal disinterest. For girls, this compensation is not so readily available. If they complain outside the family group about fatherly neglect, they are, to an extent, implying their own unattractiveness. This is somewhat similar to the later situation with boyfriends; if boys reject girls in an unkind way, many girls see this as a function of their own unattractiveness rather than of male discourtesy.

Parents have conflicting needs about the growth of their children into adulthood. Mothers and fathers may both be reluctant, unconsciously, to see their children grow up. Because girls are more obviously dependent than boys, this is more likely to be a problem between mothers and daughters than between mothers and sons.

In a serious and meaningful way, parents may find their children questioning attitudes, beliefs, and behavior. Some parents perceive themselves as growing with their children, others find it almost intolerable to have their ideas contradicted and may dismiss both their children and their ideas. Children may then retire into themselves in anger and despair. The sexuality of their children may be felt as an emotional threat by parents, who may feel that their own sexual potency is declining. Parents who have, themselves, had an unsatisfactory sexual adjustment may unconsciously provoke sexual activity in their children (Johnson, 1953). The inorgasmic mother may live vicariously through the sexual activity of her promiscuous daughter (Miller, 1958). At this time, marriages that are fragile may begin to disintegrate.

At all stages of growth, children need as much responsibility as they can handle. There are no rules for this, but the growing adolescent shows his parents that they are now ready for more independence. This may be a highly indirect communication. A boy, for example, who easily becomes enraged when frustrated, may unconsciously be telling his parents that he should not drive the family automobile; driving is, after all, likely to be a frustrating experience. Overcompliant, withdrawn adolescents, or those who are excessively turbulent, are not giving their parents signals that they are ready for more responsibility.

Most girls are ready to try out their role as women by the middle stage of adolescence, but many are well into late adolescence before they feel ready to involve themselves in a meaningful way with a boyfriend. Social pressures make a difference in this respect. Dating practices vary, depending on social class, economic status, and religious affiliation (Crist, 1953). Immigrant groups often differ from the host society for two to three generations, depending on their isolation, educational techniques, and the closeness of kinship ties.

Girls from financially or emotionally underprivileged families are likely to have intercourse earlier than those from more secure groups; although girls from the upper-upper social groups tend to behave as do those from lower-lower socioeconomic groups. This is because both experience essentially similar types of upbringing; neither may be looked after by their mothers, and they have a similar contempt for external objects—the very rich because they are so easily available, the very poor because they are rarely obtained. Early school leavers and delinquent girls who are educated in residential, single-sex schools may have intercourse before equivalent girls graduating from high schools (Schofield, 1965). Girls from schools with an environment that respects the growing needs of adolescents are more likely to appreciate that boys and men can like them for themselves; others may seek sex in order to feel worthwhile.

THE ADOLESCENT GIRL

Girls who put a high value on academic achievement seriously involve themselves with boys only toward the end of late adolescence. The parents of girls who are seeking high academic status may try to discourage boyfriends because this will spoil their daughters' academic chances. Such a girl may acquire a boyfriend to defy her parents, or she may become a relatively isolated member of an academic community.

> Karen, a beautiful, nineteen-year-old student, was referred to the student mental health clinic because, despite excellent high school grades and SAT scores over 1300, she was failing academically. Her usual work load was to go to the undergraduate library for approximately six hours nightly after classes. She had one girlfriend, no other social relationships. In high school, she had had a grade point average of four and had been told by her parents that friendships with boys would mean inevitable academic failure.
>
> She was unable to accept that her life was inadequate during an initial psychiatric assessment. She went to a psychotherapist as obediently as when her parents told her to avoid boyfriends.
>
> Psychotherapy was inordinately difficult, as a healthier outlook toward life basically defied parental norms. Only when the patient understood her fury with her parents, did she become free to begin to develop as a person in her own right. Ultimately, she was a successful graduate who married a fellow student.

The competitive nature of the academic world primarily meets the needs of boys. However, some girls deal with this by becoming overinvolved with academics. Such individuals may concentrate on studies, to the exclusion of everything else, because of internal conflicts or in order to deny important feminine qualities. Sexuality is not all that matters about a girl, but without such an expression of her femininity, life is often felt to be empty. Girls who are forced into competitive situations may have to suspend important aspects of feminine psychology: tenderness, creativity, and the particular capacity to care for others. Under stress, many girls find it increasingly difficult to make meaningful and important emotional relationships (May, 1950). Further, excessive academic pressure, to which adolescents in the middle stage may be exposed, may make it difficult for them to become autonomous from their parents. The passing of requisite examinations, or earning appropriate grades in school, is taken as a sign of self-worth. Such adolescents may appear to do well at school, perform satisfactorily in the first years as university students, and then begin to underachieve. Adult status, instead of being a delight, is a threat; emotional upset is a last attempt to cling to the benefits of childhood.

Although stressful, competitive situations may seem only to delay some aspects of emotional maturation, some adolescents will become emotionally isolated and depressed. Those who come from small, isolated nuclear families, in which academic achievement is overvalued, are particularly vulnerable to academic anxiety.

ADOLESCENT LOVE AFFAIRS

Since girls mature faster than boys (Wilkins, 1965), they are likely to be interested in boys two or three years older than themselves. The more uncertain girls are of themselves, the more likely they are to plunge into prematurely intense relationships with boys or, sometimes, with very much older men. Girls who fall intensely in love at fifteen, who feel they cannot live without their boyfriends, may be unconsciously trying to repair an emotional deficiency of early years. They use the relationship to feel secure, as they leave the security of the nuclear family. Just as with their boyfriends, this relationship becomes a safety blanket that protects them from anxiety about parental separation.

Even without an excessive need for affection, a first love affair in the middle years of adolescence, unless it terminates by mutual agreement, almost always ends with pain for the girl. When girls fall in love and enter into a sexual, loving relationship, they rapidly want it to be permanent. Although boys may say that they will love the girl forever, they cannot mean it before they are well into adulthood, as their primary psychological task is environmental mastery. In sexual relationships, they do not accept long-term responsibility until they feel secure in their vocational responsibility.

Very quickly, a girl discovers that, if she tells her boyfriend that she would like the relationship to continue indefinitely, or that ultimately she would like his child, the relationship becomes tense. So although increasing intimacy should be possible, the girl learns to keep her own counsel to maintain the relationship. For those individuals who need the relationship to reinforce a sense of security and self-worth, its end may lead to a feeling of being unlovable, and unloved. This may happen with either sex, but it appears to be more common with girls.

A satisfactory feeling of womanhood is associated with a capacity to feel creative and imaginative, to be productive in academic or vocational achievement, and to bear a child. When a girl falls in love, these needs come to the fore. In relationships between the sexes in middle and late adolescence, the intensity and completeness of physical intimacy is rarely balanced by an equivalent emotional experience.

SIGNIFICANCE OF SEXUAL RELATIONSHIPS

In the young, the wish to experiment and test capacities is a necessary preliminary to constructive adulthood. Adolescents need to find out about themselves in relationship to another person; this includes the need to discover their own sexual capabilities. Until a boy has actually had intercourse, he cannot know for sure that this is something he can do; until a girl has experienced an orgasm, she does not know whether she has this capacity.

Adolescents in their middle years may have sexual intercourse, but the intensity of exploratory needs as against tender loving needs may lead to conflict, especially in those who feel that human integrity is important and who have developed a capacity to be empathic. A boy may not necessarily boast about his sexual activity, but unless he is unconsciously seeking a mother substitute, the need for a tender, loving relationship with a girlfriend is likely to be secondary to his drive to obtain genital pleasure. In girls, these needs are reversed; their primary need is for a tender, loving relationship; only secondarily, at any rate before they have had sex, have they a need for sexual exploration and excitement.

Girls find dependent needs tolerable and emotionally acceptable; intense sexual excitement may occur only at the culmination of intercourse. A girl first must allow herself to feel and to be dependent on a boy for feelings of sexual readiness to receive him to come to the fore. At this point, glandular and vaginal discharges occur; most girls do not experience this as a frequent sensation without an actual sexual relationship.

By the time a boy engages in a heterosexual relationship, he will have ejaculated many times, having experienced a solitary orgasm either in masturbation, nocturnal ejaculation, or both. In a heterosexual experience, boys seek an enhancement of an experience that, to an extent, they have already had. Only secondarily are they likely to seek a loving tender relationship. Along with a possible wish to feel in love with a girl, the exploratory wish for sexual experience is more conscious with a boy than with a girl. Loveless sexual intercourse indicates that a girl undervalues herself; this is less likely to be true with a boy.

PROBLEMS OF SEXUAL PERMISSIVENESS

Sexual permissiveness poses a dilemma in present-day society. There is still parental and societal pressure against premarital intercourse, but there is also an implicit social pressure to early active heterosexuality. A girl who remains a virgin, even in mid-adolescence, may feel that she is missing out on special experiences that she suspects her girlfriends are having. The pressure among mid-adolescents to ignore parental interdictions is reinforced by some parts of the communications industry, although adolescents who are able to conform to family standards may be able to resist this.

The acceptable moral attitude is appropriately protective of the emotional needs of girls. A compromise in parental attitudes because of a fear of rejection by their daughters is unhelpful. Acceptable moral codes may or may not be listened to, or even apparently heard, but a potential way of life is offered young people that even those who ignore it may ultimately adopt. If adults understand the needs of boys and girls, and if this is reinforced by a girl seeing her own loving parents, then these codes can be heard. When an obviously happily married mother talks about human needs to her daughter, the girl will find it hard to believe that her mother sees all men as predatory when she is urged to restrain her sexuality until she is older. When a parental marriage is unhappy, a daughter may feel that her mother is trying to prevent, in an envious way, a relationship that she herself has never had or has lost. An unloving parental home, or being raised without an involved father because of death, divorce, or constant absence, is likely to harm a girl's capacity to make loving relationships and may drive her to seek them in sexual activity.

Reluctance to explain the nature of heterosexual relationships may be due to parental embarrassment, and may be seen as an unconscious encouragement to become involved, or it may produce acute anxiety.

> Mary, at the age of fifteen, did her best to make herself unattractive to boys. This followed an episode when, at the age of twelve, while on vacation, she had been chased on the beach by two fourteen-year-olds, who had "touched" her. Mary said, "My mother told me about periods, but never said anything about sex. She suggested I read a book, which did not help much. When I came back crying and told my parents what happened, they asked if I had been hurt and then suggested I go swimming."

Children need to know about sex, to be aware of certain situations when it is dangerous to wander alone, or to go off with a stranger. They should also be made aware that certain types of behavior, even in family friends or relatives, are unacceptable. Insofar as sexual behavior is concerned, an updated type of Victorian conservatism, liberally applied by loving parents, is the attitude that is likely to be most helpful. It is reasonable for parents to expect to meet their mid-adolescent daughter's boyfriends. To visit strange homes, where the parents are going to be out, is not felt by children to indicate that such parents are loving, whatever might be said. It is helpful to middle-stage adolescents for parents to be fairly restrictive, to insist, for example, that their children be home at night by a certain time. In some, this may arouse a feeling that parents are being overprotective; young people will angrily complain that their parents are old-fashioned and that restrictive behavior keeps friends of the opposite sex from being interested. When their children are angry with them, parents face the problem of feeling unloved; there is no doubt that it is easier to say "yes" than to say "no." But an angry daughter is less likely to be emotionally hurt than a daughter whose parents cannot tolerate her anger when immediate gratification is denied. Those young people who have been surrounded all their lives by loving and caring adults can weather many storms. A rejection that to one individual is only hurtful, to another is a painful blow, which may temporarily hinder further emotional development.

SOCIAL ASPECTS OF FEMININE IDENTITY

The attitude that achievement is less important for girls than for boys ("they can always marry") is now less usual than previously. There is an awareness, particularly in the West, that both marital partners will need to work just to maintain the equivalent of the parental living standard. This may not be possible for women with children, even among those who are affluent. This may lead to emotional difficulties, for infants who do not have an appropriate mother/child stability and maternal stimulation suffer developmentally. Furthermore, mothers who are forced to accede to economic demands miss out on significant gratifications of child-rearing. Many middle-stage adolescents begin to be aware of this as an issue as they appreciate what they have lost through having working mothers.

All adolescent girls need the opportunity to understand the needs of infants, but for these who bear children, support centers for unwed adolescent mothers appear to reduce child neglect and abuse significantly, by teaching such girls about child-rearing and, at the same time, offering them consistent, supportive "mothering" relationships from a permanent staff. When girls are given the opportunity to look after little ones, they usually enjoy it; it becomes important for them to be able to babysit for their own small brothers and sisters, as well as for other people's children. This need to care for others is reinforced when school and youth groups offer opportunities for looking after others. This can take the form of adolescents from the upper grades tutoring children from the lower grades.

In one private school in the Chicago suburbs, at the graduation ceremony, the eleventh-grade boys and girls, who are present at the ceremony have children from the first and second grades sitting on their laps. At an adolescent treatment center for emotionally disturbed youth, also in Chicago, a highly valued activity among the residents of the center is to be a member of a volunteer group that cares for retarded adults. If young people are part of a social network, the opportunities to be helpful to others are more easily arranged, and highly valued.

Career choice begins to be an issue in mid-adolescence. Tasks that are repetitive, unimaginative, and not involving responsibility, produce an alienation from the self. The individual is not emotionally involved with the work at hand; only partial involvement takes place. With such employment, other outlets to prove self-worth are necessary.

Apart from the fact that the American school system is, compared to other countries, educationally deficient (A Nation at Risk, 1983), the imaginative and creative potential of both boys and girls is neglected by the high school system (Vernon, 1968). Those few schools that value the artistic endeavors or unusual imaginative potentiality of pupils may have to deal with the fact that SAT scores and grade-point averages are seen as an indication of worth by universities. In the public school system, the refusal of local communities to support school taxation has meant the cutting back of vocational and nonacademic studies, a lack that school prayer will not modify.

Education in a society that offers either service activities, or, for many, positions in technology that are not stimulating, needs to assist individuals to know how to use their own time to avoid the inner experience of boredom. Excessive television watching, or drug and alcohol abuse, may be the price paid by the young for educational failure to stimulate physical, emotional, and creative outlets. A failure to reinforce a sense of self-worth is likely to lead to an overpreoccupation with the need for immediate gratification. This preoccupation may become very obvious in the last months of school. Sex may be used to fight off potential feelings of being unloved and unlovable. When adolescents use each other in this way, the relationship is felt to be excessively clinging and demanding, and one or the other partner is likely to be devalued and rejected.

Some girls attempt to ward off the psychic tension of being vocationally and socially devalued by behaving toward boys as they imagine boys behave toward them, moving promiscuously from one to another. Other girls may be isolated, depressed, and withdrawn.

EXTERNAL CONTROLS FOR MID-ADOLESCENTS

If parents are loved and respected by adolescents, the latter behave in a psychosocially appropriate way because of what is requested by the parents, or felt to be acceptable to parental wishes, rather than fear of what the parents might do to them. To physically control adolescents at age fifteen or sixteen and over is impossible, and physical struggles with boys and girls of this age are an unhappy way of trying to assert parental dominance.

Family codes should, by now, be significantly internalized in children, and parents should be able to reinforce them on the basis of mutual respect rather than by coercion.

Parents, however loving, cannot protect adolescent daughters when stress becomes excessive. Parents are not omnipotent, but adolescents under stress appear to retain this childlike concept that they are. When adolescents find themselves hurt by life, they may irrationally blame their parents for not having protected them. An equally difficult problem for parents is that they can no longer protect their children. When young people are hurt, parents tend to blame themselves (Jersild, 1963). It is very difficult for loving parents to accept the helplessness that is now inevitable in relationship to their children's lives.

In the middle years of adolescence, daughters still need advice about many things; boyfriends, jobs, and girlfriends. Thus, although parents can offer protection, they cannot insist upon it as their child grows up. The situation may be more difficult as, from time to time, some relationships appear to be designed to provoke a parental response, and simultaneously, to prove that parental love is still present, along with the necessity for the adolescent to feel autonomous. Such mid-adolescent behavior may appear in chronological late adolescence.

> Janet sought help at the age of twenty-one because she was afraid that she was becoming promiscuous. The daughter of a controlling Jewish mother and a distant father, she began her first love affair at age seventeen with a nineteen-year-old college student. She lived with him for three years and was happy with him. Although he was Jewish, her parents disapproved of him because he was too much of a "hippie." She ended the relationship and then had an intense affair with a gentile boy that lasted three months. She was so afraid of what her mother would say about this relationship

that she never told her parents about it. This boy abandoned her. She then fell in love with a twenty-three-year-old medical student who was also Jewish, and her parents approved. After three months, despite a happy sexual relationship with him, she felt herself attracted to a gentile law student.

It is clear that Janet sought autonomy from parental domination by picking boys of whom they disapproved; at the same time she provoked their intense anxiety.

At mid-adolescence, some young people, beyond parental control, refusing to take advice or direction, are individuals at risk. Inner controls are not usually strong enough to offer self-protection in present-day society. Such adolescents may, at best, repeat in their friendships the disappointment they already feel in their relations with their parents.

SEXUAL RELATIONSHIPS OF MIDDLE-STAGE BOYS

The boy in his middle adolescent years is still assessing his manhood relative to his own age group; such boys are not yet ready to begin mature relationships with girls. Their main interest is in taking rather than giving, in a semipublic rather than a private heterosexual relationship. For example, boys of sixteen or seventeen may not object to rather exhibitionistic public necking at parties. They commonly adopt a take-it-or-leave-it attitude to girlfriends. They will rarely admit to their male friends that any girl has the capacity to hurt or influence them. Boys often discuss the details of highly intimate sexual experiences with male friends, and the opinion of a friend of the same sex matters more than that of a girl.

A boy of fifteen or sixteen, who is actively interested in possible girlfriends, may find it difficult to find a girl of a similar age. However, boys who were in the active growth phase of puberty at the age of eleven or twelve may be physically very mature males at fifteen; older girls of sixteen or seventeen may find them interesting. It was once a prevalent idea that older girls might involve themselves with younger boys because they were less sexually threatening. This is untrue. Some older girls may choose physically mature, fifteen-year-old boys who may still have a strong need to be mothered. Because of the strength of their physical needs, as against their relatively weak emotional controls, these boys are more likely to seek impulsive gratification in a full sexual experience than are older boys at the same stage of physical maturity. Physical maturity is not a measure of emotional maturity, but expectations are often based on it. Too little may be expected from those who mature late, too much from those who mature early. Usually, fifteen-year-old boys are not sexually interesting to girls of the same age, who are looking for older boys. Thirteen-year-old girls, who might find sixteen-year-old boys interesting, may not interest them. A boy of fifteen to seventeen thus tends to go through a develomental stage in which there are few girls available; this period of sexual frustration allows many boys to sublimate sexual drives into other important areas of masculine mastery and development, both educationally and in sports.

Not all adolescents have celibacy thrust upon them. For some, sexual intercourse in essentially a self-referent relationship that may begin in early adolescence. Despite the fact that earlier intercourse is becoming more common among middle-class adolescents, those who have regular early sexual intercourse are less likely to become academically trained members of the community.

Mid-adolescent boys, although still struggling against dependent wishes, begin to feel more autonomous by the end of the age period. Parents begin to notice an increased capacity on the part of their children to care for themselves.

There is much discussion about adolescent rebellion, less about adolescent conformity. Adolescents are highly obedient to consistent societal demands. When these are inconsistent, when words and deeds are contradictory, implicit rather than explicit demands tend to be followed (Reames and Sadler, 1959).

EXTRAPARENTAL ADULTS IN MID-ADOLESCENCE

All through adolescence, adults that are known, liked, and respected primarily by young people themselves, and by their parents, and secondarily by society at large, are important in emotional development. These necessary grown-ups may be the parents of childhood friends (usually these are made before the age of ten), or they may be adults who occupy a significant role in an adolesent's life. In the school system, athletic coaches and drama, art, and music teachers have an interpersonal relationship long enough to be of developmental value to adolescents. With the exception that highly charged, brief relationships may be significant, other teachers rarely relate long enough to their charges to become important as role-models. Often, neighborhood adults may provide the emotionally meaningful extraparental figures in the lives of middle-stage adolescents. As discussed earlier, one set of local parents will provide a home away from home for a whole group of young people. Sometimes they hold open house even when their children are away. These are people who have a particular quality of warmth and tolerance that appeals to the adolescent. They may be older than most parents. They often offer an emotional, safe, culturally more stereotyped picture of mothering, plump, not-too-well-groomed mother figures are the ideal image for adolescent boys, particularly if they are not their own mother. These adults may provide a friendship network that is used by boys and girls in two ways. First, they are a refuge in times of crisis; their home can provide a haven when an adolescent feels at odds with his own parents; it is somewhere to go where they are accepted. Second, as young people strive to move away from the dependent feelings of childhood, since they now struggle less with the turmoil of puberty, they can involve themselves emotionally with other people. To prove that they are no longer children, they may move away from home and literally put distance between themselves and their families. In any case, they engage in some degree, in an emotional withdrawal. Some adolescents may stop communicating with their families; adult friends then become important both to provide an anchor point from which growth away from the family can take place and to become role-models and individuals who are identified with by the adolescent.

Nonparental adults are used differently by boys and girls. Girls especially need to feel valued by extraparental adults in early adolescence; boys have this special need two or three years later, especially in the middle stage. At the time when adults are most significant to boys, girls are beginning to seek heterosexual relationships with older boys. Boys in mid-adolescence form relationships primarily with other boys, secondarily with other adults, and only when they are more mature, with girls.

Adults who are liked and respected may be seen by boys as people they would like to resemble. How such adults are seen does not depend only on what they actually are, but rather more on the way the individual adolescent looks at them. Parents are the initial significant models for their children, implicitly showing them what it is like to be adult. Adolescents, particularly boys, cannot agree that they wish to be similar to their parents. A five-year-old boy may say that he wants to be just like his dad; this statement, ten years later, is transformed into the announcement that the boy has no wish to be like his parents, becuase they are at best old-fashioned, at worst stupid. The qualities a boy admires, however, as he sees them in others, are usually very similar to those of his parents; he is unaware of this.

Adults outside the family obviously widen the horizons of young people, not only because they provide ideas, but also because they offer themselves as models of human beings who are different from the adolescent's parents. Thus, contact with grown-ups helps enlarge both an adolescent's way of looking at the world and the adolescent's own personality. Although adolescents do not usually learn better just because they like the teacher, this quality of child/teacher relationships is still present in the middle stage of adolescence. A good relationship with an adult enhances the value of formal academic and vocational education.

As young people grow through the middle years of adolescence, they begin to take on more adult responsibilities. There are many ways in which this can be done. By the time this age is reached, money and its spending begin to be seen quite differently by parents and their children. Boys may begin to earn part of their spending money, and, in some countries, all of it; if they don't, they resent having to ask their parents for a weekly sum. The value of saving money for future activities, such as going to college, becomes important; how to handle money may be taught through opening a checking account for the mid-adolescent.

PROBLEMS OF ACADEMIC EDUCATION

It is questionable whether adolescents who do not enjoy academic work should be pressured to go to college. If they are, they are likely to find the years through adolescence burdensome. Many who do go on, when they have no real wish to do so, do not last in a university course. They either drop out of a university or fail to make the grades that would be expected, according to their intellectual potential (Wise, 1958). Early specialization, or an early commitment to a specialty, is likely to make the problem worse. This is a particular problem with the children of doctors, when the wish to study medicine represents a childlike, early identification with a parent and has never become a part of the adult self. When maturation does occur, such young people may abruptly leave medical school. In some medical schools, this is known as the "doctor father" syndrome. Often, however, the successful offspring of doctors who study medicine consciously identify more with other physicians than with their fathers. Some adolescents who reject the idea of academic study, in the middle stage, may embrace it, when they are more mature.

During mid-adolescence, formal, propositional, or abstract thinking develops (Piaget and Inhelder, 1958), although the process of change from concrete thinking has been going on throughout puberty. Formal stage thinking means that possibilities can be considered and consequences appreciated. It is common for formal thinking not to develop fully, even in academic adolescents, although it does in most. Some adolescents can match standard problems with standard solutions, others work on inspiration, although often they have no idea why they think as they do (Dulit, 1972). Divergent thinkers often freely develop a variety of answers; standard method users are convergent thinkers, who focus down, in a concrete fashion, on the right answer (Hudson, 1966). The modern school system generally seems to prefer the latter type of thought, which may explain why convergent thinking is common, even among those who, potentially, could be divergent thinkers.

If all goes well during the middle-adolescent years, the move toward independence will go smoothly. Parents will be able to offer their children increasing responsibility, which they will be able to handle. During these years, parents may expect to meet their son's male friends, but they should not necessarily expect to meet their son's girlfriends. Neither should they expect to hear detail's of their son's intimate relationships with such girl-friends. Boys and girls who need to tell their parents intimate details of their sex lives are usually failing to develop a satisfactory sense of self.

ADOLESCENTS AND WORK

Now that the days of craft apprenticeships are over, except in the skilled trades, with strong unions, adolescents who become fully employed usually do not make their first job their final one. Rarely do adolescents find work that will meet both their vocational and emotional needs. Adolescents do better in those firms that are interested in them as a total personality. Tasks that do not involve the whole personality tend to be badly performed. Adolescents are able to be actively and vigorously involved in their jobs, provided that personnel of firms are prepared to care about their work life. If the relationship between the management and adult employees is unsatisfactory, the same is likely to be true between adult and younger workers. If adults take long breaks and are interested in a maximum return for a minimum involvement, adolescents gather that this is desirable behavior, or at least, that they too can get away with giving less, especially if the job is boring. Trainees may be criticized by senior employees for failing to perform tasks they are asked to do; but the young people may only be copying the world of immediate self-interest and greed they see around them.

Idleness is particularly demoralizing for young people, and Western society is likely to pay dearly for high youth unemployment, for decades. Even those adolescents who have jobs find that their jobs do not demand enough in terms of time or energy. A shorter working week may be appropriate for the middle-aged; if the task is interesting, it does not meet the needs of the young. The routine nature of some industrial work makes interest and concern from their superiors, as well as adequate opportunities for further education and recreation, essential, if tasks are to be well performed.

Boys in the middle years of adolescence still use older adolescents and young adults to obtain emotional support. They need the continuing opportunity to mix with them in social and recreational settings. Middle-stage boys vary their relationships to their peers as well as to adults, depending on their emotional needs, which is a function of internal experience as well as external reality. Sometimes social activities with peers are sought, sometimes constructive activities with adults. At times it may be preferable to laze the time away; sometimes the opportunity for constructive activities in the community is essential.

The middle years of adolescence are a time full of the excitement of discovery. The world feels new and fresh, and the young feel that it can be changed. They are critical of adults and themselves, and they are intolerant of failure. Only with adulthood do the young first begin to discover that there is often very little they can do to change the life they see around them; only in late adolescence can they begin to develop a real tolerance for the weakness of others.

REFERENCES

Bath, J. A., and Lewis, E. C. (1962), Attitudes of young female adults towards some areas of parent–adolescent conflict. *J. Genet. Psychol.*, 100: 241–253.

Cole, L., and Hall, N. I. (1964), *Psychology of Adolescence.* 256–259. New York: Holt, Rinehart and Winston.

Crist, J. R. (1953), High school dating as a behavior symptom. *Marriage Fam. Living*, 15: 23–28.

Dulit, E. (1972), Adolescent thinking à la Piaget: The formal stage. *J. Youth Adolesc.*, 1(4): 281–301.

Erikson, E. H. (1968), Psychosocial identity. *An. Social Sciences*, 7: 61.

Hudson, L. (1966), *Contrary Imaginations.* New York: Schocken Books.

Jersild, A. T. (1963), *The Psychology of Adolescence.* 28–29, 246–147, 254–255. New York: Macmillan.

Johnson, A. M. (1953), Factors in the psychology of fixations and symptom choice. *Psychoanal. Q.*, 22: 475–496.

May, R. (1950), *The Meaning of Anxiety.* New York: Ronald Press.

Miller, D. (1958), Family interaction in the therapy of hospitalized adolescent patients. *Psychiatry*, 21: 277–284.

National Commission on Excellence in Education "A Nation at Risk" (1983) Dept. of Education. Washington, D.C.

Offer, D. (1974), *The psychological world of the teenager.* New York: Basic Books.

Piaget, J., and Inhelder, B. (1958), *The Growth of Logical Thinking from Childhood to Adolescence.* New York: Basic Books.

Reames, H. H., and Sadler, D. H. (1959), *The American Teenager.* Indianapolis: Bobbs-Merrill.

Schofield, M. (1965), *The Sexual Behavior of Young People.* London: Longmans Green.

Vernon, M. D. (1968), The development of reality construction in children. *Br. J. Psychol.*, 39: 102–111.

Wilkins, L. (1965), *The Diagnosis and Treatment of Endocrine Disorders in Childhood.* Springfield, Ill.: Charles C Thomas.

Wise, D. M. (1958), *They Came for the Best of Reasons: College Students Today.* Washington, D.C.: American Council on Education.

Chapter 5

The Later Years of Adolescence

PHYSICAL CHANGES

The late stage of adolescence is still a period of physical growth in the male. As male genitals reach their maximum size, usually between the ages of sixteen and eighteen, there are changes in the hairline and a well-formed "widow's peak" appears. The larynx reaches its maximum size at about the same time, and more body hair may appear, usually, the typical male distribution of pubic hair with a hairline stretching to the navel. Skeletal growth continues until age twenty or twenty-one, and it is not until then that adult levels of seventeen ketosteroids and testosterone are reached (Hamburger, 1948). In girls, adult physical status is reached somewhat earlier (at sixteen to seventeen).

Late adolescence, however, may stretch beyond that age as part of the moratorium available to young people who are still training for more sophisticated adult roles in a highly complex society. Unlike the first two stages, late adolescence is a psychosocial rather than a biopsychosocial developmental period. It is not a significant developmental stage for those who reach adult vocational, sexual, and social roles at age seventeen to eighteen. Late adolescence is not, then, apparent in most societies of the world, except for their more highly trained elite.

THE COPING PERIOD OF LIFE—ITS AGE LIMITS

The late adolescent is basically concerned with trying out the personality structure that has been built over the years, and with learning to cope with the complexities of adult society, and to adapt to the stresses of everyday life. This is, to some extent, like the middle-adolescent years, an era of personal consolidation, but environmental mastery is now possible. An adolescent with a firm sense of self learns to cope with the complications of adulthood. Since late adolescence does not depend on physical development, definite age limits cannot be given for this period. These depend on social class, economic status, nationality, and ethnic group. The psychology of this age period is, to an extent, a consequence of the mixed feelings of society about those in training roles. Late adolescents are rarely paid for their primary task so that economic self-sufficiency hardly is possible. In the United States, it is not unusual for a student to work his way through college; such an individual really holds two jobs—one, unpaid, as a student, the other, paid, but often as a relatively menial worker. The social structure of education puts the student in a highly dependent position; sexuality is tolerated, but marriage is rarely possible. The student is expected to behave as an adult, but is offered minimal personal and social responsibility. Students are given grants or loans; therefore, they should be appropriately responsible and not make a nuisance of themselves.

For young people who go to universities, late adolescence covers the years between seventeen and the early twenties. For young people who go directly to work, late adolescence lasts a much shorter period, it may be over by eighteen or nineteen, or it may not occur, depending on society's expectations.

Young people who go out to work, except in certain trainee posts, are expected by the age of eighteen or so to take on adult responsibilities. Unlike students, young workers are encouraged by society to spend their not inconsiderable earnings with a degree of irresponsibility; if they marry, however, most of them find that their incomes will barely support adult sexual maturity. The establishment often appears less preoccupied with the aggressive "antisocial" behavior of young workers than with the behavior of university students.

Approved use of alcohol by late adolescents is a direct cause of alcoholism in early adolescents. Those late adolescents who remain in conflict with authority and who have not developed a capacity for empathy—to understand the feelings and experience of others—are willing to sell and offer alcohol to younger boys and girls. Similarly, immature, late-adolescent boys, who still have a sense of omnipotence, are only too willing to drink and then drive. Politicians who need the votes of eighteen- to twenty-one-year-olds to be elected have, in some states, been extremely reluctant to raise the legal drinking age to twenty-one. This had led to the creation of death alleys, the highways between one state, where the drinking age is higher, to one where it is lower.

Society attempted to resolve its confusion about young people by making them legally adult at the age of eighteen. Mixed feelings about this are demonstrated by the fact that, in England, late-adolescent delinquents stay in the residential care of children's authorities until they are nineteen. In the United States, on the other hand, adolescents of seventeen are tried in adult courts and may be sent to adult prisons.

MATURITY OF LATE ADOLESCENTS

Late-adolescents should be able to forgive both mother and father for their failures and omissions. In doing this, a boy will be able to establish a true loving relationship with his girlfriend. He will forgive her "maternal" nagging, which he himself may provoke; he will be seduced by her feminine being; and he will accept her feelings of loss and anxiety without anger. He will understand the depths and variations of his girlfriend's moods and understand the variations in her trust in him, both sexual and otherwise. Both sexes need a loved individual to bolster their self-esteem and feeling of worth.

While retaining attachments to her mother (Lample de Groot, 1928), the late-adolescent girl is able to vary between intense involvement with herself and with her boyfriend. When she marries, she is the mainstay of the family structure, and her husband is almost totally dependent on her for his sense of masculine worth, although his vocation and support from male friends are also significant. Yet, in the modern world, she may compete equally with a man for jobs and economic status. There is a need for an understanding of the behavior that may occur as part of a response to her menstrual cycle; she may be especially vulnerable to psychic pain just before menstruation begins. The love affairs of late adolescents as they plan a future are the grown-up version of "house" played by children. To reach full sexual maturity, a woman needs conditioning and training of her sexual organs in coitus with a man she loves. An adolescent girl may think she is unable to have an orgasm because she has had occasional intercourse with a boy she does not love. There is no evidence that this is so unless she fails to reach complete sexual satisfaction in a loving, long-term relationship. Orgasmic insufficiency, then, is often due to a failure to accept physical femininity, a need to have pain inflicted, a desire to thwart masculinity, all of which are due to a failure to resolve those infantile dependent and sexual conflicts which may be aroused by relationships in the nuclear family (Bonaparte, 1953).

Hopefully a girl has avoided full sexual experiences in early and middle-stage adolescence. In late adolescence or young adulthood, in fields other than sexuality, signs of mature behavior should be very apparent. Maturity can be measured by a capacity to be loving, to wait for emotional satisfaction, to consider the future, and to control aggressive and hostile impulses. The future will be influenced by actions in the present; an adult can tolerate anxiety without an immediate need to act to alter the situation irrespective of consequences. The issue of maturational age is still important during late adolescence. Variations in physical maturity, emotional growth, and, hence, academic achievement still occur, reflecting early or late maturation. A late developer is likely to continue to experience earlier feelings of insecurity that have not yet been resolved by time. However, during late adolescence when, paradoxically, there is generally less disparity between maturational and chronological age than there was earlier, society is less rigid about age as an indication of potential, particularly in the academic field. Performance expectations are no longer related to age by society, but immature adolescents may experience difficulty because of their own expectations. This is particularly an issue in sexual and social relationships. Hard data are typically difficult to acquire, but it appears in clinical practice that a significant number of nineteen- to twenty-year-old students with anxieties about their sexual attractiveness have reached physical maturity later than others of their own age.

THE ACADEMIC ADOLESCENT

Provided that the foundations of personality integration have been satisfactorily laid during childhood and early and mid-adolescence, the late adolescent can try himself out as an individual. Late adolescence can also allow for further emotional growth. This may be especially necessary for those whose lives have been unduly complex; many academically able adolescents fall into this group (Kinsey et al., 1953). This means that many late adolescents begin their higher education still vulnerable to reality stress, which adds to the task of schools and colleges. More is involved than preparing them for a vocation; universities have a responsibility to help their late-adolescent students to be young adults who have to learn, along with the enrichment of intellectual sensibility, to cope with a general responsibility to society, to develop a sense of personal worth, and to ensure a sense of continuity with their society and cultural and human heritage. Quite apart from the problem of late maturation, an educational system that values an early forcing of academic achievement inevitably produces a large number of late adolescents who are still emotionally immature. Yet most institutions involved with education during the late teens behave as if the psychological foundations of the personality have been quite firmly laid in each of their charges.

Universities appear to have abandoned all responsibilities other than in the provision of student mental health services for the emotional care of their charges. Adolescents in universities may live in dormitories with no support-ive social structure, few rules, and no adults with interpersonal relationship skills in charge. This is one reason why students are so easily recruited into cults. Those who are unsure of their own sense of self, and who are anxious, lonely, and socially unsupported, may accept the preliminary invitations of such organizations. The "Moonies," the Hari-Krishna, and those funda-mentalist Christian and Jewish groups that are alien to parental religious norms, promise a fellowship that offers interest, emotional support, and often food. The price paid is indoctrination, which is pushed with intensity, while the student is seduced away from his or her usual emotional and sometimes educational contacts.

Industry, like education, appears to accept little responsibility for the emotional well-being of its charges. The current interest in Japanese man-agement techniques, which are seen as a threat by American management, appears to follow the recognition that one price paid for this lack of responsibility is low productivity and poor industrial relationships. Interest-ingly, the armed services provide a structure of emotional support for the young. Those who are still struggling to achieve a sense of worth need to be given significant opportunities to feel useful; in the Navy, Army, and Air Force, such individuals normally are given this opportunity. In the United States, the Vietnam war temporarily interfered with a system in which dependent needs could be met in a socially acceptable way, thus supporting a satisfactory sense of self.

AUTONOMY STRUGGLES OF LATE ADOLESCENTS

All adolescents should have as much freedom as they can capably handle and as much responsibility as they can tolerate. They should have "caring for" duties and an opportunity to be useful to the community-at-large. The separation of late adolescents from the caring roles in society is likely to be much more painful for the girl than the boy because her mothering needs are greater. If late adolescents are given too much or too little responsibility, they retain the capacity to behave in highly self-destructive ways: quitting jobs, dropping out of school, or being almost senselessly aggressive.

The wish to leave school does not always stem from the failure of the immediate environment to meet needs. Sometimes it may be an attempt on the part of the young people to free themselves from what they feel is a childishly dependent relationship with their parents. The more a high school or a university meets the needs of late adolescents, the less likely it is that youth will see dropping out as a way of asserting independence. In some societies, there is a natural time gap between leaving high school and entering college. Entry into college is gained two semesters before actual admission, which gives late adolescents time to explore their world and themselves by wandering freely throughout their own and foreign countries. This is normally true in England. In the United States, however, entry in the fall semester immediately after completion of high school is almost always obligatory. This allows the process of education to continue, uninterrupted, but does not give adolescents a necessary period of exploratory freedom.

EDUCATION OF WOMEN AND MINORITY GROUPS

One major stress of late adolescence comes with social mobility. The adolescent from a nonacademic family who goes to college often changes his views and the way he expresses himself, and a degree of alienation from his family may result. This is often a problem for children of immigrants, who leave behind both the language and the culture of their parents.

The child of the black ghetto who obtains an academic education is likely to have a similar conflict with his nuclear family. The black American may find that education threatens his tenuous sense of cultural identity; education for a poor black, as for a poor white, may begin to move the individual into a different social class, with different communication techniques. This may partially help to explain the apparent failure of integration of minority students in universities. Faced with some hostility, minority students often fantasize that the world-at-large is far more hostile than it actually is. Clinging together in the face of real and imagined hostility also tends to reinforce group identity. Socially mobile black students, however, are also fighting their own wish to move away from their ethnic background into the ranks of the affluent host society. Thus, minority students often sit together in classes, and socializing between ethnic or racial groups is rare (*The Michigan Daily*, 1972). The well-documented studies on the effect of education on communication techniques (Bernstein, 1961), when applied to black

Americans, may help explain the apparent hostility and anxiety felt by many. The hostility is perhaps a manifestation of identification with the aggressor, the white host society. It may also represent anxiety about being pulled away from still-important ethnic roots. The ethnic identification of Africans depends on their tribal roots: the Hausa are not the same as the Yoruba, although they share a common skin color. Blackness is no more a measure of ethnocentricity than is "whiteness." So black Americans, when they try to identify with an African Hausa may be in the same position as the descendant of a Scotsman who seeks a common identity with a European Serbo-Croat. Given the nature of the black American identity, those who are acquiring the upwardly mobile skills of the larger society may find it difficult to know who they really are. The anxiety created by this also creates intragroup hostility, which leads to tensions among black students. As one individual said, "We are putting each other down." The black student faces a somewhat similar emotional situation as do British working-class university students who gain entry on the basis of scholarship; they, too, feel the loss of their cultural base. The latter, however, are not admitted on the basis of ideology, as is often the case with the student who may help the affirmative action program of a university by filling its minority quota. If such a student feels pulled away from his own group by education and consequent social mobility, his conflict is that much greater. Hence, the black student must cling to his peers to reinforce a sense of ethnic value about which he is, at least unconsciously, ambivalent.

Mixed feelings about education are also present in minority-group parents and in those lower socioeconomic groups whose children achieve academically. On the one hand, parents are immensely proud of the academic success of their children; less consciously, the response of nonacademic parents to their children's academic progress is often resentment. Such parents may fear the "loss" of their children. The adolescent from a nonacademic family may reciprocate this feeling. The attitude that is conscious and dominant makes for academic success or failure (Taba, 1953). In some ways, the minority student is better off than the socially mobile white student. Although there is intragroup hostility, the former has peer support, at the very least, as well as larger group reinforcement both from the majority and minority. The white student who is conflict-ridden as a result of social mobility is offered no support either by peers or adults in his college. In many large universities, students have no effective contact with faculty members. Even where universities have a tutorial, or an advisor, system, in which there should be a close relationship between staff and student, staff members are often unaware of the psychological stresses their students are undergoing. The tutorial system is, in any case, no substitute for confidential guidance on intimate problems. Students are unlikely to tell their tutors about their worries, partly because they fear that these confidences may prejudice the references they need for future employment.

Girls often cope with anxiety by allowing themselves to feel dependent on their parents. When girls move up in the world and go to college, they do not lose their particular need to turn to their mothers. It is not uncommon for anxious girls to feel that if they continue their academic education their life will be intolerable; they are afraid of finally losing their mothers. Such girls often give up further education because of physical health, because they do not want to go on, or, sometimes, because of an emotional breakdown. Another solution is to try to seduce a young man, who, the girl hopes, will want to make the affair more serious. She begins to feel that if the young man really loved her he would want to marry her. This is like the problem that exists with some girls earlier in adolescence. The nineteen-year-old man is usually not willing to commit himself to a permanent relationship. Such a young man is often assessing his manhood by trying out the role of a "husband"; he is not yet ready to make this a formal step. The girl is anxious to stabilize the relationship because she feels that she has lost emotional contact with her own parents. She becomes depressed when the relationship ends, particularly because the "loss" of her own family leaves her with no one upon whom she can rely.

Sometimes parents may create confusion by trying to change the way of life of their children by new educational techniques, compared to the family as a whole and its tradition. An artist who leads a bohemian life will cause some anxiety to his children if he educates them at a school that inflicts rigid middle-class value systems upon them; a family that is out of touch with its own inner world has problems when its children are exposed to a creative and imaginative educational experience. This does not mean that parents ought to try to bring up their children so that they are not different, but the effect of differences and, in particular, how these influence mutual attitudes and communication between parent and child, should be considered.

PARENTAL ROLES IN LATE ADOLESCENCE

Although by late adolescence parents may have very little overt influence on their children's personalities, they can, however, still create emotional comfort or discomfort for their young. The role of parents in late adolescence is really to help confirm their children's steps to final adult roles in society. If they fail to do this, the split between generations is likely to be reinforced; those late adolescents who reject the standards of official authority, to an extent are rejecting the standards of their parents. This is desirable, for otherwise society would remain static; the problem for parents is to accept the idea that their concepts may be rejected by their children. This does not mean that the parents are necessarily rejected as people. If parents have been successful in that role, their children, as free, independent adults, will inevitably disagree with them on some issues, although they ultimately tend to agree on fundamentals.

Late adolescents often reject parental beliefs and attitudes if they feel these have been imposed for hypocritical reasons. Parental oversensitivity as to what the neighbors might think creates a social face that is sometimes one reason given by adolescents for rejecting parental standards. Adolescents who are themselves intensely conformist may reject their parents' norms as too conformist, although to different standards. For example, parents who go to church on Sunday, but who otherwise do not observe their religion, may have children who reject organized religion, but who join different religious or political organizations with a fervent religious zeal.

Late adolescents often identify with the attitudes they claim to deplore in their parents' generation. A group of young people, prepared to bully and hound those they consider dissident, will criticize the older generation for allowing fascism to develop and for bullying minorities; but, only the victims have changed.

In this last step before formal adulthood, it is almost inevitable that some young people will have conflicts both with society and with their parents. Problems with authority at home may still be present. Late adolescents should see themselves as adults in their relationships with their parents. However, at the end of childhood, holdovers from earlier parent/child relationships are almost inevitable. In the modern world, young people have difficulty mastering the environment and face impotence in many areas of life. The anxieties of the final step to adulthood arouse a temptation to return to childish dependence. The presence of parents can be a provocation to behave in a childlike manner. Angry defiance may be a way to struggle with dependent needs aroused by the imbalance between social stress and the ability of the individual to cope with it. Family quarrels may result from a projection of conflicts about dependence. In late adolescence, some degree of intergenerational clash is almost inevitable if the adulthood of a child is accepted with difficulty by parents. Some have problems because they recall, consciously and unconsciously, the small children they reared as they relate to grown-up sons and daughters; other parents spoil relationships when they want to lean on their children as they grow up. The strength of childlike feelings in the late adolescent may be matched by a parental need both to infantilize and, unconsciously, to be an infant. This may lead to adolescent withdrawal from any family contact. The possibility of an extended family in the next generation fades; the overconcentration on the nuclear family, which causes so much stress to individuals within it, is thus perpetuated.

All human beings play a number of different roles and the "self" that is apparent in one may not be the same as in another. Sometimes, an adult role in the community is not a measure of independence within the family. The highly successful businessman may not be autonomous in other ways. Children may settle for being only sons or daughters. Overdependence on the original family is a common cause of marital breakdown.

> John, a twenty-two-year-old student, who was highly dependent on his parents, married a twenty-year-old nursing student. His marriage to a potential nurse seemed to represent a wish on his part to continue to be looked after. The girl, however, was a product of a broken home and was herself seeking to be fathered. The more dependent she became on John, the more he withdrew, alleging a need to study. Sexual relationships between them almost ceased, and finally she made a suicidal gesture.
>
> In a joint interview with a psychiatrist, a condition of relative safety, John announced that he wanted to leave his wife—"she can have the apartment and I will go home to live with my folks." He had been unable to be frank with his wife, previously suggesting only that if she went home to her mother she could be well-looked-after "for a week or two."

If the parent/child dependence remains intense during late-adolescent years, the precursors of the forty-year-old adult clinging to a seventy-year-old parent may be present.

Intense rivalry between siblings, with much aggressive competitiveness, is almost always a measure of difficulty between parent and child, and not surprisingly, unresolved dependency conflicts may be played out in quarrels between siblings even in late adolescence.

> Kenneth had an intense struggle over dependence on his mother. An eighteen-year-old student, he would go home on the weekend and tell her all the details of his university life. He would also call her on the telephone each week. However, whenever he went home, he would quarrel violently with his about-to-be-married twenty-two-year-old brother. Father, a withdrawn accountant, was a distant shadow in the house. Kenneth had sought therapy because of his anxiety over sexual conflicts, which were related to his inability to allow himself to be close to anyone. The patient perceived his brother as being controlling, bossy, and demanding; all qualities possessed by his mother but not consciously perceived by him.

When sibling quarrels continue into late adolescence, they still may be a projection of tension. It is not unusual for one sibling to criticize or dislike in the other qualities that are unconsciously disliked, either in a parent or the self. Kenneth, in the above clinical example, thus showed a typical response:

he was unable to feel close to his brother because of unresolved rage with his mother. As he matured in therapy, he became more distant from his mother and aware of warm feelings toward his brother.

TASKS OF LATE ADOLESCENCE

The late adolescent learns to cope with life with minimum support from parents. In a very remarkable way, this reproduces some of the emotional situations of earlier childhood. Children learn new skills attempting to cope with a variety of testing situations: climbing trees, playing at some distance from their mothers, fighting and tumbling about with other boys and girls. They cope with these activities successfully, providing their mothers are available. If they should hurt themselves and if their mothers are not there, children either lose trust in parents, become overdependent on peers or baby-sitters, or withdraw from meaningful emotional contacts with others. Children use new-found physical powers to conquer physical obstacles and assess their own skills; late adolescents do the same in relationship to life in general with their newfound personality strengths. They test themselves against the real world and its demands to prove their own competence as adults in work, school, play, and social and personal relationships. If the relationship with parents is good, turning to them for help and advice does not imply a loss of personal integrity. If parents are not available, because of earlier personal or social difficulties, the late adolescent, who feels unable to cope with sexual or aggressive impulses, turns to another adult or to his peer group, or he gives up a serious attempt at autonomy. Alternately, he abandons further attempts at personality growth, foreclosing his identity. The perpetual student falls into this category:

> Frank, a twenty-seven-year-old medical student, began to have academic difficulties in his junior year. He repeatedly failed examinations and was referred to the medical school's psychiatrist for an opinion about his academic underachievement. He was the son of rigid, overcontrolling, Roman Catholic parents. He was brought up with an overwhelming sense of how sinful it was to give in to one's own impulses—thus, he denied his own capacity to be loving and sexual. He was polite to, but distant with his parents. After completing his undergraduate degree, he sought a postgraduate qualification in physics. Two years before his doctorate he became dissatisfied and, one year later, applied and was accepted for medical school, providing he took certain postgraduate courses.
>
> His answer to his own dilemma of failing as a medical student and feeling happy with it as a chosen career was to apply to go back to

physics. His plan was to complete that and then return to medical school. He could not envisage the possibility of psychiatric help, nor was he prepared to accept "advice" from his counselor, his parents, or his peers.

Late adolescence, which seals the individual's sense of continuity with his family and his ethnic, racial, and social group, is also the period of separation from childhood (Terman et al., 1947). As with all transitional stages of development, new roles are tried out before they are consolidated into the personality. These involve separation from a previous way of life. Late adolescence may, in a sense, be a series of transitional experiences designed to help in the final consolidation of autonomy. Temporary separation from home is one way of doing this. The three-year-old who first plays away from home casts an eye to make sure home is still there; late adolescents may make a significant physical separation from their home by going on vacation without their parents. This has a different emotional meaning from going away to school, in that a vacation away from the nuclear family is much more a free-choice decision. The identification with parents is often clear, and the type of vacation taken by an adolescent is often similar to that of his family. Relatively affluent adolescents may choose to hitchhike, even though they can afford the fare. The type of vacation taken by parents, however, is unconsciously copied; Blackpool, England, becomes Rimini, Italy; Miami Beach becomes Cannes, France. Children who have always been sent to camp, in later adolescence may vacation with parents; parents who have always traveled in Europe by car have late adolescents who take a jeep to Turkey or to India.

Vacations are not just a way of identifying with and separating from parents. Late adolescents wish to see the world through their own eyes. A vacation may be a wish to be adventurous, to meet new people and to explore new situations. Experiences that in the past could be obtained in day-to-day living are now sought by young city dwellers in their travels. An unplanned vacation is commonly used to find a sexual partner who will provide new forms of sexual experience without the risk of incurring the responsibility inevitable in long-term relationships.

> Judy, an eighteen-year-old girl, was allowed by her parents to travel in Europe over a long summer vacation. At home she had a steady boyfriend but had never had an orgasm while having intercourse with him. Apparently, to have done so would not just have meant her acceptance of his masculinity, it also implied an emotional dependence. While in Greece, France, and England, she had short-term sexual relationships with three boys; in each of these she had orgasms. A later, brief relationship in her home town was as unsatisfying as the longer-term one had

been. She understood in her psychotherapy that, among other things, the short-term relationships abroad represented a freedom from the risk of being vulnerably overdependent.

Vacations offer the opportunity for the equivalent of shipboard or clubcar relationships; intense intimacy is possible with none of the problems involved in long-term ones. Frankness is safe because it comes with no strings.

Late adolescents have other techniques to enhance the weaning process from childhood. Even when they live in the same city as parents, many prefer to share an apartment with friends, often returning home on weekends only to do their laundry. Very often, particularly in the first year or so at school, children who live some distance away return home two or three times a semester and then may quarrel with their parents, as if to reassure themselves that their parents are still there and to prove to themselves that their parents are not needed. Sometimes individuals leave home before being ready to do this:

> Faye, a nineteen-year-old girl, was angrily dependent on her parents, so much so that they still applied a curfew when she went out at night. She decided to become independent. Her parents suggested that she move into a dormitory, but she refused to consider this, being unable to find a roommate. She moved into an apartment by herself. She did succeed in having a loveless sexual relationship for a time. Nevertheless, the whole experience was one of intense isolation. The failure of this attempt to reach emotional autonomy and independence led to her return home. She then sought psychiatric help for a fairly severe depression.

Faye's overdependence on her parents led to a futile rebellion, rather than a transitional move to autonomy. A move leading to social isolation is an unsatisfactory attempt to resolve dependent feelings and does not indicate the likelihood of creating an autonomous way of life.

Apparently, socially acceptable situations may be used as a way of defying family standards. Superficially conformist, but really defiant, domineered young people may choose a partner of whom their parents disapprove; often their choice is as domineering a person as in the original nuclear family. Unwittingly, individuals may repeat the emotional experiences they seemingly wish to escape most.

Often marriage is used as an attempt to gain freedom from overdependence on the nuclear family. The overdependent partner is likely to seek an inappropriate level of emotional support from a spouse. Marriage is not a solution to late-adolescent maladjustment; "If only he would marry," should be "If only he were able to marry."

Sexuality may be used as part of an attempt to assert autonomy in ways other than matrimony: the choice of sexual partners of whom parents will disapprove; exhibitionistic sexual activity of which parents are aware. Pubertal boys overdependent on mothers may leave masturbatory traces on their night clothes or sheets, a seductive and provocative gesture. Late adolescents may similarly take sexual partners to their bedrooms in the parental home. Whether this represents provocative self-assertion depends on the family codes. Some families accept extramarital sex; others regard it as anathema. Some girls may tell their mothers about a first sexual experience, but healthy adolescents do not discuss details of their sexual affairs with their parents. Young people who believe in premarital celibacy may, after an episode of impulsive lovemaking, marry or promise to do so in an attempt to expiate guilt. The sexually more experienced individuals may use the sexual relationship to fight their partner's parents. A relatively passive, dependent young person may then have the unconscious satisfaction of watching the struggle of powerful people, the spouse and parents.

> John, a rather gentle, nineteen-year-old boy, was brought up by Southern Baptist parents. He met a twenty-one-year-old girl on campus who eventually seduced him. At this point, he asked her to move into his apartment and to marry him. He took her to his home for a frozen vacation experience in which his parents complained to him about his girlfriend, and his girlfriend complained about his parents. After his return to school, be began to suffer from premature ejaculations as well as a reluctance to have intercourse with his girlfriend. He sought counseling help for this.
>
> It was apparent that he was now as angrily dependent on his girlfriend as he had previously been on his parents.

Parents who are permissive in their attitudes toward sexuality may have children who have to find other techniques of self-assertion; drugs that differ from those used by the family are typically an attempt to show autonomy.

When parents use alcohol, marijuana is commonly taken by their defiant children, who unconsciously identify with parental techniques. The children of marijuana-abusing parents, a generation now reaching high school and college, move onto other drugs of abuse, particularly cocaine.

Educational underachievement in the children of ambitious parents is a passive–aggressive technique of self-assertion (Goldberg, 1962); the rebellious thwarting of parental wishes is mistakenly believed to create emotional independence. The failure of late adolescents to equip themselves for the world may ensure continuing dependence, if not on parents, then on society or one of its subgroups. The academic drop-out may be as highly a dependent and rebellious a person as the lower-class juvenile delinquent.

Late adolescents may not ask their parents' opinions about ethical, racial, political, and religious beliefs. All through their developing years, however, children have been picking up parental attitudes about these. This is demonstrated when a parent of a late adolescent dies. A surviving child may handle mourning by identifying most obviously with the dead parent and seemingly become exactly like him or her. This is only possible when all these attitudes are already internalized, even if they were not previously obvious.

Most late adolescents have a fairly smooth passage to adult life, but all the way through childhood and adolescence there are things children do to justify anxiety and concern. Most of these are the equivalent of minor roadblocks on the road to maturity, but overanxious misunderstanding may give some of them more weight than they deserve. More usually, the difficult behavior of adolescents may carry implicit requests for assistance. If these are ignored, early maladjustment can become more serious later.

The success of the late adolescent in accepting and enjoying adult responsibilities depends on the extent to which early childhood experiences have helped develop the capacity to trust, and of how responsive his family environment, society, and school have been in meeting his needs.

Adolescence is the last of a series of stations on the way to adulthood, which is demonstrated by a capacity to love and by the attainment of cognitive, creative, and physical potential. The adult woman may have a career, but she is quite willing to acknowledge her wish to bear children; she is able to give and receive sexually in a love relationship. The adult male enjoys parenting, is vocationally productive, and is capable of a tender loving sexual relationship with a woman.

By the end of adolescence, individuals personally affiliate with such symbols as the flag, national songs and dances, and the nation as a whole; they also have an individual identity as well as a collective one. Mature individuals believe in the importance of their national and ethnic groups and should be able to participate in their own culture. Collective identity also depends upon communication through language, the sharing of moral values, and a political organization to shape group policy. This depends, partially, at any rate, on society's setting up social organizations through which identity systems are maintained. In other words, the social organizations of society must provide the mechanisms for maintaining the individuals' interest in large organizations as well as making possible a sense of personal identity. In adolescence, particular social organizations are significant in the reinforcement of individual and social mental health. These are necessary for personal and cultural identity, and give a sense of personal and social continuity. They are the family and its extended networks and the educational and religious systems of society. The failure or success of the latter, given the disintegration of extended family networks, are crucial and justify separate consideration.

REFERENCES

Bernstein, B. (1961), Social structure, language and learning. *Educ. Res.*, 33: 163–176.

Bonaparte, M. (1953), *Female Sexuality.* New York: International Universities Press.

Goldberg, M. (1962), *Research on the Gifted.* New York: Teachers' College, Columbia University (Mimeo).

Hamburger, C. (1948), Normal urinary excretion of neutral 17-ketosteroids with special reference to age and sex variations. *Acta Endocrinol.*, 1: 19–37.

Kinsey, A. C., et al. (1963), *Sexual Behavior in the Human Female.* Philadelphia: W. B. Saunders.

Lample-de-Groot, J. (1928), The evolution of the Oedipus complex in women. *Br. J. Psycho-Anal.*, 9: 332–365.

Taba, H. (1953), The moral beliefs of sixteen-year olds. In *The Adolescent: A Book of Readings*, ed. J. Seidman, 592–596. New York: Dryden Press.

Terman, L. M., et al. (1947), *The Gifted Child Grows Up*, Vol. 6. Stanford: Stanford University Press.

The Michigan Daily (1972), Editorial. March 18.

Chapter 6

Youth, Society, and the Family

SOCIAL NETWORKS AND PERSONALITY GROWTH

It is apparent, from the consideration of personality and physical development, that for successful emotional, intellectual, and physical maturation, adolescents need both to be able to face pressures in the immediate environment and to be cushioned against them if they become excessive. For all people, maximum emotional support is gained from caring human relationships.

Except for those who experienced primary poverty, until the Depression in the United States and the outbreak of World War II in Europe, most children were brought up as members of a fairly stable network of grandparents, aunts, uncles, and family friends. In Africa and Asia, children, outside of a few large cities, are still members of a "tribal" society that supports individuals and makes them less vulnerable to stress from outside. There is always someone who matters, who can be turned to for help and emotional support (Bott, 1957). Child-rearing is shared among many individuals, chosen by blood ties, cultural and religious custom, and friendship networks. In Western Europe and North America, this child-rearing group is now much smaller (Riesman, 1950).

An isolated unit of parents, brothers, and sisters cannot fully meet the needs of the adolescent, however well intentioned its aims. Among some ethnic groups, Roman Catholicism still provides, through its church groups under the leadership of the clergy, a developmentally significant supportive network for young people. Fundamentalist protestantism performs similar roles. Those religious groups who do not significantly engage young people occupy only formal societal roles. Teachers no longer impinge significantly on the personal lives of children, and there is a dearth of emotionally involved youth workers. Even for those adjudged as minors in need of supervision by juvenile courts, or considered delinquent, the probation service has failed to provide meaningful support (Citizens Committee for Children for New York, 1982).

Adolescents find it very difficult to bear the dependence they feel when their immediate family offers its direct emotional support, and this is even more difficult in a one-parent family. Unable to accept this from their fathers and mothers, they often have no one else to whom they feel they can go (Kandel et al., 1968). Anthropologists have argued that the nuclear family is not even the basic and elementary social unit of mankind, although a mother–child bond and a father figure are necessary in a child's life (Fox, 1967). In the past, a large social group encompassing many ages provided a haven when an individual's conflict with his parents became too much for him. Youngsters were involved with people and a way of life they could admire and adopt. From this viewpoint, it was not harmful if adolescents attended schools that failed to consider emotional needs. Teachers were not necessarily the only significant adult models for their pupils, and the social organization of the school did not necessarily have an implicit way of life with which young people might need to identify. As the networks of family friends and relatives disappear, particularly in large cities, and as society becomes more fragmented, a greater responsibility is put on the extra-parental adults an adolescent knows. The paradox is that children in parochial schools, who may have other sources of social system support from church groups, are much more likely to receive teacher support than those in public high schools who need it more. Small private schools generally offer such adult involvement.

ADOLESCENT TECHNIQUES OF COMMUNICATION

Society-at-large exposes youth to increasing stress. But even small social organizations fail to provide the necessary supports in many ways. One of these is by not recognizing the implicit message in disturbed or difficult adolescent behavior:

> June had good parents who provided her with a stable home. But they were an isolated family, and the girl had no links with grandparents, aunts, and uncles, or family friends. The family occupied an apartment in an affluent suburb. Her school was one of the best in the neighborhood, being very well equipped, but most staff did not appear to understand that many children in their care needed them as significant adults in their lives. They were also apparently unaware that the sheer size of the school quite overwhelmed some children. As is usual, June and her friends were not able to look on the school as a place they could use after school hours.
>
> At thirteen, June began to smoke marijuana. She and her friends frequented a cafe near the school that was known to be a center for drug pushers. When this was discovered, June's parents and teachers, believing that the drug was not addictive, responded just as if she had been caught smoking tobacco. For the following year she smoked marijuana regularly either after school or after breaking out of her bedroom at night. At fourteen, she began to have sex with a musician whom she thought was twenty-two—he was actually some ten years older. One day she told her mother that she thought she was pregnant, and she was at last referred for possible help.

June was behaving as a troubled child for a year before anything was done. Neither her parents nor the school social worker had understood the importance of the request for help implicit in the marijuana smoking. More and more it appears that such drug use by an early adolescent has come to be as acceptable as the use of alcohol by adults. There was no evidence that other school staff had any training in the techniques of talking with children in individual interviews. June felt that the school social worker, who was responsible for the emotional care of some 1800 children, was hopelessly inept: "All she does is lecture at you." June's father called the attention of the police to the cafe as the source of his daughter's drugs, and a number of drug dealers were arrested, but the place continued to be a source of drugs for local teenagers.

Even when adolescents make their distress explicit, their words may not be listened to, even if they are heard. Most children who attempt suicide tell someone of their intent. Perhaps because the idea is so shocking the response is usually based on denial of the significance of the statement. Nothing is done, although this threat should always be taken seriously and help sought. "I wish I were dead," as an expression of despair, does not have the same meaning as "I feel like killing myself."

IMPORTANCE OF SCHOOL–FAMILY COMMUNICATION

If there is no regular contact between the school staff and parents, teachers are likely to be unaware of a pupil's family difficulties; they will not realize that upset behavior at school may be caused by these troubles, since most are not well trained in adolescent psychology. Furthermore, teachers usually do not see an individual pupil for more than one class period a day for more than two semesters, so they are often unaware either that there has been a change in the way a youngster behaves (for example, from being withdrawn to becoming restless) or that such a change in behavior may be a request for help:

> John, fifteen-and-a-half, went to a technical high school in the inner city that was largely for young people who did not have sufficient ability to be successful in an academic program. The administration was interested in the school's extracurricular groups; in particular, its band. The principal was interested in proving how academic some of his pupils might be, in spite of earlier failure. He therefore tried to ensure that as many high grades as possible were obtained in the twelfth grade.
>
> John, whose father was a crane driver and whose mother currently worked in the school canteen, was thought to have academic potential. John had gone to see a family practitioner complaining of several months of recurring headaches; the doctor thought he was too withdrawn and sent him to a psychiatrist. Although he had been frequently absent from school, the school administration always assumed that he was medically ill. When the psychiatrist asked about his progress, the reports from his counselor were that the staff did not think that the boy had reached his academic potential. He said that the boy's home was without problems and that the staff could not understand why John had become a little restless recently. This restless boredom had been criticized by his teachers, but it had not made them feel that there was anything particularly wrong. His change in behavior was not thought to be particularly significant.
>
> In his first interview with the psychiatrist, John was shy and withdrawn for about 30 minutes; then his story emerged. For the last two years his father had been very depressed; for weeks he had spent hours kneeling on the floor weeping, watched by John, his mother, and his brothers. Because of this depression he had lost his job, the family had been short of money, and for this reason his mother got her job at the school.
>
> The boy also made a complaint more typical of his age group. The eldest of three children, he felt that he got no special privileges; for example, he and his younger brother were sent to bed at the same time.

In a second interview, John spoke of his sexual anxiety; in particular, he was worried about masturbation. He thought he did this too often and as a result would be "weakened" and would be less successful with girls when he was older. He also complained bitterly about the quality of the teaching at his school. He said that the teacher read from a book and expected the boys to spend most of the period taking notes.

In reply to a question, John said that he could never speak in a relaxed way to teachers in his school. He couldn't remember spending any time with an adult other than his father; more recently, the family practitioner had tried to talk to him for the first time.

The boy had no idea what career he wanted. He did not see himself as an unskilled worker, but neither did he wish to work in an office. He said that, since he had to leave school soon, he thought he might as well give the whole thing up now and take any job that came along. Nobody had ever discussed with him what he thought about himself, what he might do when he left school, what books he might read, what were the possibilities of further education. He seemed to feel that only one teacher cared at all but "he is busy." His father mostly watched television, or "he tells me what to do." Psychological tests showed that John was bright enough to obtain good grades. When he knew this and realized that if he worked hard enough his chances of passing were reasonably good, he relaxed.

In a third interview, thinking about his wish to work outdoors and meet people, he began to wonder about the Post Office as a possible career. By this time his headaches had ceased, and he was no longer intermittently absent from school.

If John had not had a perceptive family practitioner, which is a matter of considerable luck, it is highly probable that no help would have been available to him.

WHY ADOLESCENT DISTURBANCE IS NOT HELPED

When adolescent disturbance is recognized, it is enormously difficult to obtain competent assistance for young people. Partly this is because the biopsychosocial determinants of behavior are not recognized, and federal law, which mandates proper education for handicapped children (P.L. 19-142), does not mention psychiatry and medicine as having a role in their care. Partly it is because disturbed behavior is the final common path through which adolescent disturbance shows itself and the persistence of this behavior produces a coercive adult response. The ambivalence of society toward its young is demonstrated by its failure to provide adequate resources either for education, child-care, or treatment for those who are emotionally and physically handicapped; and this process is worsening steadily.

Even when resources are available, however, requests for help made in action or by verbal threats are commonly not recognized as having an implicit meaning.

To be more effective with young people, adults need to understand the nonverbal signals of adolescents, whose words are often not as meaningful as their actions. It is evident that John's acute withdrawal, shown by shyness and headaches, was not "heard" by most adults around him as shouting his distress to the world.

A lack of interviewing skills can also lead to adult failure to help young people, even though intense efforts at help are made:

> Peter, age fifteen, went to a boarding school at the age of nine. At ten, he and two other boys were seduced by one of the teachers. This came to light because his mother noticed that he was more and more withdrawn when she and her husband went to see him. Finally when the story came out, the principal urged her to seek advice from a psychiatrist to try to discover whether or not the boy had been emotionally damaged by the episode. The mother became extremely angry at this. She said later that she felt that the principal was telling her that she was a failure as a mother if she could not handle the situation herself. She withdrew her son from the school. Through the ensuing years the family noticed that the boy seemed to be unreasonably bad-tempered: he was unusually difficult with his younger brother whom he would hit in an apparently impulsive and meaningless way. From time to time he stole from his parents.
>
> Evidence of psychological damage was also apparent from his failure to develop many of the "normal" interests of boys of his age. Although he was physically well into puberty, he had no awareness of, or interest in, sexual feeling. Nevertheless, the family went along assuming that the boy would "grow out of it." At the age of fifteen-and-a-half he was involved in stealing at school. He was then referred to a psychiatrist for an opinion.

Why was Peter not helped at ten? One major factor was surely the school principal's unawareness of how frightening his suggestion of psychiatric assistance could be, with its possible implication of madness. He may well have tried to use his authority in a way that turned out not to be helpful. The parents felt that he was really responsible for what had happened to their son. His mother was, in any case, anxious that she was not a sufficiently good parent. This is a typical case of failure of communication between young people and their parents.

A further reason for the failure to help emotionally disturbed adolescents is that too many people still see these difficulties as frightening. Often, adults overlook anxieties and tensions in young people and are content that the youngster looks normal and does not offend them. Sometimes disturbance is recognized, but there is a reluctance to seek specialized help. For example, teachers are often afraid to tell parents that they think a child needs psycho-logical help. They may often worry if one boy or girl sees a psychiatrist; they think the expert will make unreasonable demands on the school or that other children will react with hostility. Sometimes school staff actively oppose a child getting much-needed assistance:

> The principal of a junior high school in a Chicago suburb in 1982 called the parents of a child who was to be admitted to an adolescent treatment center. He had never seen the place, but told the parents that he was convinced that what they were doing was unnecessary and harmful.

Although an adolescent may be ashamed of his first visit to a psychiatrist and may tell his friends that he is going to the dentist, he almost always tells them the truth afterwards, and it is very rare for him to be teased unless he is in a generally unhappy school. Initially, a fear of madness may deter adolescents. When they see a psychiatrist this usually ceases to be a continuing concern.

Resistance to psychiatry is more common among adults than adolescents. There are still some grown-ups who think that psychiatry is nonsense, and others who think that a psychiatrist is involved only in the treatment of the disturbed and cannot express an opinion on "normal" youth.

MEANING OF EMOTIONAL DISTURBANCE

The idea that the needs of the emotionally disturbed are fundamentally different from those of others is quite naive, as is the idea that there is an absolutely healthy and an absolutely ill personality (Menninger, 1963). Most people swing between mental "health" and mental "illness." An episode of bad temper, for eample, when young people become overwhelmed with rage and incapable of adequately appraising reality is, in a sense, "sick," but this is something that many human beings experience on many occasions. Like-wise, withdrawal from the real world and a preoccupation with what is going on inside oneself—being "lost in daydreams"—can be evidence of "illness," but it is also something that most human beings, particularly the young, experience from time to time.

NEED FOR STABILITY

People need a sense of place and a sense of where they belong. This requires relative permanence—in location and in psychosocial stability. Insofar as the latter is concerned, school changes occur too often at times that are maturationally inappropriate. The junior high school system, which often covers grades seven through nine, creates a school change usually at age twelve and again at age fourteen. This means that children lose the external support provided by the teachers and contemporaries they know, when the psychological tension of puberty is at its height, and most are besieged by internal turmoil.

A brief glance at development from childhood on makes it clear that change should not occur just before and after the pubertal period. Certainly, there is no indication that it is necessary to separate the different age groups of adolescence from each other. Ideally, children would not change schools and would remain in the same educational setting from kindergarten through twelfth grade. Only then will they firmly identify with their school as a social system. The fact that private schools, even in periods of recession, seem to have little difficulty in raising funds from their alumni, whereas the products of the public school system cut educational funds, might be thought to confirm this.

Children at the age of five have already some emotional involvements outside their own families. They are obviously interested in learning and playing with other children in the neighborhood, and they should feel comfortable in being away from their homes with other children for a few hours at a time.

At puberty, as they experience increased emotional turbulence, the young begin to seek significant emotional involvements outside their own family. Because of this, they have a particular need for the support of known adults and stability from the social environment. By just over thirteen-and-one-half it would appear that, in the United States, most boys are well into puberty, as measured by growth of pubic hair and testicular enlargement; most girls have nearly completed this developmental stage in that menstruation has begun (Group for the Advancement of Psychiatry, 1963). The logical school-changing age, if this is to occur, is thirteen-plus. If high school encompassed five grades, this would allow a preliminary testing of adult worth and make identifications outside the family easier, providing always that children had a more consistent contact with their teachers.

Immigrant groups have a particular need for social stability. In the United States, these include immigrants from the southern to the northern states, as well as those from other countries. There is a certain social and psychological blindness shown in some educated majority and minority attitudes toward the black population and other ethnic minority groups in the United States in the search for integration. Similar attitudes also exist toward immigrants from India, Africa, and the West Indies in Britain. It is generally held that the concentration of an ethnic group in certain areas is bad, and it is argued that these groups should integrate as quickly as possible into the host society. The wish for rapid integration is put forward by those anxious to destroy racial prejudice; it ignores the fact that an ethnic community provides social stability, and even when affluence allows mobility, groups are likely to live close to each other.

In all societies throughout history, immigrant groups have lived together in certain localities. Even in relatively tolerant societies, it has usually taken several generations for immigrants to melt into the population. This was true of the Huguenot refugees in Britain in the seventeenth century and of the Jewish immigrant wave from the Russian territories around the Baltic at the beginning of the twentieth. By keeping together and retaining their cultural identity, present-day immigrant communities in Britain and the United and adolescents than does the native population which has lost social stability based on ethnic, religious, cultural, and family networks. When immigrants can maintain the extended kinship and social networks the natives have lost, their offspring, in this respect, are more likely to be secure, although other factors, such as educational and economic deprivation, expose them to additional stress. Many black Americans, on the one hand, seek a reinforcement of an attenuated ethnic identity; on the other, they seek a mutual tolerance that history shows only an integrated society can produce. The resources necessary to provide a decent environment and adequate vocational and social opportunities to ensure that blacks and others have the economic and social possibilities enjoyed by sections of the white population are, nevertheless, not made available. Islands of low-cost housing in more affluent neighborhoods and poorly conceived tower blocks are not a substitute for adequate employment opportunities and neighborhood enrichment.

EDUCATIONAL STRESSES AFFECTING YOUTH

If there is conflict among adolescents in most school systems, such disturbed behavior is almost automatically blamed on the pupils. The issue may be thought to be race; sometimes parents are blamed, sometimes the innate badness or the sickness of individual children. There is little tendency to look at the social organization of the school and at pupil/staff relationships for possible causes. As a result, there is little discussion of the failure of the general social organization of the American junior high and high schools to meet adolescent needs, although much is written about classroom teaching (Miller, 1973). A preoccupation with reading scores cannot hide the fact that, in most schools, there is no recess period, often only twenty minutes may be allowed for lunch, and the classroom period may be fifty-five minutes long with five-minute breaks (Miller, 1970) for children to get to their next class. One thirteen-year-old boy may be part of six to eight groups a day, with an equivalent number of different teachers. As a result, despite the heroic efforts of some individuals, it becomes difficult to know individual young people, particularly those who do not call attention to themselves.

On the whole, nonacademic adolescents are more likely to leave school at sixteen. Non-tracked classes are often taught to accommodate the academic pupil, but not his less able contemporary; this disillusions nonacademic pupils and makes them all too likely to drop out. The school drop-out is ill-prepared to make a vocational choice for social, academic, and psychological reasons.

Children with learning difficulties and attention-span problems are badly served in most school systems. Special classes are likely to mix every type of difficult child; the intellectually impaired and the drug "burn-outs." In mainstream classes, these children are often ignored. The problem is that the biosociopsychological diagnosis of such difficulties is not made so adequate interventions occur only by chance.

In many societies, academic adolescents face difficulties that are equivalent to those of the nonacademic. In Britain, in order to obtain the requisite examination standards, adolescents are forced to choose a series of subjects they may come to dislike. They can then find no way out of their choice without expense to themselves psychologically—and to the state and their parents financially. Also, changing university entrance requirements, and standards, make it difficult for adolescents to know the level of academic achievement expected of them. Academic adolescents in the United States are forced to chase grade-point averages in order to enter prestigious universities, which often exploit undergraduates with huge classes taught by teaching fellows in order to finance and maintain the standards of graduate education upon which their reputation stands.

SOCIAL STRESS AND ADOLESCENT TURMOIL

It is clear that adolescents often respond to a lack of social support by disturbed behavior. Maximum delinquency rates are found in the conurbations, particularly in the "un-neighborhoods" of big cities, among the towering apartment blocks and sprawling houses, as well as in obviously derelict slum areas. In Chicago, gangs have developed a system in which children of eight or nine become junior members. As in many underprivileged ghettos of the United States, and in slum districts in Europe, they define their own areas, map out their turf (Block and Neiderhoffer, 1958). Rehousing, which has often ignored social interaction, has not changed this pattern and in some cases has reinforced it.

Rapid change in a community can create adolescent turmoil when previously it was not apparent:

In the space of five years, a Scandinavian industrial town increased in population from 50,000 to 80,000. In place of the old tribal environment, there were now large numbers of small families in the town. Individual adolescents became isolated from sources of social support. Being aware of changes in teenage life in other parts of the world, they became very discontented. There had been for many years in the town a religious sect that insisted on puritanical conformity from its adolescents. Compared to the larger adolescent group, these young people behaved in an unusual way. Until the change in population, there had been no community problem and good relationships had existed between adolescents from the religious sect and the larger adolescent group. As the population grew dramatically, this sect was assailed as a "minority group." Large groups of adolescents from the town jeered them as they left their church, and these jeers led to fights. The town authorities responded superficially and punitively by increasing police patrols.

Young people would find life difficult enough if their only problem was a loss of the "tribe," but they tend to be exposed to increasing social stress without a corresponding increase in social support. Some of these stresses are imposed by inconsistent demands from adult society: It is important to work and earn, but jobs are hard to find and depend on money being spent on goods with a relatively short life. Sex is healthy and natural, but it is not supposed to happen before marriage (alternately, whatever moral code an adolescent might have, there is a tendency, because of social pressure, to feel that one does not rate as a virgin). Marriage is a sacrament, but the divorce rate in the United States in 1982 approaches 50%, in Britain, 33%. Parents go to church, but religious education is not allowed in school. Education is important, but lack of money forces schools to function with fewer resources in staff and supplies. Frustration must be borne, but every effort is made to prevent children feeling it. Magical solutions are purveyed to the population nightly on television, passivity is constantly reinforced, but young people are urged to be constructive. The threat of nuclear warfare as a possible coda to their civilization, as well as the constant pollution of the earth by industry, shows adolescents that it is perfectly possible for them all to be obliterated by the action of their elders. Adolescents perceive an amorphous unresponsive "they" as responsible for the balance of terror; this is a significant cause of adolescent turbulence. It is an identification with this contempt for life that makes many talk of violent death so acceptable. It is no accident that only in the age group of sixteen to twenty-four has the mortality rate increased in the last thirty years. In white youth, suicide is the issue; in blacks, homicide; accidental death in an automobile is a major threat (U.S. Department of Health and Human Services, 1980).

Apart from issues of self-destruction and violence to others, all these uncertainties and rigidities make it hard for boys and girls to develop a satisfactory feeling of self. Those who reach adolescence with great personal and family security can cope with this; the vulnerability of others is reinforced. In many towns and cities throughout the world, on any fine evening, scattered throughout the major squares or streets, there are dozens of young people sitting, watching the world go by; they have really nothing to do and nowhere to go. This is a clear demonstration that they feel there is nothing valuable and worthwhile for them. This is true in New York and London, in Ann Arbor and New Haven. In Greenwich Village, King's Road, and Carnaby Street, the restless moving to and fro proclaims the inability of young people to find significance in their lives.

More stress occurs because present-day society seems to have lost the technique of assessing how much responsibility adolescents can handle. Sometimes they are given too much. Parents may go out and leave their fifteen-year-old to have parties with no adult present. Sometimes there is too little responsibility. Society does not appear to value what adolescents are able to produce; the money they earn is often not needed by their families. Academic young people can all too easily fail to get the higher education they seek as with the rising costs of University education, funds are no longer available. Normal ways of relieving tension and finding coping mechanisms to assist in handling aggressive and sexual impulses are hard to find.

Those who have suffered childhood disturbances can find in adolescence a second chance for mature development if they are lucky enough to be with people who understand and can meet their emotional needs. As personalities change, young people can reorganize their way of seeing the world: The failures of infancy and childhood can be rectified in adolescence. Although not all authors agree (Masterson, 1967), some children who have felt persecuted by life can, in adolescence, almost automatically correct this emotional distortion. In addition, there are some parents who cannot get on with small children, but who can help those who are more grown up. Some young people, unlucky enough to have had a disturbed childhood, are thus more fortunate in adolescence; their age presents them automatically with surroundings that meet their needs.

The Spartans exposed their young to physical stress in order to toughen their society. This was a conscious decision, but, eventually, so much was demanded that by killing its young the society destroyed itself. A youth subjected to too much social stress may have a similar effect in the Western World.

Our society has been called permissive. It is true that the range of stimulant and sedative drugs available to young people has increased; the decline of sexual prudery has led to doubt for many about acceptable sexual behavior. Nevertheless, society might more appropriately be considered confused and anxiety-ridden. As a result, the world of adults often appears neglectful, uncaring, and alienating in the eyes of the young. Many people are apparently preoccupied with surface behavior and appearance, but few show that they consider the feeling and sensitivity of others. For example, neatly dressed delinquent boys may arouse little public concern; long-haired, untidy-looking "freaks," who turn their aggression in on themselves by taking drugs and who see themselves as "heads," are thought to be a particular menace, although they are less dangerous to others.

TECHNIQUES OF REDUCING SOCIAL STRESS

Young people need to find physical outlets to release the inevitable tension produced by growth and social pressures; they need opportunities for goal-directed constructive behavior. Changing society, as a whole, is an unreal wish, but sufficiently motivated, smaller social systems can more easily be changed.

The organizations that could be more responsive to the needs of youth are schools and youth clubs. Schools should not merely be centers of learning; they should also provide anchor points from which adolescents could develop their personalities and reach out into the community-at-large. Of all the adults who work with the young, teachers are the most significant. Schools could become places in which the potential of their pupils is enhanced. Schools can be centers of learning with the opportunity for creative activity and the goal of teaching pupils how to live (James, 1968). If adolescents enjoy education, as they should, school should improve experiences in the real-life situation of the community. The better the school and the neighborhood the easier this becomes; in underprivileged areas, particularly, good schools are most needed. The Israelis, at one time, put the best schools with the best teachers, who were specially paid, in the most underprivileged neighborhoods.

Rich and poor schools both need to provide social systems able to meet developmental needs. Youth activities provided by churches and other voluntary bodies should not just offer guided vocational and recreational activities; the opportunity to help the aged and the underprivileged is particularly needed by young and old (Miller, 1973). A youth center to help bridge the generation gap, with trained volunteers and minimal planned activities, is needed, along with centers that provide a variety of other activities. The youth organizations in any one community could work together to ensure that they did not reduplicate facilities; thus, they would give young people the opportunity to move spontaneously to the type of activity that would meet a current emotional need.

Exceptionally, there are schools and youth organizations that are sensitive to adolescent needs in the total community, but most youth facilities, of whatever type, are not aware that changes in society have thrust upon them a new role—one for which they have not yet equipped themselves. Resources are not being made available to youth but the issue remains, when change does occur, as to how they should be spent.

PARENTAL UNCERTAINTY AND ADOLESCENT STRESS

Since the end of World War II, many parents are uncertain as to how they should behave; thus, they turn to experts for advice, which, paradoxically, can cause greater parental confusion. There are fashions in advice-giving: books telling parents what to do (Ginott, 1965) have been replaced with Parent Effectiveness Training. Even if all the experts agreed, a highly improbable situation, if parents behave as they are told, rather than in a way that is spontaneous and natural to themselves, they appear to their children as false.

Individuals who are unsure of themselves may seek security in the written word, but the security they receive tends to have shaky foundations. There are many reasons for this. No author can assess the capacity for understanding of his readers. If more is expected of children than they can produce, they are made anxious and uncomfortable; the same is true of their parents. If people are offered advice about how to behave and then are unable to follow through with the actions required, they are likely to be very uncomfortable. It is rarely helpful, for example, to tell a mother who cannot stand up to her son's angry feeling that she should. Had she been able to, the chances are that she would already have done so; the advice will only make her feel guiltier.

Today many parents, unfortunately, have little capacity to value themselves. It does not help to tell such people how to treat their children. The temporary feeling of security that may be obtained by being told what to do may have two effects. It may increase parental uncertainty, so that dependence on advice becomes greater and greater, leading to the economic success of the advice purveyor. On the other hand, if the ideas offered are seen as foreign, they may convince people of the uselessness of their own opinions; good advice may then be rejected or, worse, slavishly followed. In any case, if adults doubt their own capacity to be good parents, telling them how to behave may make them feel transiently better in that it may relieve their immediate worries, but it will not make them value themselves. People can be comfortable about being told what to do only if their own ideas and wishes, which for some reason were felt to be unacceptable, are confirmed. Forcefully presented foreign ideas may make people temporarily submerge their own feelings; they lead to no permanent solutions. Apart from this, many attitudes are based on social class and ethnic group customs, while experts are often middle class in their behavior and judgmental orientation. Such experts may be unaware of this, and unwittingly try to inflict on their eager listeners a foreign way of life. If parents act their roles as fathers and mothers with a newspaper column, a paperback book, a social worker, or a family practitioner as the stage director, this will create within them and their children a feeling of confusion. Children are not fooled when parents do not behave naturally and spontaneously, and they sense that something is wrong in their relationships, although this feeling may not be articulated.

Parental uncertainty is a reality and increases adolescent turmoil and stress. The fact that direction is rarely helpful does not make help impossible. One principle of adult psychotherapy is that the individual patient should not be told how he or she should behave. Good therapy respects the ability of adults to make their own decisions. Knowledge about the reasons for human behavior may be of real assistance. Understanding offered without strings respects the ability of people to make their own decisions and reinforces their sense of worth.

PARENTAL CONFUSION

There are a number of reasons why parents should be confused about the behavior of their adolescent children and doubtful about how to respond. Fathering was less than adequate after World War II. Many of today's parents of adolescents were born in the 1940's and grew up with either absent fathers or fathers who were insecure about their own role. By the time they were in their own teens, society was becoming highly mobile and many grew up without the support of an extended network of family, extra-parental adults, and stable peer relationships. This can mean that the fathers and mothers of today's young people may not have a firm sense of self and may find it very difficult to tolerate their child's anger. Furthermore, parents themselves find it difficult to tolerate frustration in interpersonal relationships, and so significant numbers of today's children are likely to be living in single-parent families, following the divorce of their parents. As a result, when boys and girls have to struggle with their mothers to fight their own internal wish to be mothered and to thus develop a sense of autonomy, there may be no father there to offer support in an involved, caring role that is markedly different from the mother's. It is not unusual, then, for adolescent children to commute between parents, as if they could thereby free themselves from dependent needs that are a threat to autonomy and work out the complex feelings about both parents that give a satisfactory sense of identity, both sexual and otherwise. Confusion about parental roles, which is currently being elevated to a philosophy, reinforces parental anxieties. Insistence upon equal roles for both parents lays a foundation for generations of disturbed adolescents. It can hardly be accidental that the increase in the number of both parents working, along with an increased divorce rate, parallels an increase in the suicide/accident/homicide rate, the incidence of drug abuse, and the largest adolescent rate of illegitimate conception in history (Miller, 1983).

The Depression and World War II led to an intense dissatisfaction with the nature of man. It was thought, rightly, that if man were less anxious, he would be less violent. Changes in child-rearing techniques were proposed, and the fashion since the 1940s has been for parents to try to consider the emotional needs of their children as they show them in day-to-day relationships. This led to child-rearing dissonance between the generations, which may partly explain the student turbulence of the 1960s. Many of those students are now the parents of children who are becoming adolescents. There has been consonance between the way these children are reared and the manner in which their parents were raised. Some, who were brought up by parents who were uncomfortable with concepts of demand feeding—children are fed when they show behavioral evidences of hunger—and the modern concept of toilet training—children are trained when they demonstrably are ready to be clean (Spock, 1965)—are now much more comfortable as parents. If there is a recognition of an infant's need for constancy in its environment, the generation of teenagers who will be going through the next decade should be even more comfortable in their role as parents. The decrease in parental confusion about child-rearing should, other things being equal, produce greater security among youth. The recognition of stages of human development (Gesell and Ilg, 1943) meant that many people knew of probable behavior at certain ages and had expectations on the basis of this. The independent striving of two-year-olds gave rise to the phrase "the terrible two's." Parents who were aware of this tended to handle situations with "Let us do this together," rather than "Do it." "Let us clear up your toys" replaced "Put your toys away." The easy relationships of the three-year-old to his world gave rise to the phrase "the trusting threes"; the competitiveness of four-year-olds to the "ferocious fours"; the equableness of five-year-olds to the "fabulous fives." These catch phrases generally make today's parents more secure about their children and so long as the age norms are not excessively rigid, there will be greater security for adolescents.

Thus recent significant changes in child-rearing have taken place, with a very real effort made on the part of parents and health educators to meet children's needs. Obviously, some who do not physically suffer may still be neglected and emotionally deprived, an almost inevitable state among the underprivileged. Confusion between needs and wants, when people do not recognize that "I want" is not the same as "I need," may lead to similar emotional deprivation among the more affluent; but one hopes that the consistency between upbringing of the generations will make this less common.

If the divorce rate drops, it is possible to be more optimistic about the next generation of adolescents, and the beginning fall in the incidence of drug abuse and suicide may well continue.

Whatever fashions may dictate child-rearing techniques, the child who is not fathered, apart from difficulties in developing a firm sense of self grows into an adult with no intuitive feelings of what a father's role has to be. Mothers handle and feed their infants as they themselves were handled and fed; they cannot successfully be both father and mother.

Without an imprint of the experience of having their needs met when they were children, and lacking support from their own parents, the insecurity of adolescents is reinforced. Wars compound the problem of adequate parenting, because the husbands who return from the inevitable deprivation of wartime military service seek undue mothering, at any rate initially, from their own wives. Thus, children who were born just after the father returned from a wartime experience are likely to feel intensely competitive with him.

Children need the security of parents who are genuinely sure of themselves or, at least, who are honest with themselves. A child is likely to be in difficulties if he has a parent who, although uncertain about what to do or how to behave, pretends certainty. If there is an absolutely right way to bring up a child, which is doubtful, it is better for a parent to be wrong with conviction that right with uncertainty. An adolescent is more likely to be mentally healthy and develop into a secure adult if parents comfortably and unwittingly do the wrong thing than uncomfortably try to do what is thought to be right.

Those of today's parents who were involved in the escalation of drug and alcohol abuse, which accelerated in the mid-1960's, will not be the parents of adolescents until the late 1980's. Not until the next decade will the effect of this parental behavior be seen. The present generation of parents who are themselves the children of divorce do not have a built-in concept that only joint efforts between adults can offer appropriate emotional support to adolescents; explicable perhaps because they did not themselves grow up in a stable society in which adults and children communicated with each other. Not surprisingly, problems and confusion continue to exist about adolescent sexuality and the parents of this adolescent generation, who were the first generation of television watchers, now collude in the passive stimulation offered children by video-games.

Parents consciously try to give their children a better youth than they had themselves; often they then envy children for enjoying something not previously available. The decline in affluence may make this less of an inter-generational problem.

Not all parental uncertainty is due to a difference between the parents' upbringing and the way they rear their children, nor is all adolescent un-certainty due to a conflict between the way parents live and how they try to educate their own children. Some people, because of their own upbringing, may be unsure of themselves as people and, thus, as parents. If one parent is emotionally healthier than the other, and if fathers and mothers love and care for their children, the resilience of human nature may mean that emotional difficulties are not passed down through the generations; never-theless, family problems sometimes are carried, like the color of a child's hair or shape of his body, from grandparent to parent to child. Depression may be a genetically inherited illness; it may also be the result of emotional deprivation transmitted through the generations.

TELEVISION AND FAMILY RELATIONSHIPS

A particular developmental stress, brought about by the use of television, has been perpetrated on children since the 1950's. Apart from absenteeism from mothering produced by both parents working, the use of television for many hours a day as a baby-sitter and as a parental entertainer may cut down very significantly the amount of time parents, and particularly mothers, spend with their children. Just as their parents, as young children, today's teenagers may have had insufficient meaningful emotional contacts with people and things. If a family group is watching television, there is little direct interaction between parents and children. They are all observers artificially stimulated by action on a screen with little talk one to the other. The attempt of children to act out the violence they have seen on the screen may, however, be controlled in an aggressive way by parents. Thus, screen violence is reinforced by intra-familial aggression. In homes that severely limit the amount of viewing, small children spend a great deal of time under their mother's feet. Household tasks may be more difficult; the child interrupts, imitates, and in a whole variety of ways clamors for his mother's attention. Turning the television set on may make things very much easier. The child is put in front of the screen to watch, sometimes for hours. Television distorts reality in a way a child cannot understand; all actions have an instant, instead of a long-term effect; time, in terms of years, is meaningless; objects are easily acquired; violence is meaningless, or clean and neat; youth is cruelly exploited. Apart from all this, and as important, is that television implicitly puts children in an extremely passive position (Stein and Frederick, 1971). They experience constant stimulation from outside, with no participation themselves (Murray, 1971). This may mean that, when adolescence is reached, young people may expect their "needs" to be met with little effort on their part, a difficulty that may increase because of the confusion in adolescence of needs with wants. Those adolescents develop an implicitly passive approach to life, expecting to be entertained by it. There is a remarkable similarity between those adolescents who take drugs for their vivid visual impressions, which they inertly and passively watch within the picture frame of their own minds, and those who sat as small children in equivalent positions watching a television screen.

In the United States, the knife and the gun are glorified on television. There is no proof that television alone has contributed to the spread of violence, although it is difficult to believe that it does not have something to do with it. Children are very imitative, and it may well be that violence seen on the screen may encourage some disturbed adolescents to express their own feelings violently (Arkin et al., 1968). But most psychiatrists cannot find clinical evidence of this, although reports of sadism in newspapers and on television can produce a crop of imitators (Miller, 1969).

There has been some public discussion as to the effects of television on the reading habits of the population-at-large, but little about its effects on educational techniques or human relationships, in general.

Television also offers magic solutions. The anxiety of many young people about their sexual attractiveness is supposedly relieved by the application of one or another skin lotion. All this may cause as much difficulty as the amount of violence seen by children on television, which has caused so much public concern.

Information given by the mass media in many other ways may increase the problems of young people. The division of the world into rich and poor nations poses particular problems for perceptive youth in the West. They are made aware, if they use their eyes at all, that they are members of a generally rich society in which most people do not die of starvation. However, even if there was no television, it would be difficult to deny the presence of the poor. In America, the ghetto is just a block down the street in large cities; in Britain, starvation stares at well-fed young people from numerous posters advertising famine relief in Africa. Affluent adolescents in the West are uneasily aware that they are envied by the less privileged; they may guiltily feel they have done nothing to deserve their worldly goods. Some, perhaps, as a result of conflict about this, feel that the appropriate response is either to drop out of a society that they see as alienating and selfish or, alternately, to look deprived. Television also affects personality development because it exposes the private lives and behavior of well-known people. If they are to develop mature personalities, adolescents need to have hero figures, preferably real people they can genuinely admire. In a healthy psycho-social environment, the ideal image of the perfect parent is projected onto a "hero." The identification with such a hero, on the one hand, helps free the youngster from overdependence on the parents. On the other hand, the ideal is then reintegrated into the personality and assists in development. The media exposé of the flaws in people's personalities and, in particular, television's superficial approach to problems, may mean that the adolescent's need for a hero cannot be met. Even those young people whom they think of as possible heroes to emulate, are often exposed as having feet of clay. The failures, deficiencies, and sometimes dishonesty of public figures are available for all to watch, so there is little possibility of young people idealizing anyone. Thus, the struggle for autonomy from parents becomes more intense as this support to growth is not available.

Heroes ultimately undergo a symbolic death and, with the present generation's preoccupation with youthfulness, this death may be associated with aging. Paul McCartney, one of the Beatles, was rumored to have died in late 1969. The excessive mourning of many adolescents signified his departure as their hero figure. On the other hand, Jim Morrison of The Doors, who died in his twenties, is currently rumored to be still alive.

FAMILY ISOLATION

Social isolation is one of the major pressures that twentieth-century living inflicts on the young. It is also relevant to the parental world, which is usually not as uncaring as angry, frustrated youth often suggest. A particular problem may develop for both parents and children in large cities and in areas of rapid social change. Because of the breakdown of social networks and the idea that late-adolescent and young adults should not live with their parents, the tower blocks of large American cities are filled with young isolated individuals who search for meaning in their life; but fulfilling human relationships and emotional depth will never be found in the world of singles bars and frenetic sexual activity.

To some extent, stable neighborhoods in the United States developed ritualized ways of having newcomers meet others. These rituals are relatively meaningless, however, since people do not really become involved with each other until they are sure that separation is not imminent. American children are, thus, in much the same situation as those in societies that have not even developed informal rituals to make relationships possible. A particular problem of affluent suburbs and city areas is the isolation of families from each other. Parents may not have friends with whom they can discuss the growth and maturation of their children. There is no network of caring adults to support a youngster, so the latter's involvement with parents may be one of hostile dependence and the parents may become preoccupied with their offspring.

Social isolation also means that parents will believe what their children say happens in other families, whatever might be the truth. A lack of parental knowledge is shown by adolescents' demanding that parents stay away from home when they are having a party. Adolescents insist that this is what their friends' parents do and claim that they will be humiliated if their fathers or mothers behave differently. Parents isolated from other family groups are likely to give in to the request; if their relationships with other families are tenuous, parents will not be able to get support from friends when they resist their children's pressures. Finally, the isolation of the nuclear family puts a marriage under greater stress than otherwise might be the case. A father may seek the phony intimacy of the bar, the pub, or the golf course—club-car situations in which people appear to care about each other but the interest does not extend beyond the confines of the activity. Mothers who have more free time when their children reach adolescence may take jobs in the community much below their potential ability, watch television soap operas, or become depressed. Some return to school, however, and when they do this, or are otherwise successful, it is clear that their children admire them.

Most parents intuitively understand a good deal about adolescence, but they often convey this understanding by a series of complaints: their children are difficult, rude, impossible to please, untidy, careless, and unappreciative. It is less usual for parents to talk of the way their adolescent children are expanding their interests in life and becoming more involved with the world. The excitement of youth is less often noted, although many are well aware of this. In a larger social network, some of the assets of adolescence, as well as the liabilities, will be discussed.

It would appear that society is polarizing the development of its young people. On the one hand, the adolescents who weather the numerous stresses placed upon them are healthier, more mature, more outgoing, and more giving perhaps than any previous generation. On the other hand, a significant number are exposed to so much stress and are offered so little in the way of community, and other support, that they turn in on themselves, become significant drug and alcohol abusers, and function academically or vocationally at far below their potential ability. These adolescents are in need of psychological and other help.

Most young people would be considerably assisted by changes in our social organizations, schools, colleges, universities, and community agencies. Almost all psychological help for the disturbed young requires assistance from the people within the institutions in which adolescents spend most of the day. Unless the people who are in constant contact with youth improve their skill in forming and keeping relationships with adolescents, expert help for the disturbed is attenuated, and psychological growth impeded.

REFERENCES

Arkin, G. C., et al. (1968), *The Effects of Television in Children and Youth; A Review of Theory and Research*. Rev. ed. Vol. 6 of *Television and Social Behavior*. Washington, D.C.: U.S. Government Printing Office.

Block, H., and Neiderhoffer, A. (1958), *The Gang*. New York: Philosophical Library.

Bott, E. J. (1957), *Family and Social Network*. London: Tavistock Publications.

Citizen's Committee for Children of New York: Report quoted in *The New York Times*; November 21, 1982.

Fox, R. (1967), *Kinship and Marriage*. Harmondsworth: Penguin.

Gesell, A., and Ilg, F. L. (1943), *Infant and Child in the Culture of Today*. New York: Harper.

Ginott, H. (1965), *Between Parent and Child*. New York: Macmillan.

Group for the Advancement of Psychiatry (1963), *Normal Adolescence*. Report No. 68. New York: American Psychiatry Association.

James, C. (1968), *Young Lives at Stake*. London: Collins.

Kandel, D., et al. (1968), *Adolescents in Two Societies*. Cambridge: Harvard University Laboratory of Human Development.

Masterson, J. F. (1967), *The Psychiatric Dilemma of Adolescence*. Boston: Little, Brown.

Menninger, K. A. (1963), *The Vital Balance*. New York: Viking.

Miller, D. (1969), *The Age Between*. London: Hutchinson.

—— (1970), Adolescents and the high school system. *J. Community Ment. Health*, 66: 483–491.

—— (1973), Adolescent crisis: Challenge for Patient, parent, and internist. *Ann. Intern. Med.*, 79: 435–440.

—— (1983), *Behavior Disorders. Etiology and Treatment*. In press.

Murray, J. P. (1971), Television in inner city homes: Viewing behavior in young boys. In *Television in Day to Day Life Patterns of Use*, Vol. 4 of *Television and Social Behavior*, ed. E. A. Rubenstein et al. Washington, D.C.: U.S. Government Printing Office.

Spock, B. (1945), *Baby and Child Care*. New York: Cardinal.

Stein, A. H., and Frederick, L. K. (1971), Television and content and young children's behavior. In *Television and Social Learning*, Vol. 2 of *Television and Social Behavior*, ed. J. P. Murray et al. Washington, D.C.: U.S. Government Printing Office.

Chapter 7

The World of School

PROBLEMS OF CREATIVITY

Although "generation gap" is no longer a currently used phrase, significant intergenerational alienation continues. Although it does not apply to everyone, the isolation of youth from adults is common in all Western societies. This is the result of the inability of society to offer emotional anchor points to adolescents, especially those in extended family and tribal type relationships. Furthermore, it is increasingly difficult for society to give young people an opportunity to be creative. The failure of society to provide for the adequate education of young people is produced partly by economic deprivation, partly by the lack of awareness of what constitutes appropriate education. Well-fed youth often appear to be increasingly aware of inner feelings of emptiness and desolation; deprived young people are either inert and passive or, despairingly, seek excitement from sex, violence, or drugs. With the view that the present generation should pay for the misdeeds of the past, political leaders who claim to represent ethnically deprived minorities seem to demand that their constituency get their share at the public trough. The insistence on meeting personal and group needs at whatever cost to others, with a pseudointellectual justification, is the same attitude that led to the creation of the out-group. Young people may see their parents' generation as boring, dull, complacent, self-centered, unimaginative, and materialistic. This projection may have some accuracy, but it also reflects the anxiety that this is what they are themselves. The failure to encourage creativity and imagination, to respect the physical needs of man, and to stimulate thinking as well as learning in the young is a failure that ultimately may lead to the disintegration of society. Waterloo may have been won on the playing fields of Eton, but the British Empire may have disintegrated with such speed because the meritocracy was taught that fairness to the weak was appropriate, bullying an anathema.

The future of the United States depends on educational processes in the public school system, and currently, the future looks bleak.

Education in the classroom has generally led to an inhibition of creativity and an enhancement of passivity. Passive obedience to a highly rigid system leads to alternations between compliance, alienated conformity, hostile projection onto minority groups and ideas, and intermittent rebellion, which may be violent (70% of adolescents are reported to have used drugs or alcohol; 40% are regular users). It is not just that children who are unsure of themselves feel empty and bored, they *are* bored.

Many intelligence tests have been standardized to measure cognitive functions, retention, reasoning capacity, and the ability to make abstractions (Torrance, 1962). The lack of interest in creativity and imagination is evident in that these cannot be assessed by any standard tests that are easily and accurately applied to large numbers (Getzels and Jackson, 1960). Tests of creativity do have validity, but it is apparent that standardized tests of IQ are given much more weight as an indication of ability.

Children brought up in a reasonably optimum way—loved, fed, nurtured, and respected for their sexuality as boys and girls—are able to be creative, the extent of this depending on a mixture of genetic endowment, nurture, and personality development (Speigal, 1958). In grade school, children's enjoyment in their capacity to be creative in playing, in imagining things, and in painting, building, and playing games begins to plateau at about the age of nine. However, after only one to two years of standard closed-system, classroom teaching in grades one and two, many children are already somewhat unsure of themselves and unwilling to take intellectual chances without the permission of the teacher. A grade-five teacher commented to a group of parents that if she told the children to follow the written instructions in a book, most of them felt obligated to check that this was what really was wanted. British grade schools have used the so-called open classroom for many years, but until recently, and still in many situations, there was a change in classroom structure at age nine from small-group teaching to a standard checkerboard of desks, with teachers isolated at the front of the room. At this point, creativity declines, and children start to talk of their teachers as "they."

In the United States, grade-school teaching has rarely been as highly imaginative as it is in good British primary schools. Until very recently, group teaching had not caught the imagination of American grade-school teachers, who have been preoccupied with teaching by reinforcement and tend to put themselves at the end of an oblong classroom as a means of maintaining control; the open classroom, however, has never meant abandonment of control.

Americans are generally concerned about the need of people to get on with each other; it is remarkable, then, that the social environment of the school system, even in grade school, makes this difficult, because consistent interpersonal relationships are insufficiently valued. Although grade schools are concerned with the child's use of creative imagination, stress is placed on a high degree of conformity, on being obedient, and on keeping up with certain age norm standards. The American concept of democracy may discourage strong ties between friends, who are often encouraged by their parents to "play with others."

Achievement in an academic field is given particular status by most schools. When school taxes are not passed, nonacademic subjects tend to be jettisoned. In any case, an either/or situation, creative and imaginative against academic and intellectual, is implicitly assumed. In one affluent school system that was economizing, children in grade ten who took academic subjects could not, if they wanted a balance of science and humanities, also take art or music. The preoccupation with academic achievement for intellectual adolescents is partly based on the demands of society. But creative learning requires teachers who are able to make meaningful, positive emotional relationships with their pupils; it is no accident that it is in the art room of many schools that teachers are felt and seen as real people. Art teachers do not normally hide behind status and desks.

Creativity is most inhibited when the child becomes pubertal, at the beginning of adolescence. There are many reasons for this, some in the psychology of this age period, some in the organization of the school. Puberty produces a situation in which adolescents seem able to be creative in fits and starts; many of their imaginative resources appear to be used in daydreaming. When puberty is over, boys and girls are psychologically more free to be creative. Creativity at the end of the pubertal period also assists in the mastery of emotional conflicts (Blos 1962), as is obvious both from the poetry of fifteen- to seventeen-year-olds and from their paintings and sculpture. But in most Western countries, the right to pursue higher education depends almost totally on intellectual, rather than on social or physical achievement. Many potentially academic young people have creative talent; overconcentration on examinations, aptitude tests, and grades does not necessarily destroy this, but it hardly represents good education. In many, however, an artificial peak of creativity may appear before individuals get enmeshed in the conformity of society. This peak often occurs when puberty is over, at the end of early adolescence, a period of maximum sexual potency and rebelliousness (Bernfield, 1924).

SCHOOL SYSTEMS AND PERSONALITY DEVELOPMENT

Many adolescents at the peak of pubertal turmoil, usually at twelve to thirteen, leave grade school to enter junior high school. Thus, they are moved to a new environment at the time they are coping with the inner turmoil of puberty, so internal and external confusion occur together. Another school change at fifteen also interferes with personality growth. Children in early adolescence need to test out the personality strengths of the adults in their environment they hope they might use as models for personality development. Entering high school at the beginning of a period of identity consolidation means that adolescents have to go through another period of testing different adults. Even if consistent relationships with teachers were possible, scheduling usually negates this. Finally, in grades ten, eleven, and in the first semester of grade twelve, the pressure is to obtain high grades for college. In addition, academic achievement tests—ACTs, SATs—distort education, and some children are sent to special tutorial classes to ensure high scores in these. So creativity of the mid-adolescent period that might bloom tends to be inhibited by both the organization of the educational system and by its teaching techniques. The decline of creativity reported by psychologists (Wolfenstein, 1956) as a function of "the adolescent process" may well be due to the negative reinforcement of the educational system.

In Britain, the potentially academic student might expect to have five years in the same school from the age of thirteen. There is a greater likelihood of having the same teachers for two to three years. There is an inappropriate push toward taking entrance examinations at fifteen or sixteen and then a further examination two years later. This system, which produces emotional stability, still inhibits creativity by a demand for convergent thinking (Blos, 1962).

In the British system, the essential demand of examinations, with essay-type questions lasting about thirty minutes, is that the adolescent be willing to forego a creative interest in one particular aspect of a subject in order to answer all the questions on the examination paper. A highly imaginative, creative adolescent may find it almost intolerable to abandon the proper study of a subject; such young people may feel that they must answer one question in depth. These individuals are likely to be discarded by the British system. Examination failure due to reluctance to answer all the questions on the paper may be related to a refusal to compromise. It is necessary to answer all the questions because the first 50 percent of the mark on any one question is easier to obtain than the next 30 percent. The multiple-choice examination of American education uses a different technique, but except for the especially able, creativity is inhibited. Because of technology and increasing leisure time, society can no longer afford to slight creativity as it hopefully improves intellectual stimulation and achievement.

There are many forms of creativity, some associated with genius and talent, others with less dramatic forms of imaginative productions. Some types of creativity are highly agreeable to society. Obviously, creativity in adolescent boys is acceptable when it involves activity and competitiveness. In most ethnic groups, a boy's need for more feminine, tender creativity, also a part of manhood, causes anxiety to some people, and then to the adolescents themselves. Cooking and caring for babies may be temporary, if important, creative activities for adolescent boys. The white Anglo-Saxon male is allowed to cook at a camp-out, with an outdoor barbecue; this is not seen as effeminate. Although this is changing somewhat because both parents work, cooking in his mother's kitchen is often felt not to be desirable for a boy. In a British School for delinquent boys, the toughest youngsters chose, as a preferred activity, a cooking class. Initially, only sweet cakes and cookies were made, then the boys began to make preserves and cook for others, and not just themselves.

Creativity among girls is rarely supported when it involves woodworking or furniture making, and in vocational schools, instruction of girls in these areas is still relatively rare. The cultural variation in acceptable creative tasks is striking: in the United States, flowers are mostly grown by women, in Britain, mostly by men.

Creativity may invoke talent, genius, or both. Talent can be defined as a special natural ability; nowadays it usually implies an excellence in art, literature, or science, involving more than an ordinary capacity. A genius can be defined as an individual having a highly superior ability to perform in a particular area, especially creatively; a talented individual is creative in a particular area, but may not be superior in other aspects of intellectual achievement.

PROBLEMS OF TALENT

Talented adolescents of both sexes are likely to have different kinds of problems. Talent makes those who possess it feel unique, and they may never quite know whether they are loved for themselves or their talent. For boys, there is not only the stress of not being sure that their activity will be economically viable, but, depending upon their field of interest, during adolescence, they may be perceived by many peers and adults as being insufficiently manly (Guildford, 1959). In mid-adolescence, when identity is being consolidated, it is difficult for adolescents to decide that their talent will be their life's work. Many wish to keep a foot in the academic camp, but developing their talent isolates them from both school activities and their peers. It is usually impossible for such young people to have full lives and obtain high grades. A ballet dancer is not normally also a mathematician. Those adolescents whose primary emotional involvement is in their creative talent have unique problems (Wilson, 1956). Many artists appear to take longer to develop a firm feeling of self than those without such talents. When they seek higher education, however, the talented are more fortunate than others: admission to good art or music schools depends on the quality of work produced over a period of time rather than on grades and academic achievement tests. Still, such students often face particular emotional problems in colleges; they find that it is difficult to develop as a professional painter, sculptor, or singer, for example, and also to study for those academic courses that may be required for graduation. The jury system may expose vulnerable students to intense pain, particularly if the staff is insensitive:

> Karl, an artistic nineteen-year-old, was being treated for severe depression. This had followed the death, by suicide, of his alcoholic father when the boy was twelve. Slowly in the course of therapy, the young man developed a sense of his own worth. As with many talented people, this depended on his feeling that his art was valued. He held a one-man show in his home town during a vacation and the selling of some pictures was immensely supportive. When he returned to school, his professor told him, at a jury, that a picture of which he was particularly proud was "shallow and pretentious and showed a lack of masculinity." Two weeks later the boy killed himself by suffocating himself with a plastic bag.

Modern trends in painting, for example, which attract the adolescent, do not offer much in the way of personality support. Apart from Karl's particular experience, art teachers often comment about the personality of their students in a pseudopsychologizing way on the basis of their art.

Vulnerability is the hallmark of the talented. Both artists and musicians tend to see what they produce as direct extensions of themselves. To criticize a flautist's playing may be a severe personal criticism; to tear a painting apart may be to shatter the artist.

Those who study the fine arts, as distinct from the practical arts, find it difficult to establish a role for themselves in society. They are often told that they must know how to express themselves in their chosen media, but it is difficult for them to see how they can produce works that will be sold. Because they fear not being able to earn their living, some adolescents abandon their wish to use their talent in order to comply with the system that values less creative endeavors. Creative impulses may be channeled into socially acceptable paths or abandoned.

> Hillel was the eighteen-year-old son of a rather passive, distant account-ant and a swamping, overpowering mother. He sought treatment because of a fear of homosexuality, but actually he was unable to get close to anyone, male or female. His homosexual wishes, which he felt as forbid-den, made it possible for him to refuse to involve himself with anyone. With economic motives in mind, he was taking advertising because he felt that if he committed himself to art he could never be successful. After therapy he abandoned both his homosexual fantasies and his advertising goal; he became a heterosexual artist, struggling for recognition.

Some talented adolescents have an intense creative drive and resist the conformist pressures of the educational system, but the sheer volume of work required in some fields may discourage them. If talented youngsters are to be assisted, they almost certainly need special schools; schools for music, art, and drama exist in some major U.S. cities for high school students; for older adolescents and young adults, special schools for musicians, artists, dancers and actors have a long history throughout the world.

PROBLEMS OF GENIUS

Another group of adolescents with particular problems are those who are geniuses. A genius has extraordinary intellectual power and may also be talented and possess a special artistic aptitude; however, there is no reason why a genius should be talented, or vice versa. The problem for the genius is that advancement in the educational system beyond the usual age norms does not allow boys or girls to make satisfactory comparisons about non-academic achievement with age-group peers. On the other hand, when such children are held back to their age norm in school, they become restless, bored, and difficult to handle (Hollingworth, 1939). If genius is not to be wasted, there is probably no alternative but to opt for a situation that allows an adolescent to advance at his or her academic pace. By adolescence, however, the genius is less mature, as measured by a capacity to tolerate frustration in non-academic fields, than a less able peer. Similarly, a genius is likely to be chronologically older than peers before developing a capacity either for an active sexual life or a tender loving relationship with a member of the opposite sex.

Robert, age twenty-two, entered college at sixteen and medical school at nineteen. He sought counseling help at twenty-two because, "I have never had a girl—whoever heard of a virgin of twenty-two?" He showed no marked evidence of emotional disturbance, but in his sexual relationships was more like the usual, somewhat diffident sixteen- or seventeen-year-old. A year later he was involved in a passionate love affair with a girl he later married. He had been seen three times in all by a psychiatrist.

TEACHERS AS SIGNIFICANT ADULTS

The more society fails to cope with the problems of adolescence, or even hinders adolescent growth, the more is the responsibility for personality development placed on the schools. Since teachers may be unprepared for the role thrust upon them, this can be quite frightening; it is not surprising, then, that many teachers tend to blame pupil disturbance on the youngsters themselves, or their parents, rather than admitting any contribution of their own inadequacies.

Many teachers are overwhelmed by the demands of parents and children for help; they feel unable to assist because they lack training. They say their job is to teach, not to look after disturbed children; social workers should cope with difficult families. Unfortunately, teachers often manage to avoid responsibility for such children in their care. Although they are present in the classroom every day, schedules in which teachers see 120 different children each day allow many not to notice those who are disturbed, unless their behavior is grossly disruptive.

There is also confusion about the appropriate goals for a school (Silberman, 1970). It is generally felt that schools should provide children with a formal education, according to their ability. Society has devised ways in which young people with academic ability can be recognized, but those young people who do not have the ability should not leave school feeling that they are inadequate, that they have not successfully graduated into life. Adolescents often leave high school crushed by sterile competition—labeled failures because they are not academic or because they develop slowly. Teachers know now that if they track groups of children according to their academic ability or place them in subject sets of differing standards, the results tend to be a faithful reflection of the teacher's original opinions (James, 1968).

Schools should be living organisms: they should teach not only academic subjects, but also a way of life. Adolescents are highly likely to conform to the expectations of their teachers. Society, as a whole, and schools, as a part of society, fail to recognize the significance of emotionally meaningful human relationships and the necessity to struggle to maintain them. Further, identification with small social organizations, such as schools, is essential for high morale. Schools, however, fail to inculcate either of these value systems because, in their very organization, they negate both.

EFFECTS OF EMOTIONAL DEPRIVATION ON ADOLESCENTS

Confused notions of human intelligence have led to the apparent belief, in some circles, that all students could succeed in an academic course, if only the school and social environment cooperated. This is, of course, fantasy. There are innate differences in intelligence.

There is no doubt, however, that emotional and intellectual damage in early childhood impairs human potential at all levels. Emotionally deprived children are most often found among the very rich and the very poor, since neither group of children receives consistent parental handling. The rich tend to be looked after by nannies, who are likely to change; the poor are farmed out to a succession of friends, babysitters, and elderly relatives.

Deprived children, brought up in poverty, are likely to have their intelligence impaired by physical and emotional deprivation. Parents from these groups do not know how to talk and play with their infants, often because they were not so treated. Commercial toys that stimulate intelligence and imagination cannot be afforded, and parents do not know how to improvise. Poor schools reinforce the inadequacy; they do not create it. Children who suffer from a variety of disorders of attention and who experience extreme emotional lability do not have the etiology of their difficulties properly looked into, nor is adequate educational intervention available.

The answer does not lie in just raising the economic level of the poor, although this is important, nor in just providing work for fathers, so that their sense of worth can be reinforced; it lies in the structure of society. Reducing the divorce rate would help. Although society offers resources to train people to function well as single parents, it would do well to try to help adults understand how divorce injures children. Some deny that single-parent families are more stressful to children than families that stay together (Wallerstein and Kelly, 1980), but there is no study of the effects of divorce on the capacity of individuals to make loving, trusting relationships when they become adults; yet, the successful rearing of future generations depends on such relationships. There is no doubt from clinical studies that this is the significant effect of parental separation, and the parental conflict that is inevitable in divorce (Chess, 1983) is a clear risk factor. It is no accident that the incidence of divorce is higher in the children of divorced parents.

Enrichment is needed in the lives of impoverished children in infancy and childhood. Headstart having been prematurely abandoned in many areas, the current fad is to try to provide this through day-care centers. The great disadvantage of these, however, is rapid staff turnover. Children are overwhelmed by multiple handling and the instability of adult/child relationships. A better technique is to teach mothers how to play creatively with their children, rather than encouraging them to watch television. Then, from the age of two-and-one-half, approximately, when separation from parents becomes acceptable, children can go to day-care centers for about two hours daily, which, one hopes, will lead to an excellent grade-school experience. Many experts are unaware that this technique was successfully applied by the Israelis to the deprived ghetto children of North African immigrants. It was noticed that these children seemed unable to make the adjustments necessary for them to learn to read. As children, they played only with sand, never with blocks. When the mothers were taught to show their children how to play with building blocks, reading skills at age six markedly improved in the children who had been taught this at three, compared to those who had not been so taught.

HOW SCHOOLS CAN HELP PERSONALITY GROWTH

Art, music, drama, and topic and project teaching all assist schoolchildren in the development of academic and imaginative potential. Along with this, a major goal of a good school should be the development of a mutual caring relationship between the children. To make this possible, the structure of a school should allow for constancy in teacher/pupil relationships; many staff will need to be taught how to relate to children in a way that will be felt as meaningful and caring. Another goal should be to develop the personalities of young people, so that they are capable of personal initiative, and flexible enough to envisage at least one major occupational change in their lives as desirable, as well as inevitable. These goals make many arbitrary demands of adults look quite irrelevant. A preoccupation with school prayer and saluting the flag is still seen as the answer to the malaise of the young. Written disciplinary codes with tariffs of punishment and a legislative preoccupation with the form of prosecution become a substitute for caring.

Those systems that seek simplistic "magical" solutions produce in the young an identification with that approach; coercion produces individuals who use similar techniques; neglecting the young as total people means that as adults they will do the same to others.

If schooling imposes rigid intellectual conformity, it may force bright questioning pupils to use their emotional energy to try to maintain personal integrity with a hidden "no." Such a conflict is most evident in those countries where schools are particularly rigid and where asking teachers questions is traditionally seen as currying favor. It is difficult for young people from such backgrounds to ask questions later on, at a university lecture or with politicians. Those who get around to questioning often fail to wait for answers.

Some teachers still behave toward adolescents as if all that is needed to produce personality growth is to tell children what to do. If repeated orders fail, they then apply a variety of punishments, as if all the school wants is passive compliance. The complexities of relationships are understood intuitively by many teachers, but the rest have not learned them.

The adolescent personality is, in many ways, very plastic. A judicious placing of children in particular classes and subjects can help resolve anxieties and conflicts. The example below was taken from a British high school. It is most improbable that this technique could be used in America, where, although classes can be hand-scheduled, this is usually done by a computer. The changeover of teachers is also more rapid than in the average English school, and drama is not used routinely as part of the teaching of English.

> An inhibited boy in a boys' school found it quite impossible to express normal aggressive impulses in a constructive way. John was shy and withdrawn and not as academically successful as his level of intelligence would have led one to expect, although he was not a total academic failure. John was considerably helped by his environment. Instead of being put in an art class and allowed to do the rather meticulous compulsive paintings that he liked, he was directed by his art teacher toward a more slapdash dramatic form of expressive art. In school plays, instead of being typecast as a weak, inadequate person, he was put in the position of having to play out a more aggressive, more definite role. The school avoided any temptation to use a carping tone in his school reports that would only have made his parents worry. John reacted by becoming more at ease, and there was some improvement in his academic work.

Except in cities in which there are private schools, the uniformity of the high school system makes the recommendation for a transfer to a more suitable teacher or subject unlikely. This is, however, changing. In some junior high schools, a small house system is being devised with continuity of teacher/pupil relationships; some large high schools have created "free schools" within their walls, in addition to a more conformist type of education. If a school cannot provide a wide-enough range of subjects to meet a pupil's needs, it may be possible to recommend that the youngster change schools.

> Tom, who had a bossy, anxious mother and a father who was often away on business, had always been difficult at school. His mother nagged him and demanded that he do many household tasks, such as cooking and housecleaning. When he became angry she beat him with a riding crop. Although he had the potential to be academic, his school

achievement was lamentable. His school was preoccupied with grades, valuing only very good athletes and conformist behavior.

Tom was moved to a school that provided many varieties of nonconformist physical activity and the opportunity to construct furniture and play musical instruments. These gave Tom outlets for his pent-up aggression, and they also allowed him to feel acceptably masculine. Within a year, there was also a dramatic improvement in his academic work.

Children who are so damaged in infancy that they cannot make meaningful human relationships will probably not be helped by a normal school environment. Special classes in the average high school may contain them, but these are the individuals who become runaways, academic drop-outs, drug users, or juvenile and, later, adult delinquents. Young people who can form only dependent childlike relationships because their capacity for further maturation has been damaged may remain emotionally tied to their school, where, at least, these relationships were possible. The least inadequate may make an apparently satisfactory social adjustment, but will, if they go to college, often become intensively and almost exclusively involved in alumni associations, subsequently. Others may make an apparently good adjustment at school, but become passive and unable to function independently when they leave. They sometimes find a solution by living and working in highly structured schoollike environments, such as the army or in highly bureaucratized organizations, typically, some large industries, universities, hospitals, and government. In a sense, they never grow out of school.

Emotionally vulnerable girls, in particular, may find it difficult to free themselves from the relationships established in sororities. They may remain emotionally involved with their adolescent friends for the rest of their lives, not by choice, but because they are rigid, psychologically.

THE SMALL HOUSE TO PROMOTE EMOTIONAL GROWTH

A number of relatively inexpensive changes can be made that should make possible a happier and more tension-free educational environment. Even if they do not solve all the problems created by adolescent tension, they will create situations in which the two sexes, and ethnic and social groups, become more aware of each other as people. Separation of teachers from their pupils appears to be built into the educational system. Scheduling of classes seems to ensure that teachers will not know their pupils. Worse, no effort is made to ensure that children can be in classes with their friends, although it is perfectly possible to schedule a youngster's day so that at least one-half the classes are taken with the same pupils. Traditional classroom design symbolizes the educational system's unawareness of what makes for easy and comfortable human relations. Putting a teacher at one end of a rectangular room, with pupils arranged in serried rows, makes it very difficult to relate to any of the class at any one time. Teachers with powerful personalities can conquer this type of room arrangement, but many teachers cannot. Customarily, in the class there will be a group of children who sit by the window, whose attention wanders to what is going on outside; a group who sleep at the back or who do their best not to be noticed; and, finally, the difficult children at the front, who are often those who seek attention or who want the approval of the teacher. The typical classroom may allow isolated children to be virtually ignored for years by their teachers, providing they hand in passable work. Thus, some children go through school without talking in any meaningful way to their teachers.

Group relationships are generally insufficiently considered in the typical school, and opportunities to make emotionally meaningful contacts lost. The maximum number of people any one person can easily relate to at one time in one place is eight. If a teacher has a class of thirty children, classrooms should be arranged so that the teacher can relate to four groups of eight children and is not faced with the impossible task of always relating to the larger whole. In very large classes, so much discipline is required from the average teacher that a warm pupil/teacher relationship is practically impossible. In the classroom arranged in groups, the teacher will have a central, rather than a peripheral relationship to the children.

Ironically, there are well-designed primary school classrooms in Britain and in the United States where children are taught around tables or in small groups, and there are similarly conceived science laboratories for adolescents. Tradition alone, perhaps based on the image of the preacher, has made for the typical classroom. If the logic of small-group teaching is inescapable for infants and scientists, it is equally inescapable through all parts of the school curriculum and for all ages. If furniture and classrooms were designed to make this possible, the effectiveness of teachers would improve, for it would be harder for staff and pupils to hide behind their status and their desks.

The emergence of ever larger high schools has made many wonder what arrangements can best promote secure relationsips, especially since a pupil needs to relate to teachers over periods of time *longer than a semester or even a year*. There is no reason why one-half a school day should not be spent with the same two or three teachers, and the other half in modular classes. It may be argued that one of these teachers could be less than satisfactory, but children also have to learn that all human relationships are not satisfactory and develop techniques of dealing with this.

The concept of a small house, essentially a subdivision of the larger unit, with a viable social group of its own, has never been widespread in the United States. Yet a study of morale in the British Royal Air Force clearly showed that men do not receive emotional support from identification with a larger unit, and can only identify with relatively small groups (Ministry of Defence, 1966). The homeroom teacher, with a primary task of being particularly helpful to a group of pupils in their psychological, social, and educational needs for one year, seemed to be an attempt to provide the equivalent support of the small-house unit. The fact that in many schools homerooms disappeared with a reduction of budgets indicates that this role failed or was not understood by either teachers or administrators. The problem is partly that homerooms often offered the only sense of stability in a pupil's schoolday that was not highly structured; therefore, much tension was relieved there. Not understanding this, many teachers responded repressively. Furthermore, teachers often do not understand the need for group stability and adult/adolescent relationships that last more than one year; usually the homeroom teacher changes with the grade.

A number of alternatives to the small house are possible. If a year–long teacher travels up the school with pupils, a group of adolescents will have the same adult relationship for a number of years. In some European schools, a change of teacher takes place after the children have moved up a grade, one change taking place in September, the other after Christmas. But ideally, children in the mid-adolescent period of development need relationships for three or four years to develop a healthy identity.

In the house system, a given number of pupils stay in one house for their school career; one or two staff members have a teaching role, but also act as personal and educational advisors. This system does not split the staff into pedagogic, disciplinary, administrative, and personal counseling roles. When this split is made, adolescents tend to see people only in their subidentities; they are not provided with whole personalities upon whom they can model themselves. The same applies to teachers. In one high school, if a pupil missed a number of classes, the teacher did not ask why or tell him he was missed; the pupil was sent to a counselor to be disciplined. If it was thought that the individual had personal problems, he was then directed to the school social worker. Adolescents communicate in actions as well as in words, and to look at difficult behavior, a possible request for personal help, only as an end in itself helps no one.

A house system only produces a structure for human relations. When house staff fail to understand the needs of children, the house may then promote only intramural competitiveness. It is probable that even a perceptive man or woman cannot know more than forty children well. If there are more than forty children in a house, other staff members must take special responsibility for different youngsters. It then becomes important that the school hierarchy does not conspicuously esteem certain categories of staff members above others.

Whichever system is used, the key factors are that non-parental adult relationships and peer-group attachments are essential for the development of adolescents and that one adult can only relate satisfactorily to a certain number of other human beings at any one time. It is also important to young people that they be able to maintain emotionally meaningful relationships through a large part of their school careers. If some teachers who teach academic subjects are to change, then other teachers involved in the more personal side of pupil's lives should continue to be available to them.

Just as forty children to a class are too many for a teacher, so are forty staff members to a principal. Since a school usually has a staff over ten, it will clearly be necessary for a principal to put himself in a position akin to that of a managing director. Ultimately he will find himself relating to heads of departments, each of which will break down into groups of eight to ten. The heads of departments will be his "managers" and his main relationship will be to them, rather than to the other teachers and the pupils themselves.

In large high schools of 1000 to 2000 children, a high degree of autonomy for different parts of the organization is required, and probably overcentralization, by a principal, is not needed. In most schools, academic and vocational departments have a high degree of autonomy, but it is not recognized that small social units also should be stable and autonomous. Each huge school could be a collection of smaller units of two to three hundred, each sharing common educational facilities. Otherwise, helpful relationships between staff and pupils cannot be created. At Eton College, in England, a relatively large school of 1200 pupils is broken up into houses of approximately 100 each. The pupils see themselves as belonging to the larger school, but their first and most important emotional attachment is to the smaller house. It is this type of emotional belonging that helps adolescents understand how organizations work.

The recognition in parts of the United States that the school day is too short, and academic subjects such as mathematics, the sciences, history, and English are too easily avoided, requires change in these areas. Alteration in these is not enough; if the positive value systems and nations of Western Civilization are to survive, a considerable restructuring of school systems is required.

TEACHER/PUPIL RELATIONSHIPS
IN THE ETIOLOGY OF DISTURBANCE

The relationship between school boards and management, administrative and teaching staff sets the stage for the relationship between teachers and pupils. When a class becomes unruly, the staff should look at their own social organization and their relationship to the youngsters instead of projecting all the responsibility onto the pupils, their ethnic and social subgroups, or their parents and society. All behavior is multidetermined, but it is remarkable how when there is, for example, racial tension, usually everything is considered except staff relationships, social system structure, and the psychological needs of the individual young people concerned.

If schools are to fulfill the role given them by society, teachers must be seen as valued. Perhaps, in unconscious revenge for the errors of past pedagogues, society refuses adequate support for school systems.

The responsibility of the community is to educate children to become productive members of the larger society; this responsibility the community largely passes on to the schools. Adolescents normally identify with the way of life they perceive in their environment. But the qualities they acquire most easily are those possessed by their parents and their circle. If their school is totally unlike their family, they will find it difficult to identify with it. For this reason, schools should consider the needs of the local community; they should not unthinkingly expose children to culture shock by imposing a way of life quite unlike that learned in their homes and primary schools (Bernstein, 1967). This is a major issue in school integration problems. Teaching white or black children black history may be desirable; it is no solution to the problems caused by an impersonal social organization weighing on individual adolescents. When the significance of personal relationships is really understood by American high school administrators, then the communication problems of differing ethnic and social groups can genuinely be taken into account.

The secondary school cannot widen the horizons of all its pupils. But it can be the catalyst for future change for many of them. The school, alone, cannot reverse the damage inflicted on an adolescent who has suffered severe emotional deprivation, but it can offer good emotional experiences.

REFERENCES

Bernfeld, S. (1924), Vom dischtenschen Schaffer der Jugend. *Int. Psych. Verlug. Wein.*

Bernstein, B. (1967), Social structure, language and learning. In *Education of the Disadvantaged,* ed. A. H. Pasow et al. New York: Holt, Rinehart and Winston.

Blos, P. (1962), *On Adolescence.* 181: Glencoe, Ill. Free Press.

Chess, S., et al. (1983). "Early Parental Attitudes, Divorce and Separation and Young Adult Outcome. Findings of a Longitudinal Study. J. Am. Acad. Child Psychiatr., 22(1): 47–51.

Getzels, J. W., and Jackson, P. W. (1960), *The Study of Giftedness, A Multidimensional Approach.* Washington, D.C.: U.S. Office of Education (Co-op Research Monographs No. 2).

Guildford, J. P. (1959), Three faces of intellect. *Am. Psychol.,* 14: 469–479.

Hollingworth, L. S. (1939), What we know about the early selection and training of leaders. *Teach. Coll. Rec.,* 40: 575–592.

James, C. (1968), *Young Lives at Stake*. 181–185: London: Collins.

Ministry of Defence (1966), *The Benson Experiment*. Science 4 (RAF), Memo 50, Appendix H. London.

Silberman, C. E. (1970), *Crisis in the Classroom: The Remaking of American Education*. New York: Random House.

Speigal, L. A. (1958), Comments on the psychoanalytic psychology of adolescence. *Psychoanal. Study of the Child*, 13: 296–309.

Torrance, E. P. (1962), *Guiding Creative Talent*. Englewood Cliffs, N.J.: Prentice-Hall.

Wilson, C. (1956), *The Outsider*. Boston: Houghton Mifflin.

Wolfenstein, M. (1956), Analysis of a juvenile poem. *Psychoanal. Study of the Child*, 11: 450–473.

Wallerstein J. S. & Kelly, J. B. (1980) "California's Children of Divorce. *Psychology Today*, 13: 67–76.

Chapter 8

School Integration: Familial, Racial, and Sexual

HOME AND SCHOOL

How home and school interact and how the interaction affects maturation and integration are poorly understood. Even if schools could offer emotional support to their pupils, many pupils would still have problems because of the intense struggle between the dependent and independent needs of adolescents, their inability to contain their own internal conflicts, and their need to project distaste for a part of themselves onto others. Possible dependence, because of the threat it poses to a sense of autonomy, particularly in those adolescents who are psychologically troubled, may cause rebellious behavior. Since no social system is perfect, some degree of in- and out-group prejudice is inevitable during adolescence.

Adults are, in a sense, in a no-win situation in relationship to adolescents; even good schools are likely to have difficult pupils. Parents often do not understand the causes of this turmoil, so particularly with their younger adolescent pupils, teachers get little help from the home. If there is no understanding between parents and staff before any upsets occur, they are unlikely to be of mutual help in a difficult situation. Parents and teachers tend to blame each other or their children. Many school principals believe that calling parents when their children have been difficult, or suspending the children from school, will automatically solve misbehavior. Suspension from class may temporarily relieve the school system of responsibility, but it is not the solution. Suspension is often based on a largely middle-class assumption that parents want their adolescent children to go to school. If the misbehavior reflects problems in the home, referral of the child to its parents will make matters worse. If the cause of trouble is primarily related to tension in the school system, however, the parents are put in an impossible situation. Suspension has been described by one school board as an immoral act (Ann Arbor School Board, 1970). An understanding of the etiology of the disturbed behavior, and real home and school cooperation, is needed.

Antisocial behavior may be a symptom of an emotional upset, even if only temporary, but it is also a sign of social system tension. The tendency is to regard conduct disorders as arising from children, as if they were unrelated to anything other than their badness. Teachers, school administrators, or parents may not understand that misbehavior is one way in which an action-oriented adolescent attempts to relieve internal tension and also to communicate a need for help. The appropriate action is thought too often to be only to control the antisocial action.

White middle-class parents often seek psychological assistance for their children; the economically deprived parent, from any ethnic group, does not know how to do this, cannot afford the cost, or is filled with shame. Some parents may deny difficulty and blame the school, some do not appear to care. Referral to the juvenile justice system is common in this group.

Cooperation between home and school requires mutual understanding. First, the goals of the adolescent, the parent, and the school may differ. The adolescent may, deliberately or not, play off the parent against the teacher or the teacher against the parent. The adults may, in their turn, withdraw from or become angry with each other. The adolescent may then see school as a refuge from home or vice versa. Even when parent and teacher are full of good will toward each other, if they are unaware of their differing goals and have no way of communicating, good will is not enough. Often parents of adolescents over the age of fifteen do not understand that a good teacher will not automatically tell them about difficulties their child may have; a teacher's respect for the pupil's striving for autonomy may cause parental anxiety.

Another problem may be the result of the parent's comparing the structure and atmosphere of a work situation and that of the child's school. In some sociologically sophisticated environments, the world outside home and school, the world of industry, is gradually becoming less coercive (McGregor,

1960). Japanese industry, as noted earlier, has shown that when workers feel involved and interested in what they produce, they are far more apt to be effective than if they see themselves as being exploited by assembly lines. The multiple recessions in the automobile industry in the 1970s and 1980s showed that the threat of unemployment did not solve the problem of poor quality control. This can happen only with a change of management style. Parents who are fortunate enough to be in jobs that offer emotional satisfaction may have the bewildering experience of seeing their children fail to get satisfaction in school. It may not occur to them that anything can be done, or they may not notice that their children are being alienated by the school.

> A group of parents of thirteen-year-olds, many of whom were on a university staff, attended a "capsule night" at a local junior high school. They made no complaint about the fact that their children had but twenty minutes to eat lunch. The parents were apparently not distressed by the absence of recess and did not seem to register the effect of the barren, tiled, lavatory-like walls of the school. Even when a homeroom teacher boasted of the fact that she would not let the children move from their seats (after a day of being educationally harried), the parents sat in silence.

It may be the children who find abundant interest and fulfillment at school, whereas the parents may get no real emotional satisfaction at work. These parents may be attacked by their children as being dull and uninteresting, or the children may find themselves unable to communicate with them. What is still usual, however, is that parents and children find themselves in a similar "work" situation. The parents may work in a factory that treats them as automatons; their children may go to schools they perceive as equally impersonal and authoritarian. Just as many managing directors see the well-being of their workers as secondary to profits, some principals and administrators see their individual pupils as secondary to other goals: apparently successful integration, academic achievement, and conformist behavior. Some principals insist that all decision-making must flow from them. The authoritarian school contains the seeds of its own destruction in that it has no way of listening to its pupils. Their words may be heard, but their teachers are not encouraged to respond. Students give up trying to communicate with many staff members, who, in turn, resent being put in charge of children they do not know. The pupils are, therefore, often seen by teachers as indifferent, unwilling to attend, or needing a high degree of control.

Adolescents in such a setting are alienated; they do not have their whole personality engaged; they are placed in the role of pupils with specific tasks, attending school as if it were a factory, for a given number of hours a day. Parents must then coerce their children to conform to the school's requirements. The parent may reject this—and come into conflict with the school—or may accept it—and clash with the child. Furthermore, groups of children are given and accept labels that vary from generation to generation: punks; greasers; jocks; freaks; straight. They may then be treated according to this label, rather than as special, unique individuals.

Given the poor quality of the educational experience of many adolescents, it is surprising that there is so little local pressure for change in schools insofar as social organization, educational methods, and curriculum are concerned. School systems, furthermore, can avoid change by playing democratic games, pretending that no change can take place without community participation. This can easily become an excuse for administrative inertia. Local control of school systems via budgetary restraints and school board elections make innovative changes in education difficult. Lay people tend to be unduly subservient to teachers, or they may see themselves as experts in education and psychology. Even if a school system opts to change, this may be stopped, as the aims of parents for their children may differ from those of the staff. Parents often want schools to prepare the children for life only as they have known it. A school that gives a child an education too different from the one the parents had may be in trouble. Thus, a school may develop the artistic sensitivities of the children of a rigid accountant or give an academic education to the children of an unskilled laborer. Both these enrichments are desirable but they may hinder communication between generations, not just because their interests differ, but also because different communication techniques are used. They may also alienate adolescents from their local environment. If teachers fail to recognize the pressure placed on such young people tragedy may occur.

John was a black youth age sixteen who was admitted to a psychiatric hospital after throwing himself from the roof of a three-story building. Astonishingly he was physically almost undamaged. A child of a fragmented ghetto family he got 100% financial aid to an excellent private school when he was ten. He felt it alienated him from his local friends who perceived him as "oreo", black outside, white inside. He felt condescended to by his age mates in school. Many school staff members had failed to recognize the nature of the community from which he came; and the quality of life in his home and social environment until the self-destructive crisis occurred. All too often this failure, particularly with less privileged pupils, spoils attempts at integration.

> A junior high school's staff were preoccupied with the acutely aggressive behavior of six black girls, age thirteen to fourteen. The black staff were as concerned as the white and both tended to project blame, although in different places. Neither took note of the following simple facts: The disturbances almost always took place after the lunchtime break, in

which the children, after lining up in an inadequate dining area, had fifteen to twenty minutes to eat lunch and return to classes. The girls' day, however, began at 6:30 A.M, when they went to the local community center for breakfast. As well as looking after smaller, grade-school children, they had to clear up after them. At 7:10 A.M. they caught the bus to school and, having traveled across town from the ghetto area, they reached the school at 7:30 A.M. Since the building was not yet officially open, they then waited in a vestibule, between two sets of doors if the weather was inclement. After starting classes, they were allowed ten minutes between class periods to move across the school and only at 11:30 A.M. did they get lunch.

School systems are apparently unaware of the develomental needs of adolescents; class periods exceed the attention span of these pupils; a five-hour stretch without a satisfactory break period for free physical movement and play is a torment for the pubertal youngster. Not surprisingly, these girls projected their hostility onto the weaker group of the white establishment, which they felt as oppressing them; they terrorized the middle-class pupils, but did not bother the children of blue-collar workers, because they knew they would fight back.

It would appear that each generation of children faces increasingly impersonal attitudes in schools, but the present generation of parents, brought up in such a system, does not demand anything better. The computer schedules classes, and personal needs as regards friendship, liked teachers, and the need for group stability are not data that are fed into the machines. A class in physical education does not take the place of the unstructured free play of a recess period, which adolescents need at about two-hour intervals. Teachers' breaks occur every one-and-one-half to two hours; children are not given such breaks. At conferences, teachers rarely start on time; pupils are harried for being late.

Schools should have roots in the community they serve; those children who are bused into school are at a disadvantage compared to those who are from the immediate neighborhood and who can play and socialize together on the way home. Communication on a bus is not the same as free interchange on a walk home or with a small group on bicycles or in a parental automobile.

Although home and school should cooperate with each other, the need of adolescents, and, indeed, all children, to separate themselves from their immediate home environment means that it is important for them to feel that home and school are separate institutions. This is first demonstrated by kindergarten children who will not tell their parents what happened at school; later, some adolescents may resent special parental visits to their school, seeing it as interference. To avoid this, parents' visits to schools should be routine; a parental visit is not then felt as unusual. School and home should be considered by adolescents as separate places with common aims: the less conflict there is between them the better. To use parents to help in schools that their own children attend is less appropriate than having them help in other schools.

It is the responsibility of parents to see that their children go to school, the responsibility of the teacher to see that the children learn to enjoy academic and vocational work. Parents should not feel that it is their responsibility to see that homework is done, although they should, of course, try to provide opportunities for their children to do it. Adolescents need to feel that parents are interested in the type and quality of the work they do, but its production is the responsibility of the teachers. If parents are unable to provide conditions under which homework can be done—for practical or emotional reasons—it becomes the responsibility of the school to provide both space and time. On the other hand, parents who nag their child to work may be resented. Adolescents who underachieve are particularly unlikely to be helped by this parental prompting, often because they consciously or unconsciously resent their parents' actions.

The school report, before it became a computer printout of grades, was one link between parent and teacher. It gave the teacher the opportunity to assess a youngster's progress and to make suggestions on what he *ought* to be doing. It could also be an invitation to parents to talk with their children's teachers. The absence of a school report that describes the child in his life space means that communication is mostly with the parents of children who have demonstrated unusual academic failure or conspicuous disturbed or antisocial behavior. The parents of difficult pupils, however, may feel completely helpless when they continually receive complaints about their child. Teachers do not seem to accept responsibility for poor classroom achievement; they tend to see the fault as in the child or in the child/parent interaction. Parents feel quite helpless in dealing with inadequate teachers, especially when the child's lack of success stems from immediate domestic pressure the parents do not know how to change or from personality problems they can neither recognize nor alter if they could. Further, the relationship between parents and these young people has often broken down, and the parents cannot control the child.

From the primary stage onward, defensive and inconsiderate behavior by teachers can destroy communication between home and school. On the other hand, a sympathetic attitude on the child's first day can set the tone for years of good parent/teacher relationships. In one large English high school, the parents of newcomers are summoned to a meeting by the principal, told how they should behave, and then asked if they have any questions.

Usually, children's communication techniques are consonant with those of the nuclear family, even allowing for the action-oriented communication of the adolescent. However, by mid-adolescence, academically educated pupils begin to put a high value on the use of words and attach less importance to action. In those families in which action communication remains highly significant, techniques of parent/child communication may be lost (Bernstein, 1961). Sometimes an adolescent is worried that he is learning too much for the parents to bear, or he begins to believe that they are stupid. Some parents may envy their child's opportunities and in subtle ways attempt to sabotage their achievement because they fear the social and communication break in the family relationships. Some children may have difficulty doing homework not just because there is little room in the house or because there is no tradition of reading, but rather because their parents more or less insidiously oppose it.

By the end of the middle stage of adolescence, active involvement of parents is of less help because of the drive of youth for autonomy, but adolescents are still susceptible to implicit, if not explicit, parental suggestions. It is self-evident at this stage that socially isolated parents are more likely to seek ways of hanging onto their children, even if these are unconscious. Those techniques—asking for obedience to implicit expectations, which adolescents grant—may slow academic growth. In non-academic families, lip service may be paid to the concept of a university education as a way of progressing socially, but the threatened father will constantly criticize the "long hairs" at the local university. Parents may still tell their daughters that some education is acceptable, a nursing program, for example, but a postgraduate course, such as medicine, will be "too much for you."

Socially deprived adolescents may be highly imaginative and creative, but their thinking may remain concrete. They thus find it difficult to deal with the abstractions that are required for an academic education. Furthermore, they may sense the anti-intellectual attitudes of their parents and find it hard to accept a way of life that values education. Such young people may also wish to leave school at the earliest possible moment because the school is inadequate and does not understand their special talents and problems. Often these points are not consciously appreciated by the adolescent, the school, or the parents. The adolescent may try to solve the conflict by working less well; the teacher may respond to this change by rigid instructions and punishments; the parents may not understand why they want their son or daughter to leave school and look for a job.

Many grade schools ask parents to come to the school to discuss their child's progress with individual teachers, and they enlist the help of the parents. This practice is less common in high schools. Unfortunately, the parents of children who worry teachers most are least likely to come to the school, even when asked. The anxiety of parents about the education of their children might be somewhat allayed if they knew their children's teachers. But teachers in the United States and Western Europe are usually unwilling to go to their pupil's homes and think that group contact in a capsule night is enough. There is a tradition in parts of Eastern Europe that a teacher calls on a child's family three times a year. A crisis visit by a school social worker or truant officer is not a substitute for this.

Adolescents learn most easily from people whom they, society, and their family esteem. It is easier for pupils to see that their teachers are valued by their parents when the school has been specially chosen, for example, when parents move into a neighborhood so their children may enter the local high school or when they send their children to private schools. The latter, through individual consultation, annual parents' days, and the like, manage to keep a relationship with parents that gives the teachers a certain mystique in the eyes of both parents and children. In good neighborhood-based high schools, parents will be less likely to devalue staff in the eyes of their children; teachers will be likely to lose respect only through personal inadequacy.

The adolescent who grows up as part of a large family in a stable social environment may look on adults with mixed feelings, but clearly a network of adults is valued by his immediate family, if only because they are part of it. If there is no such network available, school teachers and all youth workers need to be valued by parents as though they were members of an extended family and social group. Where they are not, society can, to some extent, compensate by valuing them as conspicuously as possible. If the staff are not so supported, the school cannot replace the missing networks and anchor points that are necessary for adolescents to mature.

Schools that are not chosen by parents, especially those that children are directed to attend, have a particular problem. When children are bused across town, in the interest of integration, it becomes difficult for the parents to value teachers, and the teachers often do not respect the parents. Black and white parents tend to view teachers of the opposite race with suspicion; the poor feel exploited, and middle-class parents whose children are sent to lower-class neighborhoods feel that they are being offered second-rate education at the behest of impersonal administrators.

Parent/teacher associations may perform many valuable tasks for a school as a whole, but many do not necessarily improve the relationship between the school and the local community. Quite often they will be preoccupied with such topics as whether to provide a Coca-Cola machine in the school corridor or new draperies for a classroom, rather than evaluate the essential work of the school. As a potential threat to some school administrators, the groups may be maneuvered into becoming rather sterile; alternately, they may be used to impede change. Sometimes a visiting speaker once a semester talks to a group of parents and is introduced by the school principal or his deputy; this may be the only function of a PTA.

The best schools and neighborhoods tend to get the most effective parent/teacher organizations. The sterilized PTA has its equivalent in Britain and other European countries, where there is often resistance among teachers even to the setting up of parent/teacher associations. The more rigid the school, the more likely does this appear to be the case. It may well be that teachers in such schools are so defensive about their role that they are fearful of the criticism they may get from parents.

The breakdown in communication between teachers and parents means that usually, unless there is a crisis, teachers may not tell parents what is happening to their youngsters; sometimes the parents only know that something has gone wrong when a child is suddenly sent home for misbehavior. Many teachers see themselves as having a purely academic or vocational role in their relationship with the child; they do not consider themselves responsible for total personality development. Not surprisingly, many teachers are fervent believers in behavior-modification techniques, in which they do not have to take note of the dynamic subtleties of interpersonal relationships, and they justify the boredom of much of the high school curriculum on the basis that it is necessary to reinforce factual knowledge.

The impersonality of high school—with most parents having no knowledge as to what individual within it, if any, has any special knowledge of their child—makes it possible for parents to fail to inform teachers not merely of a child's current circumstances but even of events that could seriously affect other children:

> A fifteen-year-old boy who had taken many LSD trips was sent to a psychiatrist by his parents. John had managed to do reasonably well at school because he had abstained from tripping when he was to take important tests. But he and a group of other boys had taken LSD intermittently during the year, and in quantity since the end of the school year.
>
> When his problem was discussed with the parents, they were reluctant to take the matter further. It never occurred to them that they had any responsibility to inform the school or the parents of the other children.

Adolescents will often act out at school the tensions resulting from family conflicts; for example, parental separation can lead to a dramatic decline in the quality of school work:

> Peter had a brilliant academic record at school until his mother took him to a motel room when he was thirteen and told him that she and his father had separated. Peter seemed to take this in a very matter-of-fact way; it was four years before he was referred to a psychiatrist for help because of his poor academic performance. He began to function again only when he understood his own rage and grief.

The tensions resulting from school conflict may also be acted out at home:

> Kenneth was a sixteen-year-old pupil at a rigid, religious school at which boys were beaten for poor work. He was rude to his mother and physically assaulted his father. After six months at a co-educational school with few formal rules, but a high morale, his parents said he had become a different person.

The structure of the school may, in itself, cause quite severe emotional problems:

> Jane, a thirteen-year-old girl, was referred to a psychiatrist because of lack of appetite, sleeplessness, and isolation from her peers. Her parents said that she had "no friends," withdrew from the family, and seemed "angry" all the time. They had moved to a new location some nine months earlier, and Jane had not seemed to settle in. They had taken her back to her old home the previous Christmas, and Jane had appeared to enjoy herself. However, she had refused to go again.
>
> Jane was a small, postpubertal girl whose menarche had appeared when she was twelve. She said that she had had "lots of friends" at her last school, but "here no one wants to know me." She then described how on her first day at school, she found it impossible to get to know anyone. She knew the names of no children or teachers, all of whom "seemed to know each other." Jane was in six classes a day with six separate groups of children. She had no special talents, but was an average, bright child. She was driven to school by her father daily, and the move to the school had taken place in the fall.

It is easy to see how Jane could become isolated. She was offered no stable peer group against which she could be tested. To each teacher she was one of 120 children to whom they were exposed each day, and none felt particularly responsible for or interested in her. Since she dealt with anxiety by depression and withdrawal, they never noticed her; and because Jane's family had moved in bad weather, there was no easily accessible neighborhood social life, as there might have been in the summer. Her depression and isolation were a function of a highly insensitive social organization, the school she attended. If Jane has been with the same children for a considerable part of each day in academic and nonacademic situations, her peer group would have put her through a variety of unconscious initiation rites, but she would have been isolated for a much shorter time period (Bettelheim, 1956).

If there is a breakdown in communication between school and home, or if such communication has never existed, neither parents nor teachers will appreciate the importance of the other in cases of difficult behavior. When children misbehave, many schools are still far too likely to send for parents and order them to make their children conform. Teachers may prefer to blame parents for a child's difficulties and unconsciously treat them just as they were treated by their own parents in childhood. Similarly, parents may project fantasies from their own childhood onto the schools of their own children and look on teachers with awe, fear, or ill-disguised contempt. Parents may see teachers as police officers who control antisocial behavior, as knowing nothing, or as experts in bringing up children. At a previously mentioned capsule night run by a PTA, a parent obsequiously told the homeroom teacher who boasted of making the children sit still that she knew more about child-rearing than the parent herself.

Much is made of the rebellious nature of adolescents, but not enough of their conformity to consistent or implicit expectations. Nowhere is this more evident than in the relationship between parent and child. There is an important interplay between the wishes of a parent, stated openly or not, and the wishes and actions of the adolescent. The healthy conform to overt expectations, the insecure tend to obey those that are covert. They may look rebellious but really are not. The emotional disabilities of children often meet the unconscious needs of their parents. The mothers of boys who abuse drugs, especially marijuana and alcohol, sometimes seem to unconsciously collude in a situation in which normal masculinity is not reached and they essentially have a drugged, dependent, incompetent child. The mothers of promiscuous girls, although they may appear to be distressed by their daughters' actions, sometimes obtain satisfaction from hearing the details of their sexual behavior. The fathers of aggressive boys often seem to obtain satisfaction from talking about their sons' exploits (Miller, 1965). The mothers of boys who wet their beds have been known to become severely depressed when their sons recovered. The wish of an adolescent to remain an irresponsible child may correspond to the parents' wish to keep him in that state. In these cases, it is difficult to help the youngster unless expert assistance is being given to the whole family.

The adults within the adolescent's network of relationships should be able to communicate with one another freely. It is quite unrealistic to expect that they will always agree with each other, and it would not help young people learn about the complexities of life if they did agree. But if the adults who are the important inhabitants of the adolescent's world respect each other's integrity and do not allow themselves to be manipulated, one against the other, home and school can assist the young to develop into caring adults. If adolescents need the extra-familial world to mature into adulthood and if this world consists of peers and adults, the school is a microcosm of the world. Even though adolescents are likely to stay within their in-groups, if the school is neither overrigid nor overpermissive and if it plans the childrens' day appropriately, some mutual understanding across racial, ethnic, and class barriers is possible. It is not enough to deposit white children in black schools, or conversely, rich white children with poor Appalachians; a complex social mix requires a sophisticated social system to produce a tolerant integrated society.

SEXUAL INTEGRATION IN HIGH SCHOOLS

There are remarkable similarities between the problems of educating boys and girls in the same school and those of educating children of different ethnic groups together. When Chinese and Jewish groups were the victims of more open prejudice than exists today, they attended neighborhood schools and after school their own schools taught them about their culture and religion. This, along with a strong drive for advancement, made such segregation tolerable. It may be that single-sex schools were acceptable when any boy or girl could spend the rest of the time in a stable mixed environment. But when a number of other people are not seen outside school, single-sex education is a psychologically harmful setting likely to damage personality development. A similar truth applies if a population is a victim of prejudice, has lost its ethnic identity, and lives in ghettos.

Single-sex education in the United States occurs in the correctional system, in some private boarding schools, and in the Roman Catholic parochial school system.

Deprivation in all-male societies leads to certain specific types of social pathology. In closed societies, as in the correctional system, boys may be morbidly preoccupied with sexuality up to age sixteen or seventeen. If adolescents in these circumstances are tense and unhappy, those who are least able to tolerate anxiety and loneliness may turn for solace to homosexual activity. Particularly toward the end of early adolescence, masturbation between boys is common when they are members of all-male societies. This would appear to have several causes: if a boy has made no firm identification; if girls are not present for any type of relationship; if the boy feels lonely and isolated and needs *emotional* contact, he may need to experience *physical* contact with another boy. Boys are often taught to masturbate by others, and in isolated, emotionally depriving, single-sex settings, physically bigger boys may use smaller ones sexually. In boarding schools there is rarely any physical violence in homosexuality, although in the delinquent groups threats may be part of the seduction. The more harshly boys are treated by the staff, the more likely it is that bullying homosexual behavior will occur; the more isolated the group, the more likely it is to also include coercive homosexual activity. If this is not acceptable, and since to lower-class boys, masturbation is not tolerable, the absence of self-solacing techniques may mean that such youths become violent with each other.

> In Boise, Idaho, in 1982, a group of six late adolescent boys were isolated from other prisoners in a county jail, given no privacy from each other, not supervised by staff, and then given minimal opportunity for

recreation. They spent their time harassing the weakest member of the group and ultimately such a boy was killed after having been intermittently beaten by the rest over a two-day period.

If staff members are at loggerheads, violence may also be intense.

> In one section of a youth prison, a woman social worker dominated the male staff and talked to the boys in such a way that they felt she was contemptuous of all men. In the living quarters controlled by those staff members in conflict with each other, small boys were being assaulted both sexually and otherwise by bigger boys.

Homosexual conflicts that are not expressed may torment the individual. In schools for boys in which the environment is too rigid or overacademic, boys can often be terrified of showing any sign of affectionate feelings toward another; they are afraid other boys will label them as "fags."

> A seventeen-year-old school boy, academically successful and a football player, was referred to a psychiatrist because he had an acute episode of withdrawal from everybody. For five months previously he had been tormenting himself with the idea that he was going to be "gay" because he had felt fond of another boy six months younger than he. He had no feelings of sexual attraction toward this boy, but was afraid to show he liked him because of what others might say.

The deprived school in an underprivileged neighborhood produces a similar social pathology. Release of tension is sought by early heterosexual or homosexual experiences, bullying, assaults on teachers, gang-related violence, verbal backbiting, and massive projection of anger onto the larger society. When children in such settings are from ethnic minorities, they either project hatred onto other racial groups or internalize it. When rage is internalized, the taking of drugs, principally marijuana, alcohol, amphetamines, sedatives, and hallucinogens are usual. Sniffing glue or other substances that give a high is also common. Other types of self-destructive behavior, including adolescent suicide, increasingly occur.

In single-sex schools for girls in which the children are unhappy, in- and out-groups of girls are formed. The girls who see themselves as most select will treat other girls with verbal cruelty; there tends to be an atmosphere of bitchiness. It is rare in girls' schools, however, to get any degree of physical bullying, fighting, or homosexual behavior, although these appear in penal institutions. Girls in deprived segregated schools see themselves as sexual objects and are filled with unresolved hostility toward men.

An unsatisfactory school environment for boys helps to produce antisocial behavior and self-destructive activity, and it prevents some boys from developing to their full emotional and intellectual potential. The equivalent situation for girls is likely to produce many depressed, isolated women whose sexual and intellectual adjustment is never really satisfactory to themselves or their families.

A genuinely coeducational school is better educationally and psychosocially than a single-sex school; similarly, a truly desegregated school provides a better education for all children, underprivileged or not. However, just as having girls and boys in the same school is not necessarily coeducational (Miller, 1969), mixing ethnic groups and social classes is not in itself integrated education.

True coeducation is rare because of the failure of most schools to recognize the special educational needs of girls. If girls in early adolescence are to establish a firm feeling of femininity, they need affectionate, essentially platonic relationships with males other than their fathers and brothers. They also need shifting one-to-one relationships with other girls and with boys, initially without sexual activity. Girls in isolated families, who are not members of a "tribal" environment, find it difficult to mature satisfactorily if they are educated in schools that often have a high percentage of women staff, and the assumption is often implicitly made that they will automatically relate better to women than they would to men. For example, in one school system, male social work students may not work with adolescent girls; it is thought that seduction is too likely. This is similar to, if an exaggeration of, the system in most high schools, where lack of stable relationships with extra-parental adult males can hinder the maturation of girls. Neither is there the opportunity for stable asexual relationships with older boys. Age segregation because of junior high school/high school separation cuts off any possibility of such relationships between younger and older adolescents. With these deficiencies it follows that the social and academic capacity of girls will be impaired; for example:

> A junior high school that was bedeviled with typical institutional tensions was overwhelmed by the notorious behavior of a group of angrily destructive black girls. A black social worker saw that efforts at control by the staff were disintegrating into a sterile confrontation. She called the local high school, got in touch with the president of the black students' association, and a group of grade eleven and twelve male students came over to the school. They told the girls of thirteen or so to cool it and behave like ladies. The trouble immediately subsided.

These girls were deprived by the structure of the school system of the opportunity to feel valued by older boys, neither could they worship them from afar or project with some safety sexual fantasies onto these young men. The effect of the isolation of girls from a stable, older, peer-group and adult attachments is to force feelings of alienation with an increased likelihood of early promiscuity, drug involvement, or just general unhappiness. The hostility to men may well be a reaction-formation against feeling grossly devalued from an early age.

It is well known that after puberty, girls tend to become less academically successful than boys (Abelson, 1972). Too few able women use their talents in the community or take up occupations that demand intellectual training. The reason often given is that this is a result of a male-dominated society or that women are too involved with the process of mothering. Whether or not this is true, the higher education of girls is unsatisfactory. Clinical evidence shows that they tolerate unimaginative education less well than boys and are more likely to be damaged by the grade-point-average rat-race. Girls have a greater need than boys to develop their imaginative and emotional potential; as a result, they cannot easily tolerate an educational system that, albeit inadequately, puts cognitive achievement at a premium and that undervalues esthetic and emotional expression. Girls are more future-oriented than boys of the same chronological age; they have a greater capacity to empathize with the feelings of others and have a much greater need for emotional sensitivity (Undeutsch, 1959).

Since boys in early adolescence are considerably less effective in height, intellectual efficiency, and imaginative potential than the equivalent-age girl, they find competitive situations with girls intolerable. It is thus no accident that the honor rolls of junior high schools are occupied mostly by girls; boys would rather not compete, preferring to believe that they could, if they so wanted.

On the other hand, girls who want to be attractive to boys, and know that boys have this feeling, are themselves likely to do less well; they do not wish boys to avoid them. Girls who can neither understand or tolerate their own sexuality or the sexuality of boys are more likely to retreat to an academic hideaway.

In a coeducational setting, it is, of course, desirable that boys and girls should treat each other with mutual respect. This means that they have to feel respected by their teachers. If the teachers do not respect the integrity of their pupils, it is unlikely that the pupils will respect each other. The proper education of girls is not the same as for boys, with domestic science as an optional extra. Their need for groups is different, their sense of privacy is not the same, nor is their need for physical activity.

"THERAPEUTIC" ROLE OF COEDUCATIONAL BOARDING SCHOOLS

American schools differ from those in England, with some exceptions, in their overall conformity and in the lack of variety of schooling provided. Even in the state educational system, there is a shortage of special schools, both day and boarding, for emotionally disturbed children. There is also a shortage of good coeducational boarding schools available to all children as well as to those in emotional difficulties. These are not panaceas for disturbed adolescents from broken homes, but they can at least provide a framework and some support. At best, the boarding sector of the educational system shows that stability for a number of years can be provided for boys and girls within an environment that they can perceive as valuable and which values them. They can then successfully identify with the people in it and its way of life (Atherton, 1966).

Although coeducation is preferable, it is still possible for the all-male boarding school that is not isolated from the community-at-large to educate boys satisfactorily if they stay until age seventeen or eighteen. Through this period, the development of a satisfactory male identity in a boy depends to a great extent on his being able to relate to other young males.

Many private schools offer scholarships to able low-income students but they may still be attacked as "elitist" by some. Nonetheless, those with boarding facilities are able to hold and support the less stable with the more stable. On the one hand, this has lessened the burdens on the already strained state system; on the other, it has allowed the British health services to "neglect" to provide hospital beds for disturbed adolescents more than most Western nations. "Progressives" in England often demand that boarding schools for privileged children be added to the state system. This might be democratic and egalitarian, but it would certainly be disturbing. Their society would then be confronted suddenly with many more intractable adolescents than it had imagined existed. It would have to try to find new ways to cope. An alternative, which is much needed in the United States, is to create new coeducational boarding schools that could be helpful to disturbed youngsters and do more than merely contain them.

> Thirteen-year-old Clive kept absconding from a large, all-male, English boarding school. He was a big, overgrown, early developer who was, in many ways, severely disturbed. He had fantasies of being beaten and homosexually attacked. He was also addicted to barbiturates, which had originally been prescribed as a sedative. His parents lived in the country, and they had no network of relationships to assist Clive. For such an isolated youth, boarding education had many advantages, but the restricted male environment of his school increased the homosexual pressure he was experiencing. A psychiatrist recommended that he go to a co-educational boarding school with some 300 pupils. A school much larger than this might have overwhelmed him, and he would have gained little from such an environment. The school to which Clive was sent was not a school for maladjusted children. The presence of too many disturbed children in one setting might well have made it useless. Within six weeks, Clive was getting on well with three members of the school staff and, in particular, his housemaster. For the first time in his life, he had made friends with both sexes. For this boy, a new environment did not in itself mean that no more help was needed. However, the school did provide a network of people and a way of life for him.

Such a boy in the United States would almost certainly require treatment in a good residential treatment center and the chances are that such a center would not keep him for two or three years; also, it is more expensive than a boarding school.

Academically, good coeducational schools have been shown to produce better results than single-sex schools. Although there is a mass of research (Dale, 1966) on this topic, controversy about it continues. However, when the major surveys of academic achievement in Britain since 1921 are brought together, the evidence is unequivocally in favor of coeducation. This should be more widely known; the adherents of coeducation themselves are often unaware of it and quote only the social, nonscholastic advantages of coeducation. Many parents who can afford it and have academic ambitions for their sons send them to single-sex schools. Where parents can choose between types of schools in those countries where boys go away to school prior to puberty, there tends to be a withdrawal from coeducation at the school change age of thirteen.

In boarding schools, the amount of alcohol and marijuana used nowadays rightly gives cause for concern. But a greater concern of many parents is of precocious sexual activity. There is little evidence, however, that bacchanalia take place more frequently in coeducational schools than in other schools. It appears that if the limits of sexual exploration are implicitly laid down in a coeducational school, intercourse between the pupils is less likely to occur than is homosexual behavior in an all-male environment.

Coeducational living situations do not force physical intimacy between the sexes. In a well-designed, coeducational setting, whether school, hospital, or group home, when children are shy of their bodily development, they should be able to withdraw from contact with the other sex. Since coeducational living is a healthier environment and more likely to meet youngsters' needs than a single-sex setting, promiscuous behavior is likely to be less common.

Promiscuous behavior in all-female living environments may be fairly usual, if the girls need to prove their femininity to other girls. In one girls' day school in London, it is usual on Monday morning for girls to boast of their sexual prowess over the weekend.

The same type of conversation occurs in girls' group homes in the United States, and in penal settings for girls. In such places, after a leave, girls find it necessary to talk of their conquests to their friends. The talk in such settings is not just in terms of boys being "in love" with them, but rather of boys having had intercourse with them.

The clinical evidence from Britain seems to indicate that children in coeducational boarding schools are more likely to care about each other than are those in single-sex schools. This suggests that their moral standards are higher. As long as emotional needs of their pupils are met, they are clearly very much happier schools. A study (Atherton, 1966) shows that children who attend coeducational schools describe their school experience afterwards as happier than children who attend single-sex schools. This is hardly surprising, as the implicit message of the single-sex school is that relationships with the opposite sex are to be avoided.

If children and adolescents have been exposed to bereavement through the death or separation of their parents, it is self-evident that boys who lose their mothers will be more likely to be helped in coeducational settings with women as teachers, just as girls who lose their fathers need male teachers.

The same concepts apply to the American penal and therapeutic systems for disturbed and delinquent youth. Many psychiatric facilities overrigidly separate the sexes, and residential treatment settings may be single-sex. Those, that have been specially created to treat emotionally disturbed youth, often appear too ready to send their difficult pupils away because of staff worries; because students abscond; or because individuals fail to respond fast enough to, for example, behavior-modification techniques. It would appear that those settings that are more rational in their general disciplinary approach are often more reluctant to accept irrationality and disturbed behavior in their pupils. They are overanxious about the effect of individual disturbed behavior, which is only contagious if a residential setting is unhappy because of tensions between staff and pupils. They also tend to be unaware of the effect of physical surroundings on their pupils. The environment in which children live gives a clear message to them as to how much adults care about them. For example, for years the adolescent service of a well-known university hospital, even when financial support was not a significant excuse, had furniture built by the prison service, brown tile walls, inadequate lighting, and toilets with no privacy. The patients' eating area was drab and often dirty. That this situation was allowed to exist is perhaps a measure of the ambivalence of society toward its youth.

PROBLEMS OF RACIAL INTEGRATION

The most important recent development in secondary education in the United States is the widespread attempts at racial integration in schools. The argument for racial integration is that it can provide a better, all-around education for all children than can be provided by schools that try to concentrate on the needs of one particular group. It has also been suggested that schools automatically will break down social barriers and improve the quality of the education of the underprivileged. This view is extremely naive (Silberman, 1970), as there was no evidence prior to the racial integration of the school system that it produced social integration, although clearly the availability of a general high school education produdes social mobility among some members from nonacademic groups. The children of a blue-collar worker, however, whatever their intelligence, are statistically less likely to go to college than are middle-class children. In a large high school, children whose parents belong to the country club rarely mix socially with children from the "wrong side of the tracks." Since there are many differences in the behavior and communication techniques of different social classes in the same society, merely dumping children of these groups together increases their isolation.

An unthinking mixture of academic and nonacademic, black, Hispanic, and white children from different social backgrounds—with staff whose experience is restricted to children of one particular group or who are unaware of how the difficulties involved in such a mixture may be resolved—may create serious problems. The two following examples are taken from English schools in which a socially more comprehensive environment was being attempted. In that type of education, little attempt was made to understand the different needs, communication techniques, and social attitudes of children from different social groups. The third example comes from an American high school where the same problems, compounded by skin color and ethnic group, apply.

A bright middle-class boy of fourteen was referred to a psychiatric clinic for help because he had outbursts of temper, could not bear to have any of his things touched, and spent long periods of time arranging everything meticulously or obsessionally doing his homework. His school had no complaints about him and was surprised when his general physician sought a psychiatrist's opinion. Some of this boy's trouble was due to the emotional instability in his home, but it also stemmed from his school life. He was in an accelerated academic track in a large comprehensive school. The intention was that he should complete his schooling by the age of sixteen-and-one-half and then be ready for college. The boy was very small and said that his friends in his form were about his size. He said they were looked on as being square, sissy, and so on by bigger, less academic boys. He felt that he and his friends were envied by these other boys, because "they feel the teachers prefer us." When asked about the unnecessary time spent on homework, he said that he was terrified of losing his place in the academic track. If this were to happen, he felt that he would be placed with the larger boys. They would bully him; he would be helpless. He accurately detected a very real feature of the school: he felt rather like a Jew expected to leave the safety of the ghetto in the Middle Ages.

Jenny, a middle-class girl of thirteen, was attacked after school; she was kicked and beaten by a group of lower-class boys at the school they all attended. She had previously told her teacher that this group had been responsible for bullying her brother. In doing this, Jenny broke the code of the boys, who saw the adult group as a hostile authority; they were a bad "they" against a good "we." The boys felt that the girl must be taught a lesson. Just as Jenny had felt that she had acted properly in reporting the previous bullying of her brother, the boys felt justified in attacking her.

Carla was the sixteen-year-old daughter of an automobile assembly-line worker. Although she was very light, she was black. She was bused into a high school that had little or no feeling of social solidarity. Carla made no mention of her racial origins, although she did not deny them; she was sexually teasing and provocative to some of the black boys, although much of this behavior was unconscious. She sought help from the school social worker because she had been threatened with knifing by a group of black girls for "trying to take their men" away from them. Because she had not defended herself to the group by announcing her own black origins, she was referred to a psychiatric clinic for an opinion as to what was to be done. She talked there of being tired of being thought of by her black brothers and sisters as a "white nigger" when she lived elsewhere in the state. She had decided, when her parents moved, to make no mention of her racial origin to see if that would be any better.

It would be wrong to assume that the only causes of the attack on Jenny were differing class attitudes or of that on Carla, racial tensions. The English school was so unable to cope with the tensions in its children and its staff that six senior boys were taking LSD for many months without being noticed, even though they were in a small class taught by the same teachers over a long period of time. Although smaller classes and teacher continuity are necessary, it would be naive to assume that they are not always effective in preventing or recognizing behavior problems.

These youngsters were appearing in the school in clothes grotesque even for young people. They were obviously drugged and "spaced out," and showed scant ability to concentrate on their work. With Carla, who was in a public high school with larger class size and frequent changes of teacher, racial tensions were, to a considerable extent, a result of the children's projection of anger onto each other because of the overall tensions in the school. No effort was made by the staff to produce any sort of social cohesiveness around life at school. The teachers who taught 120 children a day rarely knew them. Six weeks into one semester, some fifteen-year-olds did not know the names of many children in one of their math classes. The only educational technique of which the teachers talked was reinforcement.

The various social and racial groups will only learn to understand one another if they get the opportunity to stay with the same peers for a number of years and if these stable groups are taught by an admired teacher who is a role model for the children. It is no accident that the most integrated groups in high schools are sports teams and music and artistic groups. They tend to keep the same relationships for two to three years. Even so, there is little evidence that such young people from different backgrounds will wish to be friendly outside the classroom. Comprehensive education does not automatically break down the barriers of social class, nor does integration, as currently practiced, lead to significant improvements in race relations.

Mixing social and racial groups in childhood and adolescence, thus, does not automatically increase understanding. The best that often occurs is that children from different social groups in the same school may appear to relate to each other, but meaningful positive emotional contacts may not occur. There is some evidence that a social mix may raise the standards of academic education available to underprivileged children and adolescents, but the absorption of greater academic capacity requires more sophistication in teaching techniques and organization of social systems than is currently usual. At present, some pupils may discover that a difference of appearance does not change common humanity. Integrated education in which the school staff do not understand the effect of social and racial differences is likely to fail. The best that may occur is separate and equal in the same local system. On the other hand, the failure of the average high school to recognize the special needs of the two sexes leads to a failure of education for some. But a continued inability to provide a satisfactory socially and ethnically integrated school environment can lead to a national tragedy. Children who are deposited in schools with those of a different ethnic group with the idea that this will produce significant racial integration must project their anger onto each other, in order to maintain any sense of identity. This projection, which is thought to be necessary by many authors (Pinderhughes, 1968), inevitably increases racial tension. This impairs the stability a school system ought to have if it is to provide a social climate in which children might grow.

Despite the wishes of some, there is no absolute norm for behavior in any one society. What is acceptable to one subcultural group and family unit is not to another. Therefore, any description of adolescent behavior must take note of the social class and ethnic or racial group of the youngster. In any one school, teachers should be aware that normative behavior for one group may be aberrant for another. If this is not understood, instead of pupil/teacher relationships offering emotional support to vulnerable adolescents, there may be an increase in tension. Mistakes may be made by assuming that color is more significant than it actually is; as we have shown in other societies, too, social-class differences are most significant. In the United States, these are sometimes thought to be covered by the color of an individual's skin; but aristocratic blacks and Hispanics who are socially mobile have more in common with equivalent whites than with their working-class siblings. The common experience of prejudice is often all they share. When immigrant groups retain their cultural identity, to some extent this protects individuals from the psychological pain produced by prejudice. The black young in America often have no such defense either against prejudice or the attempt of some well-intentioned adults to inflict a false value system upon them.

The pre-existing failure of the high school to understand the differing psychosocial development of boys and girls, and to understand the problems of mixing different maturational age and social groups, adds to the problem faced in racial integration. Thus, the need for individuals to identify with the larger group of the school as a whole is paramount if, in early adolescence, in particular, the different groups are not to attack each other or, at best, isolate themselves. As well as identifying with the institution as a whole, if integration is to be meaningful, adolescents need to be able to model themselves on teachers who are themselves of different racial groups; they also need to identify with the mode of interaction between teacher and pupil. A genuinely integrated educational environment, in which children learn together rather than just happen to attend the same school, is possible. Especially to those disadvantaged adolescents from single-parent families (particularly if the parent and child are the same sex) and to deprived youngsters in ghetto areas, such an environment is clearly an advantage. Further, individuals need to be treated as such and not be made special because of race or social class. Special permissiveness to any one subgroup is taken by other adolescents as rejection. The concrete thinking of non-academic, middle-stage adolescents poses a particular problem. No novels, films, or teaching seminars will change a belief based on a concrete experience.

A nonacademic, blue-collar white boy who is harried by a group of blacks or Hispanics, or vice versa, will generalize about a whole race. Of the more inhibited middle-class group who have conflicts about aggression, because of an internal process or family attitudes, some will become more aggressive; others will withdraw.

Differences in social class are at least as significant as differences due to ethnocentricity. For example, it has already been noted that lower-class adolescents still have sexual intercourse earlier than their middle-class peers. Views on politeness between boys and girls also vary between social classes. Middle-class children in socially mixed schools are likely to find the impulsive behavior of other groups highly attractive, on the one hand, yet slightly shocking, on the other. A middle-class boy talked about his shock at discovering that lower-class boys would push girls as they were rushing upstairs. Conflict can also occur between job-directed youth and more academic middle-class pupils and teachers. If the teachers are made anxious by the behavior of lower-class groups, they are likely to try to inflict upon them a middle-class conformity. It may well be that teachers, in demanding middle-class behavior from children, can start a process of alienating them from their family units. Sometimes behavior that is unacceptable to teachers on a class basis is falsely labeled as being characteristic of a racial group.

If teachers are to be acceptable models for children, they will be tested as to their worth as adults. An effective way of doing this is for adolescents to use a different racial status as the basis for an attack. A black teacher may find written on his chalkboard "Up the KKK." The response to this provocation will indicate to the whole group, black and white, something of the individual's personality strength. As the children as a group try to establish an identity with their teacher, some will accuse others not just of "sucking up" to teacher, but also of selling out their race. Given the necessity of adolescents being able to work out their tensions in relationship to a stable peer group and a known adult, over a period of two to three years, it is not surprising that the failure to provide these makes for difficulties. Finally, teachers need a level of training in understanding personality development that is rarely offered.

The race of such individuals is usually irrelevant, if they are well trained. Perceptive, long-lasting adult relationships makes true integration possible. Apart from the pupils, it appears reasonable to suppose that well-adjusted teachers would prefer such a situation; to shift the social system of schools to provide this would not be more expensive than present educational costs.

Those human relationships in schools that are necessary for real integration, whether sexual, racial, or social, are clearly not easy to introduce. Because human beings are conservative in many things, it is possibly unrealistic to expect many individuals to want change. Integration requires an active cooperation between schools and parents, a real relationship between home and school. Since most parents love their children, if parents and schools really work together, some interracial and social class suspiciousness would also break down. Nevertheless, if the educational system is to meet the demands that are put upon it by the changes in society, particularly in large cities, there should be a planned and widespread change to a genuinely integrated school, not the type of school that is created by busing children across cities and dumping them. The coeducational errors of the past that still persist should not be reinforced with social and ethnically vulnerable groups.

REFERENCES

Abelson, P. H. (1972), Women in Academia. *Science*, 175: 4018.

Ann Arbor School Board (1970), Minority Report of Citizens Committee on School Disciplinary Policy. Ann Arbor, Mich. (Mimeo).

Atherton, B. (1966), Co-education in marriage. *Where*, November: 25–26.

Bernstein, B. (1961), Social class and linguistic development: A theory of social learning. In *Education, Economy and Society*, ed. A. H. Halsey, J. Floud, and C. A. Andersen, 288–314. Glencoe, Ill.: Free Press.

Bettelheim, B. (1956), *Symbolic Wounds*. Glencoe, Ill.: Free Press.

Dale, R. R. (1966), The happiness of pupils in co-educational and single-sex grammar schools. *Br. J. Educ. Psychol.*, 36: 39–47.

McGregor, D. (1960), *The Human Side of Enterprise*. New York: McGraw-Hill.

Miller, D. (1965), *Growth to Freedom, The Psycho-Social Treatment of Delinquent Youth*. Bloomington: Indiana University Press.

—— (1969), *The Age Between: Adolescents in a Disturbed Society*. London: Hutchinson.

Pinderhughes, C. (1968), *Unconscious Factors Affecting Black Youth Today*. Symposium on Contemporary Issues of Youth.

Silberman, C. E. (1970), *Crisis in the Classroom*. 110–111, New York: Random House.

Undeutsch, U. (1959), Neue Untergudengen zur Altergestalt der Pubeszens. *Z. Esp. Ang. Psychol.* 6: 578–588.

PART II

ADOLESCENT PROBLEMS: SCHOOLS AND SOCIAL SYSTEMS

Chapter 9

Conformity, Alienation, and Violence

CAUSES OF STUDENT ALIENATION

Students in higher education are exposed to particular stresses over and above those of younger students. For middle-class students, in particular, the current difficulties of the educational system in high school and college can be partially understood if a comparison is made between what is overtly and covertly expected. Explicitly, higher education demands sophisticated formal thinking and an ability to be a creative, imaginative person capable of original thought. Implicitly, there is a demand for conformity to a series of papers and examinations, which often test memory and the capacity to reproduce on demand. If children have been reared in families that ask for investigative attitudes and that value their capacity to make judgments, they are unlikely to feel other than alienated unless they are in educational systems with similar values.

Teaching staff at the high school, undergraduate, and graduate level may not allow students to question the way they are taught. Some faculty resolve anxiety about their role by overidentifying with the young, whereas others cannot allow any questioning of value systems. Others may apparently listen, but nothing seems to happen. The demand for bland conformity is less usual in primary education than thereafter. Grade schools may be more responsive to psychosocial pressures and move to a concept of more creative education. As children grow older, there may be inconsistency between these attitudes and those of junior high and high schools.

In Britain, the emphasis in schools with a high reputation has always been on the intellectual achievements of an elite group. Many such schools have recently become more sensitive to the emotional, creative, and imaginative needs of their pupils. Although often strait-jacketed by an anachronistic examination system, a large number of British schools are trying to encourage the fine arts and such creative activities as music and drama, as well as academic performance and sport. In this way they are ahead of the American educational system, which often seems unaware of the values of imaginative creativity.

> In one junior high school, an art teacher would not allow the children to put pictures on the walls of the corridors because it would spoil the walls. In another, a child who refused to draw in exactly the way she was told was isolated from the rest of the class.

Paradoxically, European schools offer children a larger range of subject choice than do American schools although, even in this decade of educational deprivation in the United States, they are less affluent. This is because they do not teach the same subject at the same time every day: If subjects are taught three times weekly instead of five, a greater choice becomes possible.

Modern educational techniques do not distinguish between creative, imaginative, and cognitive achievement. Those schools that are themselves creative in their teaching do not inhibit the creativity of their pupils. French as a living language, science in relationship to life, project teaching, investigating topics rather than being taught subjects, all allow young people to feel and be creative while acquiring conventional knowledge.

Students who are not developing a firm sense of themselves as autonomous people may have a particular problem in the higher educational system. Such students who are educated in a high school environment that demands conformity in behavior and rarely values nonacademic, imaginative, creative outlets may appear to be doing well while they receive the ongoing emotional support of their families or of the known environment in school; not uncommonly, they break down in their first year of university. Such individuals often have an acute feeling of uncertainty about themselves; they internalize their anger and see themselves as worthless when the support system of home and school is withdrawn.

Timothy, an eighteen-year-old student, was suspended from one of the universities for failing grades at the end of his first year. He had attended a rigidly academic school and had obtained entry to college when he was just over seventeen. Shortly thereafter, he began to feel depressed, but this feeling was for a time relieved by the onset of the summer vacation. Then he began to feel he had taken the wrong path, "I spent all my days daydreaming or living vicariously by going to the movies. I have too much imagination but I have never known what to do creatively. I have tried to do some paintings, but they are not much good. At school all they cared about was that I behaved like a jock, got good grades, and did not express unpopular opinions."

If these individuals who go to college away from their home towns return to schools near their families, with appropriate supportive counseling, they may become both academically successful and personally secure. Often students who are alienated underachieve, so, notably in high school, they lose all chance for significant higher education. This group may abuse drugs and alcohol significantly.

Apart from conflict between home and school, within the educational system itself, and that created by the personal problems of individual students, educational alienation may be created in high schools because of criteria for university admission.

Most schools try to ensure that their more able students obtain a university place at almost any cost: The schools maintain the teaching standards demanded by the universities. Nevertheless, because it is important that late adolescents be as cooperative as possible, if they complain about the quality of high school education, schools often try to obtain their compliance by agreeing with their complaints. Good teachers tend to explain away the fact that they have to teach in a rigid fashion by blaming the admissions office of universities; the necessity for good grades and high SAT scores as a measure of academic excellence is stressed. Overinsistence on these issues, however, is likely to inhibit creativity. If this blame is directed toward the university, students are likely to have very mixed feelings about admission even before they go to college. Many see a degree as a necessary ticket to an economically viable life; others arrive with a guarded "wait-and-see" attitude. Some are apparently highly motivated, but this may change dramatically toward the end of their first year. Often in universities, students do not feel valued; they are not paid either with status or money for this work, and yet they have to tolerate a dependence at a social level long past their psychological or physical need for this (Bettelheim, 1971).

Alienation may also be reinforced by the uninterrupted nature of the American educational system. Students have no time to find themselves in relationship to the world at large by enlarging their nonacademic experiences and engaging in exploratory activities. By a set pattern, for example, a medical student will have twenty years of continuous education prior to graduation. Summer vacations are often needed to earn money to help pay for a further educational year. Without a transitional experience many American students arrive at higher education feeling anxious and hostile. Backpacking through Europe later, or membership in the Peace Corps may change this, but these are outlets for the few.

In large universities the student is immediately exposed to an alienating impersonal system. Classes are full; courses are often obtained by what seem to many the underhanded means of seeing professors directly rather than through course counselors who often appear to students to be confused, overwhelmed, or disinterested. Members of the staff make no effort to get to know students. A further area of stress and, hence, alienation for freshman students, in particular, is that the universities appear to have abandoned all concern for their emotional and moral well-being. Dormitory living no longer provides a social structure with significant adult input within which students might grow. Only fraternities and sororities offer group support as an alternative to faculty interest, and these offer little in the way of adult direction. Many freshmen with permission to live off campus feel isolated in their apartments.

SOCIAL RESPONSE OF STUDENTS

These stresses placed on students produce a variety of responses: Many, particularly those who conform to the wishes of their nuclear family and who plan to take up postgraduate training for well-developed roles such as law, engineering, or medicine, pass the hurdles of the system and are apparently satisfied with themselves and their society. They know that they can expect consistency from the world. Late-adolescents, just as those who are younger, have a psychological need to conform as well as to rebel, to be dependent as well as independent. For these individuals, their sense of inner security depends upon their taking up roles that society values, both economically and socially. They obtain satisfaction in their lives because the work they do is valued and gives them economic satisfaction. The issues connected with their work tend to be ignored. Such people, essentially obedient and conformist, are looked on with favor by the authority structures of a bureaucratic social organization. Unless they encounter inefficiency, consider themselves badly paid, or are made redundant by economic game plans or technical change, they do not challenge the authority structure that has given them security. For them radical change is unnecessary, as conformity pays social and economic dividends.

Those individuals who are unsure of their ultimate role in society are under greater personal stress than those who know what their place is to be. The pattern of education for fine arts students, for example, is not generally as alienating from their creativity and imagination as for others. Often they do not need to conform to an alienating experience in high school when they wish to go to art school. Their admission to higher education may depend on their talent, as determined by the work they have produced over a period of time, not just on their grades. These students do not suffer so much from the feeling that the right to obtain such an education depends on a grade-point average. Unfortunately, once undergraduate status is reached, many students find that universities are preoccupied with this, even in art, music, and drama departments. Furthermore, once art students have entered schools of art, it may be very difficult for those with a particular talent in, say, painting or sculpture, to involve themselves in the wide range of studies demanded for a degree. A particular additional stress for those who study fine arts, as opposed to those whose vocational interest is more economically viable, is that they often find it extremely difficult to see a role for themselves in society. Partly because of this and partly because they tend to see what they produce as an extension of themselves, such students are very vulnerable to staff criticism. Some may protect themselves by projecting blame onto the staff. This is not difficult because the hierarchical authority structure of many art schools alienates students and junior staff from senior staff administration.

It is not surprising that nonconformist student behavior should appear most obviously in many art schools. The inability of art students to assess whether society will value their productivity is one reason why they have not conformed to usual social demands since Victorian days. As art schools become bureaucratized, diffuse nonconformity for many becomes focused on the school staff in an open rebellion against the system; thus, many art students drop out.

Students of the arts, such as English and languages, have always had more difficulty in establishing their final adult roles than science students, although until the last decade they were looked upon as an intellectual elite. However, the change in the economic climate has begun to create a semi-educated class of B.A. students many of whom, nowadays, find it impossible to find jobs that have any relationship to learned skills. So, arts students tend to be much more insecure than do students of technology. The latter have generally made a firm vocational decision and thus do not experience as much anxiety about obtaining employment after college, but those who are heading for postgraduate work are likely to be extremely anxious as to where and whether they will be accepted. This is a particular issue in medicine and law, and techniques of entry into these schools become a major preoccupation.

Social science students are particularly likely to be critical of the established order of society. The rigidity of the general social systems they study is likely to make them turn their attention to the organization of their own departments. Thus, they, like students of political science, tend to direct criticism at their teachers.

Students of social work and psychology, both postgraduate courses, are in an extremely difficult situation. The jobs available are few and often their teachers no longer practice in the professions about which they teach. Those students who wish to teach are in a similar situation. The irony is that the need for their services remain; it is that those in need no longer receive them.

STUDENTS' PERCEPTION OF THE UNIVERSITY

When those high school students who feel alienated from the way of life of the educational system reach the university, they are likely to feel that their opinions are confirmed. The university is often perceived by them as a hostile authority structure. Staff, particularly at higher levels, are seen as arrogant and privileged, often because they are so distant from meaningful emotional relationships with either junior staff or students. University administration and faculty are sometimes involved with in-group power struggles over what seem to some to be esoteric issues. Much time may be spent in meetings. Students may be present at these as token participants, but usually they seem to feel overwhelmed.

University power is despotic, but it attempts to be benevolent. Universities try to assist their students by providing a counseling service for academic affairs, and often personal counseling and mental health services for those who seek them are available. However, even if staff are appointed who are either good teachers or capable of having significant interpersonal relationships with the students, in a large university the structure of the undergraduate educational system makes interpersonal relationships between the average student and adult staff almost impossible. This is not just a problem at an undergraduate level:

> A university medical school had 225 first-year students. In the first semester, the structure of the education was such that the students had no opportunity for significant interpersonal contact with even one teacher. In ten weeks, no less than 30 students referred themselves for personal help to the school's psychiatrist with anxiety symptoms that they felt to be crippling.

A whole variety of techniques proliferate to meet students' needs for human relationships; attending mental health clinics, becoming a member of the student newspaper or marching band, joining a social or political organization, using too much alcohol, and smoking pot. The failure of the structure of undergraduate education to enable each student to have significant emotional relationships with at least one faculty member who is interested in him as a total person, leads to a proliferation of systems designed to be helpful. Too many have to seek professional help, a situation that might have been avoided if an involved interested adult had been available.

ANXIETY AND HOSTILITY IN THE ALIENATED STUDENT

The university social system is likely to produce alienation at both a graduate and an undergraduate level. Alienated individuals are particularly likely to respond to stress with anxiety and anger. These may be internalized, leading to a variety of depressive symptoms that are more or less self-destructive, or they may be directed outward. During the 1960s and early 1970s, the bureaucratic establishment of universities needed to offer only a most trivial or seemingly irrelevant pretext to students for troubles to begin. The etiology of this was multiple. Any potentially angry person may have his rage triggered by events that seem trivial to the outsider, but are felt as significant because of idiosyncratic or unconscious meaning. Isolated individuals often have a frantic need to belong to a group of peers. Some students may join organizations that offer them a feeling of security, hence the success for some cults, such as the Unification Church of the Reverend Moon or even the rigid, fundamentalist fringe groups of organized religion. These may totally submerge the individual's identity.

> Lionel was a twenty-year-old student who had a stormy relationship with the university in his first three years. He provoked his professors; involved himself with pot, pills, and acid; dressed in a bizarre fashion; and made barely acceptable grades. He was persuaded by his parents to consult a psychiatrist just before the summer vacation. He complained of emptiness and an inability to form any goals for himself, and he felt that only radical violence was the solution, "but they shoot you for that."
> He returned after the vacation to continue his psychiatric consultations wearing a large cross, but dressed neatly with relatively short hair. He announced that he had been saved, was now in communion with the Lord who wanted him to save people. He joined the Children of God. The following week, he left the university and spoke only to his parents and old friends in the presence of other disciples.

Violently aggressive behavior on university campuses ended with shootings by the National Guard at Kent State University. The large mass of students, however, do not resolve their conflicts by involvement with cults or violence, but they may live vicariously through identification at a distance with the reported activities of a few. No repetition of group violence is likely, unless the large mass of students collude in its presence (Redl, 1949).

UNDERSTANDING STUDENT VIOLENCE

The violent behavior of students can be understood in many ways. Riotous behavior by students is not new; in England, the night of the Oxford and Cambridge boat race is traditionally a wild, riotous occasion, when policemen often have their helmets knocked off. The last decades in the United States and Britain have seen a flurry of student violence, although this has been reported for longer periods in the Middle and Far East.

There were many general social reasons for this, but although these conditions have generally not changed, violence has become increasingly rare on university campuses, although crime statistics have risen. Regressive behavior, drug abuse, alcoholism, academic drop-out, and loveless sexual behavior have, from a clinician's viewpoint, increased. Aberration thus shows itself more in individual self-destruction. Violence is likely to appear when adolescents feel that structure is lacking. Optimally control is produced by consistent explicit and implicit social supports and mutually caring human relationships. In high schools, the absence of these is one of the determinants of racial violence and wanton property destruction; in universities, violence is directed at the establishment.

During the late sixties, youth felt itself to be a victim of gross inconsistency on the part of society. Having given their children opportunities they never had themselves, the parents of the class of 1969 to 1971, who were adolescents in war and depression, envied the freedom they saw their children enjoying; having taught them to think for themselves, they were anxious about their unwillingness to conform. Experiencing doubt about their abilities as parents, they were baffled by the apparent reluctance of their adolescent children to take notice of them. When a comparatively small number of students took revolutionary action, all the anxieties of adults in authority, particularly some politicians, became focused on them. Actions were blown up into great significance by the media, and a halo effect was created. Students began to think that revolt was expected of them, just as some feel that they ought to smoke marijuana.

> One English university student spent a summer vacation in the United States and visited other students in California. For the first time in his life, he began to use pot and his justification was "all the students at Berkeley smoke; I would have felt a fool if I had not turned on."

The same argument has been used as a justification for taking part in demonstrations and sit-ins.

Nevertheless, there are many real reasons why students should have been more than rebellious for a time, and may be so again. Students who entered universities in Britain and the United States had to bear a unique burden of guilt. The unpopular war in Vietnam in the United States was involving mostly the underprivileged; the rejection rate for university entry in Britain was reinforced by the fact that too many students applied for too few places. Many equally qualified applicants had been rejected; students knew that admission based on grades attained and examinations passed with high scores was educational roulette. Students were acutely aware of the divisions in society between rich and poor. As with all those who are rich—and compared to the poor and underprivileged of this world, students are rich— they had to bear the burden of being envied. One way of denying their own affluence was to attack the affluence of others; their own privilege was negated by their attack on the privileged. Another technique was to demand fair quotas for minority admissions irrespective of whether supporting services for such students were provided—what was sought by the affluent majority was a magical expiation of guilt.

In the last decade, there have been significant changes. Anxiety is now projected into the future; Will employment be available? Affluence is no longer so certain. The Vietnam war is over, but the politicians continue to behave with seeming irresponsibility over the future of mankind. Furthermore, American students are commonly children of those who experienced postwar affluence, so intergenerational envy, though present, is less significant.

Thus, the shift away from violence at universities appears to be due to several factors, one of which is that parents who were adolescents after the last war envy their children less. Society has become a little more consistent in its attitudes to violence; more and more of the adult population began to disapprove of the wanton slaughter of the Vietnam war, which led belatedly to American withdrawal. Just as parents who behave violently provoke this in their children, so a society is identified within its openly condoned behavior. On the other hand, some people, by their attitude to the Kent State slaughter, indicated they were prepared to collude with the murders of their own young. This took place against a background of nuclear threat, in which a balance of terror, if it is disturbed, will lead to death of all people at the hands of their elders (Beloff, 1968). Thus by threatening the life of young people, society shifted the focus of their aggression. Economic pressure was also brought to bear by threatening the withdrawal of some university funds and by the fact that it was more difficult to find work after graduation. This was all doubtlessly unplanned, but the "elders of the tribe" were seen as dangerously punitive to the young. Finally, the social demands of young people were to some extent met, in the letter, if not the spirit (Louis, 1971). The quota admission of minority groups and women to universities can be prejudice at its worst and often a rejection of academic standards, but it is a cheap way of propitiation and helps society expiate its guilt relatively inexpensively. Other demands by students, which appeared to be of two types, were rejected. The naive insistence that all authority structures be dismantled was ignored. This anarchic concept ignored the nature of the human animal to seek emotional safety in some type of power structure. The demands for representation on the governing bodies of the universities were granted in a token fashion. This did not seem to be a demand for a change in the form of the institutional structure; the students merely wanted to sit with adult authority at the triangular apex of power that inevitably alienated those at the base. As anticipated, in administrative committees, student representatives were often considered by their peers as having gone over to the "they"; the institutional weight of the system hangs heavily on those students who are not then able to produce real social change.

None of the changes associated with the great decrease in overt violence have resolved the problems of late-adolescent alienation, however.

The solution to problems of alienation rests largely with a change in the structure of universities, just as an equivalent change is necessary in high schools. Only when human relationships between adults and late-adolescents are restored can true learning begin to take place for most students.

The answer is to look closely at the present power structure of the universities, decide where and how change is wanted, and then face the enormous problems involved. Social change is impossible unless it is desired by those who run the system. They will only want this if the system, by its failure to function, makes them sufficiently uncomfortable, which is unlikely in the foreseeable future.

It is argued by some that far from producing an alienation from the self, the present social system, as it impinges on the late-adolescent, produces a valid counterculture. Reich (1970) believes that there is a new consciousness developing that "seeks restoration of the non-material elements of man's existence . . . since machines can take care of our material wants, why should not man develop aesthetic and spiritual sides of his nature." There is no doubt that many young people have been exposed to just enough stimulation of their creativity so that they yearn to get in touch with their own and other's imaginative sensibility. Regrettably, most members of the human race, when they are starved of imaginative and creative outlets as young people, are likely to become apparently dull, conformist, and rigid, living in a private world of their own. Or they become openly rebellious and destructive. Inhibition, without relieving the causes of alienation, ensures the internalization of destructive impulses. Furthermore, a nihilist and callous intolerance may cover both sloth and an antirationalist approach to life (President's Commission on Campus Unrest, 1970). There is, perhaps, then, a general disinclination to use man's capacity to be reflective. The argument is used that only the ability to experience sensations matters; sometimes this is elevated to a therapy that, it is believed, will heal magically the alienating discontents of humanity. Sometimes students become self-involved and are only concerned with their own pleasures and their own success, irrespective of the cost to others. In graduate schools, when resource papers are needed to produce academic work, they are commonly removed from libraries by anxious, greedy, ruthless students.

CHANGE AS A SOCIAL NECESSITY

Just as high schools have to learn to produce viable small social units, so must universities. The logical structure is the collegiate system, with academic staff having the ability to relate to students. The 1970s' demand for student power was also a demand for human contact with others. It was a slogan that implied omnipotent solutions. The real demand was for human contact and respect for human dignity.

A change in family relationships may put pressure on the life-style of schools and universities; if this were to occur in a positive, rather than a negative way, the inevitable changes in the latter would force changes in industry. If creativity is ever valued as the norm in places of higher education, even the boy or girl who leaves school at sixteen would find the present structure of industry and business intolerable; this might lead to a needed improvement in productivity.

Those adolescents who are exposed to imaginative teaching and who are given the opportunity for creative expression in schools, already have particular conflicts when they leave school. They tend to find themselves teased by the society in which they are to live and work. A good school attempts to give the child status as a person, so that he or she will fully develop a sense of self as valuable and worthwhile. Nonacademic students who attend good high schools find that employers are not interested in the creative imagination the schools may have fostered. One manager of a successful business said at a parent/teacher's meeting of a fairly conformist school: "I find the boys from this school excellent employees. They may not be too bright, but they work hard and do what I ask them to do."

All too often, the jobs that nonacademic late-adolescents obtain are dull and boring; they demand only a part of their attention, and there is often the assumption on the part of their bosses that they need to be coerced to work effectively. Outside their work experience, nonacademic adolescents find that life has little to offer them. If they are fortunate, they are able to find fulfilling interpersonal relationships with young people of the opposite sex. But social existence for most of them offers either the passivity of television watching, with its vicarious living, or a degree of somewhat frenetic excitement in videogames, discotheques, clubs, and commercial entertainment centers. It is no accident that drug pushers often find a happy hunting ground in such places of recreation.

Vietnam showed the violent alienation of nonacademic late-adolescents, both black and white. The assumption that the cessation of that war will resolve the problems that are hidden by "fragging" and pure heroin in Southeast Asia is naive. The war highlighted the problems of youth; it did not create them. Well-fed youth become increasingly aware of an experience of emptiness and desolation. In a panic, young people may attack the middle-aged for being dull, complacent, and unimaginative. This may be true, but it is a projection of the late-adolescent's anxious feeling that *he* is dull, complacent, and unimaginative.

Evidently many people are waiting for a hero figure they can follow. There is a mass of young people—inarticulate, often highly prejudiced, usually semieducated—waiting to be stirred to an activity that will make them feel valuable and worthwhile.

The most bitter and disaffected are among the eighteen-plus failures—those students who fail to gain admission to the college of their choice. Some start work unwillingly. Others go to a college they have not chosen, often seeing themselves as second-class citizens. Others drop out, and an unknown proportion become hippies and the like. An equivalent group is being created in the twenty-one- or twenty-two-year-olds who graduate from college, cannot find jobs, and go to work as janitors or taxi drivers. A catalytic force that exists in the United States, and hardly anywhere else in the world, is the disaffected black young. (An equivalent group in Northern Ireland is the Roman Catholic young who are the "blacks" of Ulster.) Led by disaffected intelligentsia, they light a violent fire whose coals are also present in American society.

Among these groups there is an unresolved rage that is often internalized because the individual tends to feel impotent and helpless. It is pertinent to ask whether any society can produce large numbers of disaffected young, offering no constructive solution, and survive; the evidence from history is that it cannot (Pares, 1960).

REFERENCES

Beloff, M. (1968), October for the rebels. *Encounter*, 31 (October): 48–56.
Bettelheim, B. (1971), Obsolete youth. Toward a psychograph of adolescent rebellion. In *Adolescent Psychiatry*, 1: 14–39. New York: Basic Books.

Louis, G. F. (1971), The slow road to student liberation. *Am. Assoc. Univ. Professors Bull.*, 57: 495–499.

Pares, B. (1960), *A History of Russia.* New York: Knopf.

President's Commission on Campus Unrest. (1970), *Report.* Washington, D.C.: U.S. Government Printing Office.

Redl, F. (1949), The phenomenon of contagion and shock effect in group therapy. In *Searchlights on Delinquency,* ed. K. R. Eissler, 315–328. New York: International Universities Press.

Reich, C. A. (1970), *The Greening of America.* 352. New York: Random House.

Chapter 10

The Etiology
of Adolescent Stress

EMOTIONAL EQUILIBRIUM IN ADOLESCENCE

The personality strength an individual brings to the adolescent age period is clearly the result of a variety of factors: genetic endowment and inherited vulnerability to brain biochemical aberrations due to stress; adequate emotional attachments in the first two years of life, so there is a well-developed capacity to form trusting relationships with others; positive interpersonal relationships within the nuclear family; and the family's relationships with its total environment. The latter provides children with economic and social stress or support and the opportunity for peer-group and extra-parental adult attachments (Bowlby, 1969). Meaningful emotional contact with non-parental adults are significant in personality growth, although in childhood parents are probably most important; in adolescence, peers and other adults are most needed (Miller, 1970). The loss of one of these throws particular stresses into the relationship with others, but in both childhood and adolescence, the nuclear family alone cannot successfully rear its offspring. In adolescence, the absence of peers makes successful personality development almost impossible; the absence of significant extra-parental adults is almost as bad.

Adolescence can appropriately be called an age of anxiety. Young human beings have to cope with anatomical, physiological, and psychological changes; the drive to autonomy leads to changes in family relationships; new demands are made by the world; and adolescents have new expectations of society (Freud, 1958).

The success of the adolescent in dealing with stress makes it possible for the adult he or she becomes to cope with psychic pain. The capacity to cope with frustration should be firmly developed during adolescence.

Behind all stressful adolescent behavior is a level of tension and anxiety the youngster cannot contain within himself. There is a spillover to activity that either relieves or avoids *Angst*, the experience of tension. The behavior may alter the environmental situation so that the precipitant of the tension is automatically removed—when the adolescent is seeking external controls and gets them—or the situation may be worsened. For example, anxiety caused by rejection may cause behavior that leads to further rejection (Miller, 1966), or the adolescent may convert an inner experience of feeling tormented into an actual experience of reasonable or unreasonable coercion.

Anxiety, which is an awareness of tension, can be understood as the result of the balance between stressful and supportive factors that play on the personality of the individual. The individual's physical development, environment, family, and perception of the world offer either emotional support or emotional stress; these interact with each other. The goal, for the individual, is to experience minimum anxiety, either by producing a series of coping devices (Menninger, 1963) or by acting to alter an external situation directly and consciously. If normal coping devices fail, the threatened disorganization evokes tension that produces special devices to maintain equilibrium, a variety of symptoms are produced, aspects of the conflict are repressed, or there is a misperception of the situation. Unconsciously, attempts are made to alter the situation. Thus, a homeostatic balance with environment is reestablished (Cannon, 1939).

Early adolescents, in particular, have a difficult task. At a period of maximum internal turmoil, they are likely to face maximum external confusion; external pressure comes both from the school system and the social environment at large. For both girls and boys, adolescence introduces an element of extreme peer-group competitiveness. Boys, by comparing themselves with agemates, make important assessments of masculinity, which are stressful if the individual perceives that he is inadequate. In a relationship with a particular friend, or a closely knit peer group, the adolescent may also get general emotional support.

> Jim, a sixteen-year-old boy who did extremely well academically and was perceived by his family and their friends as extremely well adjusted, sought help because of his anxiety about "excessive masturbation." Just

prior to puberty, his best friend had left town, and he had not found another. He masturbated once or twice daily, but had no way of discovering that other boys "beat off" with the same frequency. He did not feel able to ask his father because he was striving to free himself from the dependent feelings of childhood.

Thus, a social lack exposed Jim to particular stress; this made him feel more isolated and increased the frequency of the masturbatory act. His family attitudes also added to this stress. Apart from his struggle for autonomy, the parent's overmoral attitude toward sexuality made him feel that he himself was unduly interested in pornography because he liked looking at pictures in *Playboy Magazine*.

Jim's difficulties were compounded by a not unusual adolescent family struggle and the absence of psychosocial support from a close friend with whom he could talk intimately. Furthermore, his anxiety was enhanced by his criticism of his own bodily self. During a physical examination, which should be routine in all adolescents who seek psychological help, a medical student examining Jim noted that he had a slight indentation in his lower sternum. The student's inquiry about this led Jim to talk of how uncomfortable it made him feel. Jim said that his body was unsatisfactory, his head was too large, and his walk was ungainly.

This bodily preoccupation and self-criticism is typical. Jim felt, however, that his muscles were good, and he thought that his penis was as large as that of the other boys; he especially noted this when he showered with them. Thus, his bodily perceptions offered him both stress and support.

To an extent, Jim's masturbation could be understood as an attempt to gain control over his bodily anxieties, which is one of the uses of this act in the male. It was a regressive act due to the stress he experienced. On the other hand, it was also a way in which sexual fantasies became associated consciously with the genital experience of tumescence and detumescence (Reich, 1951). Finally, it was a way in which control over a bodily experience was reinforced, and it reduced the anxiety associated with loneliness and sexual tension.

PLACE OF THE NUCLEAR FAMILY

Within the family, the striving for freedom from dependent feelings of childhood is confusing both for adolescents and their parents. The adolescent may become overaggressive and overassertive. Parental reactions may increase stress, provide support for the adolescent in the autonomy struggle, or both. Testing by children of parental controls is an obvious example. Parents may respond to their children's difficult behavior with feelings of obvious dislike. Because of their own uncertainty, they may be overpermissive or overcontrolling relative to the new differing needs of their child. An individual's "adolescent" reaction may worsen the situation. Parents may find that they do not know how to talk to their children; simple remarks are felt as intense criticism because of adolescent hypersensitivity. Doors may be slammed over trivia; loss of face may be experienced by the young adolescent if a younger brother or sister is given what is sensed as priority status. The physiological state of the adolescent may increase stress. The intense lability of the blood supply to the skin may cause some obvious psychic pain: blushing exposes inner conflicts to the whole world. If parents comment about this, there is more discomfort. Pleasant family experiences, such as meal times, in which the equation of food and a warm loving atmosphere should be apparent, can become miserable stressful periods. Food fads may develop; individuals are likely to feel overwhelmed by a chance remark and rush dramatically from the table. Mixed feelings about mothering may be demonstrated by food refusal.

Often adolescents seem to stop talking to their parents in an agreeable way, they only argue, and the parents may find themselves doing the same. It is as if adolescents feel themselves to be alive by being oppositional. When family friends visit, some adolescents find this a major trauma and withdraw to their rooms at once. Others run out of the house with minimal provocation. "Now what's the matter?" is a typical parental cry. During the early adolescent period, it becomes extremely difficult to perceive the family as being supportive, so relatively minor stress, which may be misperceived, may take on major proportions.

PHYSICAL CHANGE AS A STRESS AND AS A SUPPORT

The new sense of self acquired in adolescence is associated with changes in bodily shape that lead to a radical reappraisal of the body image. A major anxiety of puberty is produced by adolescents feeling that their body is out of control. Rapid growth in boys and girls may be supportive to the developing personality as it signifies maturity; if it occurs at a different time from peers, it may be stressful. The uncontrollable menarche, before premonitory warnings due to premenstrual tension occur, is a gratification; real womanhood has arrived. As a stress, bodily substances are inexplicably lost (Klein, 1932), and the activity cannot be controlled. For boys, the bewildering increase in frequency of penile erections relative to earlier years, apparently unrelated to any psychic experience of sexual excitement, means adulthood is arriving. It also gives rise to anxiety. The degree of anxiety felt by an adolescent will depend on the adolescent's perception of the stress and his support in the situation. The psychological state of the individual will realistically depend on previous interactions with parents around issues of control and sexuality and love, guilt, and shame.

The early masturbatory behavior of the child demonstrates the situation. Children whose bodily play has been respected by their parents are less likely to be troubled than those who have been handled with parental anxiety.

A late developer is especially stressed by his slowness to change physically. A boy who develops late, in comparison with other boys of his own age, sees himself as smaller and weaker and his penis as considerably inferior to those of his friends. This makes him feel inadequate as a male (Schoenfeld, 1950). Adolescents have little sense of time; what is not happening today will not happen tomorrow. Direct and indirect reassurances, including those of doctors, are not believed. A future event is not meaningful, since it has not happened. Only if it is conveyed to such an adolescent that it is understood that reassurance is not believed, can the boy get any sense of security that physical growth will occur.

CULTURAL FACTORS INFLUENCING STRESS

Cultural factors may also enhance the tension experienced by adolescents. Because of concern about the helplessness associated with loss of control and a fear of regression to infantile dependence, the difficulty that adolescents may have in controlling the expression of their feelings often gives rise to feelings of tension and discomfort. It is often felt better to keep parents at a distance with hostile behavior than admit emotional need.

> A sixteen-year-old boy was unable to sleep one night because he felt so tense and uncomfortable about the death of a friend. He told his parents that he had slept in the family basement. They were enraged because he had not gone to bed, since they felt it was one more example of his balky behavior. In a family therapy session, they were horrified to discover what had really happened; the boy said, "I didn't want to tell you I was unhappy, as I was afraid I would get upset."

Control is socially reinforced by some cultures in males. But, in these, the denial of the expression of feeling that is considered a virtue may lead to the suppression of feeling and create additional stress. Pubertal adolescents are particularly likely to find themselves suddenly overwhelmed with feelings of happiness, sorrow, or anger, and they may anxiously fight to control them. Boys are likely to see the expression of sorrow, particularly if it leads to crying, as an indication of weakness, and femininity; their need for mothering is felt as unacceptable.

In many large conurbations, parents are relating to each other to provide a supportive network to prevent their adolescents from abusing drugs or alcohol. Organizations, such as "Tough Love," are actually if unknowingly beginning to recreate a social network of concerned adults that is necessary for adolescent development. Some church groups have created elaborate social networks that take in families who have moved to their neighborhood. Some men have refused company transfers, to avoid breaking social ties that are important to their families.

HELPLESSNESS AS A MAJOR TRAUMA

Adolescents may act to alter the situation in which they find themselves, and both boys and girls use emotional energy trying to change both their social environment and the way it is experienced. Since a certain degree of helplessness is psychologically driven and inevitable, the particular aim is to avoid making it an intolerable experience. For example, overrestrictive family situations that deny adolescents the responsibilities they are able to handle may lead to a projection of a sense of unfairness onto society-at-large. The complaints about the latter may be realistic. However, the intensity of the adolescents' response may be partially due to their own internal conflicts created within the nuclear family in the past as well as to present familial tensions. That such verbal attacks may be overdetermined does not mean that adolescents who negate the values of an established social system should be called emotionally disturbed.

ACTIVITY AND INACTIVITY IN THE ETIOLOGY OF STRESS

Physical activity is an important way of sublimating feelings of tension and consequent anxiety and aggression. It can provide socially acceptable outlets for aggression, especially for boys, in competitive sports and general athletic activity. In addition, physical activity also helps an adolescent develop a feeling of being in control of his or her body. Diffuse muscular activity is used to drain off tension, and the restlessness of adolescence is so important as an anxiety-relieving mechanism that the immobilization of adolescents due to illness may not only cause nursing problems, but also create severe emotional difficulties.

It is not unusual for athletes who are immobilized because of injury to become temporarily psychotic.

John was a nineteen-year-old college football player. He was the older son of a highly overcontrolling business tycoon and a brilliant, beautiful, emotionally cold mother. In prep school he had a brilliant academic and social career and was actively engaged in all competitive sports.

A leg injury necessitated his immobilization in a cast. For the first five days of his hospitalization, he was an excessively good patient. On the next two days he was withdrawn when his family visited him. He then told them that he was in direct communication with Christ and he described vivid visual hallucinations. His personal history showed that he had been a head-banging, extremely hyperactive child. His school career was stormy until he began to engage in such sports as ice-skating and hockey; thus he became a highly successful athlete.

Even partial immobilization, for example, when adolescents who suffer from spinal deformities are put in a body cast, may cause serious, if temporary, emotional difficulties:

Sixteen-year-old Sandra was placed in a body cast which allowed her to walk and go to school in December. In May of the subsequent year she was admitted to a psychiatric hospital threatening suicide. She was acutely depressed feeling ugly and helpless. She was in any case struggling for autonomy from her powerful somewhat insensitive parents; her adjustment failed when the cast reinforced her sense of being helpless.

The adolescent confined to a hospital bed has many techniques of coping with an anxiety that may be reinforced by anything from excessive parental concern to inappropriate placement of an ill youngster with a good prognosis next to a dying patient. The regressive experience of physically sick adults in a general hospital, that all unheard professional conversations are about them, is enhanced in the adolescent age period because of the extreme sensitivity of adolescents. The unease of the age leads to an inevitable paranoia. To reassure themselves about their more mature identity, adolescents in hospitals may also be overtly sexual with staff and other patients; girls may forget to put on their robes and wear flimsy nightgowns; boys may repeatedly ask for a urine bottle or "pat the butt" of passing nurses.

Within the nuclear family, the techniques sick adolescents use to contain anxiety may enhance parental concern, and a reciprocal state of tension may then be created. An adolescent boy may attempt to resolve his anxiety by regression, with infantile and demanding behavior; alternately, psychic withdrawal may occur and the youngster becomes passive, obedient, but essentially noninvolved. Some adolescents may be extremely difficult; they may refuse to follow physician's orders to stay in bed, take medication, abstain from exercise, and so on. Immobility leads to tension, but in some adolescents the implicit dependence associated with illness is felt to be intolerable. The adolescent responses may lead to parental oversolicitousness, anger, or withdrawal.

DEATH AS AN ADOLESCENT STRESS

The significance of death as an acute stress in adolescence from which recovery is possible with minimal interruption of psychological growth differs from the experience of death as a chronic unresolved source of internal pain that interferes with personality development.

Adolescents need to feel a sense of personal immortality, and in societies with a life expectation of seventy years or so, this feeling probably remains until about the age of thirty. Prior to that general age, although one knows that death is inevitable, one feels personally immortal unless the individual has been exposed to the repeated death of significant others; doctors and medical students with their patients, for example. Whenever young people are exposed to a threat of death that feels totally beyond their control, they respond with either excessive social turbulence, depression, and emotional withdrawal from others, or with death-defying behavior. Sometimes they react by accepting the idea of death and justifying suicide as an acceptable technique of resolving difficulties. These reactions are reported in contemporary accounts of the reactions of youth during the era of the great plagues of Europe (Defoe, 1722), and the threat of nuclear war as a potential destroyer of mankind has a similar effect.

The ability to mourn the loss of loved ones depends on the maturational age of the adolescent. When formal thinking has developed and a sense of time is operative, then mourning is possible and the dead can be buried inside the self as well as in the ground. Late-adolescent children, however, still identify with a dead parent and shortly after the death of a father, individuals may comment on how like his father an adolescent son has become. Early- and middle-stage adolescents may not be able to mourn completely, they cannot deal with the irrevocable sense of loss, guilt, anger, grief, and love that is involved. They may then keep an internal image of the dead person and grieve for many years or whenever that individual is mentioned. They may also talk to their dead loved one:

> One eighteen-year-old girl whose father had died when she was eleven said, "I say goodnight to daddy before I go to sleep. It's not that I'm hallucinating but I feel he is there with me."

A not uncommon reason for attempted suicide in adolescents is the wish to rejoin the dead person who lives in the adolescent's imagination.

The death of a peer, either through accident, illness, or suicide, is exquisitely painful not just for the intimate friends of the dead adolescent, but for a host of acquaintances. Guilt and anxiety are predominant; guilt because maybe one could have prevented the occurrence or, for those with low self-esteem, the wrong individual survived; anxiety because of the threat to the survivor's necessary sense of immortality. Because high schools do not have general assemblies, and also because the problem is often not understood either by school staff or the youngster's parents, necessary ritual mourning through appropriate quasi-religious or religious services does not occur. For those adolescents who need to be in a general hospital, anxiety is created by the presence of dying or physical disintegrating adults or children. This may be denied by adolescents, and angry feelings about the age of adults are expressed, or the adolescent isolates himself from the experience by insisting that only the old die. Confrontation with death always arouses great anxiety within everyone, but particularly adolescents.

Dying patients initially deny the imminence of death, feeling that there has been a mistake; they are angry with doctors and nurses, their families, and fate because death is going to occur. Often such people withdraw into themselves, and only at the point of death do they become accepting. Sometimes both the patient and his relatives enter into a conspiracy of silence, each to protect the other. These natural psychological processes are present in all those who are dying, although sedation by doctors and nurses and the presence of pain affect how visible these responses are to others.

Death in others arouses such anxiety that even young adults are unwilling to face the issue. This is obvious from the behavior of young medical and nursing staff in general hospitals. They often withdraw emotionally from the dying and may criticize and sometimes neglect them. The emotional difficulties of young adults are compounded in adolescents, who are not yet ready to face their own mortality. Denial is the typical response of both adolescents and young adults when those near to them, either physically or emotionally, die (Kübler-Ross, 1970). Beneath this is the same variety of psychological defense mechanisms seen in older adults, but typically young people may show their anxiety many months after the episode of death:

> An eighteen-year-old, British medical student abruptly decided to withdraw from school shortly after starting in the anatomy laboratory. He said, "When they began to strip the corpse, I began to think of a favorite cousin who died a year ago, and I could not stand it. It's strange because, when she died, I didn't think it troubled me too much."

The adolescent who is dying from such illnesses as leukemia, as well as those who die because of burns and mutilating illnesses, need ongoing support from all around them. Since many do not really appreciate the permanence of death, it may easily be felt as a relief and, anxiety and guilt are then perceived about leaving those who are loved. Older adolescents who understand the permanence of death often go through experiences of enraged bitterness after the initial feelings of denial have waned.

SOCIAL PATHOLOGY AS A PRODUCER OF STRESS

Social causes of mid-adolescent anxiety are most commonly due to the absence of an extended network of people with whom they can relate, extraparental adults or peers. This is now at least as usual clinically as when the adolescent suffers from a personality disturbance such that an available extended network of people cannot be used. The anxiety may be defended against by projection: The angry feelings that are a consequence of anxiety are projected onto others who are seen as bad. Thus, individuals create scapegoats—the establishment, the older generation, adolescents who are seen as different. Sometimes these and other defensive maneuvers fail to work, and a pervasive, empty anxiety is felt. An absent feeling of self creates general despair that may be sedated by drug use.

The constrictions of the society may cause an otherwise emotionally healthy adolescent to experience diffuse anxiety attacks:

> Tom, a seventeen-year-old boy was a satisfactory scholar at school until an unsuccessful foot operation temporarily made it impossible for him to play games, thus cutting off a necessary outlet for his anxiety and aggression. His work fell off precipitously, and he was diagnosed as suffering from depression. He appeared withdrawn, was unwilling to talk, and isolated himself from others. When he saw a psychiatrist, he said, "I knew what I was thinking but I could not bring myself to say anything as I felt too nervous." When talking of his life, he said, "We live miles from anywhere and when other boys get a social life or girlfriends, I cannot. My father suggests we fish, but I don't want to do this. In any case he is too old for me. At night I feel terribly lonely and envy boys who talk about their girlfriends. I don't know what I want to do and my parents don't seem to be able to help. My teachers don't seem to care."

The apparent depression covered an acute anxiety state and was really acute withdrawal. Anxiety was usually held at bay by competitive physical activity. When this was no longer available to relieve tension and anxiety, he was confronted with inner loneliness. He had been unable to find a girlfriend; he was also acutely uncertain as to his life goals. The failure on the part of his environment to meet his needs made it impossible for him to use what the environment did offer. A circle of inadequacy was created; the world had nothing to offer.

Adolescent girls, who find themselves unable to find suitable boyfriends because none are available, may become anxious, depressed, or aggressive. Such girls may spend a great deal of their time fantasizing the love relationships they cannot find in reality. This is a particular problem for minority-group female students in integrated higher educational settings. Ethnic prejudice is often intense among black students who see themselves in a hostile, racist world. For many psychological reasons, barriers of overt, if not covert, prejudice are ignored by black men who often have white girlfriends. However, apart from many black girls refusing to have white boyfriends because of ethnic pride, black adolescent males are felt by black girls to refuse to allow them to do this. As a result, many black girl students cannot find boyfriends. Not only do they suffer severe emotional deprivation, many of them become violently, aggressively militant, sometimes hiding guns for revolution against white society.

Mid-adolescent boys who cannot find girlfriends usually do not fantasize love relationships with imaginary girls, but rather sexual intercourse, often with older women. Hence, the interest of this age group in magazines such as *Playboy*, or in more obviously pornographic pictures.

The ongoing malaise of youth has many determinants: the threat of nuclear warfare; a bureaucratic society that loses touch more and more with individual needs; widespread unemployment; the loss of social stability; and the breakdown of tribal networks in large cities. The manifestation of this malaise depends on a number of societal factors and has varied from student rebellion in the 'sixties and early 'seventies, to massive and widespread drug abuse in the late 'seventies. More recently, there is an apparent conformity, with an unwillingness to tolerate significant emotional frustration without impulsive actions to alter the situation.

SPACE NEEDS OF ADOLESCENTS— THE PLACE OF ARCHITECTURE

Architecture and town planning are among the most powerful forces available in creating or destroying communities and family structure. The typical modern house or apartment—with a small kitchen, a communal living space, a hall, and bedrooms—does not meet the basic needs of the nuclear family. For example, adolescents cannot get away from their parents unless they go out or to their bedrooms, if they have bedrooms of their own. Often, soundproofing is inadequate.

A large amount of space is often wasted on bedrooms; with the same space, better provision could be made for psychological needs, which include in a typical family, a large eating area in the kitchen, because of the equation of food and love, and space for passive isolation or intimate talk. Children and adolescents need an area for activity away from parents where they can be noisy. The basement or "family room" may answer this need, but all too often it has become, for the middle classes and the more affluent workers, the symbolic space to which children are banished when guests arrive.

In the community-at-large, children and adolescents also require space to be both constructive within and safely destructive outside their home; they need to be able to roam and to test themselves physically. They also need to feel safe. The destruction of the core of cities is creating a social problem that is worsening in a geometrically progressive fashion, particularly as social organizations of society are allowed to decline.

> Paul was an eighteen-year-old inner city black youth. He entered a state hospital because of a toxic psychosis, almost certainly due to a combination of alcohol and drugs.
>
> He was a well-built, pleasant young man, whose father had died when he was ten. He had dropped out of school at fifteen and had never worked for more than one or two weeks. He had shown some flicker of interest in girls at fifteen and at seventeen had attached himself to a woman of twenty-two from whom he apparently caught gonorrhea. He started taking drugs, in particular, amphetamines and wine. He settled quickly into the hospital, showed obvious evidence of unresolved mourning for his father in that he wept when discussing him, and he was capable of making meaningful emotional relationships with others.
>
> It was thought that a treatment program should contain the following: an opportunity to work through some of his feelings about his dead father and an activity program that would help him resolve his sense of guilt, enhance his masculine identity, and train him for a gainful occupation. Not one of the physicians in the hospital were of American birth or had English as a native language; their caseload was high, and they had little or no psychotherapeutic training. The occupational therapy area of the hospital was understaffed and underequipped, and Paul had two hours of activity, other than ward cleaning, a week. The vocational area of the hospital could take forty patients and was not prepared to keep patients who could not at once work a full day in a productive way. Because of the lack of space, treatment was not even started.

Paul returned to the inner city, disenchanted with the white establishment and presumably, was ultimately lost in the black scene. In his turn, he is likely to breed more damaged human beings whose deprivation will be ignored unless pain is inflicted by him on the larger society. He is then likely to be incarcerated in a prison system that is a disgrace to a civilized society.

If society ever makes an effort to rebuild the inner city, neighborhoods, homes, schools, and youth-club facilities that cater to our urban adolescents, are more necessary than tower blocks. If new homes are built, it should not be beyond the wit of man to organize them so that no one is too far away from the natural countryside or large park or the means of getting there.

A major solution, the creation of bicycle paths in large cities, may offer important exercise outlets for young people; space restrictions, however, work against this solution.

It is now generally accepted that high-rise apartment buildings have a detrimental effect on family life. If small children play a long distance away from their mothers, they manage well, unless there is a crisis; then they need the solace of their mother's presence. In this situation they begin to learn that mother is not to be trusted because she is not there when she is needed. Alternatively, they are deprived of the experience of playing with others unless their mothers are able to accompany them. If high buildings were wide enough to allow several families to live on one floor, with enough space for the children to play with each other indoors, these buildings might be less damaging, psychologically.

Large schools, also, do not meet the emotional needs of their students, particularly those of developing personalities. Primary schools tend to be small in size and number of students, but the large complex of buildings found in many secondary schools can be overwhelming, arousing anxiety in both parents and children. If adolescents feel dwarfed by bricks, mortar, steel, or glass, they will enter a new school for the first time with unnecessarily increased anxiety. This does not help their relationships with each other or the staff.

In large schools, relationships are distorted by distance and inaccessibility. The interdepartmental memo is no substitute for relationships. The breakdown of the neighborhood school means that schools are not just isolated from the local community by their size and campus design, but also by the distance the children have to travel to reach them.

Tall school buildings also create problems. Human beings do not communicate if they have to go up too many stairs, and elevators do not help communications. As in high rises, where families are isolated, tall school buildings mar the formation of a coherent social structure. As noted, the checkerboard furniture arrangement of a typical classroom creates distance between teacher and pupil, and similarly, architecture may separate teachers from pupils. Even staff whose primary task is the emotional care of pupils may have their offices in a corridor away from the mainstream of school activities. This makes it much more difficult for the pupils to contact them. The isolation that pupils in emotional difficulty are likely to feel is reinforced.

Anxiety is, then, the result of an obvious interplay between physical, psychological, intra-familial, social forces. Within each of these, there is a capacity for support for the individual, but also a possibility of the individual being put in a state of stress. It is the balance of these factors that creates an effective human being or an anxious, dependent, inadequate, or overaggressive personality.

REFERENCES

Bowlby, J. (1969), *Attachment and Loss*. Vol. 1. London: Hogarth Press.

Cannon, W. B. (1939), *The Wisdom of the Body*. New York: Norton.

Defoe, D. (1722), "A Journal of the Plague Year." London: New English Library, 1980.

Freud, A. (1958), Adolescence. In *Psychoanalytic Study of the Child*, 13:255–277. New York: International Universities Press.

Klein, M. (1932), *Introduction to Child Analysis*. London: Hogarth Press.

Kubler-Ross, E. (1970), *On Death and Dying*. New York: Macmillan.

Menninger, K. A. (1963), *The Vital Balance*. New York: Viking.

Miller, D. (1966), A model of an institution for treating delinquent adolescent boys. In *Changing Concepts of Crime and Its Treatment*, ed. H. Klare, 99. Oxford: Pergamon Press.

——— (1970), Parental responsibility for adolescent maturity. In *The Family and Its Future*, ed. K. Elliott, 23–38. London: Churchill.

Reich, A. (1951), The discussion of 1912 on masturbation and our present day views. In *Psychoanalytic Study of the Child*, 6:80–95. New York: International Universities Press.

Schoenfeld, W. A. (1950), Inadequate masculine physique in the personality development of adolescent boys. *Psychosom. Med.*, 12:49–56.

Chapter 11

Aggression and Violence in Adolescence

AGGRESSION, ANGER, AND VIOLENCE

Aggression in man has two meanings; first, it is associated with the drive for environmental mastery, and as such carries no violent connotation. Although "aggression" in animals is used as a synonym for violence, in man it is probably better to consider aggression as implying socially acceptable mastery, violence carries the implication that behavior will be hurtful—it is destructive aggression. Thus, aggressive behavior is at the root of man's success or failure in coping with his environment (Lorenz, 1966). It is also associated with the physical changes that prepare the body for mastery tasks, and the word aggression is better not used when feelings of anger are involved. It implies an enjoyable experience, depending on its intensity. Behind every aggressive act of mankind is an attempt to cope with a potentially unpleasant experience of tension that is externally provoked (Scott, 1958). There is a gradation in the expression of human aggression, from the controlled use of language and physical activity to feelings of anger, to an uncontrollable or barely handled turning of destructive aggression against the self or others; aggression then becomes violence. One way in which individuals deal with violent impulses is to project them by fantasizing the other person as violent, provoking that person to violence, and then controlling it.

There are two types of violent behavior in man; one is controlled violence, which implies a planned use of violence either in words or actions. This involves excitement, but not intense emotional turbulence; it is seen in hunting behavior, and its equivalent in animals is predatory violence. The other type is "affective" violence (Miller, 1978), in which intense, rageful emotion is seen following a real or perceived frustration; its most acceptable form is a temper tantrum; its least acceptable, violent assaults on people or things.

LANGUAGE AS A VEHICLE FOR ANGER

Language is one way of expressing and beginning to relieve angry feelings. The English-speaking world is fortunate; as a language, English is particularly rich because accent, intonation, and word forms carry implications not only about the role and status of the user, but also about degrees of anger (Johnson, 1948). Furthermore, language has always been used to show group cohesion, often against an outside aggressor. The Welsh and Israelis revived their ancient tongue. The Quebecois try to eliminate English as a significant language of their province. The black American, whose language is remarkably like the eighteenth-century English of the indentured servants of the South and whose use of swear words is almost similar in color and frequency to that of the London Cockney, uses language to create a sense of black pride.

Subgroupings within the youth culture are reinforced by the use of special language. Slang words may have an idiosyncratic meaning to an in-group, when translated they become aggressive; adolescents do not see "panhandle" as being pejorative; "begging," however, is deplorable. It is acceptable to be "stoned," not to be "drunk." The language of adolescence changes regularly, the phrases of the seventies are now obsolete, and the street language of gangs changes even faster. Adolescent language is taken over by the adult world, and new words are then introduced by youth. Apart from private language within their family group, adolescents, particularly among the middle classes, often use words both to shock as well as to assert autonomy. An adolescent, using the language dissonance between himself and his parents, told them in the late 1970s to "cool it" and to "get their act together." Language, as an attempt to reinforce feelings of separateness and autonomy, may also be used to show defiance. Mixing rebellion with independence, employing language similarly to the use of clothes and hair styles, adolescents attempt to demonstrate the gap between themselves and the world of adults. Since language, like all fashions, is taken over by adults, adolescents then have to devise new slang.

USE OF LANGUAGE

The use of a special language for certain groups, prevalent throughout all societies, means that accent may be used aggressively. Superior groups in the social scale use one sort of language to show their dominance over those they consider inferiors. In recent years in Britain, the use of working-class English has come to be thought of as acceptable in association with the overtly assertive needs of some of the present generation to reverse many traditionally held beliefs; a similar process occurs with middle-class black Americans, whose youth now goes out of its way to use the language of the black ghetto.

LANGUAGE AS A REINFORCER OF GROUP COHESION

The development of language skills in children is partly related to how much a child is talked to from infancy on. Mothers who talk consistently to their infants, other things being equal, seem to rear children who develop language skills early. Initially, the child imitates the intonation of the parents, then real words are used. Some parents encourage the use of language in children by talking with them, others are relatively silent and their play with their children and interactions with them may be relatively non-verbal.

Later in childhood, children defiantly use the swear words the parents use themselves, but do not wish their offspring to use. So long before adolescence, language may be part both of the technique of self-assertion and of peer-group acceptability. This becomes obvious as soon as children, who are highly imitative, begin to make special friends. When they play outside their own immediate social groups, especially in socially and ethnically integrated grade schools, they may acquire a language that is unacceptable to their nuclear family. Correction may follow, and the children may then learn to speak with two tongues; one at home and one at school. Initially, in an unthinking way, they may bring the unacceptable language to the family table. Later, the unacceptable language may be used aggressively against parents. Thus, developmental behavior can once again be used, rebelliously, to establish autonomy.

The success or failure for the individual in an aggressive use of language depends on the codes of the individual's nuclear family. It is a concern of many parents when their children go to grade school that they will learn bad manners and language, the definition of bad being determined by the individual family. Bad language does not just consist of swear words and vulgarities; it also involves grammatical construction. In later adolescence, language may be used by educated offspring to separate themselves from their less well educated parents. Typically older children handle rivalry with younger siblings by using provocative language to goad and provoke. This may be an identification with the early use of language by parents. When a new baby is born, this generally changes. The language of love may now become criticism. "Don't do that"; "Leave your sister alone"; "Be quiet, mother is busy."

SWEARING

Some swear words are common in Britain and not in the United States and vice versa. "Son of a bitch" is unknown in England, and "mother-fucker" is extremely rare; "bloody" and "bugger" are not significantly used in the United States. Just as aggression and sexuality are clearly mixed, behaviorally (Kinsey et al., 1948) so many aggressive words are sexual. Literally, a bugger is a sodomist; the swear word has lost this meaning. Some words acquire a sexual meaning in one culture, but not in another. In Lancashire, to be "knocked up" means to be awakened in the morning. "Keep your pecker up" is northern English colloquial slang to keep cheerful.

Just as parents may perceive the language of their children as impolite and angry, the reverse may also be true. Sometimes proper language is felt by children to be mysteriously obscure:

> A nine-year-old boy reproached his mother saying that he thought that she never lied to him. His mother, who prided herself on her honesty with her son, was more than a little offended. She asked him what he meant. He told her that she had not told him the truth about the word "penis." The mother wondered what on earth he meant. She was then told that the proper name of it was "prick."

At the age of nine, this boy was beginning to feel that the language of his age group was more personally appropriate than that of his parents. Having established its nonacceptability to his parents, the word can now be used in the service of aggression; "you prick" will be said to his agemates.

Bad language may be disapproved of on moral or religious grounds; it may also be considered poor taste. The dictionary definition of "vulgar" shows the class bias associated with swearing; it is "coarse, impolite, common, of the people."

The use of swear words develops in all societies around subjects that arouse special anxiety (Montague, 1961).

Words that are associated with conscious or unconscious conflicts are used to express anger. In Tudor England, expletives were especially associated with religion. The absence of concern about doctrinal questions of religious belief now means that swear words associated with them are no longer bad. The British swear word "bloody," originally associated with the idea of God's Blood and the wounds of Christ, is a diminutive of Shakespearean England's "Od's Blood." It no longer causes a commotion in polite circles.

Anxiety about maternal chastity is more significant in some cultures than others. It is particularly likely to be an emotional issue for adolescents. The stronger the unconscious maternal tie and the younger-looking the mother, the greater is the unconscious incestuous threat to the male. A mother known by her adolescent son to be sexually promiscuous causes the oedipal conflict to be more intense because of her obvious availability. "Whoreson" was freely used in Elizabethan England; nowadays in the United States "son of a bitch" is in aggressive use (Ross, 1961). An even more angrily abusive term for one young man to howl at another is "mother-fucker."

The constant repetition of swear words in books, plays, television, and the movies has much the same effect on young people as the use of their adolescent language by their parents. The four-letter words eventually cease to have meaning as terms of abuse, and have to be replaced. The need to swear does not change; the actual words used may. Furthermore, if the forbidden conflicts behind the swear words change, new words have to be used that express what the culture then finds unacceptable.

Many individuals suffer from sexual anxieties. Until recently, in the United States, these were mostly about normal sexuality, so sexual words describing genital organs became thought of as swear words. These are often acceptable between men or boys in their own groups, but are considered unacceptable in family circles. Despite the aggressive identification of some women's political groups with apparent masculine norms, this remains true between men and women or boys and girls. However, words that boys might be unprepared to use to their mothers may now be said to girlfriends. A late-adolescent boy may comfortably say "fuck" in the presence of his girlfriend; he is less likely to in the presence of his mother. So societies that are particularly conflict-ridden over normal sexuality use the vulgar words for sexual organs and sexual activities as swear words. Angry boys will call each other "prick"; to be particularly offensive they use colorful words for the female genitalia, "you cunt." Boys will tell each other to "fuck off." Such swear words are particularly likely to occur in all male groups cut off from female company. Young women may now use these words, as a sign of their liberation. In some circumstances, the erotic quality of these words that, in normal heterosexual societies tends to be much overlaid by their angry connotation, comes to the fore. Men may unconsciously express their homosexual anxieties by the use of such language.

As normal sexuality has become less a source of anxiety in the community-at-large, the sexually abusive words have tended to leave the area of sexuality that is acceptable to the larger group. More words carry specific derogatory meaning for one socioeconomic or ethnic group, or in one part of the country. Sometimes the same social group may change the meaning of a word over a few years. For example, in northern England, "queer" means strange; in the south of the country, it is offensive for one boy to angrily call another "queer," for this implies homosexuality. "Queen" and "camp" are two homosexual words that moved into fashionable and theatrical language and almost lost their sexual meaning. Adolescent girls in some parts of London who wish to abuse another girl of their own age may call them "lesbians." English boys call other boys "cock suckers"; American boys are aggressive to other boys by asking if they "suck." Early-adolescent girls and boys call each other "fags," and in this sense the word seems to have lost its sexual connotation. "Fag," in the United States, is still slang for homosexual, as is the word "faggot." In England, a fag is a younger boy who acts as an unofficial servant to an older boy in the private school system. Sometimes conflict-ridden individuals who are biologically vulnerable, develop uncontrollable bodily tics with a most devastating symptom; uncontrollable obscene words. Typically, this may first appear in childhood and adolescence. This is known as Gilles de la Tourette's Syndrome. Even though this has a biological etiology, the words that are used manifest conflicts about sexuality and aggression in the individual who is suffering from the disease. In an ejaculatory way, they scatter swear words throughout their conversation (Hollander, 1960).

It is not clear whether the syndrome is genetic (Eldridge et al., 1977). Appropriate medication stops the verbal explosion; it does not resolve the underlying conflict.

VIOLENCE AND THE USE OF LANGUAGE

Until recently, men and women have been prudish over natural excretory functions. A whole euphemistic language grew up around the use of the toilet. Even the formal words are confusing: A "lavatory" really is a place to wash, yet it is used in England to describe a "watercloset," the official description there of a "toilet." A "closet" in America is a "cupboard" and has no bladder or bowel significance. A "toilet" is really a place to adorn oneself. A lavatory in England may be called a "loo," in America a "John." Some middle-class American women refer coyly to "the little girls' room." The vulgar words for urination and defecation are still replaced in many families with a whole variety of apparently innocuous words: "big job," "BM," "wee," and so forth. Only in the last two hundred years has the flight from a naturalness over natural functions occurred. It was perfectly acceptable for Chaucer to write of the parson in the *Canterbury Tales*: "What needeth then a shiten shepherd and a clene shepe," and nowadays "shit" is commonly used as a swear word. In case generations of schoolboys were corrupted, Victorian morality replaced the word with "dirty." Shakespeare freely used the word "piss."

Adolescents today are less liable to need to be imprecise in their use of excretory language: "Piss off" is still abusive, but an almost acceptable description of rainy weather is that it is "pissing down." The relationship between parental use of language and adolescent aggression is again apparent. If parents use euphemisms for urination, their adolescent sons are more likely to tell each other to "piss off." If "piss" is the parental word, the adolescent will be much less likely to use language in this way.

Excretory words in the twentieth century are particularly used to express anger and there is a clear relationship between such language and violent behavior.

Each family and each society decides on its own limits and techniques of control. Physical assault, when angry, as from parents to children, is tolerated in some social groups (Miller and Swanson, 1958). Some fathers will hit their sons until the latter are big enough to hit back. In other families, physical assaultiveness is very rare, if not unknown (Miller, 1980). Nevertheless, acceptable outlets for anger have to be found. Those parents who believe that they should never show anger convey to their children the idea that anger is very dangerous. Alternately, they may be felt to be dishonest if children know their parents hide angry feelings. Parents who completely repress their own anger either create children who are incapable of self-assertion, those who fear that their anger may spill out dangerously, or both.

If anger is not to be expressed in assaultive behavior, it would then appear inevitable in healthy personalities that the violence will have to appear in words. Swear words are the safest and least cruel way of showing anger. Personal security can be destroyed more effectively with polite and cutting language than with violent words. Parents may make distinct efforts not to swear in front of their adolescent or younger children. The justification for this is that parents do not wish to set a bad example, but it is important to give children safe areas for defiant and angry behavior and at the same time to show that parents, too, are not perfect.

All parents have secrets into which they do not allow their children to pry, for example, bedroom behavior. Adolescents have inevitably experienced situations over years in which parental language has only been partly understood. Furthermore, most parents swear at each other when they are enraged. In healthy families, children know that special words are associated with mutual parental irritation; sometimes these are swear words. Social hypocrisy still exists about this: An embarrassed mother will pretend that her child's bad language has been picked up at school.

Children have a relatively unchanging language and lore of their own, handed down through the generations (Opie and Opie, 1965). If all swear words were to be banished from all homes, they would still continue in the world of children, just as their games and rhymes are transmitted. The private language of adolescents needs to be seen by them as bad in the eyes of the adult world. This concept is part of their need for their own in-group.

Adolescents have a need to defy the openly stated norms of adult society. To accept bad language is to deny to adolescents a whole area of potential defiance that is relatively safe. If bad language between parents and children is totally forbidden, the probability is that young people will conform as they do in many areas of inter-family functioning (Macoby et al., 1954). Other outlets for anger will then have to be found. If bad language is disapproved of, but implicitly condoned from time to time, it will be used when adolescents wish to show defiance. If all language is permissible within the family setting, words again cease to be a vehicle to express anger.

It is possible that ethnic and social groups that do not develop a concept of forbidden language are inevitably beset by a greater likelihood of physical violence. Almost all people swear and use bad language when they are angry. If defiance is taken out of the use of language, children and adolescents may then feel forced to act out their anger in physical ways in the world-at-large, rather than by the use of words. The old phrase about sticks and stones breaking bones but words never harming has validity. In spite of biblical injunctions, it is better to take the name of the Lord in vain than to be physically violent with other human beings.

VIOLENT BEHAVIOR

Both predatory and affective violence involve the physical expression of angry feelings—inflicting damage on inanimate objects, the self, or others. In the former, the object is personalized; adolescents suffering an acute loss of ego identity (Erikson, 1968) may attack their family furniture as an expression of their rage with their parents, whom they perceive as preventing them from developing a sense of autonomy (Miller, 1967). Anger turned against the self is evident in a whole range of self-destructive behavior, but, apart from outbursts of rage directed against others in temper tantrums, physical bullying is the most usual form of outwardly directed personal violence in the young. "Perhaps, our most unpleasant characteristic as a species is our proclivity for bullying the helpless" (Storr, 1968). Beyond this, angry and violent behavior toward others is particularly likely to occur during childhood and adolescence. The streets of both the inner city and the schools may be made dangerous by violent and aberrant youth. In England, alienated youth haunt parts of London to attack isolated Pakistanis whom they perceive as helpless. Disturbed adolescents are likely to persecute others who are weaker than they are for three reasons: They cannot yet control their anger when frustrated. Bullying and violence is not felt to be wrong because the victim is dehumanized; during violent outbursts, the usual awareness of what is felt to be wrong is suspended. Typically, individuals or groups are scapegoated and, although weak, are felt to be powerful (Cohn, 1967). Scapegoats are assigned qualities by individuals that they find intolerable in themselves or in their environment; they are felt not to be the same as the self, but at the same time they possess the powerful inner badness of those who bully.

Adolescent boys may get sexually excited when involved in aggressive behavior. At all ages, particularly in the male, sexual feelings and angry feelings are easily mixed, but in adolescence this mix is enhanced.

ETIOLOGY OF THE INCREASE IN VIOLENCE

The increase in violent behavior among young people in the present decade appears to be absolute in the countries of the West. For example, between 1959 and 1976 the rate of death by homicide of white males aged fifteen to nineteen rose by 177 percent and the rate has increased each year from 1969. There is much preoccupation with causes. It is sometimes thought to be the result of changes in child-rearing techniques, but there are many more positive results from these than otherwise. New ways of bringing up children are thought to be part of a permissive society that is said to have created a moral turpitude in the young. However, society is probably more confused or rejecting than permissive. Single parent families; the breakdown of social networks; a shortened school day when no parent is at home; the toleration of drug and alcohol abuse; all have led to adolescents' feeling neglected and not cared about. Some may identify with this and become uncaring adults. Others are raised without the recognition that needs are not the same as wants and should, if possible, be met. Many parents are aware that children are not just extensions of themselves; children who are raised with the recognition that they have valued personal integrity become adolescents who do not value violence and who also feel that respect for the integrity of others is important.

In this respect, the comments from some deans for student affairs in medical schools are pertinent. The class of 1972, generally born in 1947 or 1948, were angry, often impulsive, and had a high withdrawal rate, even if this was only temporary and due to psychological reasons. This was the class that was, as undergraduates, part of the destructive wave of campus violence. The class of 1975, born in 1951 or 1952, were apparently more perceptive, thoughtful, and hypersensitive. Although there may not be a relationship, by 1950 changes in child-rearing techniques, particularly among the middle classes, were firmly under way.

Although most young people have become less inclined to use physical violence, as antiwar and anti-nuclear demonstrations have shown, crimes of violence have increased in the deprived, underprivileged, and drug-dependent groups of society. It is associated with the polarization of society into haves and have-nots and is also related to individual alienation, an aspect of human development for which the school system has apparently some responsibility. Rigid school systems usually do not provide acceptable physical outlets for anger for adolescents who are not particularly physically able, and for whom physical education classes are not enough. This, along with tension produced by forcible, and from a psychological view, unplanned integration has led to excessive tension among underprivileged members of the majority and minority groups. An unthinking ethnic and social-class mix has removed a neighborhood base for many children and placed them too far away from their parents, in social settings where they are not understood. The presence of a school counseling system means that the average teacher often opts out of feeling any responsibility for interpersonal relationship with pupils.

> A group of teachers in a discussion session suddenly realized that if an adolescent missed one of their classes they did not usually tell the individual that he or she had been missed. A teacher would only send a note to the counselor who would determine whether or not disciplinary action was necessary. If he thought the adolescent was emotionally upset, the child would then be sent to the school social worker. Furthermore, none of these levels of staff, if they were to call the youngster's home, would ask for him, irrespective of age. Parents were always told first.

Parts of the adolescent's personality are thus isolated from each other by a social system. Because an intra-familial striving for autonomy is not recognized, the adolescent is further alienated. In addition, the rigidly or-ganized school day means that there is little opportunity for freely permitted social interaction. Middle-class and white adolescents are more prepared to say what they feel rather than act it out, but even they begin to demonstrate a hostile "we/they" attitude toward their teachers. The obsession with be-havioral conformity has led, in many places, to the use of behaviorist teaching techniques, but these have not resolved the social, educational, and psychological problems of the young.

Physical bullying and its verbal equivalent, teasing, can be understood in two ways. It is related to the capacity to tolerate frustration and handle angry feelings and the degree of inner security an individual might feel. Bullying, a provoked or unprovoked physical assault on a weaker individual, is an idea children develop with the growth of conscience. Without a concept of actions as right or wrong, the awareness that one is bullying does not occur. Physical bullying is more usual in boys, verbal teasing in girls. In England, girls rarely bully; boys quite often tease. However, physical violence among girls is much more common in the United States than in England. In the United States, it is not unusual for racial violence to break out among girls in school locker-rooms; usually less privileged black girls try to physically intimidate whites whom they perceive as more affluent. The placing of policemen or human relations counselors as an attempt to stop this is not unusual; without control, the situation could be worse, but controls alone cannot succeed.

There is less adult concern about taunting behavior than physical bullying, so the adolescent who indulges in verbal assaults takes longer to give these up than does the adolescent who physically attacks other students. Adolescents who would not persecute others in a one-to-one setting may do this in a group. The stage performer who disappoints an audience may be given a slow, measured handclap instead of applause; everyone present joins in this behavior.

Conscience about the control of physical assaultiveness first appears around two; parents show disapproval when it is directed at other children. This disapproval is perceived as a loss of love, so the child initially avoids such behavior in sight of his parents. At about three or four, recognition that weaker children should not be hit is expected. In nursery schools, physical attacks will be controlled and disapproval shown. However, in free play, the concept of nonviolence may be honored more in the breach than the observance. It takes many years before the internal image of parental and adult disapproval becomes a well-developed conscience that automatically controls behavior. Kindly behavior is not always consistently present among three-year-olds, nor is it always present in early adolescents. Angry behavior in children and adolescents is related to anxiety; the more potentially anxious a child may be, the more he is likely to fight. Violence is therefore more common in environments in which children's needs are not met, in poverty-stricken neighborhoods in the United States and other parts of the West.

SOCIAL SYSTEMS AND VIOLENCE

Violence is present in the male in many cultures, and particularly in early-adolescent boys. They have a great need for semiviolent physical contact with each other. The friendly punch and the playful wrestling bout is typical behavior of adolescents to help the control of aggression, the assessment of physical strength, and the provision of a sense of boundaries due to developmental distortion of body image. This may easily spill over to become bad tempered, violent, and bullying.

Rigid social systems that do not respect the individual needs of adolescents are more likely to elicit violent behavior than are those that respect the integrity of the youngsters in their care. A vicious circle tends to be created. The more rigid the system, the more rigid is likely to be the response to violent behavior (Morris and Morris, 1963). So a situation can develop in which schools never allow unsupervised activities because of fear of how the children will behave. This is presumably one of the factors that has led to the disappearance of recess in most American high schools.

BULLYING

Small children report bullying to parents and authority adults; adolescent boys consider it antisocial to tattle. This in-group loyalty can mean that a boy may be bullied and scapegoated for a considerable time before it comes to the attention of adults. A typical site for early-adolescent bullying is in school toilet areas, perhaps in a social way confirming analytic observations of the relationship of anality to anger. It also occurs in poorly supervised school showers. Often those bullied are least physically developed; the sexual implications are obvious.

Most adults do not have optimum control of their own angry feelings, so parents may be unduly defensive when told of their child's bullying behavior. Others, in an attempt to demonstrate that bullying is forbidden, may bully their offspring themselves.

> A three-year-old boy angrily bit a two-year-old for taking his toy away. The boy's mother, when she learned about this, immediately bit her son.

The intention undoubtedly was to show that biting was wrong. The message probably given was that to get away with biting, one should be bigger and better than the opponent.

By school age, after the child enters the latency period, a strong enough conscience to prevent bullying from occurring, except under conditions of intrapsychic tension, should have developed. The relationship of cruelty to humanizing and dehumanizing is obvious in children. These children who learn to humanize animals do not behave with cruelty toward them. Cruelty directed toward other children is associated with the victim having become temporarily dehumanized. Overwhelmed with intrapsychic tension and sadism, the instigator ceases to see the other child as a person.

Children try out the strength, both of their own consciences and their own capacity to be impulsive and aggressive, by fighting other children, often in various types of war games, or in cowboys and Indians. In the excitement of this activity, children are likely to allow the impulsive break-through of angry feelings. A similar situation occurs in early adolescence. Smaller children see themselves as having been bullied in games, and an accidental blow can be felt as deliberate. It is not unusual for the ritual of a game to allow bullying under the guise of play. This may be fairly frequent and obvious between brothers and sisters who are jealous of each other.

> A group of ten-year-old children, having heard about the Spanish Inquisition, decided that they would have a ceremonial burning at the stake. As their victim for this *auto-da-fé*, they chose the eight-year-old younger brother of one of the group. The older boy allowed his brother to be tied up, but insisted on his release before the pyre was ignited.

Apart from the chance occurrence of bullying in games or its appearance in the roughhousing of early adolescence, children are likely to hit others who are smaller when they feel overcome with frustration and rage. The weaker child may be the victim of the frustration older individuals feel as a result of their own relative weakness. A boy who feels bullied by his parents is likely to bully others. Often the young thug of the classroom has a bullying father who does not hesitate to beat him. The moderately handicapped child is in the same category as is the child who loses control with outbursts of tears or anger. Both represent psychological threats and they are tormented so those who bully can reassure themselves that they are different. The more seriously handicapped child is generally not felt as a threat by others so may be cared for rather than the reverse.

Bullying is thus related to the ability of adolescents to handle their own angry or envious feelings and to put up with another's teasing or provocation. Adolescents uncertain about their identity and ability to handle feelings of anger and sorrow may be afraid that their own angry feelings will be uncontrollable. They may also have grave, if transient, doubts about the physical effectiveness of their own bodies. Doubt about personal weakness may be resolved by attacking that apparent weakness in others. Adolescents who have problems of personal self-control may provoke a peer to tears or anger, then scorn, mock, reject, or hit the playmate. This is similar to the smaller child, who, easily provoked to tears, is only too willing to mock another for being a "cry baby." Finally, the adolescent may enhance his own feelings of strength by imagining how he would respond if he were tormented. Adolescents with distressed feelings, whose personal controls are rigid, but weak, often respond to teasing with temper outbursts. These adolescents are likely to be bullied. They are ready-made victims for those adolescents who fear loss of control themselves and who can reassure themselves that they would behave differently. So bullies both identify with their victims' torment, projecting onto them in order to make the torment possible, and at the same time, dehumanizing them as objects of their sadism.

Early adolescents are likely to bully those they envy. Young people who make a conspicuous display of their worldly goods, particularly to those who do not have them, are likely to be set upon and tormented. Affluence is not always economic. Those boys who work excessively hard in high school and make their agemates feel guilty are likely to be pilloried one way or another. To defend against this some schools develop an ethos among their pupils in which work is always denied.

A boy or girl who works hard and enjoys it is likely to deny to others that work is ever done. Jealousy and envy are feelings most individuals try to avoid (Rosenfeld, 1957). People who are likely to be envied do their best to deny their accomplishments, since they fear the physical or verbal assault of others. The very rich often try to hide their wealth and pretend to others and themselves that economic bargains are significant. Upper-upper–class groups in the United States often do not drive new cars; in Britain, the very rich may take pride in wearing old clothes.

Transient emotional disturbance caused by circumstance, a family move, for example, may lead to bullying behavior. Some social and ethnic groups are more prepared to be violent than others. When almost all parental frustration is dealt with by a cuff, children hit others more easily and with less guilt than do children who come from families in which the physical expression of anger is controlled. Social class and ethnic behavioral differences can create conflicts between children. Such differences may cause severe social disruption, particularly in early adolescence, because this is the age of projection onto out-groups.

Trouble in a high school is often ascribed to conflicts between black and white. Particularly in deprived neighborhoods, this explanation of school riots and violence has some validity; nevertheless, the social organization of the school is highly significant. Children do not destroy school property and attack each other if the adults in their immediate environment are felt to be supportive and caring.

VIOLENCE AS AN INTERGROUP PHENOMENON

Small children who are in emotional difficulty easily refer back to the family ethos; although it may be defied, the parental attitude is consciously and unconsciously accepted as correct. Adolescents are more involved with their own age group as a function of emotional withdrawal from parents because of anxiety about childish, dependent, and incestuous feelings. They become susceptible to the culture of the group of the young people with whom they ally themselves. The groups may be quite small, six to eight, but they, in turn, are also influenced by the way of life of the larger society. For example, if most adolescents in a school come from one social class, providing the social environment meets a reasonable number of adolescent needs, the school will be comfortable and productive. Furthermore, any environmental tensions can be dealt with by projection onto groups outside the school with whom there may be little actual contact, although in adolescence, the bringing together of different groups often leads to problems in both groups. A mix of social class and ethnic groups without pupil/teacher stability means that stress may be dealt with by projection onto the other group. At best, groups may withdraw from each other in mutual incomprehension. This has happened in high schools on the basis of religion, social class, or ethnic background. The Jews sat at one table, the WASPs at another. Now the phenomenon is very evident on the basis of ethnic or racial groups, although more subtle withdrawal on the basis of social class also occurs. The failure of integration is apparent in undergraduate and postgraduate schools. There the minority groups may cluster together, often at the back of the room. They may demand separate housing on the pretext that they are harried by whites, and see prejudice when it is not there:

> A lecturer in a class of social work students commented in the course of the first hour of his lecture about a girl who was rather obviously balancing her checkbook. She happened to be black. After the break, every black student had vanished from the class.

Different social and ethnic groups become a convenient vehicle for the exchange of violence. Sometimes, one adolescent may behave in a way that fits his social group. A lack of understanding on the part of a member of another ethnic group can lead to an outburst of more or less violent behavior.

HOMOSEXUAL ANXIETY AND BULLYING

Pubertal adolescents, unsure of their own physical maturity, are likely to tease late developers. Particularly in single-sex institutions, physically immature boys are likely to be tormented by those past puberty, since once puberty is over, boys normally begin seeking heterosexual relationships. If this search is inhibited, and particularly if the boys are living under emotional stress, the immature boy is thought to be effeminate. Thus, the naturally developed fifteen- to sixteen-year-old becomes anxious about the amorphous sexuality of the prepubertal boy who is likely then to be teased for being a "fag." This is particularly likely when, in a closed male community, sexual gratification with other boys is a distinct possibility.

In closed penal settings, late-developing boys, those who are weak, or those who are younger are likely to be homosexually seduced. Often they accept the homosexual role because they feel that if they do not they will be bullied into homosexual activity or raped. In such environments, special rituals and codes develop. Tough boys may take weaker, more effeminate, boys as homosexual partners and look after them. The aggressive boy is not then thought to be homosexual. In some penal settings, boys who are flagrantly homosexual are often rejected because they pursue activities about which boys with a heterosexual orientation feel guilty. The same problem is an issue in correctional settings for girls although society seems less aware of this, perhaps because there are much fewer females in correctional institutions than males.

MINORITY GROUPS AND PERSECUTION

Racial persecution is mass bullying and assaultiveness writ large. In adolescence, individuals are bullied because they are given the qualities their tormentors fear they might have themselves. This mechanism is also present in the racial persecution of minority groups by the majority: blacks by whites or vice versa; Jews by gentiles; or Catholics by Protestants. The persecution of minorities is partly related to the belief that they are too clever, cunning, privileged, inferior, or a social and economic threat. If the majority are under pressure—economic, social, or emotional—prejudice, which produces social ostracism, becomes persecution. This is persecution by the majority of their own sense of internal badness, ascribed to others. It is also an attempt to relieve tension by acting out hostile feelings.

Adolescents may thus attack minorities for being deceitful, dishonest, dirty, mean, greedy, and sexually unreliable; these are all qualities that they have to deal with inside themselves. But national and ethnic prejudice only becomes persecutory action when the social climate puts people under stress, and often there is a political motive. Those who are responsible for the stress divert the attention of the population onto external enemies, perhaps a minority group within the host population. A psychological need to be prejudiced against certain groups and individuals within the population is then reinforced. Minority qualities are also used as a scapegoat for other anxieties. When one social group is housed with another, the host population that is not prepared to receive the new group may ascribe the inevitably disturbed behavior of those who have been moved to qualities inherent in their ethnic or religious group.

Individuals identify with their tormentors; they both believe they are right and will become persecutors themselves, given the opportunity. The boy who is bullied toadies up to the bullier, not just out of fear, but also out of admiration. The victims of prejudice may ultimately agree with the attitudes of their tormentors. They become highly prejudiced themselves about their own ethnic group, irrationally accepting the negative qualities they have been assigned. Alternately, they may implicitly agree with prejudice, as an attitude, by being as prejudiced against the larger population as that group is against them.

Just as the victims of parental child abuse are likely to become child abusers, small children who are bullied may often become bullies themselves as they grow into adolescence and become physically more effective. Such adolescents may persecute others for the same reasons they themselves were persecuted. Some social environments bring out the latent bullying qualities that exist in some adolescents; some schools are notorious for the amount of bullying that goes on in them.

The equivalent among girls of the physical bullying of boys is usually verbal backbiting. Just as one boy can become a scapegoat and be physically attacked, so a girl becomes the victim of verbal assaults. In very deprived societies and socially aberrant girls' institutions, bullying among girls is common. Then, it is even more usual for one girl to fight another girl than for a group of girls to bully a victim.

Bullying may be an identification by young people with the behavior of their elders, but any consideration of adolescent violence has to include the bullying of the old, weak, and helpless by the young. Throughout history, groups of young men have been known to wreak impulsive havoc on these groups; this has always been known in ill-disciplined armed forces. Young, ill-trained, or demoralized troops are exposed to the excessive psychological trauma of killing and brutality on the battlefield. If the social structure of the army unit does not offer enough psychological support, such soldiers are likely to act out their anxieties with sexual and murderous attacks on helpless populations, hence, the massacres in Vietnam (Gault, 1971). A relatively new historical phenomenon arose in the 1930s: the systematic widespread bullying of older people by young adults and late adolescents for ideological reasons. Nazi youth, reinforced by authority, divided the world, both inside themselves and externally, into good and bad. Jews and gypsies were bad and dehumanized; they could be justifiably tormented, bullied, and murdered. The cruelty of this was partly a function of a group process that gave individuals permission to act out their internal sadism. Also, authority was given the more disturbed sections of the populations to allow them to inflict their own angry feelings on people who represented to them a bad, uncaring world. The Red Guard in China, in the 1970s was another example of this.

A somewhat similar phenomenon appeared in the late 1960s with some university students. Small groups bullied and humiliated some of their teachers. Those hostile, violent students were protesting, among other things, against the hostile violence of society. Unconsciously, these young people identified with the very qualities they criticized. Many who insisted that they had been alienated by society treated their victims as if they were nonhuman. Adolescents who experience themselves as the respository for the aggressive fantasies of adults may repay the compliment in kind. Often late adolescents, who may complain that the older generation has treated them in an uncaring fashion, appear not to care how they relate to individuals younger than themselves.

Usually adolescents who bully older people have unsatisfactory relationships with their own parents, and the abuse of elderly parents by their adult children is regrettably common. To some extent, young bullies demonstrate the failure of family and social processes in rearing the young. Fortunately, they are a minority.

ROLE OF THE POLICE

To a great extent in America, and to a lesser extent in England, the police are seen by adolescents as bullying symbols of authority. This difference is evident in slang names: in the United States the police are called "pigs," in England, "the fuzz." Just as the individual who bullies often does this because he feels hated and taunted by his victim, so this may be true of a bullying policeman. Furthermore, as middle-class youth comes more into contact with police forces because of driving and drug offenses, they often provoke the violence they claim to deplore. It is as though such a student represents to a young policeman all the things he could not be. The violent club-waving policeman may be, for the student, a representative of the licensed violence he craves for himself.

Adult authority may reinforce the whole bullying process by using bullying techniques, behaving like the mother who bit her child. The message that the important aspect of living is to be bigger and better in aggressive control over others is reinforced. The balance of terror that is the official policy of those nations with atomic weapons ultimately corrupts the whole of society. The two atomic superpowers both behave in an illiberal way to those young people whom they perceive as defiant; the technique, in one country, may be more effective than in the other; the difference is of degree, not kind.

PROBLEMS OF PERSONAL SELF-CONTROL

The major preoccupation in handling and coping with problems of violence in the adolescent age period for young people, their parents, and society is control of angry feelings. The amount of self-control an adolescent can show in words, as well as behavior, is assessed as a measure of maturity. However, overcontrolled adolescents are not in touch with their own feelings or their inner world of fantasy and imagination. This overcontrol may be crippling, particularly if adolescents then face additional crises:

> Carl, an eighteen-year-old boy, hid from his friends the fact that he had failed to make adequate grades in his first year of college. He was the second son of Roman Catholic parents, his older brother was something of a ne'er do well, and his older sister had disappointed his father by failing to marry by the age of twenty-four. Carl was a friendly, outgoing boy until his failure, and he was referred to a psychiatrist because his parents felt he had become increasingly withdrawn when he came home for the vacation. Carl could not understand his increasing inability to concentrate and found it hard to accept that the necessity to hide his failure was an ever-present stress for him. He also denied having time for any sexual interests but sat throughout the whole interview with his hands covering his genitalia.
>
> Despite his denial that he was bothered by any of these aspects of his personality, Carl accepted the offer of psychotherapy to "see if it will help you become freer with yourself and others," with great relief.

The amount of control expected of an individual is not just a function of personality and family style; it is also related to religious, ethnic, and national identity. The English aristocracy is preoccupied with the control of behavior, and formal gestures carrying infinite nuances of meaning; the middle class is concerned with the control of the expression of feeling.

Control may also be lost because of aberrant brain biochemistry and episodes of loss of control for this reason are not unusual (Miller, 1978).

ROLE OF THE VICTIM

It is rare for the adolescent who inflicts pain on others to seek, consciously, to have this controlled; more commonly the victim of violence seeks assistance from adults. They do this despite the adolescent pressure not to tattle to grown-ups about the behavior of others; the peer group may insist this is unmanly. A request by an adolescent boy to parents for help with bullying may therefore be an unconscious question as to how masculine they feel him to be. A too rapid attempt at rescue may imply lack of respect for the boy's manliness, suggesting that he cannot solve the problem himself; but no rescue attempt may be neglectful. Adults may perceive some adolescents as being perpetually victims. Such adolescents may have become institutional scapegoats; but, when they are, they may be in severe pesonal psychological difficulties either because they identify with the attitudes of those who attack them or because they get others to be violent towards themselves, so thus their own violence is controlled.

> Kenneth was the fourteen-year-old son of a dominant, aggressive businessman and a highly controlling mother. She dealt with his aggression at home by asking how he could hurt her so much. He was regularly scapegoated by his peers, members of an extremely unhappy group who were the victims of gross overpermissiveness in an otherwise academic school. The boy's psychiatrist was so impressed by the scapegoating that he neglected to consider the psychopathology of the victim. He arranged for the boy to change schools and, when all seemed well, he left the matter at that level.
>
> One year later, he was asked to see the boy who had made a murderous attack on a younger and weaker boy with minimal provocation. An extensive interview revealed that in his former school, the patient had been provoking aggressive attacks on himself in an attempt to control his own murderous fantasies.

When adolescents complain that they are being bullied, the usual initial adult response is masterly inactivity with appropriate empathy. As most bullying is quite transient in healthy societies, most young people survive being a passing victim of the difficulties of older and bigger adolescents. If adolescents have felt secure within their family groups, and if their life experience is not that of victim, they have to learn that all life is not fair or kind.

SOCIAL CHANGE TO ELIMINATE BULLYING

As with all symptomatic behavior, any action taken to eliminate violence should depend on an understanding of the etiology of the situation. Sometimes even the action can be mislabeled and, on occasion, group bullying can become violent because of group contagion.

> A race riot was reported in the newspaper as having occurred at a local high school. A group of black girls had verbally tormented a white girl, and, when they began to push her around, she ran away. They ran after her, and in the ensuing scuffle she was stabbed.
>
> The etiology of the outburst was multidetermined. The school was a typically structured high school with generally fragile relationships between staff and pupils. The specific event occurred because the white girl had dated a black boy. The black girls were furious with the black boys because they inflicted a double standard: black girls should only go out with black boys, but black boys could date white girls. Feeling devalued,

the girls projected their rage onto the white girl; she, in turn, had been provocative in her dating habits. The stabbing occurred because the black girls felt that carrying a knife was justified because they feared attack.

A relatively simple problem can be solved by appropriate communication with school authorities, but often episodes of bullying behavior require complex social change; otherwise, the repression of one incident will only lead to another, possibly worse incident. It is not generally helpful for a group of adolescents to be told that individuals have complained about the way one of them has been treated. With a complex etiology, control is an inadequate answer. Inappropriate physical aggression can almost be eliminated from the life of adolescents if the social climate meets the needs of most of the adolescent group.

REFERENCES

Cohn, N. (1967), *Warrant for Genocide.* London: Eyre and Spottiswood.

Eldridge, R., Sweet, R., Lade, C. R., Zegler, M., and Shapiro, A. K. (1977), Gilles de la Tourette's syndrome: Clinical, genetic, psychologic and biochemical aspects in 21 selected families. *Neurology*, 27: 115–124.

Erikson, E. H. (1968), *Identity, Youth and Crisis.* New York: Norton.

Gault, W. B. (1971), *Some remarks on slaughter. Am. J. Psychiatr.*, 128(4):82–86.

Hollander, R. (1960), Compulsive cursing. *Psychiatr. Q.*, 34:599–622.

Johnson, B. (1948), *The Lost Art of Profanity.* Indianapolis: Bobbs-Merrill.

Kinsey, A. C., et al. (1948), *Sexual Behavior in the Human Male.* Philadelphia: W. B. Saunders.

Lorenz, K. (1966), *On Aggression.* London: Methuen.

Macoby, E. E., Mathews, R. S., and Morton, A. S. (1954), Youth and political change. *Public Opin. Q.*, 18:23–29.

Miller, D. (1967), Family interaction and adolescent therapy. In *The Predicament of the Family*, ed. P. Lomas, 34–57. London: Hogarth Press.

—— (1978), Affective disorders in adolescence, mood disorders and the differential diagnosis of violent behavior. In *Mood Disorders, the World's Major Health Problems*, ed. F. J. Ayd. Baltimore: Ayd Publications.

—— (1980), Family maladaptation reflected in drug abuse and delinquency. In *Responding to Adolescent Needs*, ed. M. Sugar, 1–16. New York: Spectrum Publications.

Miller, Dan, and Swanson, G. E. (1958), *The Changing American Parent.* New York: Wiley.

Montague, M. F. A. (1961), On the physiology and psychology of swearing. *Psychiatry*, 5:189–201.

Morris, P., and Morris, T. (1963), *Pentonville, A Sociological Study of an English Prison.* London: Routledge and Kegan Paul.

Opie, P., and Opie, I. (1965), *The Lore and Language of School Children*. Oxford: Clarendon Press.

Rosenfeld, H. (1957), Psychoanalysis of the super-ego conflict in an acute schizophrenic. In *New Directions in Psychoanalysis*, eds. M. Klein, R. Money-Kyrle, and P. Heimann, 207–216. New York: Basic Books.

Ross, H. E. (1961), Patterns of swearing. *Atlas*, 1:77–78.

Scott, J. P. (1958), *Aggression*. Chicago: University of Chicago Press.

Storr, A. (1968), *Human Aggression*. London: Penguin.

Chapter 12

Regression
in Adolescence

FLIGHT MECHANISMS OF ADOLESCENTS

One technique of escaping from psychological tension that is felt to be unbearable is to take flight, either literally or by emotional withdrawal from the painful reality that provoked the internal conflict. Another is by regression, in an attempt to recreate the omnipotent pleasures of infancy. This is often sought by the use of drugs. This re-experiencing of that emotional level in which tension was not experienced is attempted as an escape from tension.

Some regressive activity is usual in adolescence and it appears as a part of the normal defensive structure of the personality. The convenient escape mechanisms of adolescents are masturbatory activity and sleep (Bateson and Mead, 1962), idleness, social isolation (Greenson, 1949), or isolation with a group of other young people. A flight into fantasy may help emotional growth; not only do imagination and fantasy protect the personality from the effects of stress, they may also provide enrichment. The inability to fantasize and daydream is a severe emotional deficit and is often associated with certain types of adolescent depression (Cytryn and McKnew, 1974).

FANTASY AND REALITY DISTORTION

Youth is a time of vivid imagination, in which the world appears new and startling. Both childhood and adolescence can be ages of fantasy (Murphy, 1947). Children up to the age of five find it difficult to separate fantasy from reality; daydreams and imaginary events are thought to have really occurred, principally because this is the age of eidetic (picture) imagery, based on past and present experiences. Adolescents still retain the capacity to distort their perceptions of the real world to avoid the experience of intolerable anxiety; what is false becomes true and vice versa. The awareness of such distortions, perceived by others as lying, varies from time to time in the adolescent. An escape technique that is common to everyone is play, particularly games involving bluff. For some, the game of bluff may become a permanent, deliberate distortion of reality; for others, it becomes an unutterable personal conviction, a lie that becomes a way of life.

"Beauty is in the eye of the beholder," and, to an extent, the reality of the world is as individuals see it. Although human beings reach a general consensus as to what the world is really like, there is a margin in which one person may see the world one way, and in a sense be accurate, whereas someone else sees it differently and is equally correct. Intuitively, all parents know this. Perhaps because they are aware of the significance of rivalry between children and their own unconscious part in it, the following story, which is typical, tends to be treated matter of factly.

> Jane, age seven, alleges that her brother John, age nine, has tripped her. This is hotly denied. Both children insist they are telling the truth. Jane says that John deliberately attempted to make her fall. John says that his sister got in the way of his foot. The stories may be contradictory, but neither child necessarily lies. John unconsciously wanted to hurt his sister and had no real remorse. Jane wants her brother to be punished by their parents. The declared innocence of the brother has validity, since he feels he was not responsible for hurting his sister.

With the birth of a younger child, the verbalizations of parents toward the older infant changes. What was previously a play/informative nurturing interaction becomes one with multiple prohibitions, "Don't do this," etc. The older child, supposedly loving the younger, acts out his or her anger in a variety of ways that tends to further prohibition. As they both grow, the younger learns techniques of setting up the older one so that the negative parent/child interaction continues.

With adolescence, children are thought by adults to know what is real and what is not. However, early adolescents, in particular, are experts in making the world as they want it to be; their preoccupation with themselves means that all reality is likely to be thought of in terms of their own wants; the preoccupation continues in those who do not satisfactorily mature psychologically past this developmental stage.

A lie can be aggressive as well as regressive, a deliberate way of alienating and attacking others. It can also be a way of deceiving the self and inferentially making the outside world punitive. The need for this is common in adolescence, as it is paradoxically easier to gain a sense of mastery over the confused feeling of perceived persecution, when one is helpless, by arranging for the world to be actually hurtful. Reality that is felt to be deliberately persecutory and unfair can be made this way. Making loving adults "bad" makes separation easier, thus this technique of relating also facilitates the autonomy struggle. Finally, adolescents easily assume that the whole world feels as they do. A youngster confronted with a misdemeanor will assume others will be as angry with him as he is with them. So young people first may project; then they lie and anxiously distort reality to avoid the punitive response, imaginary or real, of others. Of course, the lie may then convert the imaginary to the real.

Early adolescents have a highly punitive conscience, their attitudes tend to be based on the Old Testament doctrine of "an eye for an eye." Thus, the concept of punishment is highly acceptable. This also relates to the fact that, at this age, the capacity to have a mixed feeling begins to be formally internalized and ceases to depend as much on the nuclear family. Prior to early adolescence, children bring their hatreds home, these are held within the family (Winnicott, 1953), and the child is able to return to the outside world more comfortably. As adolescence is reached, although some hatred is projected into the peer group, where it may be reinforced, some must be contained within the personality.

Punishment, inflicted by loving parents, is one way children learn that ambivalence is possible—such punishment is not really necessary for control and is actually associated with parental mixed feelings. The adolescent thus identifies with the concept that punishment is necessary, especially as the process of the internalization of ambivalence begins, formally, to be consolidated. Although all actions should have consequences, tariffs of punishment, based on the needs of social organizations, whether family units or schools, inevitably produce lies in those who feel that this is safer than telling the truth.

By early adolescence, most youngsters have neither developed a firm idea as to what they would like to be like nor have they developed an acceptable social conscience. Particularly if threatened by anxiety, they may lie as part of an attempt to get away with socially inappropriate ways of meeting individual wants at the expense of others. Adolescents can be honest depending on a number of factors: their inner sense of security, how much honesty has been part of the family's way of life, and if maturation has progressed past the attitude that wishes should be immediately gratified at whatever cost. Sometimes honesty is a way of proving one's own goodness to oneself and others; the motive is to obtain affection.

DISHONESTY

Lies can be of omission—when significant facts about events are deliberately omitted—and of commission—a deliberate distortion of reality. Both types of lies may have roots in parent/child relationships. The omission lie is a deliberate attempt to protect privacy. Children ask questions and adults may then respond in three different ways: They may refuse to answer and make it clear that they are doing this; they may give a partial answer—for example, parents may decide to answer questions about sex up to the point that they feel the child will understand; finally, many appear to be answering completely, and both they and the child know that they are not. The latter is the genesis of the omission lie.

Partial truth is a typical adolescent maneuver to avoid discomfort in interpersonal relationships; it is designed to appease the other person. If further inquiry is not made, the adolescent appeases his own conscience by projection; the omission lie is now the adult's responsibility. The adolescent's attitude is that if the adult had wanted to know more, more should have been asked. Often an adolescent will use this technique to test the sensitivity of adults:

> A seventeen-year-old boy was deciding how he wanted to get a battery for his girlfriend's car. He and she had two dollars between them. He said, "I was meeting a friend in the school car park who was going to go out at lunchtime and get one for me." The interviewer said, "You mean rip one off." At this point the boy, who had been tense, obviously relaxed and began to talk of how he was still stealing.

Lies of commission when told by parents to children may be a deliberate attempt to be helpful and to avoid emotional discomfort; the predicament is apparently made easier. To run away from unpleasantness is not consciously advocated, but if adults have this attitude, explicit or not, the young identify with it. Money and sex produce adult commission lies. The failure, because of embarrassment, to be honest about the "facts" of life, leads many adolescents to distrust their parents; unconsciously they may repeat such behavior in their own families. An increased allowance may be refused on grounds of poverty, even when this is inaccurate. The conscious wish is to be helpful, but with minimal anxiety for adults. Adolescents easily sense the use of the easy way out in others; they then use this technique themselves.

DEVELOPMENT OF REALITY SENSE

The developmental reason for lies can be partially understood in the history of each child's relationship to his family. Children inevitably go through a developmental phase in which they feel that their parents are untruthful because they feel promises are made and not kept. This is related to the development of time sense (Friedman, 1944a). In infancy, there is obviously no difference between an expectation and a promise. When a baby is picked up by its mother, the action may imply to the infant the built-in expectation of being fed, it has an automatic promise of fulfillment. The child then learns, through experience, that expectation does not necessarily mean promise. However, under stress this distinction is blurred. Adolescents may not see that their own actions have an implied expectation to others, or alternately they may know that they do, but since nothing was said, there is, they claim, no dishonesty. The student who goes to his room supposedly to do homework, but who daydreams or watches television may not accept himself that his action implies dishonesty; "I did not say I was going to work." At the same time, the youngster feels that parents are unreliable if their actions do not carry the commitment the adolescent expects. This is particularly clear over issues of time. When parental promises are made on the basis that the adolescent fulfills certain commitments in order to get what is wanted: "You may drive the car providing you get a B average," begins to mean "You may drive the car." The intensity of the wish drives out the awareness of the proviso. Since adolescents may still have an uncertain sense of the past (Bradley, 1947), as well as the future (Friedman, 1944b), the situation is the same as with a much younger child. A child may ask for a toy; parents may promise "tomorrow." The child's sense of time may mean that this is felt as a commitment to obtain the gift now.

A capacity to consider the future begins to develop, in particular, between the ages of five and ten, but this capacity may disappear under stress. Under psychological pressure, adolescents have a here-and-now expectation that tension will be relieved; tomorrow then becomes a relatively meaningless concept. The concept of adult unreliability can thus be reinforced for the tense and anxious adolescent. The adolescent who justifies his own conscious unreliability on the basis that the whole world behaves that way can feel that parents, in particular, are equally unreliable. It is not until the maturational middle stage of adolescence that young people develop a time sense equivalent to that of adults. So if young people still retain aspects of early-adolescent psychology in their personalities, common nowadays with the disintegration of adequate child-rearing networks, early-adolescent attitudes about honesty and reliability persist. Apart from the problems created by personality development, many parents are not completely truthful with their children. The myth of the white lie may bedevil parent/child relationships. Insofar as the demand for truthfulness is concerned, adolescents may often feel themselves to be in a world of "Do what I say" rather than "Do what I do." The belief that trivial lies that will cause no harm are acceptable further reinforces this attitude in adolescents; inevitably, their definition of trivial differs from that of adults.

The ability to separate fantasy from reality is a quality that is slowly acquired from infancy; education toward reality is a slow process, with many reinforcements for reality distortion. The mouthing movements of babies whose hunger has not yet been appeased is the basic model for the fantasy lie designed to relieve inner feelings of discomfort and to restore a sense of psychological equilibrium. Children may experience fantasies that are so vivid that they speak of them as if they were really so. This type of lying is harmless. A critical confrontation by adults about these lies makes children give up mentioning, but not necessarily experiencing, false beliefs. In those who flee painful reality into fantasy (Menninger, 1963), fantasies may become overt lies as a way of reinforcing self-esteem. If other people believe that the adolescent is important, the world outside the self will cancel out personal feelings of inadequacy.

Almost all children go through a period of telling commission lies, usually between the ages of five and seven, because at this time a primitive harsh conscience is projected onto authority figures. The inner expectation of the child is that a bad action will be severely punished. A small girl who chastises her dolls inflicts a punishment more severe than any her parents have ever applied. This reflects the retributive fantasy behind her dishonesty.

In adolescence, the fear may not be of physical punishment as such, but rather of what adolescents fantasize others may think or say. In particular the wish is to avoid feelings of guilt and anger which parental complaints may produce. When adolescents do something they know others will disapprove of, they may lie because they do not want the disapproval put into words, a situation that leads to humiliation and loss of face. To avoid this, the adolescent may tell lies and justify this by alleging it is done to avoid being nagged.

In modern societies, adolescents who are trying to free themselves from dependent family ties nevertheless need their parents to make this possible. To enlarge the boundaries of their world, adolescents may depend on their parents to provide either transportation or money. If they are planning to do something of which they feel their parents will disapprove, they may lie in advance. Some scorn a lie, and if they cannot obtain permission for what they wish, they become openly defiant—in words if parental control is still present, in deeds if it is not. Adolescents who have parents who are honest and who are consistently felt to be loving and fair are likely to be honest themselves. Adolescents who do not like themselves (although they may be highly self-involved), who lack self-respect, who often feel hated and unloved, are likely to be consistently dishonest and deceitful, although some may be compulsively and meticulously overhonest. The occasional lie of development becomes a deceptive facade to cover the anxious feeling of being unloved, which is experienced by an inadequate personality or as an aspect of an all too common self-preoccupation; wants must be met and those with no capacity for empathy ignore the feelings of others.

CHARACTER DISTORTIONS

The etiology of the adolescent character disorder is as complex as the presentation of symptoms. The youth who has to distort the personal perception of reality or manipulate the environment to avoid the experience of psychic tension reaches puberty, but may never be psychologically adolescent. Reality distortion, when it is embraced by a child as part of his personality, means that neither valid steps to personal autonomy occur nor a true sense of self develops. There are multiple reasons for this. The infant and then the child, due to nurturing deficits, do not develop a sense of trust. Typically, such children have been excessively punished or over-indulged, have not had their needs for security and love satisfied, or have not been treated with reasonable consistency; and their sexuality as a male or a female has not been respected. Not all characterologically disturbed young people have incompetent parents. Some children have a genetic or organic hyper-sensitivity to stress. In those children who suffer from disorders of mood, depression with a genetic basis, for example, the intense psychological pain they experience under stress distorts their personality, even though parental responses are appropriate. Sometimes character distortion is reinforced because of the effect of the child's behavior on the parenting environment as well as vice versa. This is particularly evident in children whose intense hyperactivity is a function of aberrant brain biochemistry, those who suffer from juvenile manic-depressive illness for example (Nissen, G. 1971). This type of situation explains why one child of a family may suffer from a character distortion when another does not. Sometimes problems begin early because of psychosocial conflicts alone, and there is no evidence of inhibited vulnerability.

> A mother was presented by the nurse with her infant to nurse. The baby was slow to respond, the mother became anxious and the helping nurse impatient. The mother became extremely tense, and the baby responded to the change in the muscular tone with which he was being held by becoming even more balky. At the next feeding, the mother was anxious even before the baby arrived.

This type of interaction holds one genesis of difficulty between mother and child. If early attachments of mother and infant are distorted, for whatever reason, an adolescent distrustful of motives of others and unable to be close to them may be created. Such an individual may become, for example, an infantile personality or a manipulative, chronically fearful liar, who, when discovered, feels that contrition is all that is required.

Sometimes when children show recognizable emotional disturbance, parents accept an unreasonable amount of responsibility, but others manage to avoid any personal sense of guilt. As many families have members who are thought to be black sheep, it is not difficult to appeal to heredity. Sometimes blame is projected solely onto the adolescent, despite the fact that only behavior that is relatively free from unconscious conflicts can be consciously controlled with ease. Parents are often blamed by society for the antisocial activity of their adolescents, but both adults and adolescents are victims when the latter are, for example, chronic liars with no sense of trust. Adults do not know how to treat such children constructively, and the children continue to try to avoid emotional pain in a sterile and nonproductive way.

Distortion in character formation is not only due to parent/child interaction, it may be the result of social system pressures. Emotional involvement with the nuclear family does not necessarily protect children from severe chronic stress applied at nodal development points. Physical or emotional disability inflicted on the child by illness or accident may produce parent/child character distortions; an absence of social support at puberty with an introduction to drug abuse may produce an individual who looks as though he or she suffers from serious borderline personality disorganization. This is a boy or girl who does not develop an emotional sense of being independent and free of parental domination. Such children become overwhelmed with feelings, usually negative, as a response to parental actions and behave with angry negativism. The origin of this is often in the early mother/infant interaction, but the picture looks similar when, in early adolescence, there is a failure of social support for autonomy, for example, just after moving into a new neighborhood.

PERSONALITY ORGANIZATION AND SOCIAL SYSTEMS

There are many ways in which social organizations outside the family influence the development of personality. Sometimes, a double standard is forced on children in school. Children may be secure at home, honest, and trustful, but this can be spoiled by a bad school experience.

Some schools may have staff who, by their actions, convey that they do not like children and that they dislike teaching even more. In such settings, lies of commission are common, lies of omission ever-present. It is unreasonable to look on children who lie in such settings as disturbed. Their reality testing may be good, and they may lie to avoid unfair and unduly harsh punishment. The culture of the streets in underprivileged neighborhoods may force dishonesty on the young. Too often in large cities in underprivileged neighborhoods there is a combination of poor schools with harried teachers, and a rule of violence and terror in the streets. Dishonesty and fraud may then be incorporated into the personality to make personal survival possible. Adolescents must not show overt signs of anxiety if they are to survive. However loving and fair parents might be, although some extended family groups offer enough support to them to do this, it is difficult if not impossible for their offspring to beat the culture of the street. One reason for this is that children, however unconsciously, feel their parents are responsible for whatever happens. Only with adulthood do we accept that our parents are truly not omnipotent. In poor neighborhoods, quite apart from the effect of these on intra-familial interactions, children and adolescents feel that their parents are responsible for them living there. They may then lose faith in all adults, including their parents. A lack of confidence in adults makes it impossible to be honest, and distrustfulness becomes pervasive. Parents become a part of the bad, unreliable adult world, however good they may be. The behavior of teachers is partially felt by their children to be the parents' fault; they, after all, send their boys and girls to school. Only when children can really see that parents are victims, too, do they begin to forgive them.

CULTURAL REINFORCEMENT FOR DISHONESTY

The attitudes of society make it likely that adolescents will attempt to use a fantasy solution for difficulties. Politicians have brought both the omission and commission lie to a high art; they are experts at the broken promise and the distortion of truth. Adolescents in conflict about truthfulness are acutely aware of the lies told by the leaders of society. It has been said that an ambassador is a man who lies abroad for the good of his country. Before the days of the mass media this may have been of little significance; today's children and adolescents may be exposed to the lies of the establishment as they appear on television. Lies from national authority figures convey to the listening adolescents a contempt for others. So adolescents justify the dishonesty of the folk heroes of their generation: "Everyone is like that." Their social errors are widely publicized, but condoned, since society does not reinforce honesty as a virtue. Like politicians, adolescents are often selective tellers of lies. The truth may be told to members of one's own group, but it may be appropriate to tell outsiders lies. Adolescent drug-takers may boast of their honesty with each other, but tell lies to others about who deals in drugs and their own source of supply.

In many cultures, people find it difficult to be honest about feelings. In some, misery must be hidden, in others, anger. Many parents attempt to hide their differences of opinion and their mutual dislikes from their children. Such transient behavior does not necessarily impinge on children, but pseudopositive feelings confuse them. The justification often given for adult denial of angry feelings toward children is that this type of feeling is hurtful, but children may then not know what action should convey what feeling. As anger cannot be successfully hidden, a loving remark with an angry look is confusing. Although it is inevitable that most lies will be discovered, the adolescent, preoccupied with his own sense of omnipotence, hopes that magically all will turn out satisfactorily. Furthermore, since only later on in the age period does a sense of the future develop, the present lie is of no significance tomorrow.

Lies may be socially reinforced. Lying is one way of manipulating the environment to create an inaccurate image of the self in the minds of others. Some environmental manipulators are considered socially acceptable. To gain entrance to prestigious universities, adolescents go out of their way to involve themselves in extracurricular and responsibility roles in school because this will look better, along with a high grade-point average and high SAT scores. The deliberate creation of a false image is, in a sense, a lie. On the other hand, the responsibility such adolescents choose to exercise in order to be acceptable may ultimately be incorporated into their personalities. An adolescent may behave responsibly in the first place for the wrong reason, but may continue this responsible behavior when the reason for it is no longer present.

In some manipulations, truth is distorted to play one person off against another. Adolescents from homes in which parental relationships have broken down, through lack of communication, separation, divorce, or death, become experts at recreating, in all their environments, the splits and differences that were so painful to them when they were helpless victims in a nuclear family. Sometimes a parent unwittingly reinforces this technique of relationships by refusing to express an opinion and then passing the child on to the other parent.

Lying as a solitary symptom is usually fairly transient in personality development. A generally secure living environment, for most adolescents, creates a situation in which lying need only be corrected in a firm, unemotional way. Lying is not, however, the same as a refusal to speak. The latter may indicate a distrust of the motives of others, as does a lie, but it often occurs as part of a sense of loyalty—refusing to tattle on one's peers in school.

ACTIVITY AND INACTIVITY

It has long been known that variations in the level of activity of adults may be related to their emotional state. Adults who suffer from depression, for example, show disturbances of sleep, appetite, waking up in a bad mood, and a general inability to be productive. Along with this, they feel depressed and often guilty. Adolescents do not normally talk of feeling depressed, instead they talk of boredom and emptiness. A variation in activity level, sleep, and appetite and some lability of mood may all be usually present in the adolescent age period; they may, however, also be symptoms of significant, biologically caused, depression (Anthony and Scott, 1960). In the latter, adolescents typically fall asleep and are then intermittently wakeful, have no appetite until about noon and are excessively irritable until about the same time of day.

Just as fantasy has an economic function in the development of personality, so do dreams. Disturbances of personality growth may show in the exaggerated use of fantasy and its distortions, and sleep disturbances similarly appear (Iskower, 1938). At no stage of development is this more clear than with adolescents. On the one hand, adolescents daydream more than adults and seem to dream less, on the other; an almost typical and stereotyped complaint about adolescents in Western society is the extent to which they lie in bed. It is supposedly impossible to get adolescents up in the morning, their rooms are untidy, they are lazy, they turn day into night, and they are extremely inconsiderate. The external chaos with which adolescents surround themselves is both a measure of their preoccupation with themselves—they cannot be really bothered with trivia—and an expression of the internal confusion typical of the age period. Common in adolescents is a striking alteration in activity levels; extreme activity, often a flight from the dependent helplessness of sleep, alternates with profound intertia. Morning sleepiness can be caused by late nights, but it is often related to the physiology of adolescence; a maximum growth spurt is a cause of fatigue. Psychologically, a reluctance to wake up can also be a depressive disinclination to face the day. It is an emotional avoidance and withdrawal because the world can be so tormenting (Schneer and Kay, 1962). Difficulty in awakening, which can begin as a physiological event, can also be a passive way of defying parents and so fighting the struggle of dependence against independence. When an adolescent girl or boy must be awakened by a parent, when no alarm clock will work, then the refusal to get out of bed is both a provocation of mothering and a denial of its need.

Besides the obvious knowledge that human beings need a variable amount of sleep at different maturational stages, the amount an adolescent requires varies from one individual to another. Furthermore, the same individual's sleep needs vary throughout development. Active children may become slothful adolescents. By the age of four or five, most children need to sleep about twelve hours a night. This amount gradually reduces until, in adolescence, an average of seven to eight hours at night is required. Young adults may make do with less than this from time to time. Associated with the variation in the amount of sleep people need appears to be a similar variation in the ease of wakening. Women often take longer to wake than men, although long hours of sleep during the morning seem more common in boys than girls. Irritability is not rare, the first thing in the morning; family breakfasts that ought to start a happy day are often tense and miserable. Particularly during their growth spurt, many adolescents need much more than eight hours of sleep in any twenty-four-hour period; adolescents may sleep for an hour or so in the early evening. Some boarding schools rationally insist that their students have a rest period during the day.

The most usual complaint is about adolescent reluctance to get up; the most important difficulty is insufficient sleep. Insomnia usually implies not being able to get to sleep; depressed adolescents, however, may fall asleep, then wake up. The general tension of adolescence makes many of them hypervigilant and hyperemotional (Menninger, 1963), and thus, restless sleepers.

SLEEP AND ITS DISTURBANCES

In adulthood, there are some who sleep less than six hours nightly and who function well, others who always sleep nine hours or more (Hartman and Brewer, 1977). It is clear, clinically, that these patterns begin to develop in adolescence, if not earlier. In childhood, those who require less sleep, generally wake earlier in the morning, later they may go back to bed, but do not sleep. In adolescence, as youngsters become more autonomous in the family, they go to bed later. The issue is adequate functioning during the day, and it becomes increasingly clear that although some adolescents function well with less sleep, others require more.

There are two types of sleep and this becomes very evident in the adolescent age period. The so-called S-sleep is peaceful relative to waking, there are no rapid eye movements and seldom are there penile erections. The deepest portions of S-sleep occur about one hour after sleep onset, and arousal at this time may lead to bedwetting, nightmares, and night terrors (Gestant and Broughton, 1967).

D-sleep is close to arousal and is associated with rapid eye movements, and in postpubertal males, it is accompanied by full or partial penile erections. In children, it is associated with movements of small muscles, and this part of sleep is a combination of general muscular immobility with active central nervous system activity and much dreaming. One-half a newborn child's sleep is D-sleep, but only about one-sixth of an adult's. This pattern finally develops in adolescence. Nightmares occur during D-sleep. They last only a short time, are usually remembered when they occur, and adolescents are normally aware of waking up after such an episode. They are, on the one hand, an attempt to relieve tension (Dement, 1960); on the other hand, they create it. A prepubertal child will cry and need comfort from parents. Adolescents will probably comment at breakfast next morning that they had a nightmare, but usually they do not wake their parents. Nightmares are relatively rare in adolescence, although clinically there is evidence of an increase in their frequency at puberty. This is associated with the reawakening of conflicts about a child's relationship to parental sexuality, and nightmares are as common as when a child is four or five. The typical dream at that age is of being attacked by a large animal (Blos, 1962). In this oedipal period, in which children feel particularly emotionally involved with parents of the opposite sex and are rivals of the parents of the same sex, there is an unconscious wish to get rid of the competitive parent. Early-adolescent dreams may be full of extremely aggressive ideas—brains disintegrating, eyes falling out, and so on. These are ways of avoiding panic and concern about the individual being damaged himself. Technically, they are fantasies associated with an earlier anal period of development to avoid castration anxiety. Children and adolescents still function with the talion law: The jealous rage of competitive parent is symbolized by the attack they experience in the dream.

With small children, these nightmares are often resolved by the child being told fairy stories before bedtime. In their original form, before they were diluted in the twentieth century, these stories were full of the badness of parent surrogates, the weakness of good parents, and blood and brutality.

However, the stories all end happily ever after; good is triumphant and evil conquered, a subtle way of reassuring children that all will be well.

Similarly, at ages four to five, children are preoccupied with successful and safe violence; guns and bows and arrows become important for boys. Four-year-old boys may offer to chop off the hands, legs, and heads of male visitors. Reassurance from the external world and in play is not as easily available to early adolescents. Oedipal fantasies about parents must be actively repressed, and once puberty has arrived can only be played out most indirectly in action. Angry behavior is controlled by peer-group relationships, but often spills out diffusely under stress. Just before tension is relieved by considerable masturbatory activity, prior to the boy's first ejaculation, restless sleep and nightmares are relatively common.

NIGHT TERRORS AND SLEEPWALKING

Night terrors occasionally appear in adolescent girls, but they are extremely rare in boys. Even in prepubertal children, however, night terrors are relatively rare. These last much longer than nightmares (usually about twenty minutes) and occur most commonly in early childhood. While obviously asleep, a child is equally terrified and apparently hallucinating. The next day nothing is remembered.

Sleepwalking, a play in action of dreams, is uncommon. Usually it is of no significance, although it may become a persistent symptom that represents a playacting of an unconscious wish or conflict. In spite of a common fantasy, death and damage while sleepwalking, a theme of numerous novels and plays, appears not to have been reported in the scientific literature. If a young adolescent is found sleepwalking he can be led back to bed, and there is no need to awaken him. The concept that it is dangerous to wake an individual in such circumstances is notable because both nightmares and sleepwalking occur after arousal from stage four of S-sleep; when people are awakened at this time they are commonly confused. To awake a youngster who is sleepwalking would thus enhance inner confusion because he or she would awake in what seems to be confusing surroundings. Sleepwalking is most usual after severe family stress.

> Jane, age fourteen, was extremely fond of her grandmother who lived with her and her parents. She had the unhappy experience of taking her grandmother a morning cup of coffee and finding her dead in her bed. She apparently took the situation relatively well, or so it was thought, as she did not appear too disturbed. Jane, however, was referred to a psychiatrist because she began to sleepwalk to the dead grandmother's room or that of her parents.

Jane was apparently attempting to ensure that more nocturnal tragedies would not happen; it was as if she were trying to reassure herself that the death had not really happened. Since a fear of helplessness or of death is one common cause of sleep difficulties, death in the family makes adolescents fearful of their own vulnerability, particularly when they are helpless and asleep. Menninger (1963) reports the case of a young woman who used to sleepwalk to her parents' room as part of a retaliation against them.

In many adolescents, anxiety precipitated during the day may provoke a situation in which the youngster wakes in the middle of the night and gets up for no apparent reason; this is usually to check that everything is safe in the house. Similarly, some obsessional adolescents need to check that bedroom windows are locked and that bedroom doors are open; they will then be safe.

Sleeptalking is quite common, but it is rare for a listener to hear clearly what is said, despite the common idea that secrets are given away because of sleeptalking. The idea behind this fantasy is that the pent-up tensions of the day are released at night.

Most sleep problems are temporary and are usually ignored or handled with reassurance. Persistent sleep difficulties in a tense, worried, unhappy adolescent may be an indication of a significant, biologically based depression. Like adults, the depressed adolescent falls asleep and then has difficulty in remaining asleep. Some sleep excessively, but this can also be related to rapid growth or be a way of escaping from a potentially unpleasant emotional experience. Most commonly, sleep disturbances in adolescents are due to situational stress. Specific crises may be occurring, or adolescents may overreact to day-to-day routine difficulties.

INSOMNIA

Insomnia is the most common sleep difficulty of adolescents; it is usually the type associated with a difficulty in falling asleep. It may go back to infancy and childhood, but most commonly in adolescents nowadays, it is due to drug and alcohol abuse. There is no indication in adolescence for the use of sleeping pills as a remedy for insomnia. Insomnia may also be related to habit. Adolescents who are not offered appropriate external control may interfere with their own sleep patterns either with apparently socially acceptable activity, such as a preoccupation with homework, or unreasonable behavior, such as excessive partying on weekends. In small children, insomnia often seems to be associated with general negativism and a bedtime battle with parents. Children may dilly-dally and be reluctant to go to bed or they may find it difficult to sleep or both. Parents often feel, angrily, that going to bed behavior has become a technique of getting attention. So an inability to go to bed or fall asleep may be associated with patterns of interaction set up between parents and child over a long period. This is most common with the oldest child in a family. Parents with a first child are often overanxious. Without child-rearing experience, they may overreact to minor child-rearing difficulties. Many new parents are not sure that all is well either when their child is quietly asleep or when it cries. A child may cry, and someone rushes to lift it out of bed. Parents may then show the child off to friends and relatives. So when the child wakes at night, or even when it is asleep, it may be brought to be cuddled and admired. An association of wakefulness at night with parental attention is thus reinforced. Sleep patterns may similarly be disturbed because children over three or four months of age are moved while asleep when babysitters are unavailable. The child may awaken and be frightened by strange surroundings. A transitional object (Winnicott, 1953), a well-loved teddy bear or other comforter, may allay this anxiety, but sleep difficulties can be created because of the ease of modern transportation. A child is moved and is then expected either to fall—or stay—asleep in new and strange surroundings.

The inability to sleep satisfactorily in some children may carry an implicit demand to be reassured and cuddled. Sometimes parents respond by taking the child to their own bed. Some children may sleep with their mothers for a very long time, but in most societies, this type of child-rearing continues to make an infant out of a child. A child may wake in order to go to the parental bed. One or the other parent may then be ejected from the marital bed by the sleeplessness of the child. By puberty, in Western culture, it is inappropriate for children to share their parents' bed at any time. The continued demand of a pubertal boy or girl to do this means that the adolescent cannot abandon a wish to be babied. It also implies an unconscious preoccupation with the sexuality of either or both parents.

This is not true in some cultures. In rural Ireland, all the family may still sleep together in one room; this also occurs in many poverty-stricken areas of the West. In these circumstances, the child may sleep cuddled up to siblings of either sex and to the parents. Such an individual is obviously exposed to the awareness of parental sexuality, but fantasies about this are obviously corrected by the frequency of the occurrence and the fact that everyone is alive and well the next morning. In primitive cultures, at puberty, children brought up in this way are moved away to special huts or they may be given a great deal of sexual freedom with members of both sexes through childhood, so any anxiety or curiosity about sexuality can be worked out through play. Any tensions inside an individual that are created by an awareness of parental sexuality can be played out in action. Cultures such as those of the peasants of southern Ireland, which do not allow any sexual freedom outside of matrimony, cause problems for their children. They are emotionally stimulated with an awareness of sexual activity, but are given no opportunity to play out tensions in action under a socially acceptable umbrella. This may partially explain the violence, alcoholism, sexual puritanism, and prurience that are common in this culture (Messanger, 1971).

The equation of bed with punishment may also be the cause of difficulty to children and adolescents either in going to bed or in sleeping. If children are felt by their parents to behave in socially unacceptable ways, it may be appropriate punishment to send them to a room to isolate them from the rest of the family. If children are locked in their bedrooms or sent to bed as punishment, such action may produce children who need to have their door open before they can go to sleep, or going to bed may become associated with parental rejection and guilt.

Sleep difficulties in children may be related to implicit and explicit family attitudes around resting. Parents may demand that everyone whisper because a nap is being taken: an association between sleep and quiet is then reinforced. Quiet may be insisted on because "baby is asleep." Thus, hypersensitivity about noise and sleep is created both in the infant and the other siblings. Parents may say that, because of some anxiety, they "didn't sleep a wink." This is rarely accurate, but a family may then relate sleep to feelings of well-being, and a child may identify with these attitudes. Sleeplessness in word and deed is therefore used both to get attention and to show anxiety. In adolescents with a long history of insomnia, the roots of the difficulty sometimes can be found in those interactive experiences of early childhood. However, there are much more usual causes. If children and adolescents are allowed a fluctuating bedtime, this can cause insomnia. A failure to offer reasonable security about the time of going to bed can cause sleep difficulties, and battles about going to bed are then invited. Whether or not this happens, adolescents almost inevitably use bedtime as an area of conflict with their parents. The battle of dependence against autonomy is fought as much at night as it is in the morning. The child may assess his parents' giving him more adult status by the demand for just another five minutes. Because of the implicit meaning of the request, it inevitably and insidiously slips into a demand for more and more minutes. Particularly in early adolescence, bedtime demands mirror the problems between parent and child.

The adolescent battle over bedtime is not unlike the mealtime battle of earlier childhood. It is a way in which a child can successfully defy his parents. A small child can begin to dominate the household by refusing to go to bed until the father comes upstairs or mother comes up to read to him. The boy or girl may insist that milk or food be given, that the door be left open, that the light be left on in bedroom or hallway. In themselves, these can be quite minor demands to make on parents, and many children need one or the other before they can settle down at night. If too many bedtime rituals are insisted on, an obvious attempt is being made to exercise control over parents. Similarly, as a child gets older, it is not unusual to try to delay bedtime because of the necessity of going to the toilet at the last minute or the need for "forgotten" homework to be done. Around the issue of sleep, in which control over the self is abandoned, parents may lose control of their child. A time extension is a way in which children are shown that growth is known to be taking place, but the anxious thrust of early adolescents to take more responsibility than they can handle often makes firmness necessary. Boys may need their fathers' insistence that they go to bed. The symbolic struggle that may then take place can be an early-adolescent boy's way of having his manhood respected just before the dependence of lying down and going to sleep is on him.

> Fourteen-year-old Peter was told by his parents that he could stay up until 10:30 p.m., as the family had company for dinner. At 10:40 p.m. his mother told him to go to bed. He totally ignored her request. She told him again and then appealed to the boy's father. Peter said, when his father told him to go, "Make me." With great good humor and firmness, Peter's father wrestled with him on his way to bed.

This typical family interaction conveyed many messages and had many possible implications. If Peter's mother had forced him to go to bed with father doing nothing—apart from unconscious incestuous fantasies that might be aroused by this—the family attitude that could have been conveyed was that the father respected neither the boy nor his mother. Alternately, it could be assumed that the father is afraid to support the boy against the mother or vice versa. Peter would be unlikely to feel that his manhood is valued. When the father intervened in the way he did, this control enhanced Peter's feeling that his manhood was valuable and that his father could control his impulsive (and forbidden) wishes and behavior.

A variation in bedtime according to chronological age is significant to adolescents. Older children, particularly in the early and middle stages of adolescence, need to see their younger brothers and sisters go up to bed before they themselves go; otherwise, they feel that they are not being given status their age justifies.

Merely going to a bedroom does not mean going to bed. Early adolescents may appear to go to bed fairly easily, but then they daydream in their rooms for long periods of time before getting into bed. This is partly a subtle defiance of parental authority, but bedtime is also that time of day during which adolescent fantasy is likely to be most intense. It is partly a flight from the regressive experience of sleep that may also be felt as a threat to personal self-sufficiency.

Sleeplessness in children and adolescents can be associated with severe anxiety. Those who suffer from obsessional thinking may experience a turning of thoughts over and over about one or another problem with the approach of a fatigue. Thus, such individuals may find it difficult to fall asleep.

SEXUALITY AND SLEEP DIFFICULTIES

Only those adolescents who are brought up with religious teaching that masturbation is sinful, or by parents who were overanxious about infantile sexuality, are likely to be anxious about this act. Boys who have trouble about masturbation may find difficulty in falling asleep. This is because self-control is weakened in the half-sleep/half-awake stage that precedes full sleep; anxiety about performing the act may lead a boy to stay awake until he becomes so fatigued that sleep is finally immediate. Masturbation in association with weakened personality controls is then unlikely. This anxiety should always be thought of as a possibility in boys who suffer from sleeplessness. Sometimes it is not the behavior as such, but rather the possible masturbatory fantasy that causes anxiety, particularly in those youngsters who have conflicts about homosexuality. Boys may also be concerned about dreams with a sexual and aggressive content, especially those in which they associate sadistic behavior with sexual excitement. Sometimes to avoid the experience of merely lying awake, adolescents may read or listen to the radio until three or four in the morning.

Toward the latter part of mid-adolescence, often at sixteen or so, when parents have stopped sending their children to bed, transient sleep difficulties may occur. The adolescent is being told in action that he is adult enough to make decisions about sleeping. This threshold of adult responsibility may arouse enough anxiety to make sleep difficult. There are, however, other possible causes of mid- to late-adolescent sleeplessness. The sixteen- or seventeen-year-old adolescent is now likely to be fully mature physically. If family relationships are strained, if the family is isolated from a network of other human beings, adolescents may be lonely. Sleeplessness may then be associated with the problems of sleeping alone.

Lonely adolescents may have an intense need for physical contact. This is evident by the fact that middle-stage adolescents will sit very close to adults of whom they are fond. They do not use physical distance in the same way adults do. When they go to bed, physically mature, middle-stage adolescents and late adolescents who are emotionally well balanced, are ready for sexual partners, not just for sexual intercourse and love-making, but also for sharing a bed. Children who are lonely and anxious may not be able to fall asleep until they are cuddled, either literally or emotionally, by one or another parent. An adolescent with the body of a young adult needs cuddling from a sexual partner. Today it is very common for young people to be emotionally and sexually lonely. Day-to-day stresses, the increased social pressures of early puberty, the attainment of physical maturity by the age of sixteen or seventeen—all these mean that many young people often crave not just sex but also a close, loving heterosexual relationship.

SITUATIONAL CAUSES FOR INSOMNIA

Sleeplessness in adolescents can be caused by a variety of acute, anxiety-provoking situations: physical illness, examinations and tests, academic and athletic competitiveness, conflicts over money, and sexuality. It may occur after long-distance air travel; jet lag disturbs the built-in time clocks of individuals. A most common cause of disturbed sleep patterns is associated with drug abuse. The alternating use, particularly on weekends, of stimulants and sedatives (speed and downers) by some adolescents disturbs sleep rhythm for two or three days at a time, and is particularly likely with those adolescents who attempt to stay up all night on weekends. Stimulants taken in very high doses may disturb the usual sleep rhythm. A poor appetite on the weekend in a pale, fatigued, irritable adolescent who does not sleep well may indicate that a stimulant drug is being used.

The proper treatment of sleep difficulties is not by the use of sedatives. These are usually prescribed because it is easier to offer sedatives than to deal with the general conflicts in the personality or the life situation of an adolescent. Furthermore, the general drug-taking of the adolescent age group is often a type of self-medication. If sedatives are then offered by the medical profession to solve emotional problems, it is not surprising if adolescents choose to medicate themselves with any of the drugs that illegally circulate.

In younger children and in adolescents, daytime hyperactivity may be associated with sleeplessness. Excessive reality demands are a not unusual cause of sleeplessness in children and adolescents: excessive homework; overcritical teachers and overanxious parents; dangerous neighborhoods; physical deprivation; peer-group tensions; and unhappy love affairs. These should be considered first as a reason for adolescent sleep difficulties.

Many of the transient upsets of adolescents occur as the result of day-to-day pressures on the individual. If these can be understood, and if the young person is offered emotional support, or the stress is removed, most upsets will subside, especially in a stable, loving family. The problem, if the cause of sleep difficulties is not known, is whether a policy of masterly inactivity should be pursued or whether more active intervention is required. Sleep difficulties lasting more than a few days are almost always an indication that specific assistance should be sought; and it should be directed toward the causes, not the symptomatic relief of sleeplessness with sedatives and/or minor tranquilizers.

REFERENCES

Anthony, E. J., and Scott, P. (1960), Manic-depressive psychosis in childhood. *J. Child Psychol. Psychiatr.*, 1:53.

Bateson, G., and Mead, M. (1942), *Balinese Character*. New York: New York Academy of Sciences.

Blos, P. (1962), *On Adolescence*. Glencoe, Ill.: Free Press.

Bradley, N. C. (1947), The growth of the knowledge of time in children of school age. *Br. J. Psychol.*, 65:197–217.

Cytryn, L., and McKnew, D. H. (1974), Factors influencing the changing clinical expression of the depressive process in children. *Am. J. Psychiatry.* 131:879.

Dement, W. C. (1960), The effect of dream deprivation. *Science*, 131:1705–1707.

Friedman, K. C. (1944a), Time concepts of elementary school children. *Elem. Sch. J.*, 44:337–342.

——— (1944b), Time concepts of junior and senior high school pupils and of adults. *Sch. Rev.*, 52:233–238.

Gestant, H., and Broughton, R. A. (1967), A clinical and polygraphic study of episodic phenomena during sleep. *Recent Adv. in Bio. Psychiatr.*, 7:197.

Greenson, R. (1949), The psychology of apathy. *Psychoanal. Q.*, 18:290–302.

Hartmann, E., and Brewer, V. (1976), When is more or less sleep required. A Study of Variable Sleepers. *Comprehens. Psychiatr.*, 12:275.

Iskower, O. (1938), A contribution to the psychopathology of phenomena associated with falling asleep. *Int. J. Psycho-Anal.*, 19:331–345.

Menninger, K. A. (1963), *The Vital Balance*. New York: Viking. pp. 138–139, 177–180.

Messanger, J. C. (1971), Sex and repression in an Irish community. In *Human Sexual Behavior*, eds. D. S. Marshall and R. C. Suggs, 3–38. New York: Basic Books.

Murphy, G. (1947), *Personality: A Biosocial Approach to Origin and Structure*. New York: Harper and Brothers. pp. 391–405.

Nissen, G. (1971), *Das Depressive Syndrom in Kindes-und Jugenalter*. Berlin: Springer.

Schneer, H. I., and Kay, P. (1962), The suicidal adolescent. In *Adolescents, Psychoanalytic Approach to Problems and Therapy*, eds. S. Lorand and H. L. Schneer, 180–201, New York: Paul Hoeber.

Winnicott, D. W. (1953), Transitional objects and transitional phenomena. *Int. J. Psycho-Anal.*, 31:89–97.

PART III

DISTURBANCES
AND THERAPY

Chapter 13

Psychological Disturbances of Adolescence and Their Treatment

As the biopsychosociological determinants of emotional difficulties become clear, it is slowly becoming more possible to diagnose the causes of such adolescent disturbances adequately. The nature of the symptoms varies, depending upon the adolescent's social environment, but those of an aggressive and regressive nature are, to an extent, culture free. Behavioral symptoms become the final common path of an attempt to relieve tension. Most labels applied to adolescent maladjustments are inadequate (Masterson, 1967; DSM III, 1980). They do not really indicate separate personality problems; effectively, they pick out symptom clusters. They do not represent specific illnesses as do medical labels, nor do they generally indicate the kind of help an adolescent might need. Some personality problems that appear at puberty, because of a combination of social stress and physiological turbulence, indicate that development into psychological adolescence is not taking place; many personality problems typically appear in adolescence—for example, anorexia nervosa. As well as indicating an inability to master the tasks of this age period, they inhibit further emotional development and produce a regression to more childlike attitudes.

Most typically, the disturbances of adolescence appear as a behavioral defiance of social norms. Society is preoccupied with a triad of socially defined antisocial behavior: sex, drugs, and delinquency. Although disturbed adolescents inflict pain on their environment, this does not mean that they themselves do not experience psychic pain. Nevertheless, particularly in early adolescence, it is almost always the pain that is inflicted upon others that produces the request for help. Most usually, pre-existing personality disturbance emerges during adolescence because more adult demands begin to be made on the personality. There is an imbalance between the stresses and supports provided by the family and the total environment as they are perceived by the young person, who then attempts to minimize the effects of this stress by a variety of defensive moves within the personality.

APPEARANCE OF DISTURBANCE

Emotional difficulties appear either at the height of the pubertal period, just after the period of maximum growth; at the beginning of the middle period of adolescence, the start of the period of identity consolidation; or at the beginning of late adolescence, a time of coping. These three peaks are generally in the middle of junior high school, at the beginning of senior high school, or toward the end of that experience, at the beginning of a university career, respectively. Some last until psychosocial adulthood finally appears, at the end of the long moratorium provided for complex roles in society. At a time of internal stress, there is anxiety in having to face a new situation, and breakdown is more likely to occur. Among those who are likely to take part in antisocial behavior, usually nonacademic adolescents, the severity of disorders of conduct peaks in the six months before the possible school-leaving age of sixteen.

Young people who leave school at sixteen, live in large cities, and have insufficient personality strength and inadequate support from without, had an unduly high job-turnover rate when there were some societies with full employment; nowadays they fail to find work. There is an increase in referral for psychological help in the six months before adolescents leave school to seek higher education or in the first six months of a college career. Students are often under such pressure to attain academic success that their emotional growth is retarded. They may break down in their first year at the university or during their last two semesters, when they are threatened by real life, when there are no further external supports able to offer a socially acceptable outlet for dependent needs.

THE EFFECT OF PSYCHOLOGICAL DISTURBANCE ON MATURATION

In trying to help adolescents in distress, the causes of disturbance within society, the family, and the individual have to be understood if damage is to be repaired. The nature of the adolescent's symptoms affect both the developing personality and the ease with which assistance can be successful. Antisocial behavior is often exciting and gratifying. Further, the distortions that disorders of behavior inflict on the world change the way it is perceived. One boy will insist that everyone smokes pot, another that the whole world is dishonest. Since the way the world is perceived partially influences the development of personality, a symptom that began as an attempt either to avoid the experience of frustration or to solve an internal conflict perpetuates itself. Adolescents need to feel that the world is consistent if they are to develop their identity; thus, they will attempt to keep their world consistent. Disturbed youngsters surround themselves with people similar to themselves, which allows them to continue to misperceive the nature of the environment. Further, maladjustment tends to produce a world that is felt as highly persecutory; the negative reactions aroused by disturbed behavior are painful to the adolescent. To deal with this, they are internalized and a personality that both torments and is tormenting is likely to be produced.

Thus, adolescent psychological disturbances affect the development of identity, that conscious sense of individual uniqueness that is meaningful in terms of past experience and is consonant with how one appears to others (Erikson, 1968). Those adolescents who cannot establish this sense of being in a way that they feel is satisfactory have no sense of solidarity with their world. They often see themselves only as part of a social out-group. Of necessity, the attachment to this is quite tenuous. Symptom clusters in adolescence may not allow identity formation to occur, and often the symptoms worsen as they are used to solve the empty desolation associated with confusion as to one's sense of being a person.

A goal in working with adolescents in whom identity formation does not take place is to assist them develop a sense of an autonomous self. The goal of the young person, however, is relief from chronic tension.

The helping adult must, in addition to this goal, assist the youngster in coping with necessary developmental tasks: being successful in school; dealing with frustration in ways such that present actions do not destroy future opportunities; being empathic to the needs of others and respecting their integrity.

IDENTITY CRISES

Adolescents suffering from an identity crisis may show their difficulties in impulsive behavioral ways. They are often filled with diffuse rage against their parents, whom they may perceive as highly invasive of their personalities. Impulsive acts of destruction may be directed at family property, often that belonging to their mothers. They may steal with little obvious gain, and they are usually caught. They may make suicidal gestures (Lewin, 1950) or enter willingly into sexual promiscuity or drug abuse. An identity crisis does not necessarily imply a pervasive failure to develop a personality; it may accompany developmental disturbances at adolescence. As is so often the case, the severity of the disturbed behavior does not necessarily imply an equally disturbed personality, at any rate a deeply disturbed one. On the other hand, the first evidences of a seriously disturbed personality may appear as an identity crisis, because the adolescent has been unable to make meaningful emotional attachments to individuals outside the nuclear family. Most usually, the more immature personality shows itself in a diffuse inability to make decisions.

The symptoms of personality disorder are often very similar to those found in a crisis of identity. The difference is in the ease of resolution and the length of the history. A failure of adequate emotional development that begins in childhood is always found in disturbances of character formation.

IDENTITY DIFFUSION

Some adolescents suffer from *chronic identity diffusion*. They are unable to settle on a vocational choice, or even whether to be generally academic. They cannot commit themselves to a sexual role, and, even if they seem to be involved with others sexually, their sexual activity is both masturbatory and self-centered. They have major problems trusting other people.

Adolescents who suffer in this way easily abandon any sense of self they might have. They are particularly vulnerable to group contagion (Redl, 1942), and seem prepared to abandon anything that conveys an awareness of their own special individual uniqueness. The drug scene particularly appeals to such young people, but even without this, they fail to fulfill their academic or vocational potential. Often they feel unable to make meaningful emotional contacts with anyone. They may have intercourse, but they do not make love. The most common cry of such young people is "Who am I?," "What am

I?," "What do I want?" Sometimes they complain of a feeling of complete emptiness.

In chronic identity diffusion, adolescents are likely to experience acute confusional states that are often misdiagnosed as a schizophrenic reaction. If this happens, and the youngster is placed in a typical psychiatric hospital in which a socially aberrant way of life is apparent, the adolescent may then affectively withdraw and appear more disturbed than is actually the case. Some may appear as drug or alcohol abusers and be labeled as chemically dependent; others may be caught in antisocial behavior and be deemed delinquent; these labels are then adopted as a description of the self; they are an answer to "Who am I?."

THERAPEUTIC ASSISTANCE FOR IDENTITY PROBLEMS

In social systems that allow meaningful emotional contact with other human beings, both peers and extraparental adults, most adolescents with a problem of identity formation can be significantly helped by an understanding adult who does not have formal training in psychotherapy. However, if identity difficulties are caused by early damage to the personality, important emotional attachments are difficult, if not impossible, and specially trained therapists in therapeutic settings may be necessary. In social systems, therapeutic or not, adolescents who suffer from identity diffusion often test out the value of other people by antisocial behavior designed to assess whether they are really cared about. The problem is that such an adolescent is overinvolved with his own tenuous sense of self, but he does not like or love himself. In order to be able to do this, he first has to introject and then incorporate the image of a loving other. To establish the value of this individual, he has to behave in antisocial ways, both to ensure that the other person is powerful enough to control violence and that the violent behavior will not lead to rejection; only then can love be felt and be relied upon. The distrust is not the distrust of paranoia; it is based on an assumption that one cannot possibly be cared about. Thus, the motives of others become highly suspect and must be tested and retested.

These difficulties are present in the therapy of adolescents. In one-to-one situations, their anxious hostility has to be understood and interpreted. In social therapy, similar distrust is likely to be initially present.

In psychotherapy, there are particular problems around its termination. On the one hand, a therapist should not fight adolescents' wishes to try out a new kind of identity for themselves when they wish to leave therapy; on the other, if therapy is abandoned too quickly, the identity problems recur. The issue is whether a desire to leave therapy is real because the adolescent wishes to test out the strength of a new personality, or whether it is to determine love—"If you loved me you would not let me go."

ANXIETY DISORDERS OF ADOLESCENCE

Some symptoms are an attempt to resolve the anxiety associated with internal conflict (Josselyn, 1954). For example, the anxious child who does not want to leave home because he is afraid of what might happen to his parents when he is away, but who wishes to go to school at the same time, may develop an irrational fear of attending school, a school phobia. Except for an acute stress response, crippling anxiety responses do not occur in an otherwise healthy personality. By the time puberty is reached, since most adolescents are not primarily fearful of leaving their mothers, school refusal is more common than school phobia. Typically, there is reluctance to go to school after the weekend.

It is impossible to conclude that specific conflicts always lead to specific symptoms. What appears depends on the psychosocial environment and the personality development of the youngster. A conflict about becoming autonomous of mother, with unconscious hostility about a fear of leaving her, with its consequent oversolicitous parenting, may appear as drug abuse in some, school phobia in others. The essential difference is in treatment; disorders of conduct tend to be consciously or unconsciously gratifying. Irrational fears and obsessional thinking, when the adolescent is preoccupied with a thought he cannot get out of his head, may be felt as painful. The individual may have to repeat an action to an extent that may seriously inconvenience his life—going back to see whether the light has been turned off, making sure doors are closed, arranging clothes in a specific way. Most such difficulties will not be resolved without expert diagnosis as to other causes and then specific therapy, however youth workers and teachers can certainly help such young sufferers by accepting that they have difficulties, but expecting the performance of which they are capable.

These difficulties always come to involve the whole family, and it is inconceivable to attempt individual psychotherapy, up until the time children leave home, without involving the parents, and to some extent other siblings. Such family treatment alone is generally as unsatisfactory as individual therapy alone; the importance of each in successful treatment depends on a diagnostic decision as to whether one or the other is to be emphasized.

PHYSICAL ILLNESS AND PERSONALITY DEVELOPMENT

Long-standing physical problems that appear in childhood or in adolescence affect the adolescent's perception of himself, his relationship to the world-at-large, and intra-familial relationships. Sometimes the pubertal growth spurt worsens the condition. Thus, spastic children who manage on crutches prior to puberty may be confined to wheelchairs when the growth spurt occurs, since they can no longer sustain their heavier body. Sometimes psychosomatic symptoms interfere with physical development; the girl who suffers from anorexia nervosa may retard her own growth if the syndrome occurs before the growth spurt.

The difference in response to chronic illness in childhood and adolescence are demonstrated in the way prepubertal children and adolescents handle such illnesses as diabetes mellitus and epilepsy. Diabetics, in childhood, are forced to be overdependent on their parents because insulin has to be administered by father or mother. Sensitive pediatric care ensures that such children are taught to give themselves insulin prior to puberty, so that when puberty is reached, the battle of autonomy need not be fought by a refusal to take insulin. Since the emotional involvement of the parents is likely to continue, this refusal may still occur, despite early teaching of a technique. So good care delivery ensures that the child has a long-term relationship with the same physician and nursing staff. Otherwise, diabetic adolescents have a self-destructive weapon they are likely to use to provoke parental anxiety, make them feel impotent, and be death-defying.

Similar conflicts appear in epileptic children and adolescents. Epileptics who have usually been given their medication by their parents have particular difficulties. Control is a crucial issue during adolescence, so medication may be refused as part of the adolescent's wish to test his own controls: Can life be managed without medication? This is felt as particularly important, since adolescents with epilepsy have the hidden anxiety that they may have a seizure during sexual intercourse. Just as with diabetics, the adolescent epileptic may also refuse medication as part of an autonomy struggle with parents.

Physicians involved in the care of these illnesses need to be felt as supportive extra-parental adults, but if they take on a parental role, they are equally likely to be defied. If a physician to whom a youngster has become attached leaves without giving the boy or girl a chance to understand and deal with the painful effect of such separation, a worsening of symptoms, or an increased balkiness in the youngster, is likely to be seen.

A number of physical conditions have a strong psychological component, and what used to be considered a "resistance" to infection is certainly related to emotional stress. The great psychosomatic syndromes of adolescence include bedwetting and anorexia nervosa, but chronic physical symptoms without organic cause are the most common indications of emotional upset in adolescents. Fatigue or vague physical ill health of no known etiology often indicate that adolescents are not coping successfully with psychological stress. Chronic tics, including nail-biting, indicate an anxious youngster who may easily become tense even though stress is minimal.

Asthma is a disease with many subtypes and although, as a chronic illness, it always affects prsonality development, not all asthma is psychosomatic. Further, conflict cannot be considered a cause of asthma because many adolescents with similar conflicts do not get this disease. It would appear probable that just as some adolescents "come down with" behavioral symptoms as a result of biopsychological stress, others, who are genetically vulnerable, have physical symptoms. The most typical symptom clusters associated with psychological causes include such diseases as migraine, juvenile rheumatoid arthritis, an irritable colon, and eczema. Functional constipation is typically associated with early problems of bowel training, and ultimately it can result from a parent/child interaction over bowel function. It is also not uncommon in adolescents who suffer from depression in which the principal etiology is biological vulnerability.

A common skin disease of adolescence is acne, but it would appear that the incidence of this may be decreasing as non-endocrinological factors seem to be attenuating—adolescents nowadays are generally cleaner and wash more frequently than their predecessors. Many are also more secure about masculine identity, as a result of the currently more sensible attitude toward sexuality.

Accidents are the commonest cause of physical deformity in adolescents. The lethal combination is the automobile and alcohol and drugs. Permission to drive is given before many adolescents have a firm sense of their own body in space, and thus are able to sense intuitively the spatial boundaries of the vehicle they are driving in. Motorcycles may legally be driven in some states without protective helmets and clothing; lack of this protection leads to an excessive number of young people who suffer from major paralysis and brain damage; they become a major human, public health, and economic problem to themselves, their families, and society.

Some adolescents become permanently physically deformed following accidents, but the degree of deformity may allow apparently near normal functioning. Facial scars, however, may lead to excessive social withdrawal, but adolescents with bodily scars initially may appear to deny their significance. Those who require an artificial limb may in a remarkable way engage in physical activities. However, anxiety symptoms commonly appear in late adolescence, when many of these young people seem impelled to avoid sexuality, because they feel they will appear unlovely to a sexual partner; this is a problem for boys as much as it is for girls.

> Kenneth, a seventeen-year-old boy, was severely burned in an accident involving a high-tension electrical cable. The accident occurred when he was with two friends: one was killed; one had a bilateral leg amputation; and Kenneth was severely burned around his buttocks. He also had a below-the-knee amputation of one leg.
>
> From being an outgoing boy with an active social life, Kenneth became quiet and withdrawn. His parents persuaded him to see a psychiatrist as they became concerned about his bitterness and what they felt was the excessive use of marijuana. In the course of therapy Kenneth said, "I can't stand to look at myself in a mirror. What do you think a girl would think if she saw my leg and ass?"

Once-weekly therapy, in which Kenneth talked freely of his undesirability to girls and was helped to see it as a projection of his own feelings about himself, led to a reduction in marijuana smoking and an improvement in his schoolwork. He found a girlfriend; the first time he had intercourse he kept his prosthesis on; he was then, on other occasions, able to remove it.

THERAPEUTIC INTERVENTION

The intervention of the sensitive adult, when young people suffer acute trauma, can be remarkably useful to the adolescent. Caring adults need to be perceptive about the underlying conflicts of the lives of the physically damaged young, and to work with them in a way that respects individual integrity. Adolescents need to be able to express their grief, anger, loss, and sense of unfairness. The initial optimism and denial present in the first weeks after serious trauma, in which the youngster seems to have a magical expectation of recovery, is very helpful in the rehabilitation process. This is usually followed not by a direct expression of feeling, but rather by a variety of actions that demonstrate the adolescent's impotent despair: a refusal to cooperate, irrational anger, intense withdrawal. This is the time when sensitive intervention to assist the youngster come to terms with his or her situation is crucial. Families too need assistance, otherwise they may collude in reinforcing the adolescent's sense of helplessness rather than the reverse. A crucial stage occurs after a youngster leaves the hospital, and the failure to provide adequate psychological assistance at this time may mean that massive efforts at physical rehabilitation may be wasted because of an inadequate follow-through of assistance. Surgeons and their staffs involved with injured adolescents need to be knowledgeable about adolescent psychology and the psychological techniques needed to make rehabilitation work.

Parents should discuss the problems of adolescence, as they affect the behavior of the child with a chronic illness, with a pediatrician or family practitioner, prior to puberty. As soon as feasible, children need to be given responsibility for their own medication, which becomes something the doctor discusses with the child. Anxiety about sexuality needs to be appropriately considered. Reassurance should not be facile, but neither should an iatrogenic anxiety be produced by telling the youngster of things he might worry about. If physicians or others have a good general relationship with the adolescent, this is the background against which concerns about chronic illness can be discussed. Dermatologists who indicate willingness to discuss the life of adolescents with them, rather than only look at their pimples, are enormously appreciated.

SEXUAL DIFFICULTIES

Sexual difficulties appear during adolescence. For example, some boys still worry about masturbation or the fantasies that go with it. They may fear that they will not be potent or that there is something wrong with them physically, but they are often reluctant to mention these fears to anyone. Sometimes they feel that the persistence of this act means that they are immature. A similar situation occurs when boys in mid-adolescence become anxious about homosexual feelings. Usually such boys are not sexually excited by the sight of another boy's body; the real issue is one of identity, with the implicit question as to whether one is sufficiently manly.

Promiscuity is a typical symptom of emotional deprivation and depression in both boys and girls. Many depressed boys who have been reared without fathers reach puberty with the concept that a man's role is to impregnate and then abandon. One three-year-old boy of a single parent, when asked what men do, said "sleep over with my mom." This, combined with a need for physical cuddling, along with a concept that masturbation as a self-solacing activity is unacceptably infantile, may lead to a wish for unprotected intercourse. Promiscuous intercourse in girls seems related to a wish to estalish a feeling of wholeness. The relationship is with someone who holds and cuddles, not with a boy as a person, but with a part of his body. A girl takes the boy's penis into her vagina as the infant sucks its thumb. Such individuals are often very demanding with their boyfriends—as clinging as an infant to its mother. The boyfriends of promiscuous girls may feel that their girls try to control them. Unsure of their own masculinity and quite self-referrent, they are unable to tolerate the neediness of their sexual partners. Even if the relationship lasts for a time, the boy withdraws if the girl becomes pregnant. In any case, a girl is liable to be rejected because the boy begins to feel that even the act of intercourse does not justify her demands upon him. The girl's fear of rejection promotes her rejection.

Adults who wish to help adolescents with sexual difficulties have particular problems. Sexually disturbed young people often find talk about their sexual activities gratifying and sexually stimulating, as can be observed from their appearance. Youngsters assume a rather glazed expression, or they may start to shift uncomfortably in their chair. Sometimes adolescents are brought to doctors by their parents, or they come themselves. Since sexuality is used developmentally as a way of asserting privacy and separateness, therapists in such situations cannot tell parents why their children seek help. The young people themselves have to decide what their parents should be told, although in action, therapists cannot take sides against parents by colluding in silence.

Whether or not adolescent girls should be given contraceptives is a significant issue. Early adolescents who behave promiscuously always suffer from significant emotional deprivation, which may be transiently related to problems in the age period, or may reflect more profound psychological difficulties. The same appears true for girls who form intense sexual attachments with older males. In the event that no treatment for the deprivation syndrome is possible, the giving of contraceptive advice may be ethically justified; unfortunately, by implication, it gives adult permission for the sexual activity.

For less deprived middle and late adolescents, those who prescribe a diaphragm, the pill, or the intrauterine device, should explain to the girl that her expectations of a sexual relationship is likely to be different from her boyfriend; the latter has less need for a feeling of permanence and may find the natural feminine request for this anxiety provoking; this often leads to rejection.

It is important when trying to help boys with their anxieties about masturbation and homosexuality not to be overly facile. They may be told that the anxiety is common; that if it does not abate they should return for assistance. If an adolescent is told not to worry and his anxiety then continues, he may find it difficult to seek assistance. The intended reassurance fails to help, and the adolescent is made to feel even odder because the problem is still present.

PREGNANCY AND ABORTION

When unmarried girls become pregnant, adults try to be helpful in a variety of ways. An abortion is more and more seen as the acceptable solution. Although this may be socially convenient, the girl often feels that the important adults in her life do not see her as fit to be a woman. If lack of security about her feminine role is the emotional conflict that has led her to getting pregnant in the first place, abortion increases one problem as it solves another.

After an abortion, an adolescent girl often appears to show no psychological effects other than relief. However, usually about six months later, when the baby would have been born, girls who are coincidentally in psychotherapy report episodes of severe depression. The clinical evidence is that many insecure girls attempt to become pregnant again at this time; partly this is to reassure themselves that they have not been damaged, partly to replace the "murdered" infant. If abortions take place after an adolescent girl has felt the baby move, she then seems to feel herself to be murderous. If the parents have helped arrange the abortion, she projects that feeling onto them, as well as onto the doctor who performed the operation. This occurs especially in adolescents whose thinking is still concrete. Girls who have this experience are irrevocably hurt by it, and abortions at this stage are more damaging, psychologically, than is having the baby.

There are no psychological indications for abortion; there are only psychosocial justifications. Adolescents who have abortions should receive counseling thereafter, because a pregnancy—like any other adolescent action with antisocial connotations—is likely to be a request for personal help. An abortion, however, is a magical solution, and, if magic is offered, talking is often felt as useless and tedious. If counseling help is offered to illegitimately pregnant girls who are to have an abortion, a relationship with a therapist should be established prior to the abortion, so it can be continued thereafter. Social and educational help is obviously necessary. To process adolescent girls through abortion clinics is a medically effective, but psychologically inadequate technique that leads to further emotional difficulties. Ideally, a clinic for pregnant adolescent girls offers counseling and reality assistance, as well as the possibility of termination of the pregnancy.

Pregnant girls who are to have their babies are still often suspended from high school; this may partly be because of society's anxiety that others will be tempted to follow in their footsteps, partly because of concern about the attitudes of other children's parents. But girls almost always know when one of them is being sexually active. There is, thus, little justification for removing a girl from school because she becomes pregnant. If the pregnancy of a girl is felt as shameful, there would appear to be no alternative but to hide; the attitude of the young in these cases, however, is generally more mature than the attitude of the older generation.

When girls are unmarried and having a child, they need emotional support and help from adults who care about them. Unfortunately, they are often the victims of society's unconscious punitive attitudes. Homes for unmarried mothers may be emotionally frigid and cold places.

The pregnancy of adolescent girls almost always inhibits emotional development and they require optimum prenatal care; commonly, they do not receive this. Their infants are at greater risk, postnatally, than the babies of adult women and require highly sophisticated medical attention. If the baby is reared by the adolescent mother, the need for ongoing emotional, educational, and physical support to assist in the rearing of a healthy infant and prevent subsequent infant neglect and abuse is necessary (GAP Report, 1984).

Society makes it particularly difficult for unmarried mothers to keep their babies, even if a satisfactory father substitute can be found. Children brought up by one-parent families without an adequate parent substitute of the opposite sex are almost certain to be emotionally crippled. If unmarried girls bring their babies home to the nuclear family, they are often in competition with their mothers for the care of the child; the girl usually loses.

Those unmarried mothers who have their babies adopted have special psychological problems. If they do not nurse and hold the baby during the lying-in period, it is very difficult for them to mourn the loss of their child, as it has never been real to them. For them to do this, and then hand over the baby with no personal counseling to help them mourn the loss, does not seem humane. Nurses, however, often project themselves into the situation and insist that unmarried mothers who are not going to keep the baby not see it. Mothers who give up babies for adoption need therapy, both to understand the etiology of their need to become pregnant and to mourn the loss. Only then is repetition likely to be avoided.

EATING DISORDERS

Because they result from interrelated factors in the physiological, psychological, and environmental experiences of the individual (Bruche, 1973), obesity (Wallace, 1964) and anorexia (Sperling, 1962) are common problems in adolescence.

We live in a society that is preoccupied with thinness; but it is notable that obesity is commoner among economically deprived adolescents, self-starvation and/or overeating and vomiting (bulemia) more usual among the more affluent. Self-starvation appears most typically at the beginning of the middle stage of adolescence; bulemia is the commonest symptom seen in girls' dormitories in college.

All adolescents show a variation in weight and in distribution of body fat, but manipulation of body size by self-starvation is an indication of a preoccupation with one's own body, sexuality, and issues of helplessness and control of the self and others. These conflicts are typical of anorexia nervosa, but self-starvation may also occur in depression, hyperthyroidism, and other endocrine conditions and a variety of malignant illnesses, such as leukemia. In self-starvation, the determination of the kind of intervention—hospital or clinic—depends on the extent of loss of body weight (a loss of more than one-third is dangerous) and whether the weight loss continues. Sometimes these adolescents have been fat as children; often their problems are related to family attitudes toward food and love. Sometimes such adolescents, particularly girls, may be identifying directly with their mothers. Anorectic mothers are likely to have anorectic daughters. A significant number of cases have been seen in which mothers have gone to work and given up cooking. It is almost as if, in a hostile dependent way, some of their children identify with their mother's implicit wish not to be bothered to cook for them. This fits the previous history of such youngsters who have often been inordinately good children "the best little girls in the world."

Gross obesity distorts adolescents' relationships with peers and adults. They are related to not as individuals, but as "fat." This, in the middle stages of adolescence, particularly affects the development of sexual identity. Fat adolescents may either be heterosexually ignored, or behave in a highly promiscuous way. Sometimes obesity may be a flight from heterosexuality; sometimes it represents an angry dependent rebellion within the family. In this, dependence on food is very similar to dependence on drugs and alcohol. It is a regressive attempt to solve the problems of anxiety, whatever its cause. Food can also be the one solace, often depending on a childhood system of reward, in an impossible situation. It replaces "love."

There are two possible approaches to the treatment of obesity in adolescence. Generally, intensive psychotherapy is difficult, and there are few reports of success in the literature (Bruche, 1973). Group therapy seems contraindicated in adolescent obesity, as the acceptability of fatness is socially reinforced. One approach that has been successful is to admit obese adolescents to either general medical wards for adolescents or adolescent psychiatric units in which group counseling ensures that the children relate to each other as people. The youngsters are put on a 500-calorie diet, which ensures that they will lose one pound a day. While in the hospital, these adolescents participate in educational recreational and vocational activities; they also see a psychiatrist regularly, whose goal is to help the reinforcement of an acceptable sense of masculine or feminine identity. When the adolescents have reached an acceptable shape, other young people do not relate to them as fat, and thus a new body image is societally and psychologically reinforced (Tolstrip, 1970).

This type of treatment can be highly successful, but it is inordinately expensive. Complications are that many obese adolescents became very aggressive as they lose weight; thus, they are very difficult to handle on medical wards. Furthermore, it is not unusual for their mothers to smuggle food into the hospital for them, and insurance carriers are often unwilling to pay for their treatment.

Obese adolescents should never be given appetite suppressors. Amphetamines in such youngsters may offer the replacement of dependence on food with dependence on drugs.

Anorexia nervosa is commonly associated with a preoccupation that if only an extra two to three pounds are lost all will be well. It is common for the adolescent to blandly deny that danger is possible, although the self-starvation can be suicidal in degree. Some adolescents appear to gain positive satisfaction from the helplessness their starvation produces around them. Food becomes a battleground in which parental figures are gleefully attacked. Self-starvation can occur in boys as well as girls, but is much rarer.

> John was a fifteen-year-old boy whose father was a master chef. At puberty he was sent away to school, but only at the end of the pubertal period did he begin to lose weight. This loss occurred at the time when other boys were beginning to be heterosexually interested, and ultimately John was sent home in a state of severe starvation. John's starvation had multiple roots. He consciously felt sexuality to be bad and was trying to starve himself so that he no longer got erections; he had never masturbated. He also got enormous satisfaction from driving his father to a fury because he would not eat his good food. When he was hospitalized he would force himself to vomit and would hide food if he possibly could. This boy fits a well-known psychological picture (King, 1963). Typically, he was highly preoccupied with food, but determined not to have it. He also had an omnipotent denial that he could be hurt by abstinence.

Apart from its physical effects, starvation produces some of the psychological symptoms that have been ascribed to anorexia nervosa, in particular, the loss of appetite and the knowledge that one is hungry or full. The syndrome is often associated with a driven need for inappropriate exercise, and the adolescent may be extremely dishonest about his or her eating habits.

In some adolescent girls, it is hard to find conscious sexual and autonomy conflicts; for them it is as if thinness and a feminine shape has become an end in itself. This has been called a weight phobia (Crisp, 1970). Often those who suffer with anorexia nervosa are one of a group of girls in a high school who are preoccupied with dieting. Those who become severely anorectic become highly important to others who talk much of the time about their self-starving peer.

Therapy for anorexia nervosa involves the whole family, as well as the individual youngster. Mild cases may be successfully treated with outpatient therapy (Minuchin et al., 1977). Those adolescents who require hospitalization do better, in this author's opinion, when treated in sophisticated adolescent psychiatric units than on pediatric wards. In the latter situation, they often become the focus of staff rage because they "deliberately" make themselves sick, whereas the other children are victims. If the child has to be intubated to be fed, this seems to represent a therapeutic failure. Weight gain is often not enough and a behavior-modification approach that does not treat underlying pathology runs the risk of suicide (Blinder et al., 1970).

MENTAL ILLNESS IN ADOLESCENCE

Mental illness is the generic term applied to those illnesses in which there are significant aspects of brain pathology, sometimes in transmission between nerve cells, as in temporal lobe epilepsy, sometimes in neuroendocrinological aberrations in which the brain produces abnormal substances or excessive metabolic breakdown products under stress.

These illnesses, genetic in origin, are neither well diagnosed nor well treated in adolescence, and this lack makes them a major social and human problem. They include those associated with mood disorders—the affective illnesses, which are major depressions (unipolar disorders) and manic-depressive types of illnesses (bipolar disorders). They also include a group of illnesses that may be diagnosed as schizophrenia.

None of them present themselves in children and adolescence in exactly the same way as in adults, and often in the lower age group they appear as disorders of conduct. There is also a group of illnesses that show themselves as associated with learning disabilities and an inability to concentrate and pay attention (Millichap, 1977). The affective disorders, in particular, have not been well diagnosed and studies indicate that adolescents in correctional centers with a history of serious delinquency show a high percentage of these illnesses, which have not been treated (Grapentine, 1982; Miller, 1982). Young people diagnosed as suffering from schizophrenia receive a label that has tended to become pejorative and often provokes fears of inevitable personality deterioration. The classical descriptions of schizophrenic syndromes as inevitably deteriorating have not changed because of tranquilizing medication, although the length of stay in hospitals has been reduced. The outcome of the illness as inevitably unsatisfactory is generally a result of illness plus inadequate treatment. The personality disintegration ascribed to schizophrenia was shown to be reversible decades ago (Miller and Clancy, 1952).

The idea that these illnesses lead to personality disintegration has grown up because their natural history in adolescence is almost unknown. Most of the clinical descriptions are based on observations in mental hospitals. If adolescents are placed in disturbed, socially aberrant environments, such as those in many mental hospitals, their personalities almost inevitably deteriorate (Miller, 1954). Most hospital routines still involve a time table in which there are hours of enforced idleness that hardly assist adolescent development. Those young people who desperately need competent psychiatric help already have difficulties in making satisfactory identifications. They are likely to deteriorate if they are subjected to the social lunacies of a typical hospital environment for more than a very short space of time. Many schizophrenic adolescents can be kept away from long-term hospitalization if they obtain skilled help from an outpatient clinic; if they have adults and other adolescents in their lives who relate to them as people; if they are offered permanence in therapeutic relationships; if medication is used to target very specific symptoms and, since long-term usage effects are unclear, for as short a period as possible. The effects of the illness on thinking ability needs to be understood by educators, otherwise these young people are unduly stressed in school.

A massive assault on brain functions is inevitable in acute or chronic conditions due either to the biochemical insults of drug abuse, with hallucinogens and alcohol, or acute neuroendocrine disturbance. Typically, there is impairment of short-term memory and a loss of capacity for abstract thought. When, after an acute episode of illness, adolescents return to school, serious stress may occur if this is not understood. They cannot easily function at their previous academic capacity, yet if they are placed with less able children, they feel hopelessly devalued.

The problem is compounded because the concept of the "least restrictive alternative" in treatment has become a legal shibboleth and the desirability of short-term hospital treatment has become confused with the need for long-term therapeutic support. Because the ideal treatment is to hospitalize such youngsters only during the very acute phase of the illness, the concept of brief treatment has been applied to this illness. Many of these children require special schooling; all need long-term psychological help, as do their families, from the same treatment personnel. Essentially, these young people need a variety of high and low intensity care regimens. Further, from a psychiatric viewpoint, these youngsters too often are treated by trainees. As is often the case in medicine, patients with the most severe syndromes are treated by the least experienced.

Schizophrenic symptoms should be looked upon as a stress response, and efforts should be made either to reduce the patient's sensitivity to stress or to reduce stress levels. Tranquilizers tend to have this effect in adults and later adolescents, but they do not appear to work as satisfactorily in pubertal adolescents who have a high blood level of hormones. Acute episodes of illness in those young people requires sophisticated therapeutic support to prevent personality deterioration; this should usually be given in a good adolescent treatment center. It is crucial to work with the family to modify their aberrant responses to their child's illness.

The problem associated with schizophrenia is that competent treatment is rarely available, perhaps because as a result of the fear all human beings have of madness. Schizophrenia may result in antisocial or aggressive behavior, but when this happens, there can be no guarantee that schizophrenia will be diagnosed.

Unless society routinely takes the trouble to listen to its adolescents, the illness underlying such behavior may be ignored.

> Tim, age sixteen, was in a juvenile detention home for making a violent assault first on his mother, then on other women. No one had spent sufficient time with the boy to allow him to say that the devil was instructing him to kill people. The world had reacted as he were a bad aggressive boy, rather than a severely disturbed, disorganized mad boy.

Not all delusional or hallucinatory symptoms are due to schizophrenia. Apart from hallucinogenic drugs of abuse they may also occur in temporal lobe epilepsy and brain tumors.

> Bill was sent to a school for delinquents in need of care and protection because he was constantly running away from home. He had not told anyone in his environment that he heard voices telling him to do this. Ultimately, Bill was found to be suffering from a brain tumor that explained his delusion.

More usually, conduct disorders including the abuse of drugs; intolerable violence and unacceptable sexual behavior may have, beneath their surface presentation, a disorder of affect.

There are clusters of symptoms that are typically associated with biologically induced mood disorders; some are culture free and some are not.

Children and adolescents who are suffering from biological depression commonly show sleep, appetite, and mood disorders. These symptoms are not volunteered, but have to be asked about. The adolescent generally falls asleep, but is intermittently wakeful in the night, and becomes particularly irritable in the morning. Often he has a poor appetite for breakfast and does not become hungry until lunchtime. If the depression is pervasive and everpresent, other symptoms will depend on whether the adolescent comes from a controlling or an impulsive family (Miller, 1980). Children from a controlling family tend to be excessively good; children from an impulsive family have many behavioral symptoms. Depressed youngsters who use bad conduct as a technique to relieve stress may initially show the same type of antisocial behavior (stealing, poor schoolwork); violence as an intermittent symptom is unrelated to a clear external precipitant. If this is not adequately treated, a developmental impasse occurs, and the conduct disorder worsens.

If, in adolescence, depression is relieved with tricyclic antidepressants, a temporary period of acute excitement that appears manic, but that acutally is an acute confusional state around the issue of who one is, appears. The known depressed self disappears, and a new sense of oneself has to be found. Other drugs are not indicated at this time, but the situation is complicated because some children with manic-depressive illness, when seen in a depressed phase, are misdiagnosed as depressed. Biological tests for depression (Carroll, 1979) are probably not valuable as they are positive in only a very small percentage of those adolescents who suffer from organic depressive illnesses. These syndromes are inherited, and a history of depression or alcoholism is found in collateral and direct family members in about one-third of all cases.

When manic-depressive illness appears in adolescence, it may be that phases of angry, or excited, behavior alternate with conduct disorders. An inability to learn from experience is a common symptom and punishment or consequences for unacceptable behavior have no influence on its future appearance. Sometimes the illness shows itself as a psychotic episode, in which the excited adolescent is filled with grandiose delusions, alternating with a perception of ultimate evil. Suicide in adolescent manic-depression is not infrequent. On occasion, the impression is gained that these young people do not, like adults, spend money; they squander the goodwill of adults by their intermittent pervasive demanding nastiness. A common misdiagnosis is of a serious borderline personality problem, which leads to treatment only by psychotherapy and social interventions in a hospital.

> Debbie at age thirteen was angry and demanding; she refused to attend school or when she did she intentionally rejected her teachers in a grandiose manner that enraged them. This behavior alternated with episodes of withdrawn isolation. She was sexually promiscuous during her angry episodes, and exercised no social judgment. When hospitalized, she refused to see a psychotherapist, and she spent ten months in a hospital with no progress until finally placement in a residential treatment center was recommended. The parents then sought a second opinion. Not only was manic-depressive illness diagnosed in her child, but her mother was found to be suffering from a serious biological depression. The daughter was treated with lithium carbonate and supportive outpatient therapy after three weeks in another hospital. The mother received tricyclic antidepressants. Two years later, at follow-up, Debbie had become a successful member of her local high school.

Many adolescents suffer, along with a variety of conduct disorders, daily, marked swings of moods. Some show rage attacks, following an understandable stress, which are grossly excessive, and many suffer from serious episodic dyscontrol syndromes (Miller, 1980). All these disorders respond to intervention with lithium, but if the syndromes have persisted for years, dramatic results are often not obtained because the personality distortions remain. Although appropriate medication makes such adolescents treatable, it offers no "magic bullet." When medication is indicated and not given, treatment by psychosocial intervention alone becomes inordinately difficult or fails.

The correctional system is filled with many adolescents with serious disorders of affect, who have been neither diagnosed nor treated.

ADOLESCENT SUICIDE

In the decade since the first edition of this book appeared, there has been a dramatic increase in the suicide rate in the United States. In the first edition, the statement was made that "there is some suggestive clinical evidence that suicidal attempts among adolescents in the United States are currently increasing in frequency, apparently associated with a decline in the incidence of syringe hepatitis and toxicity due to drug abuse."

The increased rate of suicide has paralleled the increased divorce rate and an increase in adolescent homicide. Perhaps because of the disintegration of societal social structures and the increase in social isolation due to drug abuse, more and more adolescents talk of self-destruction as a personal right. This casualness about the value of life is also seen in those politicians who talk of survival after megadeath in a nuclear war.

Suicide may be deliberate or accidental; it may result from a type of Russian roulette played with life, as when experienced mountain climbers go out alone, or a youngster deliberately either drives drunk or sits in the passenger seat with a drunken driver. It may be the result of enraged frustration, serious depression, or a pervasive inability to enjoy life ("anhedonia") (Miller, 1982).

Commonly there is a notification of intent that is ignored; sometimes it is impossible to know that an attempt is to be made. Adolescents who have never caused trouble to anyone may abruptly kill themselves when faced with adult demands for functioning that imply abandonment of inter-familial security. Sometimes an isolated, rather withdrawn adolescent commits suicide (Schneer and Kay, 1967), and often there appears to be little or nothing adults could have done to prevent it.

> Tom, an eighteen-year-old boy, was admitted to the adolescent medical ward of a university hospital with multiple physical complaints. No organic cause was found for these, and he was seen by the psychiatrist attached to the ward. The boy had not been able to make a satisfactory adjustment away from his parents, and it seemed reasonable to work with him in brief therapy over the issue of his being able to separate himself from his family.
>
> Initially Tom appeared to do very well. He discussed some of his sexual anxieties thoughtfully, his somatic symptoms disappeared, and

plans were made to discharge him from the hospital to continue therapy at home. The day before his discharge he went to the hospital chapel and covered his face with a plastic bag; a three-hour search found him dead.

He had given no clue to his competent therapist of his suicidal intent; the only evidence that could be retrospectively found was that two days earlier he said to an adolescent girl patient, with whom he was out walking, that he did not think suicide was always wrong. With this boy, as with similar episodes with others, great guilt is almost always aroused in those individuals who have been emotionally involved with an adolescent who commits suicide. Suicide is one of the most hostile acts of which adolescents are capable; it is directed at loved ones and at society, as well as at the self. The survivors are always left wondering how they failed.

Suicide is not uncommon as the result of unresolved mourning, particularly for loved parents and relatives. Children rejoin their dead who continue to live inside their own heads. At particular risk are those youngsters who have a parent who committed suicide, as this act gives hostile permission to survivors; also at risk are those who lose a peer through suicide. Since survivors are always unconsciously angry with the suicide, the mourning process is more complicated and difficult than is the case in a natural death.

Many genuinely suicidal adolescents can ally themselves with therapists and undertake not to attempt to hurt themselves without giving the helping person a chance to prevent the act. Some cannot do this; they always make this clear by hedging a commitment not to engage impulsively in self-destruction. Adolescents with disturbed personalities who make suicidal gestures to call the attention of the world to their emotional difficulties can rarely be relied upon, even if they promise not to hurt themselves; not because these adolescents are bad, but rather because their need for help is so desperate that they will say anything to get immediate approval from adults. This need to be gratified here and now is so great that they cannot predict anything of their own behavior. They are not deliberately lying; their truth constantly changes.

This type of impulse-ridden personality should not be accepted as being able to make commitments. It is certain that they, like all youngsters who threaten to kill themselves, should be taken very seriously. When threats are made, immediate psychiatric help should be sought. The problem is that many adults know that, as adolescents themselves, the thought, "I wish I were dead" was not rare. This is not the same as "I'm going to kill myself." At particular risk are adolescents who have made one attempt, however inept that may seem to have been. They have discovered how easy the act is and furthermore have reinforced the common adolescent fantasy that death is not permanent and that it is an experience that can be tried to see what it is like.

ADOLESCENT CONDUCT DISORDERS

Adolescence can be such a turbulent age that it may be particularly difficult to assess the significance of difficult behavior. As with all individuals, adolescents need to balance within themselves the wish to behave impulsively, and thus relieve tension, and the need to control this behavior. The more uncomfortable an individual becomes with his environment, the weaker the personality controls, and the more likely that impulsive behavior will occur.

One additional problem is that adolescents have to exercise required controls, yet standards are rapidly changing. Adolescents have to try to free themselves from childish feelings of dependence on their parents. They have to cope with physiological changes within themselves that cause psychic turbulence, if not turbulence in outward behavior. So it is almost inevitable, from time to time, that most adolescents will appear to be behaving in a highly unreasonable way. Most of this behavior settles down; the problem is to decide when it will do so and when adults, whether parents, teachers, youth workers, or family practitioners, should try to offer something more specific than usual day-to-day care.

People do not always see disturbance for what it is, and they sometimes tend to approach the surface behavior of children without any real consideration of underlying causes. The disturbances of adolescence usually show in some form of difficult or antisocial behavior. Just to react to this repressively is not helpful, as the problem may go underground only to reappear a year or two later. Equally, to be overpermissive will increase the adolescent's anxiety; there is a need to provide external control.

If the stresses from which the adolescent suffers lead to antisocial behavior, there should be no conflict between the needs of society for protection and the treatment of the individual; it is impossible to help a disturbed adolescent if, in the process, hurtful attacks on others are condoned. When authority figures act as if antisocial behavior has no social implications, they will not be able to aid the individual concerned. If the causes of difficult behavior are not understood, the response is likely to be appropriate only by chance. Appropriate control by a loved, admired, and respected adult, however, may be highly meaningful.

The most effective control of disturbed behavior can occur only when an adolescent trusts and likes significant adults. This becomes a particular problem in the average high school where the pupils do not have teacher contact over a sufficient period of time to respect the adult as a person. Teachers may not be seen as people, only as occupiers of roles. This forces schools to use tariffs of punishment. The carrot and the stick are inadequate ways of impressing the young. Often minor upsets that are noticed by teachers are ignored by counselors because "no one else has complained." Thus, the meaning of unusual behavior is lost. Nevertheless, inappropriately destructive behavior must be controlled, accepted, and understood; if it is not, the stress produced by such behavior may make the situation worse both for the adolescent and his environment.

All adolescents should have their privacy respected by authority adults. This means that there should be hesitation before anything more than a routine response to misbehavior is considered necessary. Otherwise adolescents are likely to feel that their private world is constantly being invaded. Before investigating some of the more private motivations of adolescents, concerned adults should consider how antisocial an action is and whether or not the adolescent will respond to a relatively superficial response. When routine attempts to be helpful to young people in this way fail, it is then that causes should be investigated. Usually this does not happen; people in the environment tend to give up on difficult adolescents and wait for them to go elsewhere, or offer support only with the goal of assisting the individual through school. It is as though supportive school staff, social workers, and the like feel no responsibility for what happens when a youngster's school career is over. Ongoing assistance is rarely found. Furthermore, such staff are not trained to understand the possible biological etiology of disturbed behavior.

All too often, when adolescents are seen in a juvenile court, they have a long history of persistent angry and antisocial behavior, to which previous adult responses appear to have been stereotyped. Sometimes the individual is so disturbed that nothing could have been done, but previously inadequate reactions may be due to the inadequacy of a school's social setting, its teachers' lack of training for the task they have been called upon to perform, or anxiety about confronting the child's parents with the idea that psychological help may be needed.

EFFECT OF ANTISOCIAL BEHAVIOR ON THE ENVIRONMENT

The behavior of the adolescent must affect his environment and his family. Thus, disturbances can become cyclic: more stress can be fed back into the individual from his environment, which is then put under greater stress, producing more disturbances. The severity of the disturbed behavior may thus be a measure of the disturbance within the social situation, not merely of that within the individual. The following episode comes from a school in England:

David, a particularly small fifteen-year-old, became more and more upset at school. He engaged in whatever antisocial behavior seemed to be occurring. He was known to be a troublemaker, and on many occasions he and a group of his friends involved themselves in a bout of marijuana smoking. He ran away from school frequently and was abusive to the staff, who felt that despite his academic progress they could no longer tolerate him, and he was expelled.

David's father had been divorced by his mother when he was seven. His stepfather was extremely fond of him, but David was still suffering from the separation. He was struggling to establish a firm sense of masculine identity. His school still used physical punishment, and David felt that if he were beaten it would be a humiliation. He was afraid that he would cry—an intolerable threat to his sense of manhood—and he was consciously afraid of the homosexual threat in having to bend over to be beaten on the buttocks. In spite of his many fantasies about the brutality of beating, David was provoking, by his behavior, a situation in which he was likely to be beaten. He asserted himself by refusing to allow this to happen and collided head-on with the authorities. He and they maneuvered themselves into a situation in which there was no going back; neither would give in to the other. The school felt that it must have control, he must conform to the rules; he, in his turn, became more defiant and difficult.

Ultimately, the school and the boy were feeding disturbed behavior, the one to the other. The only solution that the school could see was to send the boy away, and as soon as this happened he settled down. This led his parents to believe that all was now well—regrettably far from the truth. After having moved from school to school, thus repeating the loss of significant adults in his environment that began with the loss of his father, he became dependent on marijuana.

A failure to understand the significance of such emotional stress as death or divorce in the early lives of difficult adolescents is common.

One problem is that many adults are quite unsure as to the level of optimum performance for an emotionally disturbed adolescent. Disturbances are unlikely to be helped unless adults expect the maximum performance of which the individual is capable. Too much or too little may be expected:

James, an asthmatic sixteen-year-old boy with a father who was a highly successful alcoholic businessman and a mother who was a depressed, anxious woman, reacted to family stress by failing to turn in his homework. In addition, he cut some of his classes. The principal of his school reacted to this by suspending him at once and threatening to expel him if he broke the rules once more. This handed the boy a weapon that he angrily could and did use against himself and his parents. He immediately acted up again and stayed out of school.

A woman teacher, who rightly perceived a thirteen-year-old boy in her class to be severely disturbed, spent so much time in containing his upsets, and made so few demands upon him, that the morale of the whole class suffered. She oversympathized with the underprivilege she sensed in her pupil and began to take his side against the rest of the class. It was as if he became the good boy and the others became bad. The rest of the class became more and more difficult to handle as they felt, reasonably, that their teacher was not as interested in them as she should have been.

ASSESSMENT OF CONDUCT DISORDERS

Adolescents typically show disturbance by inflicting pain on the environment, rather than by experiencing pain themselves. By hurting the environment, an adolescent indicates to the adult world that something is wrong.

The extent of the adolescent's destructiveness, either directed toward the self or others, needs to be assessed. In doing this, the age, social situation, and general stress under which an adolescent might find himself have to be understood. For example, temper in an early adolescent with minimum provocation is less significant than a similar outburst in the late teens. A refusal on the part of a boy or girl to make reparation for a destructive action, often symbolized by a refusal to apologize, is often an indication of psychological troubles. The frequency with which the behavior occurs is significant and may indicate a biological etiology. Sometimes problems that were apparently bearable to the youngster at one stage of development become unbearable later. Learning difficulties are an example of this. Prior to puberty, the family can offer emotional support to children with learning difficulties, with the helplessness that is an inevitable consequence. At puberty, this support is intolerable as it threatens the child's attempt to become emotionally independent. A sense of mastery has to be obtained, and since educational systems commonly offer neither enough assistance for the disability, nor socially acceptable compensatory mastery outlets, conduct disorders ensue.

Adolescents in psychological distress often look it. More unkempt than their peers, they seem pale, listless, and fidgety; they look as if they need a good night's sleep. The daydreaming and the inability to concentrate of early adolescence may persist for years, rather than months.

Persistent behavior that deviates from the norm of the group may indicate disturbance, if the values of the system meet the developmental needs of the young. The difference between patently unusual behavior and acceptable nonconformity is the key issue. That adolescents do not conform to what they see as an unreasonable rule does not mean that they are psychologically upset. Social change is often created by the pressure put on society by young people. Conformity is not necessarily a sign of mental health; sometimes it indicates passive aberration.

Disturbed behavior may be a reaction against the imposition of what the adolescent perceives as alien values. This is an issue in ethnic conflicts in the school system, but more often it is related to social-class values or academic preoccupations about nonacademic adolescents. Some people define behavior as disturbed because they do not like it.

> The principal of a high school became extremely upset because a large number of adolescents were milling around in the halls. After berating them, he discovered that they were a group of nonacademic youngsters on a scavenger hunt arranged by their class teacher, who was delighted by their capacity to work together.

If schools impose middle-class values on black, Hispanic, or white working-class adolescents, they may be attempting to make them abandon the standards of the social group from which they come. In any school that has a social mix and that does this, persistently difficult behavior will likely occur in one or the other group. This will not necessarily indicate permanent psychological disturbance, nor will it indicate how the adolescents will behave when they leave school. This conflict is a particular issue in high schools, rather than in the primary school. Until children reach adolescence, they are more involved in the emotional life of the family than they are in the world outside. Home is the important emotional base, and it is unlikely that grade schools will create a severe conflict of values in children; when vital decisions have to be made, the child will follow the values of home. After puberty, the child's need for emotional independence from his parents makes him more susceptible to the influence of the school; if this influence is too pervasive, the adolescent then has a severe value conflict, which may lead to over-dependence on peers or an intense conflict with either parental values or those of the school.

If, in any one school, there is a social mix, it may be hard for teachers to decide whether any particular pattern of behavior is abnormal. The local norms and culture have to be taken into account in assessing its possible meaning. For example, in some schools it is not unusual for early-adolescent boys to be playing covertly with their genitals at the back of the room, but a sixteen-year-old who does this is likely to be upset. Mutual masturbation up until midadolescence should not cause undue alarm in an all-male, closed environment, but this depends on the general stress the boys are exposed to at the time. In any overrestrictive single-sex setting, homosexual behavior or preoccupation almost certainly indicates transient emotional disturbance.

The nature of such acts when they occur and the extent to which they are coercive is the significant personal issue.

Sometimes adolescents may ask for help by prolonged disturbed behavior or by actions that are highly unusual:

> As part of an assignment to write on any subject he liked, Kevin, a fourteen-year-old boy, handed in a long, highly pornographic essay. A day or two earlier, he had accidentally dropped a lurid paperback on the floor in class. His teacher recognized that the boy was in need of some sort of aid and felt that merely to punish the boy would not be appropriate. He thought that Kevin was expressing contempt or hostility for the school, and Kevin was sent to the school social worker, who talked to him in a firm but kindly way about the unacceptability of his behavior, which did not recur. There was no punishment, and the teachers reacted to the behavior helpfully on an explicit level.

Kevin perhaps was trying to show how worried he was about his sexual feelings. It might have been helpful if he had been asked about this, but the fact that the behavior did not recur could have meant that Kevin took the school's non-rejection of him as an acceptance of his sexuality. This would certainly have helped him.

Frequently adults who try to help do not know whether a problem has been solved or merely driven underground. Those people who take on the job of trying to aid the young have to bear the uncertainty of never being quite sure whether they have been useful or not.

Conduct disorder presents itself in many forms. Nowadays it is of major concern to society when it involves issues of violence including suicide and drug abuse and promiscuous sexuality leading to adolescent illegitimate pregnancy.

Of less concern is the type of behavior that insidiously eats away at an adolescent's self-esteem and reduces the likelihood of a successful, productive life. The disruptive youngster with an attention deficit disorder becomes a significant individual, even if negatively, in the school system and to parents; but the quiet underachiever may be of less concern to those in authority.

UNDERACHIEVEMENT

Underachievement (Kimball, 1953), the persistent failure on the part of an adolescent to achieve his known academic potential, often remains unrecognized as an indication of disturbance, yet it probably is a most common symptom of emotional disturbance in the academic young. This can be highly destructive to the individual, particularly in those educational systems where progress depends on age, even when underachievement lasts only a few months. The characteristic qualities of delinquent behavior are present in underachievement: it attacks the individual himself, the social system as a whole, and carries with it a perverse gratification. It may not be noticed because little has come to be expected of an individual adolescent or because it is part of a syndrome that has come to include withdrawal. Underachievement is the typical antisocial act of academic youth who commonly do not behave antisocially in the community-at-large. It is a technique of being destructive to oneself and of showing anger toward the family and the school.

Some underachievement is a result of learning difficulties, in which a youngster gives up rather than face the helplessness of not being able to perform a task. "I will not" is preferable to "I cannot." Sometimes, specific learning difficulties are produced by perceptual motor problems; sometimes they are based on emotional conflicts. Either way, the symptom is under-diagnosed and rarely properly treated. As common is the pervasive inability to function at one's individual capacity. Sometimes this is due to chronic drug abuse, especially of marijuana and alcohol. Seriously withdrawn behavior through a significant part of a school career, even if the young person appears to be functioning at a moderate level, may indicate severe psychological disturbance. This is missed as a manifestation of difficulty because conformity is so valued. In social systems that require passive acceptance, adults may not be aware that compliance, which is seen as indicating a good child, can be problem behavior. A combination of the obedient withdrawn adolescent who never does quite as well as expected, and a highly rigid school, may result in a failure to perceive severe emotional difficulties. In many situations the adolescent who never disturbs anyone is naturally thought of as being in good psychological shape. Those adolescents who never bother parents or other adults in their life are usually troubled. Such withdrawn young people are extraordinarily difficult to help, and there are very few centers in the psychiatric world equipped to treat them. They may suffer in that they cannot involve themselves emotionally with other people, either adolescents or adults. It is very difficult for adults to become anchor points for adolescent development if the young cannot relate to them.

Not all disturbed behavior, however, is impulsive or unconsciously motivated. It may be quite conscious, and it may be a direct plea for help.

> Martin, a boy at a fairly rigid conformist British school, wanted to change some of his courses at an advanced level. He could not see a way in which the school would agree to this (although the school would, in fact, have agreed to a change). Martin, therefore, decided quite consciously that the only solution was not to work. Ultimately, he would be removed because he was not working; he would then be sent somewhere else where he would be able to do the courses he wished. This highly

disturbed piece of behavior arose because the boy had assumed that the world of his school would be hostile to him, just as he felt his parents were. It is easy to see how he could assume this degree of hostility in a school where the boys felt extreme conformity was demanded.

Many university students appear to get poor grades out of choice. Often these are people who begin to resent the academic treadmill. For a medical student, continuous education under considerable pressure may have been going on for eight or nine years since entering high school. Some medical schools quite properly do not permanently drop individuals who make poor grades; rather, they send them on leave of absence for academic, medical, or psychiatric reasons. A student who wants a year off from academic studies may deliberately do poorly to get it. A not unreasonable goal is achieved by a deliberate piece of disturbed and somewhat antisocial behavior.

Schools in which teachers have sufficient contact with young people so they can recognize the situation often report that adolescents "could do better" over a long period of time; it may not occur to them that this may be a symptom of emotional maladjustment. In high schools, where teacher contact with pupils is minimal because teachers remain with students only one semester or two and have too many to whom they must relate, it is often not even recognized that a pupil is not achieving to his or her potential.

Schools that are sensitive about underachievement as a possible symptom of upset may well wait for pupils to pass through the turbulence of early adolescence, before coming to a decision as to whether there is a call for specific help. The phrase "could do better" from a school may, during early adolescence, indicate developmental difficulties only. In midadolescence, it may indicate psychological disturbance, chronic depression, an unresolved conflict, or a failure to develop a firm sense of self. The young person whose symptomatic underachievement is not resolved may remain inadequate. After leaving school, the psychological cost may be more apparent. Bright individuals find it difficult to perform jobs they find boring, yet young adults without formal qualifications often find themselves in such a position.

Underachievement may also occur in adolescents who reach puberty at sixteen to seventeen, since a late developer is preoccupied with his failure to develop physically as well as his contemporaries. Adolescents who develop late may appear to be bright, but lack the capacity to tolerate frustration as equably as others. They often underachieve because of anxiety during the usual years of early adolescence and pubertal turmoil during part of what for others are mid-adolescent years.

The commonest current cause of underachievement is dependence on marijuana. This interferes with short-term memory; it also reduces motivation and may produce a chronic unrecognized depression. It causes particular problems in retaining knowledge, if joints are smoked after doing homework and before going to bed. When the drug is used during the schoolday, the dreamy depersonalization it creates makes effective functioning difficult. Chronic marijuana smokers often report feeling "pretty stoned" until noon or later, after they have smoked.

> A seventeen-year-old boy was referred to a psychiatrist because of a sudden fall-off in academic achievement. Following the loss of his girlfriend, he had begun to smoke five to six joints daily. He found himself disinclined to work and unable to concentrate. The frequency of his marijuana use was reduced with intensive therapy and an insistence that he abstain. As use became intermittent, less than once every seven days, his grades improved.

All workers with young people need to understand ways in which boys and girls show emotional disturbance. Sometimes being a good listener is enough; the patient recognition that there is a difficulty over which the youngster has little control may make it possible for a self-righting mechanism to appear. An upset adolescent benefits from becoming aware of the positive loving qualities of people in his environment. Therapy is often directed toward reducing the feeling of persecution experienced by the world, so that the positive qualities of others can be perceived and incorporated into the personality to allow identification to take place.

The disturbances of adolescents mostly show as symptom clusters that are associated with sex, drugs, and delinquency. Each of these topics merits separate consideration, though the underlying difficulties are often the same.

REFERENCES

Aichorn, A. (1935), *Wayward Youth*. New York: Viking.

American Psychiatric Association (1980), *DSM III—Diagnostic and Statistical Manual of Mental Disorders*, 3rd ed. Washington, D.C.

Bruche, H. (1973), *Eating Disorders*, p. 6. New York: Basic Books.

Blinder, B. J., Freeman, D. M. A., and Stunkard, A. J. (1970), Behavior therapy of anorexia nervosa and effectiveness of activity as a reinforcer of weight gain. *Am. J. Psychiatr.*, 126:77–82.

Crisp, A. H. (1970), Premorbid factors in adult disorders of weight with particular reference to primary anorexia nervosa (weight phobia). A literature review. *J. Psychosom. Dis.*, 14:1–22.

Erikson, E. H. (1968), *Identity, Youth and Crisis*, pp. 155–165. New York: Norton.

Grapentine, L. Personal Communication.

Josselyn, I. (1954), the ego in adolescence. *Am. J. Orthopsychiatr.*, 24:223–237.

Kimball, B. (1953), Case studies in educational failure during adolescence. *Am. J. Orthopsychiatr.*, 23:405–415.

King, A. (1963), Primary and secondary anorexia nervosa syndromes. *Br. J. Psychiatr.*, 109:470–479.

Lewin, B. (1950), *The Psychoanalysis of Elation.* New York: Norton.

Masterson, J. F. (1967), *The Psychiatric Dilemma of Adolescence.* pp. 11–21. Boston: Little, Brown.

Miller, D. (1954), An approach to the social rehabilitation of chronic psychotic patients. *Psychiatry*, 17:347–358.

—— (1980), Treatment of the seriously disturbed adolescent. *Adolesc. Psychiatr.*, 8:469–481.

—— (1982), Adolescent suicide, etiology, and treatment. *Adolesc. Psychiatr.*, 9:327–363.

——, and Clancy, J. (1952), The rehabilitation of chronic schizophrenic patients. *Psychiatry*, 15:435–443.

Millichap, G. (1977), Learning disabilities and related disorders. Chicago: Year Book Medical Publishers.

Minuchin, S. et al (1977), Input and outcome of family therapy in anorexia nervosa. *Adolesc. Psychiatr.*, 5:313–322.

Redl, F. (1942), Group emotion and leadership. *Psychiatry*, 5:580.

Schneer, H. I., and Kay, P. (1967), The suicidal adolescent. In *Adolescents, Psychoanalytic Approach to Problems and Therapy*, eds. S. Lorand and H. I. Schneer, 180–201. New York: Paul Hoeber.

Tolstrip, K. (1970), in *The child and his family*, eds. E. J. Anthony, C. Kouperick, 311. New York: Wiley.

Wallace, M. W. (1964), Why and how children are fat. *Pediatrics*, 34:303.

Chapter 14

Social Organizations and the Treatment of Disturbed Adolescents

PRINCIPLES OF CARE

In any recommendation that is made to help disturbed youth, note must be taken of the available community resources. Psychiatric services, child care, group homes, probation services, student health centers, and a variety of free clinics all have to try to cope with an overwhelming demand, and their resources are often inadequate. The quality of care provided by a formal agency can be estimated on the basis of how well certain principles are followed (American Psychiatric Association, 1971).

1. *Each individual within the organization should be helped to achieve an optimal level of growth.*

2. *The integrity of each adolescent and his family should be respected.*

3. *Respect for the maturational level of the individual should be at least equal to that of his chronological age.*

4. *The program should respect the striving for autonomy of each adoles-cent, and the needs of the child should not be sacrificed to the orienta-tion, personal or theoretical, of the staff. Just because staff are expert in one field, they should not automatically assume that this will meet the needs of young people in their care.*

5. *The significance of parents, peer groups, extraparental adults, and social norms in the personality development of individual adolescents should be respected. Adolescents in residential care should not be "institutional-ized" by being exposed to an "emotional deficiency disease" (Bettelheim and Sylvester, 1948), or being asked to identify with a way of life that is so aberrant that it produces a variety of pathological psychological reactions (Miller, 1965, pp. 63–77). In particular, the capacity of young people to be creative in the community should be enhanced, not de-stroyed.*

6. *Imagination, creativity, and intellectual ability should be equally re-spected. The physiological and psychological needs for space, activity, and community contacts of each adolescent in care are as important as an attempt to resolve an adolescent's intrapsychic conflicts.*

7. *Each adolescent is a total person: the physical state of the adolescent should be considered as important as his emotional well-being, and vice versa.*

8. *The dependent needs of adolescents should be respected, which means that adult staff have the responsibility not to abandon young people in their care. The physical environment in which youngsters are cared for should be warm, safe and non-institutional, and respect the tactile and perceptual sensitivities of the young, as well as their need for privacy.*

9. *Since adolescents live in a drug-taking environment, therapeutic agen-cies should prescribe medication with great care.*

10. *There is no place for punishment in the residential and nonresidential care of adolescents.*

Few institutions in which adolescents are cared for meet these require-ments. To sum up, delivery systems should provide nonspecific care, that to which all individuals are entitled, in social, psychological, and biological areas. They should also provide specific care designed to meet the special needs of all individuals within the system. This includes adequate diagnosis as well as specific psychosociobiological intervention (Knesper and Miller, 1976).

Not only will society never provide the treatment services that are required, but this is elevated to a philosophy on the basis of the concept that the "least restrictive alternative" should be used in treatment. This becomes an excuse to try the least expensive type of intervention to see whether it will work. This technique is in widespread use by school systems and the correctional system. The generally unsatisfactory facilities, through which society often demonstrates its unconscious distaste for its young, have not significantly improved in the last several decades.

EDUCATIONAL SETTINGS AS TREATMENT AGENCIES

It has already been stressed that school is vital to the development of healthy young people. This is equally true of the disturbed adolescent. A good school can be particularly helpful to those young people who have specific emotional needs. And just as a good family practitioner is interested in treatment and prevention, a good school is involved with positive growth, as well as with helping the transient disturbances of its pupils. A family doctor refers for further help those few patients he cannot diagnose and, thus, cannot treat or those for whom he does not have adequate treatment facilities. There is an analogy with the school system. Most disturbed adolescents will be automatically helped by a good school; those that are not will be recognized and either specifically aided in the school by the use of school social workers, trained teachers, counselors, or appropriate curriculum adjustments, or by being sent to small alternate schools. The problem is that children are referred to specialized agencies usually only after these approaches fail. Since a significant number suffer from behavioral disorders that indicate disturbances of brain biochemistry, of which more and more is being learned, many are not adequately diagnosed and treated.

SPECIAL EDUCATIONAL SETTINGS

It is generally recognized in the educational system that special facilities are needed, either in the general school system or separately, for the mentally retarded. There is far less awareness of the needs of the emotionally disturbed. However, in recognition of the importance of the school setting, many countries provide special schools that they hope will resolve the particular difficulties of emotionally disturbed children. Children may be sent to these by legal authorities or child-care services; in the United States, in theory, if special education facilities are needed, they should be provided by school districts or made available by them. Three separate systems exist. Some children are "mainstreamed," a technique that tries to deal with the special needs of individual children in ordinary classes; often this does not help. Some children receive one or two special tutorial classes; most commonly, these are used for youngsters with learning disabilities. These problems are generally quite insufficiently treated, and such classes are all too often a token gesture toward assistance. Finally, some large high schools have smaller alternate schools within their system. These have the advantage of being smaller identifiable units, but they are often understaffed, relative to the children's needs and the many types of problems seen.

The emotionally disturbed are referred to residential treatment centers, boarding schools, and correctional institutions; often these settings are single sex. Since a coeducational environment is certainly emotionally healthier, it is striking that disturbed children from broken homes, often with only one parent, go to a school that is staffed by and that offers treatment to only one sex. The insistence of some states in not paying for out-of-state placement again reduces the availability of good residential care.

EDUCATIONAL PHILOSOPHY ON THE TREATMENT OF DISTURBANCE

Special schools and experimental schools for ordinary children often are run in accordance with certain interesting ideas; some, however, do not make for a growing environment. A popular belief is that disturbed children will be helped by being loved, but this is usually taken to mean that they should live in a permissive society in which their expressed wishes should be gratified (Berg, 1968). Alternately, it is believed that such children need to have aggression controlled only externally. The film *Warrendale* illustrates an approach that suggests that children would be helped by a type of emotional catharsis in a controlled environment. Another concept is an environment in which behavior-modification techniques are used. There is something of value in all these ideas, but a good setting fits the treatment technique to the needs of the individual child, rather than the reverse. Certain principles apply in the treatment of disturbed children. Foremost is that children need to feel cared about (Shields, 1962). Anger and violent behavior should be controlled so that youngsters find it difficult to inflict pain on themselves or on others. The opportunity must be given to play out safely their most disturbing conflicts in an understanding environment.

No resolution of internal conflict is possible without some manifestations of difficulties in behavior. Institutions that demand social conformity at any cost do not help youngsters develop to a reasonable emotional level. Staff members need to understand the difference between behavior that acts out internal conflict; behavior that relieves internal tension, due to aberrations of brain biochemistry; and acting up behavior, in which the adolescent tests the value of people in his or her world. Finally, although many adolescent children are as big as adults, they still need adequate care as children. In the case of emotionally disturbed adolescents in the educational, correctional and health care systems, loving adults are needed who, apart from child-caring roles, should preferably have another vocational identity the children can recognize and value; as, for example, vocational instructors, teachers and so on. Thus, they become adequate developmental models.

CAUSES OF INSTITUTIONAL FAILURE

Institutional failure is inevitable if an adequate diagnosis has not been made, since a suitable treatment regimen cannot then be begun. Often, treatable mood disorders are not diagnosed, nor are educational problems adequately assessed, particularly in the area of learning disabilities and problems with attention span and concentration. Additionally, care delivery models fail because society finds it difficult to tolerate change or because the schools have not been able to meet the needs of their pupils. Failure can be subtle, and disguised by the fact that difficult children are repeatedly placed elsewhere. On other occasions, an institution deteriorates very rapidly or is closed because of some scandal. Finally, many poor institutions continue, particularly in the field of delinquency, because of a variety of emotional and economic needs of society-at-large. The protagonists of the idea that love is enough do not appear to understand that it is not sufficient to offer love and patient understanding to a deprived, aggressive adolescent. They live in a simplistic world of good and bad and tend to see critics of their approach as bad, themselves as good. This belief is similar to that of the emotionally disturbed youngster who splits the world into good and bad.

With disturbed children, such splitting is inevitable, and they initially should be helped to perceive the people nearest to them as good, those farthest away as bad. In a school setting, this means that if anyone has to become a bad authority figure it is the principal. If he ensures, either consciously or not, that he is seen as the good member of the community, other staff will be likely to be seen as bad, leading to manipulation of the staff by the children, and increasingly disturbed behavior. Staff members then quarrel among themselves, and this increases the amount of disturbance in the community of children. It is no use to blame some staff for being over-authoritarian. Good administrators have to create competent organizations with some inadequate staff, and a turnover of some of their best staff.

If techniques of emotional catharsis are used, staff members sometimes unconsciously provoke disturbed outbursts in their charges, perhaps in the unwitting service of their own, rather than the children's needs. In World War II, an effective technique of treatment for battle neurosis was to allow the psychologically wounded soldiers to reexperience a traumatic experience under hypnotic drugs. The success of this apparently led to the false belief that catharsis of painful emotional experiences was a solution to the more chronic ills of civilian life.

Successes have been reported with well-planned group homes for young people and in skillfully organized settings for delinquents. These organizations always report better results with boys than girls for a good many reasons. Disturbed boys call the attention of society more dramatically to themselves; they act up in the community earlier than girls. Girls first retreat into the family, which is often acceptable to parents, and their emotional disturbance must be more severe to be recognized; furthermore, girls have illegitimate pregnancies as a pseudo-solution to their difficulties.

The common denominator for success appears to be the capacity of adolescents to recognize the value of a human relationship and accept controls within it. The recognition of the integrity of each individual lies in the use of implicit social expectation, the provision of resources to make the development of identity possible, adequate vocational and educational training, and adults who are seen as valuable and who are not frightened by the angry or seductive behavior of the young. Adults particularly need to be able to understand and help dissipate the persecutory anxiety of the disturbed adolescent.

Success is measured by the ability of an adolescent to master the socially acceptable rules in education and living of the age period; to develop an appropriate developmental capacity for empathy; to tolerate frustration; and to behave in a caring manner to others. Adulthood can be said to be attained when parents can be forgiven for their real or imagined trespasses.

ROLE OF ADULTS IN HELPING THE EMOTIONALLY DISTURBED

There are two main problem areas in the care of difficult young people. If staff, particularly men, have only child-caring roles, they are likely to threaten the tenuous sense of autonomy of the disturbed adolescent, even when they appropriately meet dependent needs. This arises because they are not seen in socially recognizable roles. If they are, such individuals can be identified with by boys and can offer girls the interest that is needed to support their developing sense of femininity. The absence of this supportive aspect of child and adolescent care means that adolescents in institutions are more likely to regress or become overtly destructive. The problem is not dissimilar to that in penal settings, where a most highly valued member of the institutional community is the prison guard. Thus, a man or a woman in a job that is a model of nonproductivity is not an appropriate identification figure for a delinquent adolescent who, unsure of his own sense of self, looks to adults for models.

Sometimes adolescents threaten young staff, often because the latter are so like the former. In such situations, if staff members are not offered adequate emotional support, they become so anxious about getting close to adolescents that they are physically neglectful: health needs of the young are not met and adolescents are treated in environments that may be clean but sterile and cold. Alternatively, they may be drab, neglected, and deteriorating.

Family relationships have a bearing on the treatment of adolescents. An important determinant of upset behavior in the young is poor or absent interactions with the family or within the family. This means that appropriate intervention with disturbed adolescents must include supportive help to parents and assistance with intra-familial disturbances. This is often a token in nature. In correctional institutions, for example, it is not unusual for young people to be placed several hundred miles from their homes. It is a convenient myth to believe that a probation officer's visit to the parents, or an occasional pass for the youngster, deals with this problem. To save some resources, under these circumstances, other resources are wasted. There may be a confused belief that if disturbed children placed in treatment, educational, and correctional centers go home to visit their families frequently, their poor relationship with their parents will necessarily improve. This has led to a system in Britain where delinquent children are placed in schools as close to their homes as possible. Intense therapeutic effort may be made with adolescents whose personality is still quite elastic. Infrequent visits from social workers with excessive case loads are thought to be enough to assist a family in which there are difficulties with individuals, and often pathological interactions.

There is some evidence that separation from their disturbed parents for older adolescents is helpful if placement is in a social setting that really meets the child's needs with skill and sensitivity. Insofar as parental help is concerned, in the adolescent age range there are two relevant approaches. First, the parents of young adolescents who return to their homes need to be helped. Otherwise, the youngster is likely to return to the same pathological environment from which he or she came, and be subject to the same problems. Secondly, older adolescents from the middle stage onwards have to learn to cope with their parents as they are. It is less necessary to expect parental change, and the goal of work with parents is to help them maintain their child in a therapeutic setting for as long as necessary. With adolescents of any age who need to be in treatment settings, the return home for long visits without skilled help offered to parent and child is likely to be very disturbing. If institutions close for vacations, the action is usually more to meet the institution's needs than those of the children.

Most emotionally disturbed adolescents should be able to receive help in a good school that is not specially designed for the sick, but that does meet general adolescent needs. Some schools are reluctant to admit disturbed adolescents because it is thought that they will be upsetting to otherwise well-adjusted boys and girls. Although this anxiety often occurs in an ordinary school, well-balanced adolescents can tolerate upset behavior in their contemporaries, although adolescents who are themselves under stress are likely to be made anxious by a boy or girl they perceive as disturbed. Early adolescents are more threatened by disturbance in others than are those from the middle stage onward; they are so anxious about their own controls and their own physical integrity that the emotional turmoil of others is frightening. As a result, early adolescents scapegoat the weak and the incompetent. This only happens with mid-adolescents in environments in which their developmental needs are not met. The sixteen-year-old who is known to have been in a psychiatric hospital runs a real risk of being tormented by his peers in a typical, impersonally structured American high school. In such settings the fantasy of "madness" of the adolescents who have been recognized as disturbed is threatening; the larger group of young people may reject such individuals by bullying or teasing, and thus provoke more disturbed behavior. The rejection is an attempt to deny their own potential for such disturbance. Bullying is part of this denial. The members of the larger group try to prove to themselves that they can control disturbed behavior in others. Thus, they believe they can control it in themselves. This behavior does not occur with healthy mid-adolescents in schools in which their emotional needs for significant interpersonal contact are met.

Psychologically, good schools in which the maladjusted can be helped can admit a certain number of disturbed adolescents and still maintain a good environment for all pupils. Adolescents respond to implicit expectation and peer-group pressure. If too high a population of emotionally disturbed young are placed in the average good school, however, with their greater needs for both nurture and control than their normal peers, they may shift the balance of the whole school. There is then a regressive pull on normal adolescents who may still be struggling with childlike needs. An outsider cannot specify how many disturbed children a school can take. Each principal must assess the strengths and weaknesses of the school, and then decide. It is probable that most school principals are too anxious about this and that the school could handle more children who are known to be troubled than are actually accepted. In the average school, about 13 percent of the population suffers from some degree of emotional disturbance at any one time; 3 percent are probably severely disturbed (Feinstein and Miller, 1980). The latter tend to be a fairly fixed group of individuals; since most disturbance is transient, the former are different individuals at different times.

In the private sector of education, and to some extent even in the public school system, there are schools that have special qualities that make them able to help some youngsters and not others. School principals are, however, often uncertain as to the type of adolescent they are best able to help. When they are in doubt, technical assistance, usually from a psychiatrist, should be sought. Unnecessary rejection of young people can produce guilt in teachers, and damage disturbed adolescents and their parents. On the other hand, to take in young people that cannot be helped may be even more unfortunate:

> A small, private, co-educational, Quaker boarding school, which was extremely anxious to be helpful, agreed to take Debbie, a girl from an unhappy and divided home who behaved in a provocative way toward authority. But the school had not faced the fact that its staff members were in disagreement; the women were more rigid and conformist in their social attitudes than the men. This led to tension between the girls and boys, and made Debbie more anxious. She did her best to allay her anxiety, becoming as provocatively difficult to the women as she had previously been to her mother; for example, she accidentally left cigarette butts on a table by her bed. Women staff members then told the headmaster how wrong he had been to take her. Her provocations became numerous: Debbie managed, even when she was wearing a school uniform, to appear seductive; inevitably the teachers were annoyed. When they became repressive, she gave them a lecture on liberal morality. Although she was doing better academically than ever before, and for the first time made real friends among her own age group, the staff concentrated on Debbie to such an extent that she became a scapegoat. The principal felt that he had no alternative but to send her home.

A major problem that any one faces in handling the seriously disturbed adolescent is knowing when to ask for expert help. Pediatricians, family practitioners, teachers, and youth workers should be knowledgeable about the major psychiatric syndromes of adolescents. In particular, they should be sensitive as to when biological dysfunction is likely to be a significant cause of difficulties. The failure to obtain early appropriate medical intervention means that symptomatic behavior is likely to continue and the likelihood of a developmental impasse is enhanced. Parents generally do not seek help, initially, in the field of psychiatry; they and their children are entitled to expect that adults who are trained professionals should know whether psychiatric treatment is likely to be of use. This requires that helping adults both get to know children and learn how to recognize the type of disturbed behavior patterns that may be symptoms of more severe difficulties. Help should be sought *before* the presence of a disturbed adolescent in a social setting can no longer be tolerated.

SELF-RIGHTING MECHANISMS IN ADOLESCENCE

To a certain degree the idea that, insofar as emotional disturbance is concerned, one can snap out of it, or, alternately, grow out of it, continues to exist, not only in the United States, but also in many other countries of the Western world. Like so many of the concepts of society, this has a kernel of truth. Because of it, attempts to get necessary help may never occur or be delayed, but it is fair to say that it may also allow young people to solve their difficulties by themselves. To be able to conquer difficulties obviously enhances an adolescent's self-esteem; this is clearly desirable. The important thing is that the price should not be too high. For example, drug dependence, especially on such substances as marijuana, is colluded in both by nonactivity on the part of many adults, schools, and youth centers and may be encouraged by adults who smoke "grass" with younger people.

The psychic turbulence of some young people's adolescence may automatically correct childhood upsets. The change in the attitudes of the adolescent toward the self and the resulting attitude changes on the part of parents, teachers, and others may create a self-righting mechanism during adolescence. The possibility of relating on an emotional level to adults who are new in the young person's life may offer a second chance for mature development. This is particularly true in a social environment in which people are sensitive to adolescent needs.

On the other hand, a change for the better may be more apparent than real; the adolescent may repress his internal conflicts and appear to function as if nothing were wrong. In this situation, there is frequently little emotional energy left to meet the challenges of the real world. The adolescent may pay the price for his superficial improvement by failing to develop his full potential.

The self-labeling propensity of adolescents may also discourage adults from referring them for help. Many are fearful that young people sent to a psychiatrist may then describe themselves and explain away their actions in terms of being emotionally disturbed: "I'm sick, I will act accordingly." The propensity of adolescents to acquire a false identity may make it very difficult to motivate some to seek help. Adolescents who abuse drugs may announce themselves to another person with "I'm a head." Young adolescents in conflict may use gang membership to reinforce their false identity.

Those who are emotionally distressed may find it difficult to say: "I am me, I am a person." Instead they are all too ready to wear the label that is available, or that society gives them, to obtain a false sense of security. So young people may call themselves freaks, straight, punks, and jocks. Potentially helpful adults are likely to worry when adolescents flaunt an eccentric label. Are they really disturbed? Or are they exaggerating a minor difficulty for effect? Can anything be done anyway?

Any labeling of adolescents is liable to create difficulties. Many are all too often prepared to adopt the identity they are given in their immediate world. When they are tagged by schools as failures by being put in low academic tracks, they tend to respond and see themselves accordingly as failures. When the young are saddled with formal diagnoses that imply a poor chance of recovery, the people around them tend to be so influenced by these that recovery is made more difficult.

FEAR OF PSYCHIATRY

A further reason why adolescents are not referred for help when they need it is that many people are both ignorant about, and suspicious of, psychiatry. Some believe that all patients lie on a couch, others that psychiatrists deal only with the insane:

> In Finland, a psychiatrist telephoned a boy's teacher and said that he would like to discuss a boy's difficulties with her. Later that evening the psychiatrist was telephoned at his home by the teacher's husband. He was highly suspicious and demanded to know why the psychiatrist wanted to interview his wife.

This suspicion of psychiatrists still exists in many societies and represents a dread of the unknown forces inside each human being. Many teachers, for example, often believe that sending their pupil to a psychiatrist implies that they have failed to perform their job adequately, or they are afraid that moral weakness and grave mental illness will be detected in the adolescent. These attitudes rub off on adolescent patients, who may say that they think the job of a psychiatrist is to see whether or not they are crazy.

If teachers do not consciously hold these attitudes themselves, they often assume that parents will feel ashamed of their child's need for help.

> A teacher at an excellent school wanted a girl who had been stealing to see a psychiatrist. The letter she wrote to the girl's mother about this was so vague, talking of a "psychologist friend of the school," that the mother had no idea what the teacher was trying to say. When the mother found out what was happening, after giving permission for a psychologist

to talk to her daughter, she was shocked and angry, she had failed to recognize that the teacher was saying that the girl was emotionally upset and needed psychiatric help.

QUALITY OF PSYCHIATRIC CARE FOR ADOLESCENTS

The concept of peer-group counseling is often applied by adults to avoid the responsibility of facing emotional disturbance in their charges. It is much easier to get an adolescent of fifteen who is smoking pot two or three times daily to talk to marijuana-smoking young adults in their early twenties and imagine something constructive is being done than to face the real distress of the youngster.

> In one high school, a drug-help group was set up in a room in the school to talk to the students who so wished about drugs. Apparently very successful rap sessions were held. Obviously no formal follow-up was possible, but a group of students said at a drug-education discussion that all the students who took part in the sessions were more heavily into drugs after the session than before.

Peer counseling is offered, in particular, to institutionalized delinquents and minority-group students; alternately a poorly trained social worker or counselor of the same race may be assigned because, supposedly, the children will more likely to be understood, irrespective of the quality or the training of the helper. This is racism at its worst. What matters is the quality of help offered; the more deprived the youngster, the better it should be. Regrettably, this is often not the case.

If an adolescent does go to a clinic, the chances of his being adequately helped are, at present, extremely small, since many psychiatrists, social workers, and teachers do not have the training to understand the problems of children and adolescents.

> A psychiatrist who specialized in treating adolescents gave the last lecture of a course to a group of graduating social workers at a well-known school of social work. In the question period one student said, "How do you talk to adolescents?" Nowhere in the course had any significant discussions about techniques of relating to adolescents been held.

Too many clinics process young people as if they were on a moving staircase, spending insufficient time with them or their families because they are overextended in the services they offer. Psychiatrists who are trained to work only with children often may find it difficult to relate to adolescents. Theirs is much the same problem as that of a grade-school teacher who feels out of his or her depth with boys or girls of fifteen.

Traditionally, adolescents have been considered difficult to help psychiatrically. Adolescents are often reluctant to see themselves as needing help of any kind from adults. They particularly resent being sent to a child-guidance clinic. To wait in a room in which parents and children are also waiting and to be seen in a playroom for small children—all this makes the adolescent feel that he is being treated as a small child. Service delivery for adolescents is also unsatisfactory. Many clinics tend to have very long waiting lists, and adolescents are usually referred for help at a time of crisis. By the time the day of the appointment has come, the adolescent is often unwilling to turn up, or in some way or another the problem seems to have faded. The need for help is then no longer considered necessary by anyone: doctors, teachers, parents, or the youngsters themselves. This is particularly likely because parents, if not schools, are always hopeful that matters will right themselves. Sometimes staff from referring agencies may become so resentful of what they see as the cavalier attitude of psychiatric clinics to their needs, implied by long waiting lists, that they give up requests for help in despair.

EXPECTATIONS OF PSYCHOLOGICAL HELP

All emotionally disturbed adolescents feel both all-powerful and helpless. These feelings do not counteract each other, but when a referral for help is made, omnipotence is projected onto the potential therapist, and too much may be expected in the way of psychological assistance. Disturbed adolescents, and often their parents, may look for immediate and dramatic improvement. Both may find it difficult to accept that psychological progress is not likely to take the form of a straight line upward, but rather a wave motion on an upward curve. Psychiatrists should make it clear in initial interviews that there can be no magical change. If they fail to do this, both the adolescent and those involved with him may prematurely withdraw in disappointment. Of course, on occasions, change is rapid, and this contributes to the unreal picture of the omnipotent psychiatrist:

> A sixteen-year-old boy was referred for help after having been troublesome for about three years. Andrew was depressed and felt that the teachers were expecting him to be troublesome. He felt that little was to be gained by staying in school. Whenever he found work difficult, he walked out. His teachers responded repressively; Andrew became more outrageously provocative. A late developer, he behaved as if he were

really an early adolescent. He was argumentative, difficult, exhibitionistic, easily upset, and in constant trouble. By the time Andrew came for help, puberty had started. The fact of referral changed the teachers' attitude toward him; they decided that he must be disturbed and, therefore, became less critical. Andrew experienced, with immense relief, the physical changes that he had thought would never occur. He was able in three or four sessions to discuss his feelings about his teachers and his late development. His behavior changed dramatically. He became a successful member of the school where it had been thought that he could never hold a responsible position. As a result, the staff began to expect equally dramatic changes in many of their more disturbed pupils. There was a flood of referrals for help, which rapidly dried up when the same "magic" was not forthcoming.

Not all adolescents can be helped in outpatient psychiatric clinics; formal psychiatric treatment, in particular individual or group psychotherapy, may have little to offer to adolescents who cannot form relationships. In psychotherapy, the understanding a patient develops with a therapist makes possible the control of disturbed and antisocial behavior. The patient then needs to develop those relationships that alone can enable him to grow.

The stormy course of some adolescents' treatment tends to become intolerably difficult for people around them (Miller, 1957). This sometimes has inevitable, if unfortunate, consequences. Because it is difficult to predict when change will occur, an adolescent may be rejected just at the point of improvement. Frequently, if adolescents feel themselves change, they automatically resist the process. The individual may engage in a burst of disturbed behavior as if to prove that nothing has changed. One is as one has always felt oneself to be; nothing is different. At this point interested adults are likely to feel that the situation is now intolerable: "We have done all we can and there is no point in trying any further."

It is essential that psychiatrists and other workers with young people should understand one another. For example, psychiatrists often feel that they get no cooperation from schools. A distance is then created between the teacher and the psychiatrist. Each has no real idea of what it is that the other expects, and makes few attempts to find out.

It is also important that school social workers be supported by psychiatrists. Without adequate psychiatric advice, expectations may be aroused that cannot be fulfilled. The better the worker, the more likely is it that he or she will discover and release disturbed behavior. Adolescents who sense difficulties within themselves usually cannot go directly to a person they know to be helpful; they have to act out a request for assistance. Once moderately upset children are helped within a school, more disturbed adolescents will surface. A school social worker will not have the personal resources to help severely disturbed adolescents, who will attempt to get help through disturbed behavior. The school social workers are then put in the same impossible position as psychiatrists who work in poor penal institutions. By their assistance to some, they may encourage young people to believe that they will get help for their difficulties; when adequate aid is not forthcoming, such individuals feel acutely disappointed and teased.

Teachers and other adults should use the psychiatrist sensibly. Some are so anxious to help adolescents they perceive as disturbed, or adolescents they have referred to a psychiatrist, that they make help very difficult. Unwittingly, they may put themselves and the psychiatrist in a ludicrous position:

> Lewis was sent for help at the age of fifteen because he had stolen $2.00 from a changing room. Despite the fact that he was warned that further bad behavior might mean supervision, he followed this with a series of minor infringements of school rules. Between his first and second appointment with the psychiatrist, he was caught by a teacher with a packet of cigarettes. He was told that he would be suspended, unless "your doctor specifies otherwise."
>
> The boy felt the school was saying: "We will reject you unless we are told not to do so." Meaning to be helpful, the school authorities effectively told Lewis that they did not trust their own judgment and they gave the psychiatrist a power over his life that could not be helpful. Lewis felt obliged to be overpolite to the doctor and found it difficult to talk freely about how he felt about himself, his parents, and the school. He thus had to be on his best behavior because the psychiatrist had such power over him.

Often, children are suspended until a psychiatrist will say they are fit to return to school. This is futile; behavior is also a function of the quality of the environment. A similar pattern is created when children who steal in school are sent home with the statement that they can return if a specialist recommends that they return. It is not surprising then that in most parts of the Western world referral to a psychiatrist is still seen as a last resort. The psychiatrist may become the policeman for disturbed young people. It is not uncommon for adolescents to be warned that they will be referred to a psychiatrist unless they pull their socks up.

NEED FOR NONPSYCHIATRIC HELP

Deficiencies in the psychiatric services and the difficulties involved in using them means that skilled assistance is needed even more from school staff. Some adolescents can probably only be helped in educational settings; schools and youth clubs can be very helpful to an adolescent who finds it difficult to form one-to-one human relationships and who thus finds it very hard to be helped by psychotherapy. The general atmosphere of a school may help such young people form tenuous and not very emotionally meaningful relationships, yet obtain satisfaction from performing useful and worthwhile tasks. Too many demands are not then made upon such adolescents, and they may find satisfaction in the numerous activities, physical, imaginative, or academic, offered.

To understand the disturbances of adolescents and how to treat them, it is necessary to sort out three factors: the type of symptoms, the capacity of the individual to form meaningful emotional relationships with others, and the etiology of the upset. It is important to consider built-in stress and supports that impinge on the individual in three areas: the family, the environment, and the personality of the individual as it affects the perception of the world. The maximum helpful effort can then be placed where it will carry the most weight. Sometimes the main attempt will be with brain biochemistry. Sometimes the goal, initially, will be to control the behavior through some type of drug, for example; a change of environment or help with the family or work on personality difficulties may be indicated at other times. Any one individual may need different kinds of help at different times, but, whatever is done, young people need a continuity in their relationship with helpful adults. If continuity of care with the same group of adults is not provided, much effort is wasted, as adolescents are highly sensitive to the loss of meaningful adults. The assumption is sometimes made that if an adolescent is in formal psychotherapy, other relationships do not matter. For example, court social workers commonly sever their relationships with clients when a decision for outpatient therapy is made. Quite apart from the fact that external controls may be needed in an adolescent's life, psychotherapy, when the therapist provides the only meaningful relationship in an individual's world, is almost bound to fail.

PREVENTION OF MALADJUSTMENT

The networks of society should be preserved and strengthened if prevention of maladjustment, which offers the most hope for the development of healthy young people, is to be possible. Individual dedicated teachers and youth workers can perform remarkable tasks in poor school systems and neighborhoods, but society cannot rely on the lifeblood of very special human beings. Many social organizations are necessary, but the stability that society lacks—and without which many adolescents find it difficult to develop—can be recreated in the world of school by skilled staff. The resilience, charm, creativity, and loving qualities of humanity can be seen in sharp focus during the adolescent age period. The destructive anger and hatred of mankind can also be most vividly present at that time.

The psychological mettle of the young is tested and retested in present-day society. In some ways we are now permissive; this is probably desirable if it allows young people to make emotional contact with each other and the world. Permissiveness, however, becomes destructive license when it exposes individuals to intolerable stress and conflict. The issue, in society, is how to allow for the creativity while containing violence. We can do this only if we learn from our own history; people can direct their energies outward in a constructive way only when they have a safe and secure emotional base from which to grow.

Before remedial action to help adolescents grow is possible, the way in which social systems fail to meet the developmental needs of the young must be understood. When, for example, community mental health organizations deal only with the symptomatic manifestations of social-system malaise, they may preserve an inadequate social organization. If, for example, distressed and disturbed youth are removed from schools, helped, and then returned, little has been done to look at the fundamental maladjustment within the organization.

A decision may be made, by helping people, not to work intensively with a disturbed family because an individual child may grow up and grow away from it. The same decision made about a social organization that significantly affects the lives of generations of young people should be made only after the most thoughtful deliberation.

REFERENCES

American Psychiatric Association (1971), *Standards for Psychiatric Facilities Serving Children and Adolescents.* Washington, D.C.

Berg, L. (1968), *Rising Hill.* Harmondsworth: Penguin.

Bettelheim, B., and Sylvester, E. (1948), A therapeutic milieu. *Am. J. Orthopsychiatr.,* 18:191–206.

Carroll, B. J., and Curtis, G. C. (1976), Neuroendocrine Regulation in Depression. *Archives of Gen. Psychiatr.,* 133(1):45–50.

Feinstein, S., and Miller, D. (1980), Psychosis of adolescence. In *Basic Handbook of Child Psychiatry,* Vol. II, ed. J. D. Noshpitz, pp. 708–722. New York: Basic Books Inc.

Grapentine, L. (1982), Personal Communication.

Group for Advancement of Psychiatry. (To be published 1984), Illegitimate Pregnancy in Adolescents.

Knesper, D., and Miller, D. (1976), Treatment plans for mental health care. *Am. J. Psychiatr.,* 133(1):65–80.

Miller, D. (1957), The treatment of adolescents in an adult hospital. *Bull. Menninger Clin.*, 21:189–198.

———— (1965), *Growth to Freedom, The Psycho-Social Treatment of Delinquent Youth.* Bloomington: Indiana University Press, pp. 63–77.

Shields, R. W. (1962), *A Cure of Delinquents.* London: Heinemann.

Chapter 15

Principles
of Adolescent Therapy

Just as in general medicine, it is self-evident in psychiatric medicine that the etiology of any disturbance has to be understood before any helpful recommendations can be made. Unfortunately, whether therapy is given by non-physicians or by psychiatrists, this concept is not generally applied. Often, the type of assistance depends on the discipline of the helping person. Sociologists think in sociological terms, psychologists in individual psychological ways, psychiatrists may have a psychological or sociological orientation, but add the use of medication. Within any one discipline, there are numerous orientations: the psychotherapies—group, family, individual; behavior-modification techniques; milieu therapy and therapeutic communities; somatic treatments. Even within these orientations, the adolescent may be offered assistance that is related to such factors as the time the therapist has available. A psychotherapist with one free session a week offers this; a group therapist with a vacancy in a group makes the place available.

In medicine, the discovery of certain drugs and surgical techniques has made it possible to improve, at any rate potentially, service delivery. In helping adolescents, not only is it important to determine whether or not there is significant brain pathology that might be helped by medication, but those social organizations that impinge on adolescents need to understand their role in helping or hindering personality development. Just as the individual diagnosed as suffering from a pneumococcal pneumonia may now be treated with the appropriate antibiotic, so children with conduct disorders may need appropriate medication, but personality development can only proceed more smoothly if the staff of schools and youth centers and extra-parental adults then respond in appropriate ways. To date, attempts to help the maturation of the personalities of disturbed adolescents are often hindered by the rigidities and unawareness of social systems.

SOCIAL ORGANIZATIONS AS THERAPEUTIC AGENTS

The necessity for continuity of human relationships has been repeatedly stressed. With this in mind, schools could become more sensitive about the use of maturational norms in academic placement (Jones, 1969). After the age of eighteen or so, when adolescents begin a university education, they usually enter an educational system that does not normally consider the individual student's age, at any rate prior to age twenty-five, as a criterion of academic progress. In community colleges, high school subjects are taken irrespective of age. The European concept is that it is not necessary to teach each subject every day; if the concept of a half-day off twice a week were adopted, if schools had a viable house system, established small-group continuity, and allowed children of different levels to use specialized central facilities for certain academic and vocational activities, what would then be needed would be more adequate training for teachers in human development and techniques of interpersonal relationships.

Within a school, one aim of a teacher should be to provide emotional support and care, while adolescents learn, along with academic or vocational knowledge, that impulsive needs for gratification cannot be met. A baby is harmed if it has a mother who rushes to give it a bottle before it cries: similarly, to meet needs before they are expressed, imprints on the human personality an unreal image of the world. An environment that does not allow an adolescent to experience frustration does not help him mature. There is, then, no evidence that it is desirable to abandon in academic and nonacademic subjects the need for a high standard of achievement and pride in productivity. It is a mistake to imagine that to be totally loving is to be nonfrustrating: too much love can produce intolerable frustration, since it makes people feel helpless and impotent (Bettelheim, 1950).

Just as school systems consistently repeat the trauma of separation from significant others, equally the psychiatric system does not offer genuine continuity of care. Children and adolescents have their emotional privacy invaded by diagnostic assessments with no follow-through; adolescents who require residential treatment have consistently encapsulated treatment experiences with no genuine continuity of care. Hospitals that place disturbed adolescents in closed wards and then transfer them to open ones as they improve, devalue the significance of relationships with other than psychotherapists.

RELIEF OF TENSION AND ANXIETY

During the maturation process, the young may not be strong enough to withstand tension and anxiety. Their wishes for the immediate relief of frustration may be greater than their capacity to delay an action they know to be unwise. Internal conflicts are then acted out on the community or directed against the self (Freud, 1920). For example, if an adolescent wants to pass an examination, but because of a general depression finds the subject boring, he is likely to forget to do his work, fall asleep, and lie to himself. Teachers are disappointed and often irritated, and the youngster suffers an unnecessary failure. If adolescents are not aware of what troubles them, or if they feel hopelessly misunderstood and ill-treated, antisocial behavior is more likely to occur. An adolescent who appreciates his surroundings will try to do his best. A common fantasy of the large high school, which has abandoned meaningful emotional relations as the norm, is that adolescents can be controlled by a tariff of rewards and punishments. Well-adjusted adolescents who feel positive about adults will accept control and will not see controls as punitive and arbitrary. A young person who feels loved and cared for by an adult can often abstain from self-destructive impulsive behavior for the other person, if not for himself. This principle applies both to education and all other types of psychological care.

It is not unusual for children who have done well academically and socially in high schools up to grade ten to fail in grade eleven and start to misbehave. This may occur partly because the youngster cannot tolerate the idea of independence, which is now imminent, partly because it is no longer possible, at sixteen, for the average adolescent to contain impulsive behavior only for the sake of parents. To do so sacrifices autonomy strivings. A poorly developed sense of the future, particularly in boys, does not deter the gratification that may be obtained from impulsive behavior. An intellectual understanding, without emotional awareness, that present behavior affects future activities is likely to increase the adolescent's level of anxiety and so enhance the probability of impulsive behavior, which becomes an attempt to avoid frustration.

John, sixteen, who had made straight A's in grade ten and D's and F's in grade eleven, was referred to a psychiatrist because he missed 120 class periods in one semester. He said, "I know my parents want me to do well and last year that was enough, but now I hassle with them all the time; particularly my mother. I want to go into a profession, but this worries me; and I can't get my head together enough to do any work."

At the start of grade eleven, John got all new teachers, and the two teachers he had liked in grade ten no longer taught him. He neither knew, liked, or valued any of the staff presently teaching him, so the social system no longer supported his autonomy strivings. In schools, the most liked teachers tend to get the best results; they are the ones who find it easy to keep a class interested and involved. It is in contact with individuals such as these that adolescents are likely to suspend difficult behavior. One year of such people is not enough. There is no reason, however, why one teacher should not be able to teach the same group of children a subject over two to three years.

Those who oppose change argue that if teacher-pupil consistency is maintained, children may get stuck with a disliked teacher. Most children can, and should, tolerate occasional discomfort, and they need to learn to handle this. "Change is part of life" is the argument for the school system not producing interpersonal continuity; that is the very reason why it should. Adolescents may never experience significant relationship constancy in our society outside the nuclear family, and it does not always happen there.

RELATIONSHIP CONSTANCY

All adolescents dislike and resent losing people who are important to them. When a "good" adult leaves an adolescent, this arouses at least irritation, at most despair. The anger of separation has to be worked out with the individual who is leaving. If it is not, the next adult will have a harder time forming a new relationship, and finally the youngster may appear to give up trying to establish a mutually trusting relationship with adults.

As a result, by the time grade twelve is reached in high schools, adolescents may expect very little from their teachers. Some teachers, however, are willing to try to create positive consistent relationships with their pupils. Those teachers who wish to respect the integrity of individuals and not repress them will try to provide a setting in which this is possible. Unfortunately, disturbed adolescents who are likely to become aggressive may see such teachers as weaklings. In a generally rigid school, the frustrations forced on them in class will be acted out in the classroom with the more understanding teacher. In such an authoritarian school, the new teacher with the attitude that rigid external control need not be a suitable teaching mechanism may be forced to be as repressive as the other teachers. The more a school fails to help its difficult adolescents, the harder it is for a teacher who has an authority role in such a setting to have a good relationship with pupils. All authority adults tend to be tarred with the brush of the environment in which they work. Very remarkable personalities may be able to hold out against this pressure; others have no alternative but to conform or leave. In present day society it is still possible to find significant other adults in neighborhoods, with the extended family, in church and youth groups. Unfortunately too many children are isolated with their parents and the only available network to provide necessary social supports for personal growth is within a school system that generally fails in this respect.

THE ROLE OF SIGNIFICANT ADULTS

Adults who are models for young people should have attitudes which are generally consistent with the manner of living in the larger social environment. When areas of conflict exist, they should be clear. The content of moral education should be consistent with the environment in which it is taught. For example: if a teacher talks about mutually caring relationships in an environment in which these do not generally occur, he is felt to be insincere or helpless. It is impossible to teach that human sexual behavior should be part of a loving interaction unless the relationship between teacher and pupil is positive.

In unsatisfactory environments, individual staff members may give real help to individuals, but they are unlikely to be used as models by the larger group of adolescents for whom they have responsibility. This is especially true when such people are insufficiently valued by the environment and what they say is inconsistent with what their presence implies.

When adolescents are seeking autonomy from their parents they are particularly likely to be influenced by significant adults. If the attitudes of these individuals are generally consistent with those of the family, identification is less stressful. When dissonance may be necessary, as in the treatment of some antisocial youth, the situation is more complicated.

The provision of good psychological treatment and general emotional care depends on the ability of an environment to meet the nonspecific developmental needs of those adolescents within it. A good teacher or counselor working in such a setting should be able to form relationships with adolescents that will help them incorporate into their personalities the positive values of the world in which they live. In a setting that fails to meet appropriate human needs, a particular problem in our society, the young are very suspicious of all authority adults. If their doubt abates, and they seek counseling, they will expose to their counselor the corruption of their own relationships and those with other adults in the system. This exposure is an implicit demand that something be done. Usually the counselor has no power to effect reforms, and the adolescent feels cheated. Any faith in authority adults that may have been developing is dissipated. If an attempt at reform is made, the institution may, with many rationalizations, try to get rid of the person who is perceived as attempting to discredit it.

When adolescents develop good relationships with adults in environments that meet their needs, they can communicate their feelings and are thus freer to cope with themselves and the demands of the world. Communication is in action and in words; the former is more important in early adolescence. Appropriate control that values the integrity of such young people helps them feel cared about.

Whatever formal role is assigned to adults who are significantly involved with emotionally disturbed young people—teachers, counselors, social workers, physicians—all have an important role in helping young people understand the complex reality of their world. Adolescents are faced with problems of general and political morality, sexual behavior, drug dependence, and the use of alcohol and cigarettes. Adolescents identify with what adults do, rather than what they say. If teachers or parents use cigarettes, any exhortation from them not to smoke is likely to be valueless. When adults smoke in their common room, adolescents are likely to do the same in the washroom. When teachers go on strike or refuse to perform extracurricular duties, their message to their pupils is that direct action is the appropriate response to grievances. Children adopt the same technique by refusing to go to class when they have a grievance against their teacher. When adults become aware of their own inevitable inconsistencies they will allow for their effect.

It is sometimes believed that group approaches to the young are simpler than one-to-one relationships. Such group approaches depend on a good working relationship between adults and young people, however. Adults should be able to listen to adolescents and help them with their difficulties— whether help is explicitly requested or not—before they can help a group with its conflicts. The individual who is empathic and is valued because of a particular skill should be able to establish an individual working relationship with young people. Then adolescents will have someone to whom they can turn as individuals, and they can also discuss the conflicts that trouble them as a group.

Adolescents, because of their fear of dependence, often find it difficult to express gratitude. Even if an adult has been helpful in an individual relationship, an adolescent may complain that "he tried to talk to me, but he was a phony." He may feel that the adult was not sufficiently understanding or did not care enough. The lack of appreciation that is sometimes shown by the young often leaves adults, who are thus made to feel inadequate, reluctant to try to help. Those teachers who have a capacity to relate to their adolescent pupils are often unreasonably put in the position of psychotherapists or personal counselors. Yet the need is so great, they really have no choice but to try to be useful. Probably no other organized group in society has the same opportunities to aid adolescents as the well-trained teacher; only after the pupil has left school may the deserved appreciation be offered. The production of successful loving people is the reward of all adults involved with the young.

THERAPEUTIC RELATIONSHIPS WITH ADOLESCENTS

All workers with young people—teachers, school counselors, probation officers, physicians and social workers—generally feel the need for more adequate training in interpersonal relationships and personal counseling techniques with adolescents.

Adolescents are creatures of their environment and are highly conformist to consistent expectations, and the adults who wish to influence the young should understand the effect of the environment on the adolescent's behavior, but they should also realize its effect on themselves. There is clear evidence, for example, that adults who spend a large part of their day in emotional contact with middle-stage adolescents adopt the latter's relationship techniques (Krohn and Miller, 1974).

In addition to specific psychotherapeutic techniques, there are some general guidelines that might be of value to those who wish to relate in a useful way to adolescents in distress. Thus it is common for specific contact to occur with adolescents at a time of crisis, and although an adolescent may ask for help in words, he more often implicitly demands help through an antisocial act. The helpful adult needs to understand what is behind the adolescent's difficult behavior, and it is tempting, in looking for the answer, to ask the youngster why he behaved in such a way. This is usually a pointless question; if the adolescent knows the answer, he may lie; if he does not, he may feel obliged to produce a specious reason. Although he may think he knows, his answer is usually inaccurate. Asking such a question is likely to make a young person feel persecuted; discussing his general life situation is much better. If the adult covers the adolescent's general social situation, work, and family relationships in an interview, the explanation for the difficulty often becomes clear.

Adults who are out of touch with their own inner experience of feeling and imagination, who are unaware of their own conflicts, and who are preoccupied with their own status find it difficult to help the young. All grown-ups interviewing adolescents should ask themselves at least three questions: What is the youngster likely to be feeling right now? How has this feeling been modified by interviews with me and other authority figures in the past (Gill et al., 1954)? What are the adolescent's expectations of the situation, how has he been told about it, what is his perception of the interviewer's role?

THE ADULT AS AN AUTHORITY FIGURE

Authority has two meanings: it can mean expertise and it can also mean coercion. Adults who see themselves as the former are commonly perceived as the latter by adolescents, depending on their state of mind. In all human beings, experiences of the past condition responses in the present. The reaction to authority in the here and now is based partly on a previous perception of authority. So if a doctor or a personal or academic counselor or a teacher in a school or university attempts to relate to an adolescent, the latter's reaction will be determined by many factors. It will be based partly on childhood experiences of authority from father or mother, partly on the experience of authority in hospitals and clinics, schools and colleges, partly on how personally secure the young person feels. Insofar as the latter is concerned, if the youngster is feeling very helpless, an authority figure will easily be perceived as persecutory. The peer group's perception of the individual staff member, who is acting as a personal counselor, is very important: How has he treated students in the past? What is his reputation in society-at-large? The issue of reputation, both institutional and societal, influences the attitudes of young people to their personal counselor. Although a reputation as an expert may not be accurate, it is generally helpful. Minority students are sometimes encouraged to feel that only members of their own ethnic group can understand them. The prejudiced individual of any race is hardly likely to be a good personal or vocational counselor, but the real issue should be the competence of an individual, not his skin color or ethnic group. Also important is the depth and breadth of a counselor's education. Not only does the identity of different ethnic groups need to be understood, but also a counselor who is a Renaissance man or woman is likely to impart knowledge quite unconsciously.

Freedom of expression with authority adults is very difficult if it is not promoted in the whole life of the community. In schools where nobody expects children to ask questions in the classroom, it is quite unrealistic to expect them to talk freely to adults in an interview.

Some adults working with adolescents are proponents of conformity to societal wishes; others may feel that this is not their role, that it is their responsibility to help young people feel internally free to choose whether to conform to the wishes of society or not. Rebellious young people may believe that their actions are based on an experience of inner freedom, but their rebellion may be an attempt to break out of an internal straitjacket.

However the helping adult sees his role, it is desirable that adolescents feel that adults are not only on their side, but are also not against parents or society. Since antisocial behavior is usually self-destructive, the adult should try to convey, without being pompous, that he wants it to cease. His attitude should be: Let us see how you and I together can be useful to you.

PSYCHOLOGICAL COMFORT IN INTERVIEWS

The basic principle for successful human relationships is to help the other person feel at ease. Even a confrontation about antisocial behavior will be more effective if the adolescent has a good relationship with the adult involved. But good will is not always enough.

Adults may know that condescension is unsatisfactory in interviews; however, what influences the boy or girl is not the intent of the interviewer, but what is perceived as his or her intent.

Those young people with whom stressful situations are being discussed are particularly sensitive to what they think the interviewer thinks of them:

> A boy with a rich, powerful alcoholic father was sent to see a professor of psychiatry because the staff of his prep school was alarmed about his frequent outbursts of temper. Harry was fifteen and a late developer; there were as yet no signs of puberty. In his first interview he was seen by the professor in the presence of his staff and students. Harry replied to all questions in monosyllables. The professor thought that the boy might be suffering from an acute personality disintegration, possibly schizophrenia, because of his withdrawal.
>
> In a subsequent interview with a psychiatrist who was not a professor, Harry said that he thought the professor was much too important to talk to him about his troubles. Harry then spoke of his feeling of inferiority because he was small; other boys teased him and called him queer. It was more difficult for him at school because his father always collected him at vacation time in a big expensive car; other boys were

critical about this. Unwittingly, the professor was repeating for Harry the painful experience that he had had with his powerful, successful father.

In this case the boy misperceived the intention and feelings of the professor, who did care about the welfare of young people. In other situations, attempts to help by those who do not like adolescents—or the particular youngster concerned—are seldom effective.

Adolescents are sensitive to their treatment prior to an interview as well as to what happens within it. An offhand secretary can greatly disturb the young; rigid registration procedures in hospitals, in which individuals are kept interminably waiting, form letters, and lateness for appointments imply a lack of caring to which the youngster is likely to respond negatively. What the interviewer actually does is as important as what he or she says. Taking notes in order to remember what is said at the time may arouse a whole gamut of feelings in the other person, varying from worry as to what is being written to a feeling that it must be critical. Sometimes an adolescent may feel that the interviewer is more interested in the quality of the notes than in his or her own feelings and ideas. If notes must be taken, it is important to recognize how anxious this might make young people and to tell them why notes are important. Much the same sort of concern can be aroused when a report is read in front of an adolescent with no comment about its content or who wrote it. If an interview is seen as criticism or chastisement, the adolescent's anxiety can prevent the adult's comments from having any long-term effect or value.

For an adolescent being interviewed for the first time, two issues need resolution: the perception and understanding of the situation held by the youngster, and the interviewer's frank statement as to his or her understanding. Adults who value words as significant communication tend to underestimate the importance of action (Sullivan, 1951). Adolescence is an action-oriented age; adolescents interpret—and sometimes misinterpret—the behavior of adults, and they themselves often communicate by their actions. Anxiety is most commonly shown by behavior: the way an adolescent sits, nervous fingers, agitated fidgeting—all these show the presence of tension. If these signs of tension do not disappear during an interview, it means that the adolescent is not able to respond and become more comfortable. When an attempt to help the youngster feel at ease obviously does not succeed, it is reasonable to comment on this in a noncritical manner. Adolescents have conflicts about exhibitionism and know when they are being observed; their automatic inclination may be to feel embarrassed and criticized when a comment is made about appearance, particularly because adults often pick on this. Adolescent hypersensitivity may turn a helpful comment into a persecutory one.

An adolescent who does not respond to an understanding remark about his tension may often be helped by a more oblique technique: "Sometimes people are so often criticized about the way they look that they get hurt by anyone noticing it." This type of comment allows the adolescent to reject an idea if he wishes.

All interviews should have a goal. It may be to understand the adolescent's capacity to be emotionally involved, to cope with frustration, and to appraise reality accurately. The interviewer should determine what he or she wants to learn or convey. It may be the control of disturbed behavior. Some feel that the way to exercise control in such situations is to apply a conscience pressure, to be an external control for the adolescent. Others believe that the adolescent should feel that the interviewer is an ally who is attempting to be useful in controlling destructive behavior.

It is naive to assume that the person who is put in a helping role will necessarily feel comfortable. Many teachers, for example, understand that there are complex motives behind the behavior and words of their pupils. Because such teachers are concerned about the adequacy of their own response, they prefer to react by avoiding the issue; they act as if no problem existed. All adults who have significant emotional attachments with young people have to face their own inadequacy and guilt. The person who wishes to feel important—or be omnipotent—should not work with adolescents.

CONTROL AND PUNISHMENT

Some adults feel that the only way to show youngsters that what they have done is wrong is by punishment, but it is arguable that punishment, as distinct from control, is ever justified when it is applied by those who do not love the individual. Behavior should have a consequence, which may be felt by the adolescent as punitive, but this should not be the intent of the adult involved. Punishment has to be extremely coercive to control behavior, but even then it rarely works well. The criminal underworld may kill informers; the police cannot function without their presence. The death penalty does not stop homicide and does not lessen its incidence. As a regular or reflex response to wrongdoing, punishment is particularly futile. For late adolescents, punishment represents a failure in development in or the inadequacy of the interpersonal relationships of their social system.

In relationships with their children, parents can always find situations in which they wish they had behaved better or been more understanding or less permissive. Similarly, significant extra-parental adults, whatever their role, may be defensive about what they have done in the past. One way to handle this discomfort is to hide behind the concept of role. Certain actions were not performed, for example, by teachers as people but only because they had to play the role of teacher. It is then assumed that the pupil, or society, will find the unacceptable act more tolerable.

Corporal punishment is a typical example. In those states that continue to tolerate corporal punishment in their educational institutions, some adults feel defensive about it; most feel uncomfortable about having to inflict pain, although they may obtain unconscious satisfaction in so doing. The conflict is eased by the conviction that beating is part of the role of a teacher or, in residential institutions, care worker, and that there is nothing personal about it. This is not how the young see it. The boy who gets beaten is likely to be a less mature member of the society; he is quite unlikely to appreciate a distinction between what is done personally and what is done by an adult playing a role. If such a boy does not value the adult who beats him as an individual, and does not feel that he is cared about, he will react either by an emotional withdrawal ("I don't care") or with fear, according to the severity of the beating. Another possible reaction is contempt. If the boy does feel valued and cared for, he will probably react to the beating with a feeling of slavish dependence, particularly if it has been painful. Advocates of "spare the rod and spoil the child" rationalize that adolescents agree with them. A pupil treated with excessive harshness may react by identifying with what has been done, so adults who may be criticized by an outside authority for such punitive behavior can often show that adolescents support them. Teachers who beat their pupils have the gratification of being told by them that the action was right. This is a similar process to that found in families. The victim of child abuse is likely to become a child abuser as an adult.

No one adult in an authority role can effectively dissociate himself from corporal punishment used in their social setting. Within any social organization, staff appear to support each other: Adolescents feel that if staff work in an organization where beating occurs, they implicitly agree with this type of behavior. Thus, there is mutual responsibility. Staff may attempt to deny this, but their denial will not be accepted by pupils.

Calling upon adolescent victims to support some particular aberration within a system is widespread:

> In a meeting of adults and adolescents to discuss a "disciplinary policy" for a local school system, a school administrator asked a fourteen-year-old girl if she thought peer-group stability was necessary. Her reply was "Oh no, I think it's so nice to have a new set of people every semester." The administrator beamed at this confirmation of a statement previously used by him to justify a no-change policy.

Some adults feel that they should try to talk to children who misbehave, but they have no real expectation that it will be helpful. They will warn a boy about unacceptable behavior and then use violence to repress it. The following story was reported in the English magazine *Where* (Miller, 1969):

George was eleven. Big for his age and very strong, he hadn't been in the school for more than a week before a little boy in his grade was brought to the assistant principal with a bruised mouth. George had hit him, "because he hassled me."

The principal tried to talk to him in a humane, reasonable, and persuasive way, but the same kind of incident was repeated three times in the next month. He decided George should be handed over to the school social worker, who had time to go into his background thoroughly and establish a good relationship with him.

The social worker reported fair progress: he thought he was getting somewhere. Alas, no, for the next victim was a girl. It was established that she called George "four-eyes" (he wore glasses) and he retaliated by striking her very hard on the breast. The assistant principal reported as follows: "I had a chat with George. I found him likable and frank, but he had, so he said, a terrible temper. I decided that he needed to be taught a sharp lesson, but held my hand until the social worker had seen the parents." He went on to say that the father, a long-distance truck driver, had taught George to use his fists, "but only to look after himself." The mother said George did as he liked when her husband was away, that he was an easy boy to be with at home, but was very rough with other boys. The social worker thought, as I did, that George was out of hand and needed checking. "I had George in and told him that the next time he hit anybody without being hit first I would beat the stuffing out of him. Within a fortnight George was brought to me for giving a smaller boy a black eye. I thrashed him and said that next time I would double the dose; I did.

"Since then, over a year ago now, there has been to our knowledge no more bullying."

George may have decided that it was impolitic to hit little girls at school, but he was not being taught that to take advantage of his size to inflict pain on another is wrong.

The more violence adolescents or adults have within themselves, the more they will see violence as appropriate for the control of others. The violent adolescent who is beaten for his violence applies exactly this same technique to try and control other people, usually with less discretion and control than the violence that was applied to his person. Such an adolescent is likely to become an adult who approves of violent techniques of control.

COUNSELING ROLES IN SCHOOLS

Personal counseling roles have been given in some schools to social workers. If this is done, more than one social worker for two thousand or more children is needed. Furthermore, the isolation of this from other roles is unrealistic; for most children, personal help is most easily accepted from someone who has a role that is understandable in the social context in which the adolescents and adults work. Some adults may have administrative authority within the school, but this should not isolate them from offering personal help to the children. Ideally, any adult should be able to help any pupil who approaches him or her. In practice, certain individuals not necessarily designated for a care role are the ones who are contacted. Some feel inadequate to deal with the emotional problems that are brought to them. This difficulty in personally counseling adolescents, and the fact that most school staff have not been adequately trained for it, have led to the idea that the responsibility for the emotional care of school boys and girls should be given to those who do not have an educational role.

The specially trained school counselor should have sufficient skills to help adolescents in distress, and should have a special role in relating to parents. But the presence of such staff may encourage others to opt out even more from a significant personal role in the lives of their pupils.

To ensure good relationships between adolescent and adult in schools, all teachers need both counseling skills and a sensitivity about the effects of social environment on human behavior. Rather than having specially trained school counselors, it would seem better to change the type of courses in schools of education and to offer all present-day teachers a chance to learn more of human relationships and of the difficulties that adolescents may experience. In many schools of education these courses are optional, and furthermore may be taught by those who no longer have relationships with children.

If human relationships in a school are well-developed, teachers may then be said to "teach" human relationships: first, by setting an example in the living social environment of the school, and next, by meaningfully imparting facts and attitudes verbally. But loving attitudes can only be imparted to adolescents in an atmosphere where human beings care for each other. Sex education demonstrates the issue. If pupils are not treated with consideration by teachers, they tend not to respect each other. It is reasonable, if sexual behavior is being discussed, to indicate that intercourse should only take place as an act of love. This concept is not very meaningful if it is offered by someone who is felt to be uncaring. Similarly, there can be no very perceptive discussion of the disadvantages of autocracy, if the teacher leading it behaves like an autocrat.

YOUTH CENTERS

More out-of-school activities should be available. Although formal classes of various sorts, usually adult education, are given in high school buildings at night, these only skim the resources. If a school has facilities for recreation and the creative arts, they should be available to the public, including adolescents, outside school hours. It is absurd to leave them unused in the evening and during school vacations. The arguments that it is too difficult to clean the buildings or that destruction will occur or that funds cannot be made available are unconvincing. In addition to whatever is provided by home and school, adolescents need various youth centers in their neighborhood. At present, these tend to be organized by churches in smaller communities; in many large cities, boys' clubs are run in association with the Boys' Club of America. In many places, however, there is remarkably little cooperation between youth clubs, which may jealously guard their membership. Often the wealthy neighborhoods have the best facilities, although the situation in most affluent suburbs, where youth facilities are notably lacking, is as deplorable if not worse, than in the inner cities. The facilities for youth in poverty-stricken areas are, however, often as run down as the rest of the neighborhood.

Adolescents do not usually move very far in cities; most of their activities occur within about a square mile of their homes. Adolescents should then have neighborhood centers with a multiplicity of available facilities; organized recreation; outlets for creativity; unstructured settings equipped with a food bar, a record player, and a TV set. In each of these, adults should be ready, if asked, to provide an opportunity for interpersonal relationships across age groups with no formally organized activity. Such youth centers can be housed in different kinds of buildings, which (with the provision that poverty is no help) should generally fit the character of the neighborhood. The interior of the youth club should be designed to meet its particular function. In smaller cities and towns, the club should be centrally placed, rather than at the periphery of the community. The hours of such centers should meet adolescent needs; a drop-in unstructured center, for example, should be open every day of the year, if it is to be genuinely useful. Professional staff need to understand the role of volunteers and should be able to train them to understand and assist with adolescent problems. This is essential if a youth center is to convince the adolescent that the community-at-large cares about him.

HUMAN RELATIONSHIPS AND SERVICE TO OTHERS

All communities have a need for service that can be met only by voluntary effort: the care of the aged, the crippled, and the helpless. All adolescents need to feel needed in the world in which they live. Service to the community should be in the school curriculum of all adolescents as soon as the turmoil of puberty is over. However, it is impossible for a school to direct its pupils toward community service, unless the pupils feel that the school is helping them. Schools that appear not to care will not convince their pupils to help others. When teachers are considered distant and uncaring, real cooperation from adolescents will not be forthcoming. They may appear to go along politely with the demands made upon them, but jobs are poorly performed; more aggressive youth merely refuse. Service to the community cannot be like a military school football game in which the attendance of spectators is insisted upon by a roll call, with punishment for absentees. Community service offers adolescents the chance to make contact with all ages and to feel valued, but they must first feel respected by the adults who direct them to this service.

This applies to young people of almost all levels of emotional maturity. In the Adolescent Treatment Center of Northwestern Memorial Hospital in Chicago, one staff member takes fifteen adolescents as volunteers to an approved home for retarded adults each week. The children, whose symptomatic behavior modification ranges from serious drug abuse to homicide, have never failed in five years to perform in an exemplary manner.

The principles of human relationships apply equally to pediatricians and their adolescent patients; youth clubs and youth workers; the staffs of penal institutions and psychiatric hospitals; and school staff and their pupils.

PROBLEMS OF STAFF TRAINING

Apart from understanding the psychosocial implications of human development, special training in understanding human relations and in counseling techniques is a necessity for adults who have responsibility for the care of the young. This may be done by regular training groups (Miller, 1967) and seminars, special vocational courses, or for the few, the sabbatical year. In an ideal society, this training would also be an integral part of the coursework for youth workers and teachers at college. The national shortage of trained people to help those who work directly with adolescents makes the planning of training difficult, and it is likely that the present shortage of such experts will last indefinitely, even though more clinicians are available as a result of cuts in social services. To deal with this problem, a self-help technique with only occasional technical input, in which people working with the young pool their experiences and learn from each other, would seem a realistic solution.

If communications between the adult and the adolescent are to be restored, caring adults should always be present in the social environment.

The essence of successful human relationships with the young is common sense and sensitivity. Though these cannot be *taught*, extra skills can be learned. Young people need relationship consistency, empathy, and an understanding of the significance of communications from involved adults.

PSYCHOTHERAPY

There are many types of psychotherapy. Supportive therapy is designed to relieve tension by offering emotional support. It consists of reality clarification, permission to express feelings, confrontation, and explanation, within the context of a positively felt relationship with a therapist. Expressive therapy is designed to convey understanding, which is both intellectual and emotional, of the meaning of experiences. It may be existential, in which here and now understanding is the primary issue; or it may involve transference, the way in which significance relationships of the past influence the present. Finally, therapy may be behavioral, which involves the management of the patient's life by behavior-modification techniques or through interpersonal relationships. Individual, group, and family therapy are labels that may indicate who is present; they say nothing about what is done.

Attitudes toward psychotherapy are ambivalent: either it is thought to require no special skills or it is considered to be a highly esoteric art. Some of the principles and techniques of psychotherapy, however, are highly relevant for those who would be of use to the adolescent in personal distress.

Because adolescence is midway between childhood and adulthood, a number of the techniques of relating to the world that belong to childhood remain during the period of adolescence, and this produces special treatment parameters. Specifically, action communication is highly significant. Verbal communication may still be much less indicative of how the youngster perceives his world, and this has implications in psychotherapy, family, group, and individual and expressive or supportive. In adult psychotherapy, verbal communication is most meaningful with middle-class adults; it is much less so with working-class adults. It is, however, even less meaningful for pubertal adolescents than for adults from any social class.

Adolescents may be sent to see a psychiatrist by their parents; it is not necessary for early adolescents to wish, consciously, for help. Only very disturbed or very manipulative early adolescents are likely to express such a wish. Parental pressure is still needed in midadolescence, but it is the responsibility of parents to have their child seen by a therapist, who, after the first interview, has to mobilize the adolescent's motivation so that a general willingness to attend without parental pressure becomes evident. In late adolescence, parental pressure may be applied, but the motivation to attend, in situations other than acute personality disintegration, generally must be that of the patient.

INITIAL APPROACH TO THE ADOLESCENT AS A PSYCHIATRIC PATIENT

The attitude of an adolescent to any treatment process is obviously multi-determined. Apart from attitudes that may previously have been created by his environment, treatment begins at the moment of referral to a psychiatrist. Most adolescents up to the maturational age of fifteen or sixteen do not go willingly. A younger adolescent who seeks psychiatric help is usually in very serious psychic difficulty. Most will have been sent to a therapist. They will not have said in words, "I want help," but will have arranged, usually by antisocial behavior, to get into a position in which help will be offered. Repetitious disturbed behavior in an adolescent usually represents a shout for help.

The adolescent's acting out a request for help puts a peculiar responsibility on the psychiatrist. Prior to the referral, the adolescent has shown the ticket of admission for assistance to school teachers, parents, pediatricians, or others. These authorities may then ask for a psychiatric consultation. An affirmative reply, but a delayed initial appointment may imply that the psychiatrist does not really think the youngster or his behavior is important. Adolescents usually request help by creating a crisis; apart from the implications of a delayed response, a long wait may mean that the opportunity to be of assistance is gone. Adolescents act out their request for assistance when the structural supports in their environment fail or when the relationship with their parents or their environment is too stressful. At the crisis point, a new personal environmental homeostasis has not yet been established, and this is the point of optimal intervention.

The success or failure of an attempt to help an adolescent may depend on the initial interview and on the relationship established with the youngster. The therapist should not know in advance a great deal about the patient. In a helping relationship honesty is crucial. It is desirable that the patient lies neither by omission or commission. The therapist who does not tell the adolescent what is known about him is effectively "omitting"; to distort the interview process by spending considerable time discussing what the therapist knows is equally irrational. The therapist should mention what he has been told of the difficulties leading to the request for a consultation; the adolescent is then in the situation that information is required from him, or her, and thus an open communication can be established.

Communication with an adolescent is most significant in a waiting room. In disturbed adolescents, in particular, conflicts about dependence pose a threat to autonomy. The interviewer's actions in a waiting room may indicate to the adolescent how he is seen. Shaking hands with the parents first and then with the adolescent has a different meaning from greeting the adolescent first and then acknowledging the presence of the parents. Usually it is better to talk with the youngster alone first and then meet with the parents and patient together. The next steps toward a satisfactory resolution of difficulties can then be discussed.

CRISIS REFERRALS

Acute crisis referral may occur when young people appear at a hospital emergency room, acutely confused from drugs or otherwise, or following a suicide attempt. Communications from professionals are highly meaningful at such a time. If adolescents are talked down from a bad trip and then sent home, they may understand that assistance will be offered to help drugs be safely used. The message about the drug's toxicity may not have been well recognized.

Suicide attempts or gestures require special care. If adolescents are sent home after a suicide attempt—once it has been established that there is no danger to life—and told to contact a psychiatrist the next day, the implication may be that neither the individual nor the action is taken too seriously. Admission to a hospital after a suicide attempt is always indicated unless it has been firmly established that there is no further risk of self-destruction. If admission is first made to a general hospital it is poor practice not to arrange immediate psychiatric hospitalization as soon as the effects of drug toxicity or physical damage have been alleviated.

> Kenneth, age 16, was admitted to an intensive care unit after having been found unconscious by his father. He had taken over 1,000 mgms of an intermediate action barbiturate which did not disappear totally for six days. The half-life of the drug was 48 hours which meant that two days after ingestion Kenneth was still toxic. Despite this the hospital sent him home over a weekend because a psychiatrist who saw him while he was still toxic felt he did not need to be in a hospital. The next day he took the family car and was seriously injured.

This was the result of a failure to take a suicide attempt seriously enough. Even though it may be clear that the patient is not in immediate danger, the attempt needs to be taken very seriously by authority adults. If adolescents are seen in an emergency room after such behavior, the emergency room physician or psychiatrist should at least make an appointment for the patient for the next day. Preferably, the same person will see the patient, although this may not be possible. Parents often need to deny that their children are suicidal, so to leave it to them to make an appointment may be as unsatisfactory as leaving it to the adolescent. Further, the necessity for protection of the patient until a thorough diagnostic assessment is made is quite crucial.

THE ROLE OF THERAPY IN THE PREVENTION OF DISTURBED BEHAVIOR

Adolescents perceive themselves as all powerful. When they relate to an adult they see as personally helpful, they project their own feeling of omnipotence and assume that the therapist is omnipotent. Adolescents in the initial stages of a therapeutic contact thus see the therapist as an extension of themselves, and this explains the importance of the contact an adolescent might have with a therapist or secretary or receptionist. If a psychiatrist has a secretary who is felt by young patients to be unpleasant, the psychiatrist is blamed, since he is supposed to know about this behavior. To an extent, adolescents who are taking adult steps to autonomy may be like the two-year-olds who are first trying to be independent. When they fall and hurt themselves, they may blame their mothers, who were supposed to know of such an eventuality. When an adolescent trusts an adult enough to allow him to be helpful, such a therapist is supposed to be prescient; he is felt as responsible for the behavior of all his staff. There is some truth in this assumption. Psychiatrists who do nothing when they hear of such episodes show disrespect to the patient.

A particular problem in the outpatient treatment of adolescents is that they will act out their tensions unless this process can be interrupted by therapeutic intervention. In early adolescents, conflict and psychic pain are projected onto the environment; others rather than the adolescent experience the pain. In the first stages of therapy, a major task is to help young people not act out their conflicts in such a way that the chances for assistance will be destroyed. An adolescent who continues to hurt society will not have such behavior tolerated, and the initial wish to be helpful on the part of adults disappears, replaced by a punitive response. To allow therapy to take place, outpatient adolescents must begin to feel positive about their therapists. With prepubertal children, therapists have more time, because the disturbed behavior of a child is usually contained within the family. A nine-year-old may tell his parents that he hates his therapist, but he is less likely to rob the neighborhood store or become drug toxic to demonstrate how futile are attempts to help. If adolescents do not begin to like and value adults who try to help them, they continue to act in self-destructive and aggressive ways. Thus, for adolescents to contain the self-destructive behavior that has brought them to treatment, therapists must be seen as omnipotent, interesting, and involved. Therapists, however, are not omnipotent; they are often devalued by society; they may not be sufficiently interesting; and the adolescent may demand an impossible level of involvement.

Some who work with adolescents seem to be successful with them while they are seeing the youngsters. As soon as such a therapist goes on vacation, however, or the apparently successful therapy ends, the adolescent is exactly where he was before, because the issue of omnipotence has never been resolved. The therapist, too gratified by the positive feelings of his patient, is willing to accept the omnipotent role; he never deals with the angry, anxious experiences that spilled over into the self-destructive behavior that brought the boy or girl to treatment.

COMMUNICATION BETWEEN THERAPIST AND ADOLESCENT

In all circumstances, crisis or not, action communications from therapists to adolescent patients must fit those in words. Sitting behind a desk implies a wish to keep a distance; note-taking may lead the patient to assume that the primary interest of the interviewer is in his data collection. The adolescent's initial intent is to try to assess the personality of the interviewer.

The usual formal method of taking a psychiatric history implicitly demands conformity; it says nothing about the adolescent's capacity to make a meaningful emotional relationship. It is crucial to differentiate this from clinging behavior and non-relating. Without an involvement with the interviewer, there is no way a youngster can use the relationship to suspend symptomatic behavior or obtain release from tension. Collecting information from an adolescent about his life, asking him to perform simple psychological tests or to name the President may only show that the adolescent can be maneuvered into a situation of obedience and passivity, if it does not imply that he is merely an object to be studied. In order to understand the adolescent, a knowledge of his or her upbringing is important, but a formal history cannot be taken as with some adults. Formal history-taking distorts the adolescent's communication technique with adults, and it is crucial to understand the adolescent's natural ways of interacting with others. The physical distance an adolescent puts between himself and the interviewer is as significant as the evidence of anxiety that does not dissipate in the course of an interview. In the initial interview, tension and anxiety are inevitable. Learned superficial techniques of verbal communication may produce apparent interaction, but unchanged tension is highly significant nonverbal communication. There are two levels of communication in an adolescent interview: what is said, and what is done. Useful understanding can be gained by a consideration of what might be communicated if the adolescent could only be seen and not heard.

Because adolescents communicate partly by play—although the play is unlike that of children—it is technically difficult to handle such communication. The adolescent in therapy, or in a meaningful emotional relationship with an adult, may play out his difficulties in action, just as small children resolve maturational conflicts by direct play activity.

> In Britain, train watching is a common habit of early-adolescent boys. They go to train stations and check the numbers and types of trains entering a main-line terminal. A discussion by a boy about a train coming in and out of a station may carry meanings similar to the play with trains of a smaller child in play therapy.

Adolescents may also play at being in therapy or may even play the role of being a young person in relationship to adults. Adolescents will talk of their play and, thus, communicate. Formal play probably has little place in adolescent psychotherapy. Some therapists have the special ability to use "squiggles" (Winnicott, 1971); others play checkers with their young adolescent patients. However, the latter is probably of value only in early adolescents who cannot yet significantly involve themselves in verbal communication because of their stage of puberty. This is the stage of development at which one silent boy said in psychotherapy: "It is not that I do not want to talk to you, nothing comes into my head and I cannot." Adolescents must try out roles—subidentities—as patients, young people, sick people, delinquents, self-involved and considerate. All these may be seen by the same psychotherapist with the same patient over a period of time. Adolescents may use themselves in a psychotherapeutic session as if they were the toy with whom they were actually playing.

> An adolescent was being interviewed in a one-way vision room, and the session was being observed by a group of medical students. Although he knew about the students' presence and had agreed to be seen, the patient was uncomfortable, had many anxieties about what the students thought, and wondered who they were.
>
> The boy, who was highly delinquent, arrived in the interviewing room before the therapist. When the latter arrived, the patient was standing by the mirror with a chair as if to break it. This threat was both a test of the therapist and a communication about the situation.
>
> The boy had not been seen before; the therapist knew little about him. Nevertheless, a highly significant interaction from the start of the interview was inevitable. The therapist had to decide whether he would try to

interpret to the boy what he thought the action might mean or whether he would try to therapeutically counteract. The therapist sat down calmly and seemed to be cool about the behavior. He said that he understood that the boy had strong feelings about the interview. He could always break the mirror if he wished, and the interviewer indicated that he would make no effort at physical restraint. If he wished, the students could come into the interviewing room, but it might be very crowded. The therapist was explicitly and implicitly telling the boy that he recognized his anxiety. In this way reassurance for the boy was counteracted; the comfort of the therapist acted as a control for the patient.

MOTIVATION AND RELATIONSHIPS WITH PARENTS, THERAPISTS AND OTHER ADULTS

Conscious motivation is usually present only in those early adolescents suffering from severe psychic pain who are very depressed or psychologically disintegrating individuals. It is not, however, unusual for family psychopathology to show itself as adolescent maladjustment. The adolescent may be the family's way of obtaining help, although in these situations the motivation is not usually that of the young person.

The pubertal adolescent is narcissistically involved with the self, and feelings and conflicts are inevitably projected into the adult world. Hence, the youngster feels that the problems are not really his, they are the world's or his family's. There are always special difficulties in the therapy of early adolescents who experience a psychic dissolution. Many such adolescents are particularly preoccupied with the need to gain control over themselves because of the physiological changes of puberty. They have little capacity for self-observation, and it is hard for them to form a therapeutic alliance with a therapist. They are more likely to see the therapist as a valuable adult with whom they might identify. Furthermore, any anxiety that may be produced by referral for psychiatric help is a further threat to a tenuous sense of autonomy. The implied dependence and incompetence are also threats to adolescent self-esteem.

The important technical problem in the initial interview is to note the marginal, often nonverbal, communications of the adolescent that convey that magic is wanted. The recognition of this unstated wish is, of course, therapeutic omniscience. If a therapist does not make clear that he knows that the adolescent wants a magic solution, and that this is unattainable, the adolescent feels cheated. Either he does not return, or he plays a pseudo-therapeutic game to appease those authority figures who sent him for help in the first place. In the initial interviews, one must be sufficiently omnipotent that acting-out behavior will be suspended and the adolescent will return voluntarily; at the same time, however, the knowledge must be conveyed that the therapist cannot be omnipotent. If adults temporarily feel that their therapist is disappointing and useless, conscious motivation may be relied on to keep them coming for therapy. With children, parental motivation has a similar effect. However, for many adolescents who see psychiatrists, communication with parents has broken down. The reason for referral may be loss of parental control; parental wishes are not carried out because they are too threatening or are no longer valued. The therapist must then keep a sufficiently positive interaction so that such adolescents will continue to attend, while at the same time trying to help them cope with their angry feelings and the world. Parents are needed to prevent an abrupt withdrawal from therapy, particularly when the patient becomes disenchanted with the therapist and the value of therapy. Since insight is valueless unless it is felt to be true, patients will not understand their anger unless they feel it with the therapist. At the same time, they must care enough about the therapist to continue. This need to sustain ambivalence is one reason for the storminess of adolescent psychotherapy. Parents, moreover, are often highly mixed in their attitudes to therapy. A sick adolescent is also a dependent child and may gratify the parents. Often parents stop paying their child's treatment bills on time as improvement begins to take place.

Given the important role of the family and parents in adolescent maladjustment, both the initial relationship between a therapist and the parents and continuing contact have treatment implications. A decision has to be made as to whether the initial contact should be with parents alone or with the youngster and the parents; an alternative is that the parents are seen after an initial contact with the adolescent.

If the adolescent is seen with parents at the start of the first interview, this carries the implicit meaning that the youngster is seen as an integral member of the family unit as a primary concept; this is appropriate for prepubertal children. If the parents are seen first, inevitably, when the interview with the adolescent takes place, the boy or girl is in the position of not knowing exactly what has been said about him or her. If the interviewer tries to relieve this discomfort with a full report, the adolescent cannot be other than defensive, if no report is given, data are being withheld—an undesirable implicit message. As has already been said, it is probably preferable to see the adolescent alone first and then go on to an interview with parents and child. At that time, subsequent diagnostic sessions can be planned.

Success in treatment is related to an accurate biopsychosocial diagnosis. A decision has to be made as to where the primary specific intervention should be and what other therapeutic techniques should be used. Treatment planning should include the setting of realistic goals.

AIMS OF THERAPY

Changing the personality structure of an adolescent is generally not a realistic therapeutic goal. An appropriate direction is to aid the normal growth process, to assist adolescents to gain autonomy from dependent infantile ties, and to help them toward making firm identifications. The therapist should aim to assist young people obtain that inner freedom from conflict that will allow them to live fuller lives in today's disturbed world. Help for parents is usually directed at assisting them in the resolution of their personal conflicts and not using their child as part of a family conflict. Since there is, in a sense, a conflict of interest between parent and child, family therapy has little place as the only treatment for adolescent maladjustment.

Adolescent conflicts may so weaken personality functions that an impaired capacity for human relationships is produced. Instead of receiving a positive feeling of love, affection, and value from their world, even when it is offered, disturbed adolescents feel highly persecuted by their environment and the people in it. The people to whom they relate are felt as unloving. The parents of conflict-ridden adolescents are well aware of this; other adults sometimes accept adolescent alienation as appropriate to the youngster's age. Although disturbed adolescents may allege that they are only understood by their own generation, this often is more of a wish than a fact. Many do not feel understood by anyone. They cling to their peers as a drowning man to a lifeline, but they may feel as persecuted by their agemates as by adults. Adolescents may say they want no contact with adults; they really wonder whether adults are prepared to care for them. Perhaps the most that all but highly intensive therapy does is to reduce the amount of persecution the adolescent feels from his world, and to allow the processes of positive identification to take place. Angry feelings have to be worked through and understood in the therapeutic relationship; catharsis is not enough. In the course of therapy, the patient becomes aware that his angry feelings do not necessarily destroy good relationships. The negative feelings that become focused in the therapeutic situation may contribute to the adolescent's not wishing therapy. Moreover, people in the adolescent's world, particularly parents, may be feeling that the adolescent is doing extremely well and they are less likely to support the idea of continuing therapy. For this reason, many young people leave therapy permanently, but the feeling that all is going well, and that only the therapeutic situation is tormenting, is not an indication for termination. On the other hand, if the therapist is seen as the only benign figure, therapy is rarely going satisfactorily.

Successful adolescent psychotherapy requires, apart from a therapist, the availability of other people to whom the adolescent can relate. If these are not present and if the patient does work through some of his angry feelings, the only available positive relationship is with a therapist. Adolescents then have no way of freeing themselves from dependence on therapy.

NEED FOR SOCIAL NETWORKS

Adolescents recommended for psychotherapy need people in their world, in the past, present, and future, who care about them. Thus, social isolation may be a contraindication to outpatient therapy. An adolescent with a history of very tenuous or very negative relationships with parents or others is in a difficult psychotherapeutic position. When such an adolescent has just moved to a community, a typical junior high school, for example, it may be almost impossible for many months for relationships with peers or teachers to occur. Such distressed adolescents may not progress in psychotherapy because they cannot find people in their world to whom they can relate. Teachers are too distant, and the potential peer group is overinvolved with itself.

Again, therapy for the adolescent requires a diagnostic assessment of the stresses and supports in the adolescent's world. The potential for growth in church groups, youth organizations, and so on, may have to be considered, if a school system cannot provide adequate human relationships. Sometimes, if these are absent, psychiatric day care may be necessary. Placing a disturbed adolescent in a meaningful social network does not in itself lead to emotional growth and conflict resolution, but without such relationships, the chances of successful psychotherapy are slim.

NEED FOR RELIEF OF SYMPTOMS

An important aspect of therapeutic work with adolescents is to enable them to make firm positive identifications. Because symptoms may produce persecutory responses from the environment—for example, underachievement arouses rejection and anger; drug-taking arouses intense concern over external controls; bedwetting leads to hostility from those concerned with the adolescent's cleanliness, even if some vicarious satisfaction is gained from the activity—symptomatic relief is a necessary prerequisite to further emotional growth. Without it, it is unlikely that an environment that has been made hostile by disturbed behavior can become supportive.

Some therapists used to believe that relief of one symptom without resolution of the underlying conflict would automatically lead to the production of another symptom. This is only rarely true. That theory presupposes that environmental support and the perception of love have little effect on the development of a healthier personality. Symptom relief is necessary in those patients who have a capacity to make positive attachments to people in their environment; more emotional growth can then be expected than might otherwise occur. The technique by which the symptom is relieved is a particular issue, especially insofar as medication is concerned.

MEDICATION IN ADOLESCENT TREATMENT

In adolescent treatment, medication should be prescribed only when specifically indicated. Prescribing antidepressants to early adolescents requires sophisticated monitoring techniques because of issues of growth and the way the drugs are transported to the central nervous system. If the patient receives too little or too much, such a drug ceases to be effective.

Lithium carbonate is specifically valuable for those with a highly labile affect that is organically caused. It requires preliminary monitoring of cardiac, renal, and liver functions, and the blood level of the drug must be monitored at regular intervals. Adolescent patients with an attention deficit disorder without an underlying learning disability are likely to do well on therapeutic doses of pemoline. The appropriate use of tranquilizers in adolescent schizophrenia is more difficult, because early-adolescent schizophrenics do less well with the tranquilizers than those whose growth phase of development is over. Tranquilizers also cause psychological stress in adolescents, as most affect muscle tone, and physical activity is an extremely important way of relieving emotional tension in adolescence.

Prescribing medication also teaches adolescents that this is an appropriate way of handling anxiety and further presupposes that therapists can be magicians. Except in specific organic diseases, sedatives are particularly contraindicated in adolescents; they do not help general states of tension, and adolescent sleeplessness can usually be resolved by a combination of psychotherapy and environmental management. Therapy implies that it is difficult to work out emotional problems; a minor tranquilizer or sedative contraindicates this concept and reinforces the common message of society-at-large that escape through drugs is acceptable.

A major treatment problem today is the illicit use of drugs. As a test of a therapist's value, adolescents may arrive at a therapy session stoned. They may want the therapist to be aware that they are into drugs (that is aware of them as individuals), or they may want something to be done about their behavior. The hostility of drug-taking to the therapeutic process needs to be recognized. Depending on the substance, drug-toxic adolescents suffer from greater or lesser depersonalization; in this psychological state, they are not able to involve themselves with others in an emotionally meaningful way.

Although the capacity to reinvolve oneself with a reality situation under external pressure is greater with marijuana than with alcohol, the effects of the drug cannot be interpreted away. Whatever else may be done in such a therapeutic session, counteraction is forced on a therapist; psychotherapy ceases to be possible and the session should be terminated. Similarly, chronic drug abuse makes psychotherapy valueless and the adolescent must be abstaining from drug use if such an intervention is to be useful.

TERMINATION OF TREATMENT

The termination of therapy with adolescents poses many problems. Often an adolescent will express the idea that he wishes to try himself out in life without therapy. This attempt at autonomy should generally be respected, although it is a temptation to persuade an adolescent to stay in therapy, particularly if psychopathology is still evident. The real question the adolescent is raising is whether the therapist sees him as capable of autonomy.

The suggestion that the adolescent should reduce the frequency of sessions is not a viable option as this carries the same message of lack of confidence in the youngster. Furthermore therapeutic frequency should be optimal not subject to expediency. It is better to risk the adolescent's having to return for more therapy—though he may be angry because he was allowed to go too soon—than to crush an attempt at independent growth. It is important that this concept be understood, if only intellectually, by an adolescent's parents.

Although in the psychotherapy of the middle and late adolescent a therapist may have little direct contact with parents, he should see them at the end of the assessment phase of work with the adolescent before therapy formally begins. He should be sure that parents have someone with whom to communicate their anxieties, if this role is contraindicated for the therapist. At the termination of therapy, the offer should be made to see parents again, although this is rarely accepted.

REFERENCES

Bettelheim, B. (1950), *Love Is Not Enough.* Glencoe, Ill.: Free Press.

Freud, S. (1920), Beyond the pleasure principle. In *Standard Edition*, Vol. 18, pp. 7–66. London: Hogarth Press.

Gill, M., Newman, R., and Redlich, F. C. (1954), *The Initial Interview in Psychiatric Practice.* pp. 106–107. New York: International Universities Press.

Jones, H. E. (1969), Adolescence in our society. In *The Family in a Democratic Society*, Comp. Community Services Society of New York, pp. 70–82. New York: Columbia University Press.

Krohn, A., and Miller, D. (1974), Flight from Autonomy: Problems of social change on an in-patient adolescent unit. *Psychiatry*, 34(3):187–198.

Miller, D. (1967), Staff training in the penal system. In *The Use of Small Groups in Training*, eds. R. Gosling, P. M. Turquet, and D. Woodhouse, pp. 98–112. Herts, Eng.: Codicote Press.

—— (1969), Aggression in adolescents: *Where*, January 4.

Sullivan, H. S. (1951), The psychiatric interview. *Psychiatry*, 14:361–373.

Winnicott, D. W. (1971), *Therapeutic Consultations in Child Psychiatry*. New York: Basic Books.

PART IV

THERAPY
FOR LIFE STRESSES

Chapter 16

The Treatment of Disturbances Produced by Death and Divorce

Some serious adolescent maladjustments occur when the balance of stress and support that exists in the immediate environment of the individual is disturbed by the death of or separation from a parent. It is difficult to know which is the more painful: death, final and irrevocable, or separation, perceived as bewildering and teasing (Robertson and Bowlby, 1952). It is probably impossible for any child to deal adequately with either experience unless adults other than the remaining parent help. As the family networks of Western civilization are broken up, this puts a particular responsibility on pediatricians, family practitioners and a whole variety of youth workers.

PROBLEMS OF MOURNING

It is necessary to mourn to get over the death of a loved one. Traditional mourning is subtle and complex: the dead person is buried in the ground beneath a headstone (which perhaps reassured our ancestors that he would not return to haunt them); he is talked about, wept over, laughed about; his faults are reviewed and his abilities are discussed (Draper, 1965). He is even blamed: "How could he possibly leave me?" The grave is visited quite frequently. Often, after the burial, a party is held to celebrate his departure. These processes allow the adult to play out feelings of guilt, anger, grief, despair, and loss; paradoxically, there may also be relief that the death has occurred at last.

All the mixed feelings in the adult who loses a loved one are present in the adolescent who loses a parent. The mourning processes of adulthood, however, are not so easily available to the young. At one time, the very obvious rituals of adult mourning allowed the young to experience these at second hand. Not being mature enough to deal with death themselves, they could experience grief reactions in a way in which they could cope, through adults. Today, these formalized gestures of adult society are disappearing; it is no longer commonplace in the Western world for people to mourn in a way that meets their psychological needs. The ritual of the funeral home, with the gussied-up body and the family isolated with their grief, is no substitute for a mourning experience, as is still seen in some more primitive societies. Particularly in American culture, where the outward expression of sorrow is not particularly acceptable, the loss of a loved one causes an additional stress even for adults, because they are no longer allowed satisfactory social outlets for grief. Mourning rites are as old as man: it can only harm people when they are abandoned. The lack of these rites hinders adults from helping the bereaved adolescent by their example, because *they* no longer show how to cope with death. Some adults, isolated with their grief, have been known to die prematurely. Grieving adolescents may lose their zest for life and are likely to become cold, unloving people, whose capacity for loving and caring has withered away.

DEATH IN THE HOSPITAL

Because most hospitals forbid children under the age of twelve to visit adults, the death of a parent in the hospital means not only that the dying parent may be denied the opportunity to make peace with children, but also that children feel that a parent has abruptly and mysteriously left them. Children cannot be shown by a parent that they are not responsible for the parent's death; they cannot apologize for leaving. The policy of hospitals, intended to be helpful, ends by being emotionally painful to all.

Before the age of puberty, children do not really understand that death means a permanent separation, and even after puberty this is probably not really appreciated. The current fashion of not allowing children to go to funerals increases this difficulty. Death is not emotionally comprehensible, even to adults, until they become emotionally aware that they will die themselves. It is possible that this awareness only reaches many adults in the early thirties. Up to then, the healthy know they will die, but they do not really feel it to be possible. It is therefore hardly surprising that children and adolescents have difficulty with death.

PARENTAL LOSS IN INFANCY

A child or adolescent may cope with loss by an immediate denial (Bonnard, 1962) of feeling. If, as is likely, the survivors in the family fail to recognize that this is happening and believe that the death has been taken well, the young have an even greater need for outside help, a need of which they are often not consciously aware.

> The mother of a daughter, age ten, whose husband had just died, was unsure whether she should let the child go to the funeral. She therefore asked her daughter what she wanted to do. "Go to the funeral and then to the movies" was the reply. With relief she accepted the child's partial denial of feeling as a solution: the child's grief was apparently slight. It did not occur to the mother that more than this would be necessary to help the child over the loss.

If children cannot be helped to mourn parental death or separation, they are left, as they grow up, with an unresolved traumatic experience. The damage this causes depends, to some extent, on the age at which it occurs and whether it is the mother or the father who is lost.

Children who have never known their mothers because they were abandoned through death or desertion are likely to suffer gross damage to their capacities to be loving human beings, unless they obtain a permanent mother substitute. An infant must have mothering or it cannot survive (Greenacre, 1952). Sometimes the child who has no real mother is looked after by a series of women: this multiple handling can damage the personality and impair the capacity to develop a trusting relationship with others. In turn, this makes it difficult to develop the capacity to develop mixed feelings; the ambivalence of love and hate is not well developed. This interferes with the development of conscience, which at best, in such situations, is likely to be not only harsh and punitive, but also unable to control impulsive destructive behavior. Sometimes a consistent mother substitute is available for the first months or years of such a child's life, and then she leaves. The child will suffer parental loss, as if she had been the real mother. It is often difficult to provide children with an adequate mother substitute because they may initially rebuff adult attempts to help them. They cannot trust the new adult not to go away, and they project their anger against the lost parent onto the parent substitute. Often these children become adults who appear unable to make close and warm relationships with others; they may be helped to make a good adaptation, rarely are they able to be truly loving.

Children who have never known their fathers and who are brought up by women alone, with no father substitutes, are also likely to have severely damaged personalities (Deutsch, 1944). Boys, in particular, find it difficult to take the first steps toward masculinity if no male is available as a model and both boys and girls do not have the normal intense involvement with mother modulated by father's presence. Ultimate personal autonomy then becomes more difficult. How great the damage is depends on other factors in the environment: the degree of physical and emotional deprivation, the presence of possible father substitutes, and the inborn sensitivity of the child. Without a father figure, even if a general sense of masculinity develops, such children have no inner image of fatherhood; when such boys become fathers themselves, they do not know how to behave.

Brought up without fathers, girls may not experience asexual male love. Thus, they may have no internal image of themselves as being valuable to the opposite sex, or themselves, for other than sexuality. These problems are demonstrated by the generation who, as children, hardly saw their fathers until they were five or six—if ever—because of World War II. The girls may have a strong image of a mother, but no experience of fathers as consistent, loving, supporting figures. Thus, as mothers themselves, they have no expectation as to how their husbands should behave. Such women relate to their husbands as their mothers did to them, often in a controlling, mothering fashion, rather than as mistress, lover, and wife. Similarly, in the present decade, the underprivileged matriarchal societies that may exist among some poverty-stricken groups present a continuing problem. If the young men are not helped to be adequate fathers, they abandon their new family when they feel their children are competing for their mate's affection, usually when the infant is about three months old (Miller, 1965). So the process is repeated, and a succession of children from vulnerable, one-parent families is created.

PARENTAL LOSS IN LATER CHILDHOOD

Children who have lost a parent before the age of five or six pose special problems for adults who wish to help them when they reach adolescence. The lack of satisfactory mothering is likely to create a damaged, isolated adolescent, who finds it difficult to form a trusting relationship with adults (Miller, 1965). Those children who have experienced unsatisfactory fathering also have difficulty in forming relationships with adults, but they have suffered less: if a new, consistent relationship is available to them, they can use it after much preliminary testing.

Parental loss when a child has had the solid emotional experience of a loving parent through the first five or six years of life has a different effect. The child has an image of an apparently loving parent who has chosen to go away. This feeling that the action was deliberate is inevitable, because a child cannot conceive that a parent can be helpless, and the fact of death cannot yet be understood. The parent is felt to have been a deserter, and one possible explanation is that the parent has left because the child is bad. An older child may also feel this, but may also be angry with the parent for leaving. If the father dies, children are often enraged with the mother, for as the person who was initially perceived as all powerful, the loss must be her responsibility. This may create a bad relationship between mother and child for years.

> John, aged eighteen, had a father who had died after one week's illness when John was eight. He consciously felt that his mother had tried her best to save father, but following the death, he did not mention his father again. He became a shy and withdrawn boy, and to help him socially, his mother sent him to a prep school. There, he began to abuse drugs and alcohol. He was ejected from the school in the last semester of grade twelve and lived at home for four months while awaiting college entry. He became furious with his mother and this fury only subsided when he understood its relationship to his father's death.

Sometimes children really do not internalize the death and keep the dead parent alive inside their own head.

> Seventeen-year-old Jill was hospitalized after repeated suicidal attempts. Her father had died in his office of a heart attack when Jill was nine. She said upon inquiry as to whether she ever thought of her father, "I say good-night to him just before I go to sleep. It's not that I'm hallucinating, I just feel he's alive inside me." Quite consciously, she wished to die to join her father.

Her father was also used as a comforter; whenever she felt unhappy she thought of him.

From the age of five to the end of early adolescence, the feeling that is aroused by the death of parent is the same; the intensity of the experience is more easily handled as the individual's capacity to understand reality matures. For the adolescent who has lost a parent through death, the father or mother may have been buried, in reality, but cannot be buried by the self without outside help. The image of the dead parent stays alive inside the child and the adolescent. Feelings about this are likely to torment the individual, either consciously or unconsciously, through adult life, if they are not resolved. Many years after the death of a parent, when the mourning process ought to be finished, the adolescent may still weep about a dead father or mother, or feel a pervasive sadness when the loss is recalled.

It is difficult for an adolescent boy to accept control from his mother; the absence of a father in the house makes it hard for the boy to obtain a satisfactory feeling of self. A girl brought up without a father finds it equally hard to value herself as a woman. One way of dealing with the loss is to identify with the dead parent. A dramatic change in older adolescents may occur following parental death: a boy or girl may suddenly seem to everyone to have become exactly like the dead father.

> Judy, a fifteen-year-old girl, was placed in a juvenile detention home because she repeatedly ran away from home, became addicted to drugs, and was then picked up ill in cafes, side streets, or in the summer, on the sidewalk. This behavior had been going on for two years.
>
> In an interview, Judy told a psychiatrist that she hated her mother, but she said, with tears in her eyes, that she had loved her father who had died when she was twelve. She was asked what he was like. "He was a chronic alcoholic, he did not get on with mother. They would have a row and he would leave home and we would not see him for two or three days. Then someone would bring him home; he had passed out. He would dry out for a day or two then they would be at it again."

Apart from these internal difficulties, the fatherless child or adolescent has particular social problems. The friend with two parents is envied, and often the individual who has lost a parent when a child has the unconscious conviction that the world now owes him a living—having experienced such a loss, he feels entitled to things. Similarly, many children who feel starved for affection frequently steal from the person who they feel is depriving them (Bonnard, 1962). The adolescent who has lost either parent commonly responds with an expectation that society will provide for him. When he grows up, he is often unreliable, particularly in handling money and at work.

Guilt, anger, and depression may all be present in children whose parents are being divorced. The fact that the divorced parent is still alive, in a way, makes the situation worse than if the parent had died, for the child cannot alter the feeling of having been deliberately abandoned because the parent chose to go; with death, the child eventually can learn that the parent had no choice.

There are two types of divorce: marital divorce, in which the parents decided not to live together, and parenting divorce, in which one or the other parent ceases to behave like a parent. Either way, shared parenting is lost. In divorce, the child may have the fantasy of replacing the divorced spouse while still keeping an attachment to him or her.

> A sixteen-year-old anorexic girl went to live with her divorced father because she could not get along with mother. She said, "I thought father

would be nice with me, but he's no better with me than he was with mother." With this understanding, she was then able to return to her mother and the tension subsided.

A parent of the opposite sex leaving home is felt as a rejection of the child's identity; a girl feels worthless if father leaves. The child might live with the parent of the opposite sex apparently equably until remarriage occurs, then, the behavior of the child may then have the flavor of "hell hath no fury." The same may occur when a widowed parent remarries:

> Jane, age eleven, reacted to her mother's death by looking after her two younger brothers, keeping house for her father, and being a model child at school. Her father remarried when she was thirteen. The same week she ran away from home with a seventeen-year-old boy she had just met. Two years later, she was seen in a juvenile detention home with a long history of promiscuity and absconding. No one had discussed with her the feelings of loss she felt for her mother or her anger at her father for then deserting her for another woman.

Healthy emotional growth requires that children feel loved by their parents. Divorce or separation may imply that the child is secondary in their life, and children must come to terms with such a notion. Young people find it difficult to express to other adults their feelings about this, sometimes because they are trapped by a feeling of family loyalty and do not wish to take sides against one or the other parent, always because there are few built-in social supports for the children of divorced parents. Occasionally, adolescents will simplify the issues and make one parent bad and the other good, maintaining a facade of extreme cynicism. Inside themselves, however, they are often as grief-stricken, bereft, angry, and despairing as the adolescent who has lost a parent through death. In trying to help such young people, it is important that therapists do not allow themselves to be maneuvered into taking the side of one parent or the other. It is, however, farcical and alienating to tell an adolescent who does complain about his father or mother that he "really loves" his parents; he won't feel it to be true and will think that the adult is talking nonsense. The adolescent does not want agreement that the parent is bad; he wants recognition of the fact that he feels this. Divorce arouses intense mixed feelings if one parent deserts the other. If a father leaves home, for example, adolescent children particularly feel that their mother should have been able to stop father from going off with another woman. She is blamed as a failure. If, however, the mother successfully dates men, her sexuality becomes even more anxiety provoking. Adolescent daughters may become anxious when they have boyfriends, in case they should be as much a failure as they felt mother to have been. This may be sexually acted out. Boys partly identify with what they feel as the sexually predatory behavior of their father; they are also gratified in protecting their mothers. Yet, they also have a profound contempt for women who cannot keep their men. Boys and girls may both identify with the parent they see as a sexual failure.

> John's father had left his mother when he was twelve. She told him about the new wife with scorn and loathing, and John refused to communicate with his father. Consciously, he had no feelings, at that time, of anger or contempt for his mother.
>
> John worked extremely hard at school, was a straight "A" student, and at the age of eighteen was admitted to a prestigious university. He had never had a girlfriend. Shortly after entering as a freshman, John met a girl and after about three months had intercourse with her. He knew she was seeing another boy all the time but preferred to think this was of no significance. Four weeks after they had intercourse, John was told by the girl that she might be pregnant. This was confirmed, and two weeks later John paid $250 toward her abortion. The obstetrician told John that his girl was ten weeks pregnant, but the youth felt that that must be a mistake. John came to see a psychiatrist after the girl left him for the original boy because of acute feelings of failure, and the unshakable idea that if he had been more sexually able the girl might have stayed with him.

Identifying with his mother, John put himself at the losing end of a sexual triangle. It is no accident that, statistically, the children of divorced parents are, as adults, more likely to be divorced themselves than are children from intact families.

THE ONE-PARENT ADOLESCENT IN SCHOOL

The adolescents who are most likely to suffer in the school system are those from one-parent families. Fatherless boys and girls, particularly, need a male teacher who is prepared to be interested and involved with them over the years. Such a teacher can enable such children to live rather than just exist, if he can accept their inevitable preliminary testing of his personality. It is easier for an adolescent to accept substitute fathering than substitute mothering, because mothers are expected to involve themselves in their child's life more intimately than fathers. Substitute mothering is, therefore, that much more difficult.

Unfortunately, the school does not automatically respond to a child's loss of a father by ensuring that male figures are available. Even if they did, the loss would be rapidly reexperienced because teacher/pupil relationships rarely last more than a year. This means that significant males for such a child may have to be sought outside the school. This need is met more often for boys than girls. The girl who loses a father may be forced into early heterosexual relationships as the only way of finding a significant male figure. Often such girls seek out older men; when they are abandoned, they are again bereaved. Often they themselves precipitate abandonment, but it is still a teasing and tormenting experience. An adult who wishes to help fatherless children should be aware that they may feel teased by the very gestures that seem appropriate. An invitation home to dinner or an offer of a visit to the lake may be felt as an invitation to be a child of the family.

FEELINGS ASSOCIATED WITH LOSS

Of all the feelings that are aroused by loss, the one most socially acceptable is grief. Children are allowed to cry; adolescents are also allowed to show their misery, to an extent, even though in many cultures boys are thought to be unmasculine if they do cry (Jersild, 1963). But other emotional experiences surrounding death make it difficult to handle inside the self.

Adolescents tend to make all experiences their own, perhaps because the most unacceptable experience for them is helplessness. To avoid this helpless feeling, adolescents—even though they may also appear to disclaim responsibility for relatively trivial difficulties—will accept responsibility within themselves for the profoundly disturbing incidents that befall them. The young person not only may feel that he was responsible for parental loss, but also guilt may be increased by the realization that the competition for the affection of the surviving parent is over.

The effects of anger, personal responsibility, and grief exist irrespective of ethnic groups or social class. A vocational guidance counselor working in a Scandinavian youth employment office was concerned about a boy who had difficulties at work since leaving school at sixteen:

> Gary's father had died when he was nine; his mother had remarried when he was twelve. When he was fourteen, one of his half-sisters drowned. According to school reports, he had been very good in such subjects as arithmetic, physics, and chemistry, but he had no interest in social studies and had found religious instruction particularly irksome. He was very intelligent, but restless.
>
> At the youth employment office, Gary was given a large battery of psychological tests. These showed that he was capable of leadership, but incapable of making friends. His level of achievement was high; he was thought to be fluent and imaginative. It was deduced that he was unstable and sensitive and suffered from a good deal of anxiety. He was said to be restless, unsettled, and lonely, and to have need of reassurance.

Gary had only five interviews with the counselor over eighteen months, although he visited the employment bureau looking for jobs at least twenty times. At first he had wanted a job in a distant town with an uncle, and there had been some attempt to send him to the training school of a paper mill. The principal, after interviewing Gary, felt that he was unable to accept him. He then worked for six different employers, staying on the job for one and one-half months at the most. Whenever he had a job in which promotion prospects were likely to be excellent, he quarrelled with the foreman and was fired. The counselor felt that there was no chance of this boy ever working successfully because of his quarrels with authority. Gary's story was bewildering; he appeared to have been given every chance and it was suggested that he was really a psychopath and nothing could be done. Routine efforts at systematic help having failed, the response was to apply a label.

The story can be understood in the following way. The school had not understood the reason for his restlessness, and while he was there, no one had helped him with the underlying conflicts that helped create it. Nevertheless, the structure of the school had offered him a good deal of emotional support. When this was withdrawn, the painful experiences of his early life, the death of a father and a half-sister, were recalled. The unresolved feelings of anxiety and guilt led to self-destructive behavior. Feeling himself to be dangerous in relationships with others, Gary constantly put himself in a situation in which he could not be close to people, because those he loved might die. In addition, he was so angry with authority figures, because his father had "left" him, that he had constantly to quarrel with them, hence the difficulty with his foreman.

The youth employment officer was unaware that there could be any cause of Gary's behavior other than work shyness; he had tried to help by seeking changes and by criticizing Gary whenever he lost a job. The officer had not been able to consider changes that might have met Gary's particular needs, for example, a job in which the foreman would not be disturbed by his rudeness. It could have been explained to a potential employer that Gary needed to keep himself somewhat isolated from supervisors; the employment officer might have insisted that Gary show he could keep just one job before making further attempts to find him a position to suit his talents. This would have given him some opportunity to expiate his feelings of guilt by doing menial tasks. If his school had been helpful to him when his father and half-sister died, by giving him the opportunity to talk about his feelings to a sympathetic adult with some sensitivity to the effects of loss, he might not have been left as a late adolescent with an intolerable self-destructive burden of guilt.

Whenever people suffer anguish, they need to share the experience. It may appear that adolescents do not want to do this; they say, leave me alone, because sharing may seem like a return to childlike dependence. Although the adult may accept this stated desire for isolation, the need to share remains. Sooner or later the bereaved child or adolescent has to be able to express in actions or words his feelings about his loss. The child facing the emotional confusion aroused by parental death may not feel anything: the experience of loss may have to be denied because it is too overwhelming. The adolescent, possibly more aware of his feelings, may not be able to share them because he is afraid that he might break down and cry or in some other way show that he feels desperately unsure of himself.

Adolescents who are aware of the grief of the parent who survives will wish to be helpful, not hurtful. It may, for instance, be impossible for them to show their angry feelings. If adolescents were to allow their mixed feelings about a dead parent to become conscious, these would probably be considered as bewildering, idiosyncratic, or mad. Furthermore, adolescents may also blame the surviving parent. They may angrily feel that a caring mother could not possibly let her husband die.

In setting aside confused feelings about the loss of a parent, the adolescent is likely to find it increasingly difficult to become emotionally involved with others. Alternatively, the adolescent may act out on the stage of the real world the conflicts and anxiety that have been experienced. It is not unusual for adolescents who experience parental loss to become aggressive and disturbed at school. Because the causes of this disturbance may not be understood, the adolescent is not helped with the feelings of responsibility, guilt, and anger that lie behind this antisocial behavior. Misunderstood in school, the adolescent's disturbance spreads into the community. This is a common cause of delinquency in adolescents.

ASSISTING A CHILD TO MOURN

Adolescents who experience parental death can only mourn if helped by their environment. To assist this process is crucial for mental health. Sometimes, no specific effort need be made, sometimes children seem able to use their environment unconsciously in a helpful way. Then trouble occurs only when their self-help is interrupted:

> Richard was eleven when his father died. The boy lived in a port; his father was a fisherman. Richard reacted to the death by going down to the docks every day after school and watching the ships go out. Because of the change in the family's finances, it was necessary for them to move to a town away from the sea. This, of course, interrupted the mourning ritual Richard had established for himself. Inland, he soon became delinquent.

It is possible that as a newcomer to the district he found it easier to join boys, aggressive and disturbed themselves, who were all too willing to have a new recruit. But his delinquency was certainly associated with the inability to deal with the feelings he found rising inside himself when his mourning was interrupted.

The boy went through society's typical responses to delinquency—from juvenile court to probation officer. He landed at a correctional center, but ran away after quarreling with one of the staff. In another such institution, he continued to behave in an extremely disturbed and aggressive way. The principal asked for a psychiatric opinion. During the interview, when his father was mentioned, Richard's eyes filled with tears. (This was some three and a half years after the death of his father.) He was thought to be suffering from an unresolved mourning experience. Those staff members who spent time with Richard and knew him were asked to give him every opportunity to talk about his father, if he voluntarily brought the subject up. If he did not do this, they could appropriately raise the subject themselves—asking him what his father was like and what he might have done in a given set of circumstances. With the combination of genuine interest and the opportunity to talk about his father with people who obviously cared about him, Richard became less disturbed and a productive member of society. He was discharged after six months. Two years later, he was still a settled member of the community.

Richard was helped a number of years after his father died, but often adults have to aid a young person who is suffering from an immediate loss. The common assumption that children or adolescents should try to forget and live life as father or mother would have wanted is wrong. If a child has mixed feelings of responsibility and anger, the suggestion that he live as the parent might have wanted is likely to arouse stubborn resistance. To talk about the dead parent helps the adolescent face the fact of the death and share the experience of grief. It is not enough for a helping adult to expect the adolescent to volunteer statements about the dead parent. "What was your father like?" "What might he have done in this situation?" are appropriate questions to be raised. The mention of the dead parent will be painful, but it is by sharing pain that the adolescent can grow out of such a traumatic experience.

Mourning adolescents constantly appear to be seeking adults who will replace the lost parent; although they may experience the caring adults as not offering enough, they often apparently wish to repeat the experience of loss in their day-to-day life (Freud, 1933). When bereaved youngsters become emotionally involved with an adult they seem to provoke a situation in which they might lose him or her, as if, in order to convince themselves that they have control over the situation of loss, they try to provoke a helping adult into rejecting them—producing a loss of their own making. This is an attempt to separate the sense of being helpless from the experience of being deserted. Adolescents want to feel responsible for what happens in their world. The adult who is trying to help an adolescent disturbed by parental loss should have no expectation of gratitude. The young person in mourning is angry; some of the anger must be directed toward an adult with whom the adolescent has become involved. If adolescents, immediately after the loss of a parent, are given the opportunity both to talk about and to some extent play out their sense of despair, much subsequent suffering can be avoided. The adult who wishes to help the bereaved adolescent should be aware of the sense of confusion aroused by the death as well as his or her own feelings about death or separation. It is easy to overidentify with bereaved adolescents and, in helping them through their difficulties, to expect too little of them. The adult must use his intuitive understanding of how much to expect, too little may be as useless as the "snap out of it" attitude that expects too much.

Some common societal responses to death are misleading oversimplifications. When boys respond to the death of their father with aggressive, outwardly directed behavior, the tendency, particularly by juvenile courts and social agencies, is to point to loss of parental control. Sometimes the significance of parental loss is ignored; the decision of the helping authority to attempt to reimpose controls then represents only a partial solution. Often such young people, after a series of delinquent acts that are not understood as symptomatic behavior, are separated from their environments. Their experience of loss is then repeated, and they are sent to institutions where they will be controlled until, it is hoped, they grow out of their difficult period. This tends to produce isolated, withdrawn human beings. At best, such adolescents may make a social adjustment that is primarily an adaptation to life; but if they are not also helped with their confused feelings, they do not really live. At worst they swell the ranks of the criminal population. (It is perhaps inevitable that society should overvalue the controlling function of parents because this is the one that seems most easy to replace.)

Finally, a delinquent act that is a symptom of bereavement may also be gratifying; then this type of behavior is reinforced. Similarly, when marijuana is smoked to relieve psychic pain, it can still give a pleasurable high.

Some adolescents respond to loss by withdrawal into themselves. They tend to be in a much more serious plight than those who respond aggressively (Menninger, 1963). The withdrawn adolescent is often considered by adults to be taking the whole thing so well; there is no awareness of the danger. Withdrawal, as a symptom of disturbance, seems almost wholly unrecognized by the American educational system, in which conformity is highly valued. In fifteen years of practice in the United States, in the author's experience, no child has been referred because adults became anxious about overcompliant behavior; in England, on the other hand, withdrawal and excessive compliance were fairly frequent reasons for referral, at any rate by sensitive and perceptive teachers.

Withdrawal is more usual as an anxiety symptom in girls than in boys. If it is unrecognized, girls may continue to withdraw from others or they may react frantically, needing emotional contacts, seeking consolation in sexual contact. Promiscuous behavior may be an attempt to contact another human being, to establish a sense of femininity, and to resolve hostility. Often intercourse is the price paid to be cuddled; sometimes, however, a purely physical relationship implies contempt for the total personality. It is an attack on both the girl's femininity and, by identification, that of her mother (Blos, 1962). Anger over loss may thus show itself by an inner refusal to be emotionally involved with another person. Acute emotional withdrawal then becomes chronic uninvolvement with people and things.

Adolescents and children should not be allowed to attack society or themselves as part of their grief. Destructive behavior should be controlled, but the chance to understand and work out in a positive way a sense of loss is also required. This may be partly done by helping grieving adolescents to put their feelings into words to a helpful, interested adult. They also need the opportunity to use their environment to assist the mourning experience. When girls lose their mothers, they can, to an extent, work out their mourning experiences by playing a helpful mothering role in the family, both to other children and their father, as if to identify with their dead parent. When a girl takes over such mothering tasks, she is doing something that everyone will perceive as valuable. The risk is that she may be used by her family and unable to develop as a person in her own right.

Boys may attempt to take over the role of a dead father, but there are fewer socially acceptable ways in which this is possible for them. The schoolboy in Western society cannot easily earn wages to keep a family, and younger children will resent the attempts he may make to control them. Closeness to his mother is less tolerable for a boy than is closeness to her father for a girl. When the mother of an adolescent boy dies, it is psychologically and socially inappropriate for him to take over the housekeeping role in the family.

DEATH OF FRIENDS

The death of friends of their own age is particularly anxiety-provoking to adolescents. The mixed feelings aroused by parental loss can perhaps be more easily understood than the extreme distress that can be brought about by a friend's death:

> John was sixteen and was brought before the courts for indecent exposure; he was seen masturbating in a copse in a local park. He had no previous history of disturbed sexual behavior. Two days before the episode, he had arranged to meet a friend after work and, to make this possible, had lent his friend his motor scooter. He waited in vain for his pal, who was killed on the way to meet him.
>
> It is not hard to see that John's masturbating might be understood as reassurance to himself that he was still alive. Although he had no conscious thought of exposing himself, the relatively public nature of his act might well have stood for his unconscious wish to be punished for his own part in his friend's death. The interpretation was made to John during the course of an initial interview, that it looked as though he had jerked off to prove to himself that he was still alive. John wept profusely, talked of how he was responsible for his friend's death, and said he deserved to be punished.

Typically, when two young people are together and one is killed or commits suicide, the survivor feels guilty as well as sad. It is common to feel that if one had acted differently, the death might not have happened or that the better person did not survive.

Death poses another problem for adolescents: it reminds them of their own fragility. The necessity to deny this is the reason why some adolescents seem relatively untouched by the death of very close friends. This denial is often more apparent than real:

> Sally, a girl of thirteen, had a friend who died suddenly in the night after what appeared to be a trivial headache the day before. This happened at the beginning of the Christmas holidays, and Sally appeared to be relatively untouched. Her parents noted later that she complained she was not sleeping well; on a couple of occasions, she had reported nightmares and one night she walked in her sleep. On the first day of school, in class with her favorite teacher, Sally complained of a splitting headache and had to be taken home. It then emerged that she had been afraid to sleep during the holidays because she was afraid she would die; she waited until she was with an adult who mattered to her to develop the headache that finally led to the emotional first aid she needed.

DEATH OF SIBLINGS

The death of a brother or sister is a particular problem for an adolescent. Children feel intense rivalry as well as affection toward each other. The death of a sibling can cause intense internal and intra-familial conflicts. Apart from the ambivalent feelings of the survivors, it is not uncommon for them to become the repository of two sets of parental feelings. On the one hand, the parents may split their own ambivalent feelings about their dead child; he is loved, and all the hatred over the loss is put onto a surviving child. This is, of course, unconscious, but the surviving adolescent experiences his parents as being both unreasonably angry and at the same time overcontrolling. A son may overhear a bereaved parent say that the best child was taken.

EFFECTS OF CHRONIC PARENTAL ILLNESS

Chronic illness in their parents, their immediate families, or in boys or girls of their own age can also be very painful for adolescents. Illness arouses in the young a fearful feeling about the vulnerability of their own bodies. The pain, bewilderment, and anger that adolescents feel when a parent is chronically ill make it hard for them to be as considerate as involved adults would wish. Adolescents often need to withdraw from such a situation, and they may be overwhelmed with guilt because they feel they should be more involved. The more painful and intractable the illness, the more likely it is that the adolescent will be disturbed at school, doing poor work, constantly making trouble, or becoming irritable. Adolescents seem to need to demonstrate their own pain, and deny the parent's agony, to ensure that they will be punished for their badness in not being loving to the ill parent. When a long illness ends in death, the adolescent is likely to be even more disturbed:

> Tom's mother was dying of cancer. She had been intermittently ill since he was nine, but as her illness reached its terminal stage, and hope was abandoned, he began to behave in an increasingly antisocial way in school. Tom was perpetually in trouble with the staff, and, presumably because the cause was not understood, he was suspended. At this point his mother died. The loss of his mother and the rejection and lack of understanding he felt at school drove him to theft and assault, and after the usual interval of probation, placement, and various types of highly intermittent therapy, he was committed to a school for delinquent boys. The youth was overwhelmed; he was angry, sad, and ridden with guilt, feeling strongly that his mother's death was all his own fault because of his bad behavior. In his new school, he accidentally damaged a newly built wall that fell over on him and nearly killed him. Only after this probably unconscious suicide attempt was he given the opportunity of facing, with an interested adult he felt cared for him, his pain and anxiety over his mother's illness and death.

The disturbed behavior of guilt-ridden adolescents may occur because they unconsciously try to get their environment to punish them. They often seem to succeed all too well in this. The first response of society to the antisocial behavior of grief-stricken adolescents is usually sympathetic. When the behavior continues, the response often becomes punitive.

Despite the almost inevitable response of adolescents to the loss of loved ones, adults who feel intimately involved in the care of the young may not be aware that a parental death or separation has occurred:

> In one school a fifteen-year-old boy began to steal repeatedly. This school had no tradition of communicating with the parents, and the first his mother knew about the problem was when she received a letter with the boy, who had been sent home. At no time during the discussions that had gone on between him and the staff over the thefts had the boy told them that his father had died during the previous vacation.

Extraordinary though this may seem, it is typical of adolescent behavior. During such a crisis, the young take an attitude toward interested adults like that of the two-year-old to parents: one is supposed to know that the tragedy has occurred without being told about it in words.

In summary, death and separation are some of the most painful experiences that happen to the young, fortunately, still, to the minority. Those young people who are not helped over such crises are highly likely to become emotional cripples.

Caring adults available to young people need to be able to be sensitive to the underlying conflicts of their lives; to work with them in an emotional atmosphere that respects individual integrity; and to try, appropriately, to meet their needs. Adolescents may suffer today, but they can become part of the mature adult population of tomorrow if efforts are made to assist them through these acute conflict situations they cannot handle alone. Under these conditions, many adolescents can resiliently cope with severe stress. On the other hand, when an adolescent exposed to trauma is isolated from caring adults who can intuitively offer them help and emotional support, the best that can be hoped for is adequate, formally organized, psychological intervention. A failure to obtain this may produce a crippled, damaged, and damaging personality—both are too expensive for society.

REFERENCES

Blos, P. (1962), *On Adolescence*, 235. Glencoe, Ill.: Free Press.

Bonnard, A. (1962), Truancy and pilfering associated with bereavement. In *Adolescents, Psychoanalytic Approach to Problems and Therapy*, ed. S. Lorand and H. I. Schneer, 166. New York: Paul Hoeber.

Deutsch, H. (1944), *The Psychology of Women*. New York: Grune & Stratton.

Draper, E. P. (1965), *Psychiatry and Pastoral Care*. 126. Philadelphia: Fortress Press.

Freud, S. (1933), Anxiety and instinctual life. In *New Introductory Lectures on Psychoanalysis, Standard Edition*, Vol. 22, 81–112. London: Hogarth Press.

Greenacre, P. (1952), *Trauma, Growth and Personality*. New York: Norton.

Jersild, A. T. (1963), *The Psychology of Adolescence*, 193–196. New York: Macmillan.

Menninger, K. A. (1963), *The Vital Balance*, 200–201. New York: Viking.

Miller, D. (1965), *Growth to Freedom, The Psycho-Social Treatment of Delinquent Youth*. Bloomington: Indiana University Press.

Robertson, J., and Bowlby, J. (1952), Responses of young children to separation from their mothers. *Courr. Cent. Int. Enf.*, 2:131–142.

Chapter 17

Adolescent Sexuality and Its Disturbances

SOCIAL NORMS AND SEXUAL BEHAVIOR

Nowhere is the interplay between environmental, intrafamilial, and personal factors more evident than in the field of sexual behavior. Sexual attitudes, feelings, and activities shift with cultural and religious expectations, and conscious family effort may alter attitudes toward sexuality within a generation. A description of women's feelings about menstruation, written in the 1940s, in which concepts of dirt and shame are stressed, is now anachronistic (Deutsch, 1944). Homosexuality is no longer considered evidence of emotional instability or a personality disorder, and the more liberal concept of sexuality that was previously present in history is returning. With sexuality, as with other types of behavior, it is apparent that the definition of what is normal depends on criteria of social acceptability. The ancient Greeks saw homosexuality as normal; in India, every form of sexual activity was accepted, as is evident from their temple sculptures. A change in what society considers sexually acceptable and desirable relieves anxiety in some; with others, such a change may reinforce sexual anxiety, as guilt is less easily hidden by social constraints. Most young people are aware of the implicit and explicit sexual attitudes expressed in films, on the stage, and in contemporary books and magazines. Many have therefore come to expect a whole range of exciting sexual gymnastics from each other without any real awareness that some of these should imply great respect and love of one human being to another. Adolescents often believe that a girl's orgasm is inevitable, if only a boy is sufficiently skillful. They are not aware that sometimes this will occur only if a girl really feels in love and at one with her boyfriend. If some adolescent girls do not enjoy sex sufficiently, they may begin to feel that there is something radically wrong with them. Some become self-conscious, and then their chances of having a successful orgasm decrease. Others demand an orgasm as a right and bitterly criticize their boyfriends' failure to give them one. Because some boys feel that they are failures if their girlfriends do not respond with what they consider to be sufficient sexual excitement, security is not enhanced in either party. Nevertheless, an advantage of a decline in sexual prudery is that adolescents with sexual difficulties may now more easily seek help.

The increase in frankness in writing about various forms of pre-intercourse sexuality has begun to lead to a change in adolescents' awareness of what might be expected either of themselves or their partners. Many more boys than in the past are offended if a girl is not willing to kiss or suck their penis; few still regard this as a perversion (Messanger, 1971).

It is abusive for one boy to call another a "cocksucker," but from the evidence of clinical practice, boys who are anxious about being homosexual today talk about a wish for this type of sexual activity more frequently and more easily than they could in the past. Fellatio, which has always been accepted in some cultures (Altschuler, 1971), is now written about as a common event and is shown, by implication, in films. Often little indicates that an intimate emotional relationship might be involved. Like cunnilingus, fellatio is frequently talked about, particularly by upper-class adolescents, as if it were not more significant than any other type of petting (Gebhard, 1971). A profoundly significant human activity with complex psychological significance may be treated as a mild sexual frolic. Because in fellatio, a boy puts himself symbolically in the position of a feeding mother, he needs to feel great security about his own sense of masculinity. The boy who is fellated passively puts himself in a position of implicit trust in his sexual partner, a girl who takes a boy's penis into her mouth is conveying her immense love for her partner's sexual organ, which will give her ultimately such great satisfaction. The boy who tongues a girl's clitoris and vaginal opening similarly should convey great love.

Conscious parental attitudes toward sexuality have changed. The last generation of parents deliberately, the present generation more automatically, are less anxious about infantile sexuality. Clinically, masturbatory guilt associated with fantasy (Harley, 1961), is now rarely seen, but conscious anxiety about the masturbatory act, except in certain small towns and rural areas, has almost disappeared in a decade. Working-class youth still describe the activity as infantile, and young adults who continue the practice may feel that they should have grown out of it (Woods and Natterson, 1967).

SOCIAL CLASS AND SEXUALITY

Many lower-class adolescents from different ethnic groups are less inhibited sexually in some ways than the middle class, although from the statistics of illegitimate birth and clinical observation, adolescent intercourse is becoming more frequent among middle-class youth. Upper-upper–class groups of adolescents in both the United States and Europe are usually able to gratify themselves heterosexually with apparent ease, but as in the lower classes, there is little depth in these relationships, which are often highly self-referent and unloving.

Sexual experimentation is natural. Primitive societies (Mead, 1939) may institutionalize a period of relative license for their young. The puritan tradition among middle-class adolescents inhibits this, but for others, from the end of early adolescence, usually at age fourteen or fifteen, experimental heterosexual behavior is common. Early sexual intercourse, particularly in poverty-stricken groups, is usual. Such behavior is not usually associated with a love relationship (Giver, 1955). Middle-class adolescents tend to expect a wide variation of sexual techniques even in their first heterosexual experiences.

> A seventeen-year-old boy sought psychiatric help at the instigation of his parents because he had made a series of long-distance telephone calls with a false credit number. The calls had been made to impress his girlfriend who was away on vacation.
> In discussing his relationship with his girlfriend the boy reported that the couple had begun to have intercourse some weeks earlier and in this first experience for both they had used "oral intercourse" (his phrase) prior to the actual sex act. He did not regard the former as presupposing particular intimacy and felt it only as a variety of sexual play.

Clinically, this is fairly commonly reported among the middle-class group; it would still be considered perverse by some lower-class adolescents (Gebhard, 1971), perhaps because of its association, with what is, for them, an intolerable experience of passivity.

The reluctance to be the first person to have intercourse with a girl who is a virgin has, among the sexually active white middle class and the black lower classes, been somewhat modified, but virginity still tends to be respected. Hispanic youth who still have roots in their own culture clearly divide females into those who are respectable and marriageable and those who are easily available. Many boys from all social class and ethnic groups still retain the fantasy that at first intercourse they will impregnate a girl, and among many, although it is less usual, the double standard still continues to exist: if a girl has intercourse she would become unacceptable as a marriage partner to a male who might himself be sexually experienced. These attitudes are still fairly prevalent, although they are waning and often represent a projection of a personal conflict about sex.

> Tom, a nineteen-year-old student, sought help for academic underachievement and depression. These complaints were only a ticket of admission for his real complaint: his girlfriend was, he felt, not to be trusted although he knew this was not true. He felt that girls looked upon men's sexual wishes as disgusting and obscene; they put up with sex only in marriage. He knew this was untrue but nevertheless felt it to be accurate. These feelings were a direct projection of his parents' attitudes and the social norms, although somewhat distorted, of the community in which he had been raised.

Middle-class white mothers may still feel more prepared, than those in some other social and ethnic groups, to attempt to interfere in the sexual life and attitudes of their children. Some do this by offering contraceptive advice gratuitously with no knowledge as to whether their children intend to engage in premarital intercourse. Others are readier to warn their daughters that if they engage in premarital sex, they will become less marriageable: boys are not interested in damaged goods. General hostility is often expressed toward male sexuality; boys are thought to force their attention on girls, not caring whether or not the girl wants sexual intimacy.

On the whole, in adulthood, white, lower-class fathers who remain in the marital home appear to become closer emotionally to their sons than their middle-class contemporaries. The boy is often in closer physical intimacy with his father than his middle-class peer, and often, male activities take place without women present. The unconscious homosexual wishes of such boys are then, perhaps, both more intense and more forbidden. Early heterosexuality is more necessary. Lower-class black youth often have no involved father, and their society remains highly matriarchal.

Lower-class males from all ethnic groups may have sexual intercourse at about fifteen years of age or earlier; even with changes in sexual attitudes, most middle-class youth do not envisage carrying sexuality to this length. Sexually active young males from all social groups nowadays usually have the attitude that intercourse is to be both gratifying and experimental, even though the relationship may last for some time. They may talk of love, but they do not mean it. Most middle-class adolescents, however, still accept a basic frustration in their relationship with each other; they may be sexually stimulated to the point of intercourse and then not experience complete sexual fulfillment, as extramarital intercourse or intercourse without matrimonial intent is not acceptable.

SEXUAL FREEDOM AND ITS COMPLICATIONS

The attitude that sexuality should be enjoyed is now more widespread, and it is no longer considered, by many young people, as unacceptable outside marriage. There is, however, a tendency to oversell sexual intimacy; boys and girls come to believe that intercourse should automatically, without an equivalent emotional intimacy, be a unique experience. It is not unusual for a boy to feel that he is in some way deficient if his partner does not have an orgasm. Mutuality of love is not considered as essential as expert sexual gymnastics for fully satisfying and gratifying physical intimacy.

> Kenneth's father contacted a psychiatrist and told him that his eighteen-year-old son was in urgent need of help. Kenneth was a well-built, lithe young man who was suffering from an acute anxiety state. This was partly related to a recent operation for a benign tumor that for a while had convinced him that he was going to die. It was also related to his feeling of total sexual inadequacy. Kenneth had done a great deal of psychological reading and said, "My mother is a castrating bitch. My father does not care about me, all he does is make money." The source of the boy's anxiety preceded his operation. He said, "I have always felt shy with girls, but last spring Judy got me to go to bed with her. She didn't have an orgasm, so I felt absolutely useless. Whatever I did, she did not enjoy it enough. I am a failure, I have a girl now who wants me to sleep with her, but I won't because I know I won't do it properly. I am impotent, I think."

Although some adults now realize that their adolescents are likely to have premarital sexual intercourse, there is still an intensely mixed feeling about this. Attitudes vary from one part of a country to another and among different ethnic, social, and religious groups. In clinical practice, it is now more usual for adolescents of about sixteen, from all social groups, in both the United States and Britain, to report having had intercourse once or twice. Academically involved youth will report intercourse much more frequently than they would have ten or fifteen years ago. It is by no means certain that all tell the truth, although this is more likely in an interview with a doctor or social worker than in answering an anonymous questionnaire. Adolescents fill out forms on the basis of what is expected of them; therefore, despite figures produced in the United States and Britain, there is no way of knowing how common premarital intercourse among adolescents actually is. The idea that premarital intercourse is acceptable both supports and stresses the individual. All adolescents tend to believe that sexual intercourse among their age group is usual; apart from those with obvious conflicts, many young people who do not engage in premarital sex may feel that they lack a satisfactory identity. The idea that everyone has intercourse has led to changes in the quality of human relationships between girls and boys. Boys feel justified in pressing their sexual demands. Girls begin to feel that if they do not have intercourse they are missing out on an important human experience, an attitude that is reinforced because many of their girlfriends claim to have had sex. Some girls now demand that boys have intercourse with them.

The shift to extramarital intercourse, as a more usual social norm, has a varying effect on the emotional health of the population in general. Although it will probably lead to happier sexuality in marriage, difficulties may arise for those who engage in such an activity. Ignoring anatomy, neurophysiology, and endocrinology, many people argue that the differences in the psychology of men and women are due to social conditioning. Nevertheless, their emotional needs are not the same. Men can, perhaps, act promiscuously without impairing their capacity to be tender and loving (although this is debatable), but women do not adapt easily to a sexually promiscuous life. Promiscuity is no more normative now, at any rate from clinical evidence, than it was in the past, but prolonged and transient mating now seem common. In those tender, loving, sexual relationships, girls are generally more dependent than boys; they are more future-oriented, they have a greater need to build nests, and they feel that if their boyfriend really loved them, he would want this. Boys are much more creatures of the present; they do not want to rear children until they are aware of their own mortality. This recognition, perhaps, led to pressure from women for premarital celibacy as a socially acceptable norm. This provided a safeguard against illegitimate pregnancy and also protected girls from feeling failures as women because they were rejected by a less psychologically mature male. Love relationships in which there is full sexual activity, with no intention of marriage, are likely to cause problems, particularly for girls. One essentially feminine contribution to a meaningful relationship between a boy and a girl, one of the factors that makes the bond secure, is that the girl feels a desire for permanency. Along with her wish for love, is a wish to have children. This aspect of feminine psychology is not felt by the young male, who, if he considers the long-term future of his present emotional commitment, is likely to fear the responsibility.

The irresponsibility of late adolescents was noted by Shakespeare. In the *Winter's Tale* he wrote, "I would there were no age between sixteen and twenty-three. There is nothing but getting wenches with child." The Elizabethan situation still exists. The expression of a girl's normal feminine needs for permanency, when they are expressed as a wish, are often felt by a boy to be an unreasonable demand. When a late-adolescent girl, feeling the flowering of love, allows herself to be and say what she feels, she is likely to be rejected by her boyfriend; the young male does not yet feel ready for long-term, caring responsibilities. An unplanned pregnancy is thus likely to break up a long-term, apparently satisfactory sexual relationship. The boy irrationally feels that a girl has trapped him; the girl feels abandoned and let down by the boy's cold response.

SEXUAL ATTITUDES

Sexual inhibition is often related to parental attitudes about the sexual play of children. Children may closely examine each other's genitals, lie on top of each other, bang their bodies together, and generally act out fantasies of intercourse. Alternatively, they replay a sexual act they might have seen or heard their parents perform. For sexual activity to be loving, a child needs to be brought up in a loving environment, where it is obvious to the child that the parents are both physically and emotionally involved with each other. Thus, one of the outcomes of a child brought up by only one parent is that he or she is less able to be a loving sexual partner, depending on when the separation took place, than a more fortunate peer.

There are two stereotypes of sexual behavior that seem to be related to the type of family from which the individual comes: impulsive or controlling (Miller, 1980). The offspring of impulsive families often engage in aggressive sexual play, and some girls from controlling families find this very attractive. Often males from this group may feel that it does not matter very much whether or not their partner enjoys the act, and they often talk of sex as being overrated. In this case, sexual activity does more to fulfil a physical need than to provide erotic and loving satisfaction. A boy in such a situation feels that the girl is lucky to have his penis inside her; the girl accepts this attitude.

In both men and women, an essentially masturbatory self-reference during intercourse may be seen as indicative of satisfactory masculinity and femininity. If maturation past this point does not occur, a loveless sexual attitude is found in married couples. Men may feel that they must have sex with their wives because it is expected of them. Women may feel that men have their sexual and other rights to which subservience is necessary. A woman in such a setting may not like the sexuality of men and may not see them as loving, but her husband's and her son's sexual wishes are acknowledged without overt complaint. In such families, boys are rarely asked to perform the activities in the house that are obviously feminine—making beds, washing dishes, cleaning. This stereotype is probably still common among a considerable sector of the population, which remains relatively untouched by changing women's roles. Loving relationships are mostly fantasied; sexuality is seen as the outlet for men's erotic needs rather than as a mutually loving interaction.

> A boy of eighteen, a trainee in electronics engineering, was in psychotherapy for a functional gastrointestinal disorder. He was discussing his weekend and talked of having sex with his fiancée. His therapist wondered if his girl had enjoyed the experience. The patient looked astounded and said that it never occurred to him that it mattered. "I fucked her; she should have been pleased to have that happen."

The middle-class attitude to sexual activity has always been somewhat more constricted. The close supervision of children, which is usual in more tightly structured smaller families, makes it more difficult for boys and girls to take part in natural sex play. In adolescence, a delay in anything other than autoerotic sexual activity is still commonly associated with an expectation of academic achievement, even in socially mobile groups (Kinsey et al., 1968). This is not surprising, for academic education demands more control of impulsive behavior than vocational studies, and a greater capacity to tolerate frustration. In academic tracks, the opportunities for sexual involvement of one child with another are considerably reduced, if only because of demands of homework. Until high schools began to go on limited schedules because of financial stringency, the opportunity for free unsupervised interactions between children was rare; during the school day it is still fairly minimal because the school gives no time for unstructured interaction except for a brief lunch period. This leads to a school in which adolescents respond as if it were a factory or in which they sometimes react in an overaggressive way to each other until grade eleven or twelve.

Middle-class families tend to be smaller, relative to the amount of available space, than lower-class families; physical intimacy between the family members is less intense, and impulse expression less allowable than with other social groups. When controlling families are angry with each other, then tend to shout or be tight-lipped; members of impulsive families tend to hit out.

SEXUALITY AND AUTONOMY

Many parents can now accept that healthy adolescents do not discuss the details of either sexual activity or sexual difficulties with them. Sexual intimacy is kept secret from parents because this is a way in which adolescents develop autonomy and assert their separate identity. The privacy of sex helps prove to adolescents that they are no longer dependent children. Girls do not discuss what they feel might be orgasmic insufficiency with their mothers; boys do not discuss with fathers whether or not a particular sexual wish or activity might be perverse or whether they are sufficiently potent. This can cause particular problems in psychiatric adolescent outpatient clinics. It is increasingly common for boys of sixteen or seventeen to seek help for impotence in such settings. They come on their own and do not usually tell their parents that they are going. When these sexual problems do not respond to brief intervention and require a great deal of therapy, however, it may be impossible because of financial constraints, or illegal, for the boy to continue to come without the knowledge of his parents. In any case, if a clinic sees an adolescent over a prolonged time period without the parents' knowledge, the staff is agreeing by its actions that the parents are bad and persecutory; acting out with patients against parents vitiates successful therapy. A good therapist will help an adolescent understand the need to tell parents that he has sought psychiatric help but will still guarantee confidentiality as to what he has been told. Parents then demand from either the therapist or a social worker the reason for their child's appearance at a clinic. The request made to a social worker may cause interdisciplinary problems, particularly with those who have worked with the families of smaller children; they find it hard to accept that the problem they have to discuss is that their children cannot be frank with the parents.

Parental responsibility for adolescent sexual feelings and attitudes and behavior depends on the implicit and explicit communications made during childhood and adolescence. Often, parental anxiety about their own role is deflected onto sexual issues, for example, what adolescents should see and read, whether they should have sexual knowledge, and how it should be imparted.

CONTRACEPTION AND ADOLESCENT SEXUALITY

There has clearly been an increase in the frequency of premarital intercourse among middle-class youth in the last decade, although it is highly questionable whether there has been a change in the frequency of such behavior among lower-class, and economically deprived adolescents. The increased illegitimate conception rate indicates that knowledge of contraception does not necessarily imply its use.

More secure adolescents still are fearful of pregnancy, which remains a potent bar to unprotected sexual intercourse. There is no clinical evidence that the media-inspired preoccupation with genital herpes makes the slightest difference to sexually active adolescents. It is still common for mid-adolescent boys to buy contraceptive condoms, in the hope that the opportunity for intercourse will occur. The anxious seeking of drugstores with male clerks remains as fairly typical middle-class behavior, but most feel condoms to be unaesthetic; and many are aware of their failure rate. Most adolescent boys are convinced of their potent fertility; they fantasize that one sexual encounter will almost certainly produce pregnancy. They therefore carry male contraceptives more to impress their masculinity on their friends than to use them.

The illegitimate pregnancy rate has risen with the divorce rate, with some time lag, and it is possible that the one-parent family produces male offspring who perceive impregnation as significant evidence of masculinity. Since the role of their own fathers was all too often to impregnate their mothers and then leave the marital home, this is commonly the only significant masculine model available to many as infants and children. Clinically, the number of boys who are prepared to allow themselves to have intercourse, irrespective of possible pregnancy, has increased, as has the fact that the legal age of consent does not appear to be greatly significant. There seems to have been an increase in the number of youths who seem driven to get a girl pregnant. The wish to "ride bareback," the British slang phrase to describe condomless intercourse, is increasingly common.

It is a sophisticated attitude to understand that fertility and potency are not connected. Sterile males feel less competent in their sexual role and this internal equation is a cause of some of the psychological complications of vasectomy. For many, fertility is essential to a masculine self-concept. Many boys will insist that intercourse feels better if their partner does not use the pill. What they really mean is that they experience it as more satisfactory because no one controls their fertility without their permission.

The cultural equivalent of this psychological state can be found in India. There the male Khama (spirit) gains immortality through the birth of sons. Contraception will not be practiced by poor Indian males, nor will they allow their wives to use it, until they have sufficient sons to ensure that at least one survives (Elliott, 1970). The implication for contraceptive problems in a poverty-stricken country, where death from malnutrition and its side effects are common, is obvious.

The techniques of contraception at the boy's disposal are not particularly safe. He may use a condom, he may practice coitus interruptus, or he may quite cynically satisfy himself at the expense of the girl's peace of mind. The use of the contraceptive pill makes it easier for a girl to have intercourse promiscuously, but easy contraception poses problems both for adolescents and their parents. Parents may be tempted to encourage their daughters to use the pill or to be fitted with a diaphram. Similarly, doctors may make the same recommendation to their adolescent patients. This represents adult approval of, and collusion in, extramarital sex. Adolescents may not want this adult invasion of their privacy and may feel it as devaluing them. On the other hand, adult failure in this respect may lead to illegitimate pregnancy, with all its complications. The decision has to be made on the basis of the physician's understanding of the girl's psychosocial state. An individual driven to promiscuous sexual behavior is not going to give this up just because no contraceptive is available. A seriously deprived girl, intellectually, emotionally and economically, should if possible be prevented from illegitimate conception just as surely as she will continue to have intercourse. On the other hand, to offer a girl a contraceptive just because of parental anxiety invites the girl to have sex.

Easy contraception also brings to the fore a typical adolescent conflict between the wish to experiment with sex and thereby discover a sexual self and the human need for the physical expression of tender loving feelings. This conflict is not inevitable, a first sexual affair may be, but often is not, a love affair.

It is quite naive to believe that if parents are told by others that their children are seeking and obtaining contraceptive assistance, that in some way this will inhibit the child's sexuality. Those who are responsible enough to seek such assistance may not be conventionally moral but they are clearly attempting to be responsible. If the parent–child relationship is not one such that adolescents will communicate with their parents themselves, the situation will not be assisted by intrusive official interference.

HOMOSEXUALITY

The reason why some individuals choose a homosexual orientation exclusively, others a bisexual, and others an exclusively heterosexual one is not known. Similarly, those who are homosexual vary dramatically in their lifestyles: some identify with members of the opposite sex in their development, gestures, and speech, while others do not seem to fit any obvious variation in the larger culture. The incidence of homosexual activity is unclear because the assessment depends on self-reporting, and anonymous questionnaires are not necessarily very reliable. Although adolescents express considerable anxiety about the subject and continue to use derogatory homosexual words as terms of abuse, it is fairly common in clinical practice nowadays for young people to admit to homosexual wishes and to be in conflict only about who should know.

Conflict is thus created for some by a society that is still hostile to homosexuality and homosexuals, although the social situation is not as bad as it was a decade ago. Late adolescents and young adults who are exclusively homosexual become aware that it appears more difficult to set up stable relationships with others that are recognized and acceptable; thus homosexuals tend to cluster together in large cities. Since the divorce rate is in 1982 nearly 50 percent, it is unclear whether couple relationships in the homosexual world are less stable than for society at large. It is clear, however, that adolescent homosexuals who enter the "gay world" are able to be extremely sexually active at a younger age than those young adults who involve themselves in the world of the singles bars. Loveless sex, of either orientation, ultimately becomes unsatisfactory.

For adolescent males, the homosexual preoccupation with young beauty seems to distort their value system and appearance, and youth become inordinately important. This is the same situation as exists for very beautiful adolescent girls, who are related to only on the basis of their appearance. Homosexual conflict shows itself in adolescence in a variety of ways. Some wish to be heterosexual and want not to be homosexual; some feel lonely, isolated, and uncomfortable with their peers and parents. Some torment themselves for years with a sense of being worthless.

If an individual wishes to retain a homosexual orientation, psychotherapy may be helpful with a variety of conflicts, particularly those related to shame and guilt. Homosexuals who wish to become heterosexual are not usually helped by less than a complete psychoanalysis: behavior-modification techniques play into the passivity of many homosexuals and may produce a pseudoheterosexual adjustment. If a man is incapable of feeling love and affection for a woman, he may behave heterosexually, but the sex act is not loving.

Many boys who have a homosexual orientation present themselves as wishing to change this, but often they are seeking assistance not because they are homosexual but rather because they are afraid to become intimate with anyone. The typical paradigm of the overcontrolling mother and the distant father (Coons, 1971), is more likely to produce this syndrome, with essentially masturbatory relationships either homoerotic or heterosexual, than an emotionally meaningful relationship.

> Seventeen-year-old John sought treatment because he thought he was a homosexual. He was very attracted to boys of his own age who were handsome and muscular, as he was himself. He had an overcontrolling mother who allowed him no privacy; he was a very good son out of fear of her rages and hysteria. He hardly ever saw his father, a busy attorney, who played tennis every weekend. During the course of his therapy, he described one of his three homosexual experiences as follows:
>
> "You would think that to come over another being is one of the most intimate things you can do. When this happened I just got up and left, I wanted nothing to do with him. It was not that I felt disgusted, I just felt nothing; I turned off."

John did not actually wish to change his sexual orientation; the request for treatment was really a ticket of admission for assistance to be able to be intimate.

Homosexual activity is markedly related to societal pressures, intra-familial conflicts, and the level of personal maturity of the individual. Although the gay liberation movement has made the public discussion of homosexuality possible without criticism, anxiety about homosexuality is common to boys and their parents. Lesbian behavior is more tolerable still to Western society, and, as a result, parental and individual anxiety about lesbian activity among adolescent girls is less usual than concern about homosexuality in boys. Many more boys with a homosexual orientation are seen in clinical practice than girls. Despite the often-stated objection of parents to their son's sexual orientation, the mothers of homosexual boys commonly collude in their son's homosexual relationships:

> Paul was hospitalized because of drug dependence. He was fifteen, and he had become very dependent on marijuana in association with an active homosexual relationship with a man of twenty-three. Paul's phy-sician thought that communication with this homosexual partner was disturbing to him and recommended that the patient not communicate with his lover. The patient did not openly defy his physician, but arranged for his mother to smuggle letters from the lover to her son in her own letters.

Lesbian activity is probably less common than male homosexuality. This is because adolescent girls are less easily sexually stimulated than boys, are often markedly fearful of bodily contact with other girls, and are less needful of the physical release of sexual tension until they have actually been involved in meaningful sexual intercourse (Brunswick, 1968). A boy who obtains sexual satisfaction with another boy is using his sexual organs to obtain gratification in a way that may be masturbatory and thus a develop-mental act. The nature of the homosexual act among adolescent boys indicates whether this is associated with a transient stage of sexual ex-perimentation or whether an ultimate homosexual orientation is likely. Some boys know this anyway, others, although involving themselves in a whole variety of sexual activity, will insist that they do not wish to be and are not homosexual. Often the denial represents a wish to conform to the norms of the larger society or is related to concern about what would happen if their parents knew.

The culture and the environment in which the boy lives is relevant in assessing the significance of the behavior. In adolescence, mutual masturba-tion is commonly associated with a general sense of loneliness and insecurity, sexual curiosity, intense sexual frustration, and social acceptability within a group. Fellatio among boys is more likely to indicate a homosexual orientation in Britain, where it is a less generally acceptable form of normative sexual activity, than in the United States. The enjoyment of anal intercourse almost always implies an active homosexual involvement, as initially this is not comfortable and requires an ability to be relaxed with another male. Boys who report feeling "good" after such an episode always have a basic homosexual inclination.

ETIOLOGY OF HOMOSEXUAL ACTIVITY

Homosexual activity may be primarily a function of situational pressures. It is common in single-sex, isolated, male boarding schools, in youth prisons, and in underprivileged urban areas. The type of activity engaged in may be a function of specific pressures: gang rape may produce sodomy; fellatio may be the price a boy pays for protection by a bigger boy in a youth prison. Lesbian activity is common in girls' juvenile institutions; the absence of any males in the environment gives particular status to the butch girl and is highly pathological.

Some homosexual activity is most clearly related to family pressures. The stereotyped situation involves a devaluing mother and a passive father who is nevertheless subtly seductive to his son. This can produce a homosexual orientation, and a family row in such a constellation can precipitate homosexual activity. Homosexual activity need not imply a homosexual orientation. In British boarding schools when friends start to behave homosexually with each other, the friendship may end, although the activity may continue. Boys in conflict may be consciously or unconsciously teasing and provoke such activities only to reject them.

> A twenty-eight-year-old camp counselor did his best to persuade a seventeen-year-old boy with obvious homosexual conflicts to be his lover. He told the boy that treatment attempts were stupid, that he should accept his orientation. What pleasanter place to be in love and experience it than in the summer in the woods? The boy refused. He told his therapist, "I don't want to be as pathetic as he is at twenty-eight, having to use all that effort to try to get me into the sack with him." Although the boy had chosen to go for long walks with the man, he later rejected him.

A mature adult male should not need to feel repulsion or disgust at homosexual behavior, although it may not represent his object choice. Thus, a heterosexual male who hates homosexuals is as conflict-ridden as the homosexual male who hates women. The argument is still current as to whether homosexuality represents the behavior of an immature male in

Western society. Boys who come from families in which there is mutual security between parents, in which a husband's role is valued by his wife, and a boy's masculinity is valued by his mother may still develop an exclusively homosexual orientation, although this background is seen more usually in those who are comfortably heterosexual.

An exclusive homosexual orientation in the male may also occur when boy have been brought up in families in which there is sexual conflict between the parents and male sexuality is not respected. Lesbianism may be found in those girls who have been devalued by their fathers; just as exclusively homosexual boys implicitly may be hostile to women and girls, such lesbians devalue men.

Many homosexuals appear unable to create permanent love relationships. It has been argued that this is a result of the stress they experience from society. This pressure does exist, but many homosexuals are so intensely involved with themselves that they are unable to be loving. It is decidedly easier for two homosexuals to perceive each other as narcissistic extensions of themselves than to be mutually giving. Homosexual, as well as heterosexual relationships, when they last, do so because one partner meets the needs of the other, and vice versa. A young man convinced of his own frailty may feel he receives the strength of his male partner when he incorporates the other man's penis into his body. Equally, when he conquers his partner, his own masculine potency may be reinforced. This mutuality may also be present in all aspects of the relationship, but it is a mistake to imagine that other mutualities than those related to strength and power cannot exist in homosexual love relationships; they can and do.

SEXUAL CENSORSHIP

The censorship of school and library books in the United States is widespread and pornography remains a current preoccupation. Exposure to knowledge about sexual techniques from books, films, and plays may modify behavior, just as exposure of small children to violence on television may affect their attitudes (Lefkowitz et al., 1971), but a healthy adolescent who is consolidating his identity in midadolescence does not change his fundamental attitudes on the basis of what is seen and read. An individual's capacity to be considerate and loving with others develops through childhood and is finally confirmed at adolescence. If young people have such a capacity, a film or book, however perversely it mixes sexual and aggressive stimulation, does not modify this. Early adolescents, who have less judgment, and emotionally disturbed older youth, who are less certain in their capacities to be loving, can be influenced by portrayals of sadistic aggressive sexuality, just as they can be influenced in their behavior by aggressive individuals. The real problem, however, is the report of actual events. In the United States, a mass slaughter of young homosexuals occurred in Illinois and then in Texas in the last decade. Disturbed adolescents, whose capacities to be sexual and aggressive have become inextricably mixed, can take what is read in a book or, particularly, what is seen in a film as permission to behave in a disturbed and aberrant way, but the book or the film does not cause the confusion (Miller, 1969). The problem is that censorship, which is designed to forbid, also implies permission. If a film is given a certificate that says it may not be shown to adolescents under eighteen, those over that age may assume that what is shown is approved by the authority figures of society. This is potent permission for the psychologically disturbed, although they might have acted out their fantasies anyway at some other time.

Adolescents who have been brought up in families with mutual love will not be changed by the entertainment industry. Secure people are not significantly influenced by what they may see on the stage or the screen or what they might read in books. All they gain is information. The less secure youngster, brought up in a less loving family with less mutual respect, is in greater difficulty. The increased sexual intimacy that can now be seen on the screen and on the stage may reinforce a pre-existing lack of respect for the integrity of individuals. Very little may be wrong with two people engaging in intercourse on the screen as part of an act of love; however, the actors involved, even though they may portray it as an act of love, devalue this human activity by exhibiting themselves as part of an entertainment.

Society must decide how much freedom healthier sections of the population will give up to protect those who are younger, weaker, or more disturbed; this problem exists in the arts, in the portrayal of eroticism, and with alcohol, whose widespread early- and mid-adolescent use is a function of a lowered drinking age and adult collusion.

EFFECT OF EARLY SEDUCTION AND ASSAULT

Painful experiences inflicted on the adolescent may cause a disturbance in what appeared to be an otherwise healthy personality developing in a normal way. The most obvious difficulties are those associated with death and separation from a parent, but other painful experiences can occur during this age period. A boy or a girl exposed to coercive adult sexuality, even if they are unconsciously provoking, may have further maturation disturbed (Lorand, 1961). This differs from a situation in which a middle- or late-adolescent boy, who is aware of homosexual wishes about which he is in conflict, provokes a situation in which seduction is likely. Some who are delinquent almost consciously maneuver themselves into adult jails in order to make homosexual activity something for which they can disclaim responsibility. On the other hand, some conflicted young males who are the victims of rape in such situations become assaultive with smaller boys, as if to put themselves in the shoes of the adult who assaulted them. Both these responses are attempts to come to terms with the painful event.

Girls who have been sexually used are then highly likely to behave in a promiscuous way, but with little or no capacity to bring loving feeling together with the act of sex. On the other hand, they may withdraw from all contacts with men, repress all sexual feeling, sometimes to the extent of trying to make themselves less sexually attractive.

> Karen was a tall, potentially attractive fifteen-year-old who was admitted to an adolescent treatment center with severe anorexia nervosa. One of her stated goals was to get rid of her breasts. At the age of eight she was sexually assaulted by a sixteen-year-old boy who was babysitting with her and her small brother. She had never been able to tell her mother this. The anorexia began after a petting session with a seventeen-year-old schoolmate after a school dance.

Young people who are sexually attacked have often unconsciously provoked or consented to the incident. Most children are well taught that it is unwise to get into a car with a stranger. Some, however, forget this admonition, indicating an unsatisfactory attempt to resolve unconscious conflicts produced by disturbed nurturing experiences in their families as they grew up:

> Mary was an only child. Her father, who had always ignored her, died when she was eleven. When Mary was fifteen, she was walking home from a movie and had a choice of going down a main street or taking a back road. Though it was no quicker than the main street, she chose the dimly lit road. A car with three boys in it stopped and offered her a ride home. She accepted and was later found bedraggled and frightened on a piece of wasteland some five miles away, having been sexually assaulted.

It is easy to accuse Mary of being a seductive child, but she had no conscious awareness when she got into the car that she was putting herself at risk. The episode was just as painful for Mary as it would have been if she had been a totally unwilling victim.

Incestuous relationships cause particular problems for children. The effect of father–daughter incest generally seems to be the production of a personality that does not relate well to men, and often promiscuity is present with excessive guilt and a feeling of being all-powerful. Some mothers often unconsciously collude with this act, and it is not unusual to discover that the mothers of girls who are the victims of such behavior were themselves so treated when they were children.

All antisocial behavior has its roots in both social and personal pathology. Incestuous behavior, when it occurs in middle-class families, is associated with greater personal pathology than is the case with the impoverished, when the social pathology is greater.

> Jennifer at eighteen was seen in a university student health service after a schizophrenic episode that had occurred shortly after she entered as a freshman. She had a history of regular intercourse with her father since she was twelve. Her brother was seen at the adolescent service of a nearby city because of academic underachievement and being too quiet for the comfort of his teachers. His father had been practicing fellatio on him since he was nine. When the father was interviewed by a social worker, he explained that he felt it his duty to show his son what a vagina was like, "He needs not to be hurt on its teeth." The situation was compiicated by the fact that the whole family needed the father's salary as an engineer to survive economically.

Brother–sister incest does not seem as traumatic as that between parent and child. Father–son incest is excessively rare, but has been seen between seriously disturbed fathers and their sons. Mothers may take their adolescent sons to their beds, but this appears clinically to be a denial of the boys sexuality rather than overt stimulation. The former attitude is not rare, the latter has not been seen by this writer.

Any help for an adolescent in sexual difficulty requires the helping adult, apart from assessing the etiology of the problem, to understand the normative behavior for the group from which the adolescent comes. Even such behavior may represent an attempt by an adolescent to resolve either an internal conflict or a developmental difficulty. As has been said, postpubertal heterosexual intercourse, which is really masturbatory in nature, may be quite normal in some parts of society, but vulnerable adolescents may still use it to help resolve their internal conflicts. Lonely adolescents may have sex to buy friendship, not as an act of love or even as human experimentation.

RELIGIOUS IDEOLOGY AND SEXUAL ANXIETY

Extremely orthodox Jews are not allowed any sexual contacts, not even kissing, until they marry; masturbation is forbidden. These were perhaps tolerable restrictions when adolescents married at puberty; in society today, they present young people with intense conflicts about their own behavior.

> Karl, age sixteen, was sent to see a psychiatrist by his anxious parents because, before he obtained his driving license, he constantly took his father's car on long rides through the town. He was picked up twice for

speeding, and the referral was precipitated because he crashed the car in a one-car accident. Since the father was a local family practitioner, the police took no formal proceedings, providing referral to a psychiatrist was made.

The boy was a handsome sixteen-year-old, obviously mature physically, who showed no evidence that he needed to inhibit his sexuality. Nevertheless, being the son of highly orthodox Jewish parents he did not date, masturbate (he said), or allow himself any physical contact with girls. If he had attended an orthodox Jewish school, peer-group social support might have made life possible for him. However, such a school was not available, and he went to the local high school. Because he was in grade eleven, many boys were assessing their masculinity by successfully having intercourse with girls. Karl believed in the tenets of his religion, but was aware of diffuse rage directed against his father. This he felt to be intolerable. He knew that driving his father's car made him less tense, particularly when he drove at high speeds.

The boy did not stay in psychiatric treatment. The anxiety about possible confrontations between his profound sexual wishes and his religious and intra-familial morality was much too intense.

Some Christian churches cause similar problems to adolescents in present society: some Baptists, the Pentecostal Church, and others forbid any demonstration of tenderness and sexual affection outside of marriage. Puritanical Roman Catholicism continues to look upon masturbation as a mortal sin.

An apparent agrophobia in one sixteen-year-old boy was related to anxiety over masturbation. He thought that were he accidentally killed in the street before going to confession after masturbating, he would die not in a state of grace. The threat of purgatory had to be relieved before he was able to develop any sense of sexual freedom.

Again group support may make those restrictions tolerable; isolation from similar others increases anxiety.

PROBLEMS OF MALE POTENCY

Impotence, absolute (Ferenczi, 1950) or relative, is a common complaint of late-adolescent, middle-class boys. Although most boys are aware that they may fail to penetrate a girl successfully the first time they have intercourse, this occurrence may cause great anxiety. If they are fortunate and have a male friend with whom they can discuss the failure, or if the girl is understanding, all may then go smoothly. Effectively, they seek consensual validation from another male about the transiency of the experience. Many boys use sex so that a girl will discount their internal image of a devaluing female, which they may have acquired in their nuclear family. The dominance of the American mother and the fragmentation of American society, both of which make it extremely difficult for the young male to develop a firm sense of himself, probably account for the prevalence of sexual anxieties. Paradoxically, however, adolescent blacks seem less sexually insecure, and more tolerant of overt homosexual behavior, than their white counterparts, even though black ghetto society is matriarchal. The explanation for this may be that black mothers do not devalue masculine sexuality as often as white mothers.

> A nineteen-year-old black youth was seen by a psychiatrist because of academic underachievement. He was totally dominated by his professional father. Of his mother he said, "When I go home for a vacation, mother is concerned that my brothers and I have time to go out with girls. She worries if we don't seem to be having a good time when we go out with them at night."

Middle-class black, late-adolescent girls often appear more racist about inter-ethnic sexual relationships than their white counterparts. They may become incensed when black boys date white girls.

The impotent adolescent may appear for help after several unsuccessful attempts at intercourse, with the usual story that he can maintain an erection until he is about to penetrate the girl's vagina; at that point he loses his erection. This type of impotence, on the assumption that the boy can successfully maintain an erection and ejaculate when he masturbates himself, is often responsive to brief therapy.

In theory, there are two possible psychological reasons for impotence just before vaginal penetration: the adolescent may be fearful of women and anxious that they will engulf him, or that he may be so unconsciously angry with women that at the moment of intercourse he refuses to gratify his partner. If a therapist interprets a boy's anxiety he implies, "I know you are an anxious fearful person who is not able to be much of a man." This invites dependent incompetence and years of therapy. If, on the other hand, an interpretation is made about the aggressive teasing implicit in such impotence, the boy is being implicitly told that he is a powerful male, desirable to women, who uses his sexuality potently, if with mutual lack of satisfaction. This may produce rapid resolution of the symptom. Two cases, one from Britain and the other from the United States, demonstrate the value of interpretations about hostility rather than anxiety:

> Peter was an eighteen-year-old student at one of the colleges of Cambridge University. His father had been in the Foreign Office and was now an industrial tycoon; his mother was brilliant and witty. Peter had been brought up surrounded by art and music, and his mother's wit was

often used to quell both her husband and her sons. Peter attended a famous British school, and at the age of sixteen met a beautiful girl of the same age with whom he attempted an affair. He took her to bed, and at the point of penetration he lost his erection. He reassured himself, by talking to his best friend, that this was reasonably common and thought little more about it.

A brilliant scholar, Peter went to college at seventeen and within a few months tried to have an affair with a fellow student; the same pattern of impotence persisted. Becoming increasingly anxious, Peter failed his exams in the first term of his second year, and his academic tutor referred him for psychological help because of his apparent tension and anxiety.

A quiet-spoken, charming, handsome youth, Peter told his story in his first psychiatric interview. The psychiatrist, having heard of the controlling mother and the exact nature of the impotence, said "I think you must be one of the biggest shits I have met in a long time." The boy went white with rage, which did not abate when the therapist told him that he was "a reverse prick tease." This idea, however, obviously intrigued Peter, who agreed to return in three days.

He came back and with delight said that he had successful intercourse many times. During the first occasion he had thought to himself "I'll show that bastard." Feeling much better about himself, Peter decided he would come back only if he got into academic or sexual difficulties. The psychiatrist next heard of Peter three years later, when he was invited to the boy's wedding.

The technique had been deliberate. The use of vulgarities as interpretations were designed to present Peter inferentially with the picture of aggressive masculinity that he had to deny in himself. The interpretation about aggression made his masculinity potent. His thought about the therapist was, in a sense, homosexual; nevertheless, the relief of his symptoms led to his ability to be himself both vocationally and sexually in the future.

In another situation, a patient was to be interviewed in a one-way vision room before a medical school junior class who were being taught interviewing techniques. The patient had come in to the psychiatric outpatient clinic's walk-in service that morning. He was a nineteen-year-old student from the southern United States.

Jim was pleasant and soft-spoken, with a pronounced southern accent. He complained of a completely unsatisfactory sexual life. From the age of fifteen to eighteen he had thought of himself as a homosexual. He said that he would masturbate or "blow" the other man, usually a pick-up. However, he never got an erection himself as soon as the homosexual behavior started, although he would get hard walking to an assignation and before the sex play began. He had met a girl in his freshman year, was in love with her, he felt, and wanted to marry her. However, whenever he tried to make love to her he always lost his erection when his penis touched her vaginal orifice. He had tried alcohol and marijuana to see if this made him feel better and more successful, but neither had worked. The psychiatrist said, "You don't give anybody anything, do you? You tease both men and women and pretend that you are going to give something of yourself, but you don't." The patient became defensive and anxious and said that he never saw himself as a hurtful individual. Arrangements were made for him to return the following week.

The discussion with the students was lively. They felt that the psychiatrist had been overaggressive and they did not really understand the point of the comment. The patient, rather than waiting the week, returned to see the psychiatrist four days later. He said, "I came to thank you. I am going to get married." He then said that he had gone to bed with his girlfriend that night after the interview. He had attempted intercourse and it failed. He then, with great sadness, told his girlfriend that he did not want to tease her, that he really wanted to make love to her. She burst into tears and told him that she had thought there was something wrong with her; they then proceeded to make love successfully. They had done this several times since. The psychiatrist said that he thought the patient was perhaps treating him psychologically as he treated his male lovers sexually; he showed his potentiality, but refused to follow through. The patient was delighted with this interpretation. He said he thought it was true, but he proposed to use his energies to be a good husband and to get through school. He indicated he would let the psychiatrist know how things went. One year later, he reported good grades, no more homosexual conduct or interest, and a happy relationship with his wife.

Two short-term cases do not make a series, but it appears in both patients that the therapist had both interpreted the crippling conflict and reinforced a sense of socially acceptable masculine aggression and sexuality. Neither boy had been so anxious about his relationships with girls that he had been unable to make some physical and emotional contact with them. Such an approach would not have been successful with boys who kept at a distance from girls because they were afraid of their own murderous hostility or because they feared being totally swamped by a devouring female, although both these fears may be in the genesis of some types of impotence.

ORGASMIC INSUFFICIENCY

Both male impotence and failure to achieve orgasm in girls imply an unconscious devaluation of members of the opposite sex. Orgasmic insufficiency in girls, however, is harder to help than impotence in boys, but males who are unable to ejaculate are as difficult to treat. Boys get no erotic satisfaction from impotence, girls get closeness and warmth even though they are unable to achieve orgasm. Orgasmic insufficiency successfully devalues both male and female sexuality. Girls who experience this may play out their hostility both to their own role as women and to the male and his penis with success— even though the victory is pyrrhic. One reason for the relative failure of the treatment of orgasmic insufficiency is that unmarried adolescent girls do not feel safe in their relationships with boys, even if they seek treatment. It is hard for a girl to be totally giving to a man when she has conflicts about this—when she is unsure of the permanence of the relationship. Boys who do not ejaculate can indulge in the fantasy of enormous potency as they sustain an erection for long periods; commonly, they appear promiscuous as if they are seeking a partner who can allow them to feel safe. Since males lose their full erections within five to ten seconds after ejaculation, psychologically they "allow" their partners to make them temporarily impotent; some do not feel sufficiently trusting to allow this.

Societies that believe that the roles of men and women in families should be the same, that take away from men an authoritative family status and give this to women, are likely to produce large numbers of sexually anxious boys who either are, or fear being, impotent. They may also produce angry women, unable to establish lasting heterosexual relationships. Momism, as initially described by Philip Wylie and then again by Philip Roth (*Portnoy's Complaint*), makes it difficult for boys to reach a comfortable sexuality. Similarly, if there is no obvious mutual love between parents, girls find it difficult to accept female sexuality with all its sensitive emotional depths. As women, when they cannot achieve orgasm in a full, caring relationship, the devaluation of masculinity and femininity influences their husbands and children. An unsatisfactory marital relationship reinforces the likelihood of emotional difficulties being perpetuated through the generations. Orgasmic insufficiency may be a transient experience associated with overanxious or unloving sexual intercourse. Its appearance does not necessarily indicate serious emotional conflict. Basic parental attitudes toward loving relationships influence all adult sexual behavior in their children. At the extreme, some attitudes toward the sexuality of children are still confused. If a little boy touches his penis, inappropriate horror is still often expressed. The attitude that sex is dirty and disgusting remains too common. Many women still put up with sex with their husbands to appease and satisfy them (Rainwater, 1960). On the other hand, adolescents may pressure themselves, or feel pressured into sexual relationships long before they are capable of being truly loving.

Early heterosexuality is encouraged by the "halo" effect of the discussions about it in the various media. Adolescents are led to expect unique experiences without the necessity for a long-term, loving relationship and long before many of them develop a capacity for empathy.

SEXUAL PROMISCUITY

Most young people do not respond to the removal of psychological barriers to sexuality by promiscuously moving from bed to bed.

Promiscuity—a relatively indiscriminate, loveless sexual intercourse—is a symptom in which emotional deprivation and social pressure may be determinants. For example, a girl may take enough alcohol or marijuana at a party to lessen inner controls. In the absence of adult control, with the pressure of overt and covert sexuality that may be present, seduction by a sexually predatory youth may occur. The absence of adults at parties is often taken as permission by the young people to behave impulsively. Too much freedom given to adolescents before they are mature enough to make appropriate judgments becomes license. In such a situation, an adolescent who feels rejected, isolated, lonely, or empty may become involved in a premature loveless sexual relationship. Partly, regressive needs for infantile love may involve hostility to members of the opposite sex; cuddling may be sought by even transiently deprived girls, and under certain circumstances the price they are prepared to pay is intercourse. Since masturbatory activity is acceptable to the male his act of intercourse may be performed with less conflict. It is not rare, however, for a boy to have intercourse because it is expected of him, and some boys play out their hostility to girls by using their penis as a weapon.

> She groaned and writhed as I made love to her as if I was hurting her. She made me so mad I thought, "Fuck you!" and so I did it as hard and as long as I could. I didn't care whether she enjoyed it or not.

Some girls collect penises and neither know nor care about either their own feelings or the feelings of the boys involved. Promiscuous sex is a way of devaluing the individual's sexuality and that of the sexual partner; it also punishes the internal image of parents and effectively punishes parents in reality. The conscience is appeased by a feeling that one is unloved anyway.

Promiscuous adolescent girls are not usually treatable by formal outpatient psychotherapy. So much hostility and regressive satisfaction is contained in their sexual behavior that no therapist or therapy can titrate the level of frustration and contain promiscuous acting-out. This behavior often gives unconscious vicarious gratification to parents of promiscuous girls who are conflict-ridden about their own sexuality; this is particularly likely with sterile mothers of adopted daughters who replay the conflict about their own sterility with the unconscious wish that their daughters will bear children for them. Sterile fathers may similarly provoke their sons to impregnate a girl.

Parents of late adolescents are similar in some ways to parents of small children who must allow their children a degree of physical risk if they are to grow up as physically secure people. The former may have to watch their children take equivalent psychological chances in human relationships. In order to grow, adolescents have to match their judgment against the reality in which they live. The sexuality of adolescents cannot be controlled by adults, and many parents find this an almost intolerable burden. When their adolescent has a lover, parents face the fact that they may have lost a dependent child, as well as wonder whether the young couple can accept long-term responsibility for one another. If this is unlikely, parents will find themselves having to help heal their children's psychological wounds.

A significant number of lower-class girls who become heterosexually active during puberty do not really associate intercourse with conception. They know this is so, but it is not emotionally believed, since they may have frequent intercourse and not conceive because they do not become fertile until about three years after their first period. Only then do they begin to ovulate regularly. When, finally, impregnation occurs, many are shocked.

In some groups, there is no expectation of matrimony after impregnation, and girls are expected to produce children who will be reared by their mother or grandmother. Among middle-class groups, the greater availability of contraceptive knowledge commonly indicates that pregnancy is a result of either an unconscious or conscious wish to become pregnant. Sometimes pregnancy may result from religious belief, intellectual inadequacy, or a willingness to go along with a boyfriend's need to prove his potency. It may sometimes be an attempt to force the hand of reluctant parents to allow marriage; it may represent a wish for stability in having achieved a home of one's own.

The illegitimacy rate among adolescents continues to be high, and the relative ease of abortion now provides problems of its own. Pregnancy for adolescent girls may represent an attempt to feel whole and valuable as a woman (David, 1972). When a pregnant girl goes to an obstetrician, she may be asking this man, who society values, if he thinks she is worthwhile as a person and a woman. This question may be couched as a request for an abortion, but granting the request may imply a devaluation of the girl's femininity, and this must be understood. There are no psychiatric indications for an abortion. It is human and decent to offer abortion to a girl who is the victim of rape; a retarded girl may produce a retarded infant at great cost to society if both are well cared for, but the main indication is social pressure. A useful question to ask a girl requesting an abortion is whether she would want it if there were no such pressures upon her.

Many girls who become pregnant and claim they wish to keep the child have no idea of the demanding greed of an infant and often they are quite unable to cope with this. Physicians faced with a request for an abortion may be equally too willing to accept the content of a girl's statement at face value. An illegitimately pregnant girl may arouse the rescue fantasies of doctors when she claims that she has bad parents who must not know of her condition. Laws about the physician's responsibility to communicate with parents merely avoid the issue. A pregnant girl may project her own angry feelings about her state onto her parents and insist they will be punitive, when this is not so.

> A sixteen-year-old high school girl went to a free clinic to ask their help in obtaining an abortion. She said her parents must not be told and a physician wrote a referral letter to a clinic in New York saying the girl was eighteen and requesting an abortion. The girl had to raise $250 and she borrowed the money from all her friends. She got the sum, but her older sister found out what was happening and sought help from the school social worker. This woman persuaded the girl to tell her parents who were kind, supportive, empathic, and helpful.

The physician broke a cardinal rule. In a parent/child struggle, sides should not be taken. Thus, it was appropriate to be for the child and not against the parents. Moreover, he did not recognize the area in which she really wanted help, that is, in her relationship to her parents.

SEXUAL EXHIBITIONISM

Some degree of sexual exhibitionism has always been typical of adolescent boys and girls. Its social acceptability has varied from time to time. For a while women had to hide the fact that they had legs and ankles; men, that they had a penis.

In the Middle Ages, affluent males wore an elaborate codpiece that covered and called attention to their genitals. Clothes were colorful until the nineteenth century, and bawdy sexuality was constantly seen in the theater. After a period of approximately 120 years, men in the last two decades have once again been "allowed" to be more exhibitionistic. Many adolescent boys shrink their jeans skin-tight, thus outlining their genitals. Stylish adolescent boys' slacks from time to time appear with buttons, which are no longer hidden, to replace a zip fly. The unacceptable can become erotically stimulating, and rapid changes in fashion can cause anxiety to some. Girls who do not wear a bra may stimulate pubertal boys and be felt by them as teasing. Sometimes young women social workers or physicians wear revealing clothes that may disturb immature adolescents with whom they have contact. Similarly, a young male doctor who wears "with it" clothing may be felt by his young patients to be indicating something about his sexual and drug-related attitudes.

In general, among young people, prurience is slowly being removed from nudity, but exhibitionism as a symptom of sexual immaturity is still fairly common and is a measure of the personal immaturity of the adolescent (Kaiser, 1961). It is natural for a little boy to show people that he has a penis and that he is proud of it. An adolescent who exhibits his penis to girls or women and who masturbates in front of them demonstrates infantile sexuality. Such boys and adult men are afraid of women and at the same time contemptuous (Christoffel, 1956). Although women become extremely anxious about such behavior, it is not dangerous. Exhibitionists are not able to form close relationships with girls; neither do they attack girls. Some very disturbed aggressive boys will strip off their own clothing, however, as though to attempt rape; hence, the common feeling that an exhibitionist is dangerous.

Women too may be provocatively exhibitionistic. The girl who undresses in front of an open window in an apartment block needs to be safely aggressive to males. It is an intriguing double standard that a naked girl who behaves this way is not liable to legal penalties, whereas a boy who strikes a naked pose in front of a window where he might be observed commits an offense. Both suffer from similar levels of psychological maladjustment. There are, however, exaggerations of normative behavior. The boy who wears skin-tight jeans is exhibitionistically trying to encourage the voyeurism of girls, although an unconscious homosexual provocation may also be present (Fraiberg, 1961). The behavior may also be consciously provocative to other males. The display of a well-muscled body has the same intent. Girls who dress to encourage the sexual interests of males also encourage their voyeurism.

VOYEURISM

Just as exhibitionism is an exaggeration of a natural human tendency, so is voyeurism, the act of looking at someone else's genitals to obtain a feeling of sexual gratification. It is common and usual for small boys and girls to be interested in each other's genitals. Initially, voyeurism is part of a normal developmental stage of human sexual development. Postpubertal boys, particularly in a gang, may be involved in episodes in which a girl's pants are taken down; alternately a girl may exhibit herself to gratify a group of boys. A boy may also demonstrate his erect penis to another boy. In deprived communities, sexual exhibitionism and voyeurism coexist when a group of boys all have intercourse with a more or less willing girl in a "gang bang," as the boys stay to watch others perform the sexual act. Such a situation is also homosexual because the boys become sexually stimulated from watching the sexual excitement of their peers. It is also quite common for male spectators of pornographic films to become sexually excited by watching and identifying with the man on the screen.

In Western culture, many men gain gratification from being able to see a girl's genitals or her pants, and this can be a part of natural sexuality. This titillation of men's sexual appetites was routine in the can-can. All these types of voyeurism can be present in boys, but true voyeurs are always severely disturbed. Men and boys who engage regularly in Peeping-Tom activities, lurking around houses to try to see women and girls undressed are as disturbed as the girls and women who haunt parks and lovers' lanes to see couples have intercourse. Many adolescents who accidentally see others having intercourse will be sexually gratified from the experience and will often stay to watch, but this stimulation of voyeurism is not the same as a natural sexual relationship.

TRANSVESTISM

Unrelated to environmental pressures, transvestism is associated with intra-familial conflict. A boy who wears women's clothes, whether or not he masturbates while doing so, is convincing himself that he needs no one. When the clothes are those of his mother, the apparent masturbatory activity is highly pregenital: the boy is doing the equivalent of sucking his thumb while being held in his mother's arms. Such a boy, in fantasy, is being both a man and a woman; he is, at the same time, seeking to return to an omnipotent oneness with his mother. Those who steal the clothes of strange women are actually not as regressed, but no transvestite ever grows out of this conflict situation or reaches adult sexuality without treatment. Transvestites are commonly found out because they are caught stealing women's clothing. The type of theft demonstrates their general emotional immaturity; they do not basically *feel* that such thefts are wrong, even though they may know that they are. They are aware of the penalties society will extract, but they always feel they will not be caught.

Some aggressively and sexually disturbed boys wish they were girls and become transvestites. They enviously feel that girls have every advantage in life because they do not have a penis. A small percentage of transvestites become homicidal during sexual intercourse. In the act of sex, it is brought home to the man that the woman has a vagina and he does not. An envious rage of women then overwhelms him, and he will then kill the woman and mutilate her sexual organs. The diagnostic issue in transvestism is to establish whether or not the individual is murderous. In a skilled interview, murderous transvestites will become lost in their erotic and aggressive fantasies and talk freely of their murderous intentions (Miller and Looney, 1973).

TRANSSEXUALITY

Some individuals are brought up as infants in such a way that they really feel themselves to be members of the opposite sex. It may well be that because of circulatory hormonal stimulation prenatally, a girl is born with a boy's body or vice versa (Yalom et al., 1973). Distorted upbringing around the issue of sexuality may then be a result of the child's response to the parents, not parental psychopathology in itself. True transsexual boys are very rare, and there is no known psychological treatment for them; they are transvestites because they do not see themselves as men. They continue to demand mutilating operations, often until they find a surgeon prepared to do these. Transsexual girls cannot obtain an artificial penis that will become erect and often they appear indistinguishable from lesbians. A typical lesbian despises men and does not wish to have a penis; a transsexual girl uses lesbian behavior to fantasize herself in a male role with a penis.

In summary, in the psychological and social turmoil of puberty and adolescence, the plasticity of the human personality makes new perceptions of the world possible. The incorporation of these into the personality helps modify conflict, and the increasing freedom from childish emotional ties makes the adolescent less vulnerable.

All too often, however, conflicts about sexual identity and an incapacity to be a loving person or a doubt that one can ever be an object of affection lie behind problems of drug abuse and antisocial behavior.

Sexual maladjustment is a symptom of personality disturbance. Some individuals in need of help respond to brief, conflict-focused psychotherapy; others are immensely difficult to treat. Certain sexual behavior, although aberrant, is a source of instinctual gratification. It becomes difficult to give up a known satisfaction, even if that causes turmoil, for an unknown fantasy of a more satisfactory relationship.

REFERENCES

Altschuler, M. (1971), Cayapa personality and sexual motivation. In *Human Sexual Behavior,* ed. D. S. Marshall and R. C. Suggs, 38–50. New York: Basic Books.
Christoffel, H. (1956), Male genital exhibitionism. In *Perversions, Psychodynamics and Therapy,* ed. S. Lorand and M. Boliut. New York: Random House.

Coons, F. W. (1971), The development task of the college student. *Adolesc. Psychiatr.*, 1: 261, New York.

David, H. P. (1972), Abortion in psychological perspective. *Am. J. Orthopsychiatr.*, 42: 61-68.

Deutsch, H. (1944), *The Psychology of Women.* New York: Grune & Stratton.

Elliott, D. (ed.) (1970), *The Family and Its Future.* London: J. and A. Churchill.

Ferenczi, S. (1950), *Sex in Psychoanalysis.* 29. New York: Basic Books.

Fraiberg, S. H. (1961), Homosexual conflicts. In *Adolescents, Psychoanalytic Approach to Problems and Therapy*, eds. S. Lorand and H. I. Schneer, 84-85. New York: Paul Hoeber.

Gebhard, P. H. (1971), Human sexual behavior: A summary statement. In *Human Sexual Behavior*, eds. D. S. Marshall and R. C. Suggs, 209. New York: Basic Books.

Giver, G. (1955), *Exploring the English Character.* New York: Parthenon.

Harley, M. (1961), Masturbation conflicts. In *Adolescents, Psychoanalytic Approach to Problems and Therapy*, eds. S. Lorand and H. I. Schneer. New York: Paul Hoeber.

Kaiser, S. (1961), The adolescent exhibitionist. In *Adolescents, Psychoanalytic Approach to Problems and Therapy*, eds. S. Lorand and H. I. Schneer, 113-132, New York: Paul Hoeber.

Kinsey, A. C. et al. (1948), *Sexual Behavior in the Human Male.* Philadelphia: W. B. Saunders.

Lefkowitz, M. et al. (1971), Television violence and child aggression: A follow-up study. In *Television and Social Behavior.* Vol. 3, eds. G. Comstock and E. A. Rubinstein. Washington, D.C.: U.S. Government Printing Office.

Lorand, R. L. (1961), Therapy of learning problems. In *Adolescents, Psychoanalytic Approach to Problems and Therapy*, eds. S. Lorand and H. I. Schneer, 256-258. New York: Paul Hoeber.

Mead, M. (1939), *From the South Seas: Studies of Adolescence and Sex in Primitive Societies.* New York: William Morris.

Messanger, J. C. (1971), Sex and repression in an Irish folk community. In *Human Sexual Behavior*, eds. D. S. Marshall and R. C. Suggs, 15. New York: Basic Books.

Miller, D. (1969), *The Age Between.* London: Hutchinson.

———, and Looney, J. (1976), Determinants of Homicide in Adolescents. *Adolescent Psychiatr.* IV. 231-254. New York.

——— (1980), Family maladaptation reflected in drug abuse and delinquency. In *Responding To Adolescent Needs*, ed. M. Sugar, 1-17. New York: Spectrum.

Rainwater, L. (1960), *And the Poor Get Children.* Chicago: Quadrangle.

Woods, S. M., and Natterson, J. (1967), Sexual attitudes of medical students. *Am. J. Psychiatr.*, 124: 323.

Yalom, I. D., Green, R., and Fisk, N. (1973), Prenatal exposure to female hormones, effect on psychosexual development in boys. *Arch. Gen. Psychiatr.*, 28: 554-561.

Chapter 18

Drug and Alcohol Abuse in Adolescence

INCIDENCE OF DRUG ABUSE

Although it is extremely difficult to assess the extent of drug abuse in adolescence, particularly because young people themselves are not reliable witnesses, it can be done. In school, pupils may exaggerate the incidence of drug-taking, and those who take drugs must stick together and do not tell tales. Studies of incidence are, however, possible, with reliable cross-checking as to validity (Robins and Murphy, 1967). The conviction figures for drug offenses and clinical evidence still suggest that drug-taking among adolescents of all ages is high; at least 70 percent of high school students have used drugs or alcohol, and 40 percent are regular users. From time to time, in the last decade, there have been repeated dips in the incidence of abuse, but this continues to be a major public health problem in the United States.

The frequency of drug-taking in adolescence varies from experimentation to regular and progressive drug abuse that becomes dependence and, in some cases, physical addiction. Figure 1 illustrates drug-taking behavior and its variations (J. E. Villareal, personal communication).

Drug experimentation need not be considered evidence of psychopathology, although given the widespread preadolescent education in the problems associated with drug use, this could be taken to indicate a significant distrust of the motivation of adults. Experimentation can be defined as the self-administration of a drug (which may be taken to the point of intoxication) to discover its psychological, physical, and social effects. Even though the experience may be perceived as gratifying, intoxication, with its consequent conscious awareness of lack of control, is felt by many adolescents as psychologically threatening. In order to restore a feeling of self-mastery and a sense of control, drug experimentation is likely to be repeated four or five times after an actual intoxication experience.

Although drug experimentation in itself may not be pathological, drug responses are likely to be unpredictable and idiosyncratic. In general, experimentation with reinforcing drugs, which are addictive in that they specifically influence hypothalamic centers, is indicative of personal or social pathology. In addition, intoxicant effects related to the use of hallucinogens may be felt as intensely psychologically threatening and ego disintegrating.

Both early- and mid-adolescent drug experimentation are vulnerable to a halo effect; the more drugs are talked and taught about, the more likely adolescents are to abuse them. Identification with a valued, none-drug-using adult is more likely to lead to abstinence than the content of antidrug propaganda or classroom teaching about the subject. Good drug education implicitly and explicitly creates relationships between the teacher and the taught.

Regular drug usage is the occasional, more or less regular use of drugs because of their sedative and/or intoxicant effect. This category includes the regular use of tobacco, alcohol, barbiturates, marijuana, or any hallucinogenic or mood-changing drug, whatever its frequency. The regular user may be psychologically dependent on a drug or on the psychological "high." Intermittently, if unconsciously, the drug may be craved to relieve tension. Ease of withdrawal does not indicate absence of pathology.

Progressive drug usage with its equivalent—the habitual use of one drug—implies a variation of drug use from "softer" to "harder" drugs: for example, cigarettes to alcohol and marijuana, or in some social groups, to glue sniffing. A variety of synthetic or natural hallucinogens, stimulants, and sedatives and, ultimately, heroin, other opium derivatives, or cocaine, may be taken. Adolescents who take cocktail mixtures of drugs are progressive drug users. Commonly, but not necessarily, such individuals ultimately change from taking drugs by mouth or sniffing them, to their injection, either intravenously ("mainlining") or subcutaneously (popping).

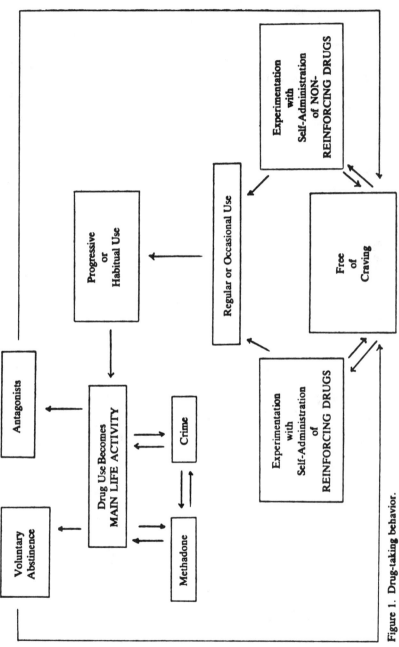

Figure 1. Drug-taking behavior.

The terminology of drug abuse is confusing. The term "addiction" has been defined as a "chronic intoxication produced by the repeated consumption of a drug." Its characteristics are said to include a compulsion to continue taking a drug, a tendency to increase the dose, and psychological and sometimes physical dependency on its effects. "Habituation" is said to differ from addiction in that it creates a desire, but not a compulsion, to continue taking a drug because of the increased sense of well-being it may produce.

Obviously, there is no clear distinction between the meaning of habituation and addiction, and in 1965, the World Health Organization recommended that the term "drug dependence" be substituted for both. Nevertheless, in 1966, the United Nations Commission on Narcotic Drugs decided to keep the old definitions.

Dependence may be on the high produced by the drug. This is particularly obvious with marijuana, and, in early adolescents, with their greed for new experiences and urgent wish to escape in a pleasurable masturbatory way from the frustrations of the age period, it may occur very rapidly:

> John was the tall, fourteen-year-old son of divorced parents. He had been an early developer and had had sexual experiences (intercourse four times), and had also used marijuana since the age of twelve. After he was caught stealing to get money to buy more, his father and stepmother moved to the country, taking him with them, where he was kept under more control than he had been when he lived with his mother. He said, "As soon as I can get back to marijuana I will. I like its effect and would use it daily. It's not dangerous, so why not? It's better than sex, since you don't have to hassle with someone else to get it. Besides sex is not as good as everyone said it would be, grass is better."

The dependence may also be on the regressive experience (Weider and Kaplan, 1969). One girl talked of how "warm and cosy" downers made her feel. Alternately, the ability of some drugs to loosen inhibitions and increase impulsive behavior may be sought. This loss of control may be psychophysiological, as with such hallucinogens as LSD which, from time to time is particularly appealing in a society that separates emotional from other experiences. It may also be an outlet for physical aggression, not uncommon in highly controlled individuals who intermittently abuse alcohol.

The liability of drugs to generate compulsive self-administrative behavior obviously varies. Precise information is lacking, although age seems to be significant. Adolescents for example, probably are less likely to be involved in this way with opiates and more likely with cannabis than adults. The commonly available reinforcing drugs that specifically influence the hypothalamus for adults rank in the following order (after J. E. Villarreal):

1. *Cocaine*

2. *Parenteral heroin, Dilaudid, morphine, methadone—"snorting" the above*

3. *Intravenous amphetamines*

4. *Intravenous barbiturates*

5. *Oral narcotics*

6. *Oral barbiturate-like sedatives with quick onset of action, nicotine (inhalation)*

7. *Oral alcohol*

8. *Oral amphetamines, solvent sniffing in some adolescent social groups*

9. *Cannabis (high doses)*

10. *Oral, barbiturate-like sedatives with slow onset of action*

Nonreinforcing drugs are not necessarily less dangerous. Hallucinogens such as LSD do not affect the hypothalamus; nevertheless, any motivation not to use them is dissipated after a variable intake in different adolescents, and their long-term effects can be devastating.

PSYCHOLOGICAL EFFECTS OF DIFFERENT DRUGS

Unsuccessful attempts have been made to equate various types of pharmacological effects of drugs with different levels of ego regression, for example, the results of taking opium (Mahler, 1968) with the psychological state in the characteristic behavior pattern of the second half of the first year of life. It is impossible, however, to draw hard and fast lines as to what the psychic effect of any one drug might be, particularly as their psychological and toxicological effects are often idiosyncratic.

Adolescents are particularly likely to become dependent on the psychological effect of drugs, and this dependence may occur with or without physical reinforcement and, hence, addiction. Those who are dependent on the drug experience show a significant degree of total personality involvement with drugs and the people who use them. They may crave either the relief of psychic tension that the drug gives them or they may seek a specific psychological sensation (Chein et al., 1964). When they take drugs, adolescents seem to be seeking satiation and contentment in the same way a baby clings to its bottle. The concept of the drug-dependent adolescent who is intolerant of frustration and is unable to make affectionate and meaningful object relationships would appear to be valid (Hartman, 1969).

ETIOLOGY OF DRUG AND ALCOHOL ABUSE

Drug and alcohol abuse can be understood, as can all other adolescent behavior, by looking at the interplay of biological, psychological, and social factors. Like sexuality, drug abuse in early adolescence is covert and known only to peers; by the middle stage of adolescence, use is more covert and defiant.

Early adolescents in Western culture first experiment with alcohol and tobacco, and it is ironic that as an attempted step to adult behavior, they identify with the infantile and sometimes dangerous habits of their parents, with drugs about which the adult world has mixed feelings. In the early 1960s, sedatives, stimulants, and hallucinogens were added, although tobacco and alcohol remain the most usual dyad.

Smoking and drinking are both related to peer-group expectations as well as adult behavior, but alcohol, other than wine, is usually rejected because the early adolescent does not like the taste of beer or spirits. Wines, particularly those with a sweet, fruity flavor, are often enjoyed, but are rarely abused by adolescents for many reasons. Wine drinking is surrounded by many cultural controls, especially because wine may be taken as part of a family, religious, or mealtime ritual. Although its use is increasingly common in midadolescence, wine is rarely used by early adolescents as part of a rebellious acting out of angry feelings directed at parents. Furthermore, the unpleasant hangover associated with excessive wine drinking spoils it as a way of reaching a state of psychic infantile bliss.

Although its taste may not be initially enjoyed, tobacco may be abused more or less regularly from early adolescence onward. Like drug taking, cigarette smoking is related to parental behavior (Emery et al., 1967). Parental attitudes about their own cigarette use are often highly mixed: "I know it is dangerous, I wish I did not do it, you must not." However, its equation with danger in the future allows adolescents to reinforce their own sense of immortality with what has come to be felt as death-defying behavior. Because to smoke is to seek an infantile experience, both early-adolescent boys and girls with mothers who smoke are more likely to become dependent on cigarettes than those who have nonsmoking parents. Because it also represents a step to adult status, early adolescents with older brothers or sisters who smoke are more likely to use cigarettes than those with nonsmoking siblings. Adults who smoke cigarettes up until the time their children are ten or eleven are likely to discover that their children's chance of dependence during adolescence is considerably increased. Because of pressure from children, parents may stop smoking when their children reach puberty. It is not unusual for twelve- and thirteen-year-olds who read newspapers and watch television to feel that their parents are being suicidal when they smoke. One boy wrote over all his parents' cigarette packets "nicotine kills." The paradox of the situation is that the very children who in early adolescence were pressuring their parents not to smoke may themselves smoke heavily later.

Early-adolescent drug experimentation is associated with early-adolescent experimentation with sex. Just as the pubertal child deals with the reawakening of sexual impulses by returning to the masturbatory activity of infancy and childhood (Miller, 1969), so drug-taking is associated with the revival of the omnipotent dependent wishes of infants.

PSYCHOLOGICAL SIGNIFICANCE OF INFANTILE BEHAVIOR

Early adolescents who do not experiment with tobacco, alcohol, or other drugs do not necessarily have particularly strong personality controls. On the contrary, failure to experiment with any drugs may be understood, particularly in boys, in the same way as failure to masturbate.

Before significance is ascribed to the fact that an adolescent cannot allow any self-experimentation that induces an infantile psychological state, environmental and intra-familial attitudes must be taken into account. A powerful parent who does not use drugs and thus gives children a consistent message may make early-adolescent drug experimentation impossible. Others may not experiment with drugs because they are very dependent on a peer-group that itself forbids the use of drugs. Some delinquent groups refuse to allow any drug-taking, and this habit is, of course, forbidden in older adolescents by many religious groups and most adults. Those religious groups that cannot allow infantile experiences—autoerotic sex or the use of drugs—may allow as substitute for these intense religious experience. Alternately, they may force individuals within their sect to attempt to resolve conflicts with various types of reaction formation, often including excessive puritanism.

DRUG EXPERIMENTATION IN MID-ADOLESCENCE

After the flurry of experimentation early in the pubertal period, there is a new episode of drug experimentation toward the end of the first year of midadolescence (Miller, 1969). Environmental pressures play a significant role in this. Early-adolescent drug experimentation that uses "parental" drugs can be an initiation rite to the adolescent group; the midadolescent who becomes a regular user of intoxicants, often those of which parents disapprove, may do this to reinforce a tenuous sense of personal identity by continuing pseudo-intense peer-group involvement.

> Douglas, a fifteen-year-old boy, was seen by a psychiatrist because of overdependence on marijuana. He smoked four or five joints daily, used the drug while in school, and began making D's and F's, having been an A student earlier. Suffering from a failure to develop a firm sense of identity, he was sent by his parents to a small boarding school with close relationships between staff and students. Of this setting he said, "The staff actually cares about you. It matters to them who and what you are and what you do. In high school, there were a few good teachers who might have cared, but they had no time."
>
> Douglas desperately wanted to belong to a new peer group. He said, "They put me in a room with a boy who got high all the time. I did not want to smoke, but some of the kids used alcohol so I started that. I get stoned on wine about twice a week. I get sick, but I need to belong."

This middle-stage adolescent felt impelled, largely because of social pressure, to seek out what was to him a new drug. Douglas's parents did not drink and, as is usual with drug use at his age, the drug chosen was less significantly related to parental behavior and attitudes than might have been the case in puberty. Adolescents are vulnerable to what the peer group-at-large perceives as fashionable: There is a feeling today that drug experimentation is the thing to do. In cultures where alcohol is the adolescent drug of choice, which is only recently true in the United States, middle-stage adolescent boys feel that they ought to get drunk. British lower-class groups take stimulant pills because they feel that they should get "blocked"; middle-class groups who use marijuana feel that they must get turned on. The first edition of this book predicted that in the United States, legislation allowing eighteen-year-olds to purchase alcohol would produce an increased incidence of alcoholism in fifteen- to sixteen-year-olds. This was optimistic; alcoholism dramatically increased in the twelve- to fourteen-year-old age group also.

At one time, a middle-class youth tried drugs and sex about two years later than his working-class counterpart, but this has changed greatly for drug abuse and has been considerably modified for sex. From clinical evidence, the end of the pubertal stage of development, about fifteen in boys, is becoming the peak age in all social classes for starting to experiment with drugs other than tobacco.

Early-adolescent drug-taking tends to imitate adult norms; midadolescents who abuse drugs act in defiance of them. Socioculturally, drugs may be used as part of a phony war against adults; adolescents who get together to use drugs have now abandoned the pseudo-philosophical justifications of the sixties and seventies and justify their behavior on the basis that they find the experience pleasurable. The adolescent who is least able to develop a genuine sense of an autonomous self is most likely to take drugs and to become dependent on them.

Mid-adolescents may still take alcohol, particularly beer, not to get drunk, but rather to participate in what they see as an acceptable adult ritual. They may also like the taste. Marijuana is rarely used in low dosage, when its intoxicant effect is mild, unless joints are handed around at pop concerts and the like. It is mostly used to get "high," although some adolescents attempt to titrate the degree of intoxication they may experience (Hollister, 1968). Those adolescents who try alcohol and cigarettes at the beginning of puberty and then stop, may become regular users of either or both during midadolescence. Those young people who are regular users of tobacco in early adolescence may become intensely dependent by midadolescence.

DRUGS USED BY ADOLESCENTS

The type of drugs used by adolescents depends on their personal history of drug-taking. Alcohol is used by many adolescents; some mix alcohol and marijuana. Early adolescents who become regular users of marijuana seem more likely in midadolescence, or sooner, to try other hallucinogens. Users of LSD seem to have a history of more than an experimental use of marijuana. The drug used also varies from one year to the next, from country to country, within institutions in any given society, and between different social groups. Drug abuse appears to vary with fashion; amphetamine derivatives may be preferred at one time and in one culture; other times, hallucinogens appear to be the drugs of choice. Lower-class black and white early adolescents may use glue and paint thinners for their intoxicant effect in parts of the United States and continental Europe. In Britain, their use is rare, except in penal institutions. Marijuana was used in Sweden for many years before it was used in neighboring Finland. Deprived and black adolescents in the ghettos of American cities, and the British working class, are likely to abuse amphetamines. Only more recently have these groups begun to use hashish, and LSD usage is rare compared to its middle-class incidence.

Stimulants and the Psychology of Abuse

Stimulant pills used by British youth have special names, such as "black bombers" (durophet) and "purple hearts" (dexamyl). In the United States, stimulant pills are "bennies," "dex," "crystals," "dominoes," "minstrels," and "purple hearts"; Dexamil pills are "Christmas Trees." In the United States, all stimulants carry the generic name of "speed." In Britain, this name is reserved for methedrine. In the United States, those young people who inject methedrine are usually known as "speed freaks." In Britain, speed is always injected. When methedrine ampoules were taken out of the pharmacopoeia in Britain, those individuals who used it injected the powdered tablets.

When the use of mood-changing and mind-bending drugs spread out of the black ghetto and the world of jazz music to the white population in the United States, the first drugs to be widely abused were stimulants, in particular, amphetamine derivatives. Prior to 1955, these drugs had something of a vogue among students who used them to cope, they felt, more adequately with examinations. In the United States, stimulants began to be pervasively used among middle-class white adolescents at about that time. About three years later, they began to be the drug of choice among working-class British youth. By 1960, the use of amphetamine/barbiturate mixtures was common in large cities and in new towns that had not been designed to meet emotional needs. Since the use of amphetamines is more culturally aberrant among middle-class youth, those who use them are more likely to be severely psychologically disturbed.

Initially, the amphetamine derivatives were prescribed by physicians mostly for middle-aged women as antidepressants and appetite suppressors. The women passed them on to their children; family practitioners did not apparently recognize that, particularly in the lower socioeconomic classes, a good drug given to mothers is implicitly prescribed for the whole family. Adolescents who felt unsure of themselves and complained of boredom, emptiness, and depression were often given their mother's pills. The underworld rapidly discovered that adolescents could take stimulants in excessive dosage and that there were enormous profits to be made. The profit in the illegal sale of amphetamine derivatives is up to 3000 percent.

Methedrine for injection (twenty-milligram ampoules) was legally used to facilitate psychiatric abreactions and in the treatment of the coma caused by alcoholism; the tablet (five milligrams) was also given as an appetite suppressor. Methedrine is abused specifically for its side effects, which include restlessness, euphoria, and extreme talkativeness. Up to eight injections a day are taken by addicts who go on runs lasting up to six days. Individual doses may be very large, and while on the run, the subject does not eat or sleep. Each injection sends an intense pleasurable orgasmic flush throughout the whole body, and the user becomes unduly fascinated with his own thoughts and feelings.

In the aggressive and sexual activity of disturbed adolescents, there is often a relationship between the implicit and explicit messages parents give their children and the latter's explicit behavior. The same is true for drug abuse. Parents say that they do not wish their children to take drugs, but act as if they do.

Larry, a fifteen-year-old schoolboy, was hospitalized because of his aggressive antisocial behavior; he began to abuse amphetamines at age thirteen. He was first given them by his doctor father because he slept excessively when having to study for an examination. The boy felt that his father was "always giving me pills," and he used this behavior to justify his own drug abuse. The father was told about this by the psychiatric social worker, and asked not to give the boy drugs. During a visit, the boy complained to his father of a headache. The latter immediately gave him some aspirin. The same day the boy absconded from the hospital and was picked up by the police one week later in a commune of boys, all of whom were regular drug users.

Amphetamines, in large doses, produce tachycardia and peripheral vasoconstriction with dryness of the mouth. Along with a transient euphoria, sleeplessness is quite common. If amphetamines are taken over several days, their psychic effect seems to be similar to that experienced when any individual stays awake past the usual barrier of fatigue. Both Preludin (phenmetrazine) and the amphetamines can cause psychosis. Cases of individuals who became psychotic after a single dose, as well as after several, have been reported (Connell, 1958). Amphetamines may also stimulate those parts of the brain that mediate violent behavior, and their use has precipitated homicidal violence in some. The capacity of an adolescent to tolerate the physical abuse of large toxic quantities of stimulants is remarkable. Some individuals die from methedrine overdosage, but most adolescents appear not to suffer permanent damage to their circulatory system. Nevertheless, abnormal electrocardiographs have been reported in adolescents on such stimulants, and endarteritis has been reported in adolescents who abuse amphetamines. After overdosage, stimulant users may be restless, overexcited, and difficult to control some twenty-four hours after the last dose has been taken.

In a toxic psychosis due to an overdose of amphetamines, the individual is typically paranoid:

A fifteen-year-old ran away from a school for delinquent boys and was later picked up by the police high on speed. The police called the principal of the school, who collected the boy in his car. As he was driving back, the boy suddenly tried to wrench the steering wheel from his hands, screaming, "We must get out. We are being attacked by a gang of murderers who are firing machine guns at us from the sidewalk."

One goal of drug use, to obtain a network of human relationships, is demonstrated by adolescents who become involved in pushing drugs. Drug users often develop a special relationship with an adult pusher and gain a feeling of security from this grown-up or older adolescent.

Rob, a seventeen-year-old boy, suddenly felt that he must have some amphetamine pills. Having no money, he went to a local cafe, notorious for its drug scene, where he knew he would find the man who could find him a supply. He found the adult pusher who offered him a drink, gave him a sandwich, and then went off to make a telephone call. He then drove Rob across town to a club, again gave him food and drink, and shortly appeared with the pills. Rob was told how much he should ask for the pills and how much he was to give the pusher.

Most adolescents who regularly use drugs discover that they are an easy escape from anxiety and frustration. They develop the notion that under no circumstances should they suffer psychological pain. The intermittent urge to use drugs as a medication to relieve psychic pain, a method similar to that implicit in the prescriptions of many family practitioners, can become total dependence:

Sixteen-year-old Michael was referred to a psychiatric clinic because he was dependent on marijuana. Two years earlier, when he was leaving school with his best friend, the latter dashed across the road ahead of him and was killed by a passing car. Michael was upset and unable to talk to anybody about the death. Two or three days later, he wandered to a section of town where drugs were readily available. In a coffee bar he was offered marijuana, which he smoked. This relieved his tension. He began to take the drug on weekends, then even more frequently. His school work steadily deteriorated and by the time he was seen by a psychiatrist, he was constantly toxic and high.

If Michael had not discovered that marijuana relieved his tension, life and the passage of time might have helped to solve his problem. Instead, he began to use the drug as self-medication.

The relationship between alcohol and sexual anxieties is fairly clear. Shakespeare wrote in Macbeth:

What three things does drink especially provoke? Marry sir, nose painting, sleep and urine. Lechery, sir, it provokes and unprovokes—it provokes the desire but it takes away the performance.

The same issue is present with amphetamines and sedatives. Quaaludes are supposed to stimulate erotic wishes and insofar as they have the same effect as alcohol, this is true. The same applies to small doses of barbiturates. Amphetamines, taken in high dosage, lead almost universally to a situation in which boys are impotent. For the boy who is unsure of his own potency anyway or who has problems of control, the ability to make oneself impotent and then potent is obviously important. One boy said, "I don't care about the chicks at all when I am blocked on Saturday, but it's wonderful to fuck on Monday." Another talked of how exciting it was to find that he could again get an erection. Some boys justify their inability to get a girl by quoting the fact that on pills intercourse is impossible.

The incidence of stimulant abuse, like delinquency, declines with the onset of chronological adulthood. Statistically (Gibbens, 1968), it has been shown that those adolescents who engage in delinquent acts for the first time at the end of puberty are likely to be conforming to the accepted social norms of society by the time they are twenty-one.

Alcohol and Sedatives

Alcohol abuse in adults was at one time thought of in two ways. There were "symptomatic" alcoholics who drank to avoid psychic pain and tension, and "essential" alcoholics, whose drinking appeared to become a part of their personality. These distinctions are no longer made, but there is a similar constellation in adolescent drinking.

Alcohol abuse in adolescence may appear as problem drinking. In this, young people use alcohol to relieve anxiety about their social and sexual acceptability; to obtain a sense of separation from their parents; to relieve anxiety, which may be provoked by reality; and to avoid the pain of depression. One or more of these may be present in the problem drinker who may use alcohol only at irregular intervals or who may use enough so that a tolerance develops. These young people may develop liver damage but chronic central nervous system damage has not been reported in adolescent age groups, although blackouts occur. Problem drinkers may be cured by a combination of abstention from alcohol and the relief of the underlying difficulty. They commonly have parents who abuse alcohol, but there is no evidence that when their internal conflicts are resolved that they cannot, as adults, use alcohol.

Alcoholics are those who are genetically vulnerable to the drug, and a family history of alcoholism is almost always present. There are two clinical types of alcoholics in adolescents. There are "binge drinkers," who, when exposed to any alcohol, given its availability, will drink to insensibility and become dangerously toxic. This syndrome has been seen in prepubertal children. And there are "drunks," who drink to the point where they feel drunk, but they do not continue to unconsciousness. They crave alcohol and go to great lengths to obtain it, unlike binge drinkers who often do not seem to seek alcohol out; the latter take it when it is available.

Sedatives and alcohol are both used by adolescents mostly after the middle stage of the age period. Tolerance to both these drugs develops apparently as rapidly with adolescents as adults, at any rate from clinical evidence. This differs from the hard drugs, in which it appears harder for adolescents to develop a tolerance, and it seems to require higher doses to become addicted. Short-acting barbiturates are typically used as downers along with such hypnotics as methaqualone (Quaaludes). Librium (chlordiazepoxide hydrochloride) is also used in this way. Adolescents, in taking sedatives, hypnotics, and alcohol do not seek sedation, but rather a high; most are not aware of their dangers. The young alcoholic behaves like his adult peer; he denies his dependence and is reluctant to seek help, but, unlike adults, adolescents feel it intolerably difficult to say "I am an alcoholic."

Hallucinogens—Marijuana

Marijuana, whose active principle is tetrahydrocannabinol (THC), is derived from the hemp plant *Cannabis sativa* and has been the subject of controversy since ancient times. It remained in the United States pharmacopoeia until 1937 and was used for a variety of psychosomatic complaints, in particular, asthma, dysmenorrhea, and migraine.

Drugs prepared from hemp vary in potency, depending on the climate, the soil, the type of cultivation, and the method of preparation. In Britain, where most marijuana comes from the Middle East and is of fairly similar potency, the terms "grass" and "hashish" were used fairly interchangeably for some time. In the United States, where much of the drug is obtained from the leaves of the uncultivated plants, marijuana tends to be called pot. The extract of the plant resin, hash, is usually more potent than grass; the best hashish is thought to come from Mexico (for example, Acapulo Gold).

Marijuana is historically a drug of protest. Its abuse to dependence is currently associated with an inability to accept the demands of reality and involve oneself in emotional interdependence with others. Among young people, marijuana has long been associated with withdrawal from the established norms of society. In the Middle East, in the eleventh century, the protest was violent. Hasan Sabah formed a secret society of Mohammedan Ismaelites to spread a new doctrine through an authoritarian, yet loosely integrated, environment. A compact force that could strike suddenly at the authority of the state would lead to its disintegration, and the new doctrine would take over. This group, with its grand master, terrorized Persia and Egypt for centuries by its sudden and effective assassinations; it became a state within a state. Hasan motivated the young members of the group by feeding them hashish after their murderous attacks. The intention was to give them a glimpse of the sensual joys that awaited them in heaven; ultimately they followed him with robot-like obedience.

The Crusaders came into contact with this group in the twelfth century and learned to know them as assassins (hashishim) from the part that hashish played in the life of the young novice. The analogy with the present century is more than apparent. Marijuana was the drug of the rebellious young in all Western societies in the sixties and seventies; in itself, it is not normally associated with violence, but it was commonly used after violent outbursts by those involved in radical protest. It is now associated with the pervasive abandonment by adult society of its role in caring for young people, with the disintegration of both the nuclear and extended family, and an inability on the part of adolescents to genuinely involve themselves with others. Marijuana proliferation is associated with the economic success of its purveyors, who market the drug to the young by word of mouth. It is sold by the young to the young, like some cosmetics are sold by housewives to each other.

When marijuana is eaten, its effects seem to last about twice as long as when it is smoked (five to twelve hours). The marijuana cigarette, or joint, usually gives an effect lasting about two to four hours. The amount smoked affects the degree of intoxication, but, unlike wine, it is rarely used only for its taste. The price of marijuana varies depending on the available supply. It may be given by adolescents to each other rather than sold, but regular users who insist they do not pay for the drug are not being honest. Young adults and late-adolescents may give marijuana to younger adolescents, but, if this is more than occasional, payment is expected.

The flushed face of the stoned early adolescent is easier to notice than with older individuals. There is a distinctly sweet smell to the drug that can be noticed on the breath and clothing of smokers, sometimes for a day after it has been smoked. If the drug is used by adolescents in school or in their parents' automobile it is reasonable to assume that they have an unconscious wish to be caught.

Marijuana intoxication, typically, is initiated by an anxious period that lasts for from ten to thirty minutes. Because of this, many individuals who suffer from nonspecific anxiety attacks use marijuana as a way of giving themselves a real reason for their anxiety. One boy experienced intense anxiety just before going to bed at night; he therefore began to smoke marijuana nightly: "It makes me even more anxious, and I get very paranoid and think the police are after me. But I know what it's about, and, strangely, I feel better." Another youth, with a childhood history of night terrors, was admitted to a hospital for his excessive marijuana use which he could not stop. When he was dried out, after some three tc four weeks, he was found to suffer from repetitious nocturnal anxiety attacks.

After initial anxiety, when marijuana is used, the individual may become calm and euphoric; the body may feel light, and visual and auditory perception is sometimes enhanced. Just as with alcohol, the individual may feel that his conversation is particularly brilliant. This is a type of chattering, and the individual who is high on marijuana is often not meaningfully communicating with others. Time sense is distorted, and depersonalization and splitting are common. Paranoid ideas are not unusual, yet the individual may appear quite unaffected by them. Under the influence of marijuana, adolescents often appear dreamy and uncaring, although they can also feel omnipotent.

Marijuana leads to a psychological withdrawal from involvement in the world outside the self, a withdrawal associated with a preoccupation with a fantasy world of daydreams.

Inso.ar as acute symptoms are concerned, the psychological effect of marijuana depends on whether or not it is taken as part of a group experience and also on the mood of the user. When adolescents feel depressed or anxious before taking the drug, marijuana is often said to make these feelings worse. Occasionally, adolescents report vivid, aggressive fantasies while under the influence of marijuana. One boy insisted that he had stabbed another to death, another that he had drowned a girl in the local river. In neither case was there any evidence that this had happened.

The effects of marijuana are highly variable and the results of studies of its effects contradictory (Grunspoon, 1969). The drug has less effect on driving skills than does alcohol; but clinical studies do not take note of a volitional disinclination to pay attention, an aspect of driving that is reported by many patients. When drug use is heavy, there are abnormalities in the sperm count. Some students, however, appear to do better in their school work when they are intoxicated; these are often very disturbed young people who use the drug as a tranquilizer.

Adolescents dependent on marijuana spend most of their days in a state of intoxication. It has been said that marijuana is less habit forming than tobacco, but the clinical evidence suggests that this is not true. The half-life of marijuana is approximately 17 hours, and its breakdown products remain in the brain for about five days after it is used. Adolescents who smoke more than once weekly are thus piling up toxic chemicals in their brain cells. The effect of this is insidious. On psychological testing, some show evidence of learning disability, evidence that disappears when the youngster has been "dry" for two to three months. A number of chronic marijuana users are thus misdiagnosed as learning disabled. Short-term memory is impaired, and an amotivational syndrome is common. Unaware of a chronic depression due to toxicity, these adolescents become passive and without initiative. Rarely, some become hyper-irritable. It takes about four weeks after the last marijuana has been taken before a change is noticed. At that time, young people will look more alert and say that they "feel better." It is just before the onset of this experience that relapse is most likely. The effect of withdrawal is variable; some report a craving for the high, others dream about smoking. Many say that if they were offered the drug, they would take it.

The long-term effects insofar as malignancy is concerned are not yet known; the smoke from a joint is at least as irritating to the mucous membranes and lung tissue as tobacco.

> Eighteen-year-old Robert smoked six joints daily, would eat inadequately, and dropped out of school. He was hospitalized because of his inability to care for himself, for a period of three weeks. He was not able

to smoke marijuana and his intense passive-dependent needs were automatically met by being in the hospital. Diagnostically, he was thought to be a borderline psychotic, and his EEG showed abnormalities typical of marijuana overdosage, with rapid beta waves. He had no obvious heterosexual wishes, but experienced an intermittent craving to "get blasted on hash." Three weeks after discharge from the hospital, while in twice-weekly psychotherapy, Robert began to smoke again. Within two more weeks, he was back on large doses, and he sought rehospitalization because he felt he could not stop taking marijuana without such support. This time he remained in the hospital six weeks.

Marijuana use may be symptomatic, as with alcohol, when emotionally vulnerable human beings use it to escape conflict. Alternatively, it may be "essential" when it fulfills a personality need.

Once marijuana is regularly smoked, dependence on it becomes more likely. It was used, for example, by a moderately depressed boy of eighteen for thirty-six hours each weekend because "I find the strain of life intolerable." Its use as a transitional object (Winnicott, 1953) to meet profound emotional needs is demonstrated by a fifteen-year-old boy who smoked grass once following an acute traumatic episode and then began to smoke five joints of hashish daily. His addiction was noticed because of a sudden decline in his school work.

The myth still continues that marijuana is a safe drug. Alternatively, and remarkably, adults still do not take its use seriously enough. Providing school work is not grossly impaired, middle-class families still take its use too casually. Their offspring usually lie about the amount they take. The attitude seems similar to those families who allow their sixteen- to eighteen-year-olds to have kegs of beer at parties. Adults do not take adolescent requests for help, implicit when they get themselves caught with drugs, sufficiently seriously. The following example illustrates this, as well as the tendency for girls who use promiscuous sex to try to solve their emotional difficulties to use marijuana also.

> Anne began to smoke marijuana when she was eleven; at that time a friend of hers was killed in a road accident, her parents had separated, and her mother was ill in the hospital. Anne liked the effect of the drug, and by the time she was twelve she was promiscuous and smoking three times weekly. She was either given joints by older boys or bought the drug from pushers. At thirteen, she tried some pills that she thought were heroin, but gave these up, and at fourteen she tried LSD once. Anne was frightened by the effect of this, although she was tripping with many other youngsters, and so she continued only on marijuana. She also took sleeping pills that had been prescribed for her mother.
>
> Anne asked for help in the following way: She was caught smoking cigarettes in the school toilet and as a punishment was told to write an essay on the evils of tobacco. She wrote one full of incomprehensible

jargon, and when seen by her teacher, she described her marijuana smoking. The teacher warned her of its harmful effects, but, apparently, thinking the drug was not very dangerous because it was nonaddictive, did nothing. Three weeks later, in a state of severe confusion Anne was seen by a psychiatrist. She revealed a whole network of fourteen- and fifteen-year-olds in a similar state to herself, and she was hospitalized. Diagnostically, Anne had never really reached the psychological state associated with adolescence for she was found to be suffering from a severe histrionic personality disorder.

Hallucinogens—Lysergic Acid Diethyl-amide, Phencyclidine (THC), Psilocybin, and Mescaline

The most commonly used synthetic hallucinogen carrying the generic name "acid" is LSD 25. It was synthesized in 1938, and discovered to be hallucinogenic in 1943; it is one of the most potent mind-affecting substances known. One to two hundred and fifty micrograms given by mouth causes symptoms in thirty to forty-five minutes; if it is given intramuscularly, symptoms appear in fifteen to twenty minutes. In small doses, LSD seems to act as a psychic stimulant; in larger doses it is a depressant. The experience associated with taking LSD, whether as a clear liquid, a tablet, or as an intravenous injection, lasts from one to six hours. Psychotic episodes lasting up to nine months, and then flashbacks may occur. Repeating the dose of LSD 25 while still on a trip does not enhance the hallucinating experience, although it may increase the duration of its effect. After a "trip," a mild fatigue is common (Hoffer and Osmond, 1967). Specifically, the effects of LSD 25 have been divided into six stages, but these overlap greatly. In general, the experience varies from a flight of ideas, with tension, irritability, and perceptual changes, to a state of preoccupation with somatic discomfort. This is often followed by confusion, perceptual distortion, and paranoia, all of which may elide into a stage of dual reality, in which the patient feels as if his inner world is being explored.

There is an apparent connection between the hallucinatory state induced by LSD and schizophrenia, and it was for this reason that it was used experimentally for a period of time on volunteer subjects to try to induce schizophrenia chemically. LSD had a vogue during the early 1960s in a type of abreactive therapy, but the results did not justify the initial enthusiasm. There is no indication for its clinical use and the drug is banned from legal production in both the United States and Britain. LSD was first used illicitly in the United States, followed by Britain and Europe. Sometimes a mixture of LSD and strychnine is taken; supposedly this gives especially vivid hallucinatory effects. Other hallucinogens reported in common use are psilocybin and mescaline. It is probable that street drugs sold as these contain neither.

Psilocybin, used originally by the Aztecs, is very similar to LSD and is the active psychotomimetic of a Mexican mushroom. It is likely to produce a chronic toxic psychosis, and the visions it generates are richly colored. Psilocybin is, however, notable in that there are never reports of erotic experiences. Its usual dose is 10 milligrams for 135 pounds of body weight. A cross-tolerance to psilocybin and LSD may develop.

Mescaline was isolated in 1896 from mescal buttons, which are used in South and Central America, and is also used as part of Indian religious rituals in the form of peyote, of which it is the active principle. Its typically toxic effect is that it allows the individual to feel removed from earthly cares. The hallucinations are concerned with perpetual changes, particularly in the areas of hearing, smell, and taste; quite often these are pleasant. The usual dose of mescaline is from 400 to 750 milligrams and very prolonged reactions are common. Phencyclidine, wrongly called THC, is used as an animal tranquilizer. It gives a peculiar warm, cozy physical effect, "like being cuddled." Steadily increasing doses are often taken, and the drug commonly produces long-standing personality disturbances. It is the most damaging of all the usually taken hallucinogens.

Response to Hallucinogens

The hallucinogenic drugs are dangerous and their effects idiosyncratic and unpredictable, apart from the fact that drugs purchased on the street are often mixes of strange chemicals.

The use of hallucinogenic drugs is most common among late adolescents, often university students and drop-outs, but it is not rare among thirteen- or fourteen-year-olds, and regular users, aged nine, have been seen. Often philosophical constructs are given to hallucinogenic usage. Many adolescents who take LSD and other hallucinogenic drugs begin to be intensely preoccupied with a type of pseudoexistentialist philosophy increasingly disinclined to do anything other than to take them. Often these adolescents appear to suffer from a borderline personality in that they show no evidence of emotional independence from their infantile involvements. It is difficult to know whether a chronic user of hallucinogens can deal with the complexities of society, in any case. Many hallucinogenic fantasies are highly unpleasant; pleasant fantasies, erotic and otherwise, are relatively rare, depending on the drug used. The latter may last for only a short period of time in any hallucinogenic experience, which in itself may last for hours or even longer.

On his seventh LSD trip, sixteen-year-old Kenneth was grossly psychotic for three days, showing every evidence of an acute toxic psychosis. He showed a classical schizophrenic picture. He heard the voices
of angels and the devil, believed everyone was about to kill him, and
became dangerously aggressive. On the fourth day, he had occasional
nightmares.

Psychological tests one week later showed no evidence of schizophrenia.

Some adolescents, perhaps as an idiosyncratic response, perhaps because
they are genetically vulnerable to becoming schizophrenic or suffering from
a disorder of affect, show one or another of these syndromes after taking
hallucinogens. One symptom commonly noticed in adolescents is that even
though they have not taken a hallucinogen recently, they cannot make
meaningful emotional contacts with others. One described this as an experience of feeling "like a tape recorder." Often they suffer from a subtle
confusional state, which the interviewer recognizes because the patient's
thoughts do not hang together. These responses are idiosyncratic in that
some get them after one trip, some after fifty; it is impossible in any one
individual to know when they will occur. Of all the drugs in which intense
psychological dependence is possible, the hallucinogens appear to be the
most apt to lead to dependency for two reasons: first, the users of hallucinogens, particularly LSD-takers, are one of the few groups of young people
who have no wish to stop when they do become drug dependent and are
aware of it; second, a marked after-effect that may last for years, a flashback,
is quite common. One doctor, for example, reported getting a flashback
for a year on hearing the same piece of music that had been playing on the
one occasion she had taken the drug.

Clinical evidence of organic brain damage after many trips may be seen.
One youth reported that he could no longer multiply six times six, but rather
had to add the sixes together. Highly concrete thinking becomes common.
On the other hand, adolescents who were dependent on LSD, may appear to
be making satisfactory life adjustments with no treatment some two to three
years after they have stopped taking the drug. Suicide on LSD trips is not
rare, and bursts of wild maniacal excitement have been observed:

A seventeen-year-old boy was having intercourse with his girlfriend
while under the influence of LSD. He suddenly became extremely
violent and attacked her and then completely destroyed the furniture in
the apartment (his father's) in which he was staying. The girl locked
herself in the bathroom for several hours, in terror; the boy was in a
catatonic-like stupor for two to three hours afterwards.

There seems to be a varying incidence of hallucinogenic use. In any one
high school or college, the hallucinogens will be commonly used over a two-

to three-year period. Then hardly any cases will be seen clinically for two to three years, and then a flurry will occur. It is as if the youth culture, from seeing the effects of the drugs on their peers, becomes aware of their danger and stops. This awareness does not remain, and then there is a resurgence of use.

Heroin and Cocaine

An unknown number of adolescents involved in progressive drug usage move from marijuana to the use of heroin and cocaine, more commonly the latter among affluent groups, gang members, and those involved in the lucrative occupation of drug dealing. There is no evidence that marijuana causes heroin addiction, although almost all heroin addicts have previously been regular, as distinct from experimental, users of marijuana. Since almost all adolescents experiment with cigarettes and alcohol, a previous experimental use of marijuana would not in itself be significant. Emotional dependence on marijuana may follow addiction to heroin after its withdrawal; many heroin users withdrawn with methadone substitute marijuana for heroin.

Heroin was isolated from opium in 1898, and since then there has been a steady increase in the incidence of its abuse. The cost of abuse is astronomical, apart from drug-related crime; treatment costs in 1977 were something over three hundred million dollars. Of young people admitted to treatment programs, some fifty percent began heroin abuse before the age of sixteen and the average age of those in drug-free programs in New York is just over seventeen (New York State Office of Drug Abuse Services, 1977). More and more addicts are white and middle class.

Heroin addiction may lead to physical deterioration and ultimately to death. Death from overdose is less common now than previously; the rate of physical deterioration is idiosyncratic—depending on the technique by which heroin is used, the degree of purity of the drug and the use of clean or dirty syringes.

> A twenty-year-old youth was offered and took heroin while under the influence of marijuana. He liked the effect and began to think he could safely use heroin. He was brought by a friend to a house full of people who were on the drug. He called a psychiatrist who had seen him previously and said, "I must have help. I cannot become like them."

It is not possible to predict the dosage of heroin that will lead to physical dependence. Some adolescents claim to have injected two or three grains of heroin daily for a period of weeks, either under their skin (popping) or into their veins (mainlining), without being dependent on the drug. On the other hand, addiction with one-sixth of a grain daily has been observed. In Britain, where heroin is pure, some disturbed adolescents will know of one person who has taken himself off the drug with no apparent ill-effect. They may then reject the risk of heroin addiction as a reason for avoiding the drug. In the United States, where the heroin is cut to varying degrees, when an adolescent comes off a dose of eight to ten caps a day, with no withdrawal symptoms, it may well be that the dosage of heroin was small. Addicts usually can tell the strength of their cap from the type of high they obtain when they inject the drug. It is usual, for example, for the popularity of any one dealer to decrease if his heroin cut becomes weaker.

Britain has a particular problem with hard drugs because it is possible to become a registered addict. Since there is no way of telling the exact amount any one addict may need, and since addicts are very often unable to mobilize themselves to earn a living, such addicts tend to live by selling the extra drug they obtain by claiming a dose greater than their need. Sometimes adolescents in Britain are introduced to drug-taking by registered addict friends who give them heroin.

> A fourteen-year-old boy who had taken heroin only once insisted that he managed to get himself registered as an addict. He said that he was given two grains of heroin and four ampoules of methedrine daily by a drug clinic.

Heroin addiction in Britain is not associated with widespread and pervasive crime to sustain the habit as is the case in America. As younger adolescents become involved in regular and then progressive drug use, the spread of addiction to teenagers becomes inevitable, although the preferred drugs would seem to be alcohol rather than cocaine and heroin.

Street cocaine is not pure and it is cut with an inert sugar, mannitol, and procaine and amphetamines. Typically, its "rush" lasts about an hour, and the myth is quite pervasive among its users that it is safe; it has replaced marijuana as the fantasized safe high. It is intensely psychologically addictive and most young users bewail the fact that they cannot afford it more frequently. At the parties given by middle- and late-adolescents in affluent suburbia, status is achieved by being able to offer cocaine.

Acute anxiety responses and paranoia are common after its use; irritability and fatigue subsequently occur. Since cocaine is "cut" with amphetamines, it is hard to know whether this is an aftereffect of cocaine or speed. The drug, in adolescence, is most frequently "snorted" through a straw or a rolled-up dollar bill, and the drug is laid out in "lines" usually on a glass-topped table or a mirror.

Chronic users of cocaine in adolescence are rare except among the affluent young who are drug dealers or members of street gangs, which are highly predatory. Runny noses are common and nasal sprays are used to contain this, just as "Visine" eyedrops are used to control the conjunctival injection that commonly occurs after marijuana use. Psychological dependence after use of two to three times weekly becomes intense and the individual becomes a slave to cocaine. Given the present abandonment of youth, if cocaine becomes less expensive, even temporarily, its use would become widespread and infinitely destructive to personality development.

THE SOCIAL AND INTRAFAMILIAL CAUSES OF DRUG ABUSE

The etiology of drug abuse can be understood if intrafamilial, social, and individual factors are considered. Only when these are taken into account can treatment plans be adequately formulated for the chronic, drug-dependent adolescent. Apart from the etiology of disturbed character formation, which finds its roots in the emotional deprivation of infancy (particularly multiple handling, parental inconsistency, and physical and emotional abuse), families can convey to their children either an attitude that all pain must be magically relieved or that some frustration can appropriately be borne. The drug scene, other than in severely deprived groups, was created in the relationship between family practitioners, their adult patients, and their children.

Many admired figures of the youth world boast of their drug-taking, particularly marijuana, and thus are adolescent role models. Jazz musicians and entertainers are often into drugs, and young teachers may make no bones of this type of drug use. Older adolescents give drugs to each other, and adolescents who deal in drugs to support their own habit have little hesitation in selling to a younger age group. In universities, it is not unusual for some staff to offer drugs to students as they might alcohol. One psychology professor regularly invited students to his house to smoke hash.

Many adults are quite unaware that obvious drug intoxication in younger adolescents is a request for help with more than intoxication. The fact that adolescents are high is ignored by others because they are unsure of what to do. Some parents choose not to see the toxicity of their children; one boy would regularly talk to his mother when he was tripping on LSD; she never noticed. Many drug-help organizations unconsciously collude with drug abuse; they look after adolescents while they are drug toxic, but make no effort to assist with the problems that led to the abuse. As the young helpers in these organizations usually do not deny their own drug use, and the organizations are adult supported, the message to adolescents who use the service is generally clear. Some parents may be obsessed with the fear that their children of sixteen or seventeen will use such drugs as marijuana, LSD, cocaine, or heroin. They seek constant reassurance from the adolescent boy or girl that they will not smoke, yet they may be aware of neighborhood houses in which marijuana is smoked, or where acid is pushed or they may know the local source of a drug, but do nothing. If parents behave in this way, their children then get the action message: drug usage is acceptable. The same attitude is reinforced if parents are themselves chronic drug users. These parents who rush to the aspirin bottle at the slightest throb of a tension headache or who take amphetamines to control their appetite, should not be surprised if their children medicate themselves as well.

Government intervention demonstrates how, in Britain and in the United States, society has not made up its mind on how to handle the problem of drug dependence among the young. The usual response is to be punitive or to concentrate on individual treatment. In Britain, where addictive drugs are legally provided when an addict is registered, a clinic set up to treat such adolescents becomes highly inconsistent. On the one hand, the explicit message to the youngster is that drug-taking is bad; on the other, society is saying in effect, "If you register yourself as an addict, we will give you drugs." Such contradictions make more disturbed behavior almost inevitable. Some drug addiction centers, moreover, appear prepared to register young addicts without telling their parents. This confidentiality encourages disturbance: the doctors are agreeing by their actions with the adolescent's idea that parents will not help. For early and mid-adolescents, this is poor treatment. It is never of use to young adolescents to agree, implicitly or explicitly, in actions or words, that their parents are bad.

In the United States, the same process goes on in methadone centers. In one state, in 1971, the National Institutes of Health authorized a physician who worked alone to give methadone; he then produced methadone addiction in those adolescents he was treating. At least one methadone treatment center offered methadone maintenance to adolescents, age sixteen to eighteen.

By accepting the concept that drug dependence is an entity in itself and by labeling young people "addicts" or chemically dependent, the youngster is given a false self by society. In those adolescents whose dependence is a by-product of intrafamilial and social factors, whose main psychological difficulty is uncertainty about a sense of self, if these clinics provide ongoing staff support after the abuse has ceased, results may be satisfactory. In those adolescents whose drug abuse etiology is biopsychosocial, clinics that do not adequately diagnose the etiology of their drug abuse, the results can be disastrous (Miller, 1983).

IDENTITY AND DRUG ABUSE

Drug abuse may be an attempt to facilitate maturation and to free the self from infantile dependence on parents or parent figures. Some adolescents, without drugs, may experience feelings of loss of individual autonomy in relation to authority figures. Such young people also tend, when off drugs, to complain of feelings of depression, anxiety, or emptiness. Before the present pandemic of drug abuse, those adolescents who suffered from identity diffusion (Erikson, 1968) behaved symptomatically in different ways: they were often delinquent, sexually promiscuous, or failing in school due to underachievement.

If the first steps to autonomy are taken in infancy and childhood, failure at adolescence may occur because of isolation from extra-parental adults. The most common reason for adolescent inability to form significant relationships outside the immediate family is not just the personal psychopathology of the individual. Social instability due to the vertical and horizontal mobility of society contributes to the increasing difficulty of forming stable, extra-parental adult relationships. When important human relationships are formed by early adolescents, especially with a teacher, school counselor, or social worker, the structural organization of the school system makes it highly likely that this adult will be lost. The pupil may, like a two-year-old who experiences parental separation (Bowlby, 1971), then forego his attempt to form other attachments.

Individual psychopathology can, of course, be significant in a failure to form extra-parental adult and peer-group relationships. Those children whose early attachments within the family were impaired are, as adolescents, likely to find it hard to establish a trusting relationship with anyone. A stable network of extra-parental relationships may protect adolescents from a disturbed parental relationship, but it is less likely to protect them from the effects of severely early deprivation.

Those adolescents who do not form significant emotional relationships with extra-parental adults whom they and society value, find it difficult to develop a sense of personal autonomy. Without attachments to such grown-ups, adolescents may fear overdependence on parents. Such young people may continue to be overdependent on peer relationships, in a manner that is more usual in early adolescence, into adulthood.

A typical group process of early adolescence is to seek awareness of commonly held feelings with peers. It is not unusual in some cultures for groups of early-adolescent males to masturbate together; they thus become aware that others can obtain the same feeling of sexual excitement as they themselves. This awareness may also be acquired through the intensive intimacy of early-adolescent friendships. In mid-adolescence, if psychological development is proceeding satisfactorily, a group of young people may use alcohol, not to get intoxicated, but rather to facilitate interpersonal relationships. Marijuana is often used with the same intent, but may instead produce an essentially masturbatory type of relationship. The adolescent on marijuana is more preoccupied with his own internal imagery and the feeling that others have a similar experience than with an emotionally meaningful interpersonal relationship. This behavior parallels the passivity of television watching. Adolescents who do not develop a satisfactory sense of self also continue, by the use of such drugs, the early-adolescent type of interpersonal group relationships. The combination of fragmented social networks and drug abuse appears to produce conformist adults who are easily vulnerable to depression, who are overdependent for self-esteem on their own pre-occupation with what others might think of them.

Within groups, some individuals who may have difficulty forming rela-tionships and establishing a sense of their own identity may not become involved with drugs, even if drugs are available. Some join street gangs, groups that see drug use as an anathema, or cults and radical religious groups; some become non-functional and are overwhelmed with tension and anxiety. Some, who are introduced to drugs in an acute identity crisis, may deteriorate because of the drug, rather than because of their funda-mental emotional instability.

Adolescents without adult relationships are extremely vulnerable to group contagion; a changing fashion of drug usage is likely to be as rapidly transmitted as is one in language, dress, or delinquent activity.

SEXUAL CONFLICT AND DRUG ABUSE

Drugs may be used in an attempt to resolve conflicts about sexuality. They may be used as a substitute for sexual intercourse, to allay anxiety about possible impotence, to potentiate masturbatory activity, or to resolve con-flicts about heterosexuality.

> Dan, age seventeen, was referred to a psychiatrist because he had run away from home three times. He described his parents as compulsively straight; they did not smoke or drink and rarely went out. The boy was academically motivated, denied any personal problems, and saw the difficulty only in that he had over-rigid parents who made him terribly angry. He said that he got "stoned on grass" every Friday and Saturday night with his buddies, and he saw no problem in this. He had no interest in girls, but was aware of feeling horny from time to time. The comment was made that surely Friday and Saturday were the nights when boys his age sought dates. He asked, "Do you suppose I use drugs to avoid girls?"

Marijuana appears to reduce the push toward resolving conflicts about sexual activity. Marijuana does not generally seem to affect sexual excite-ment, although boys say that girls who are turned on are less inhibited sexually. Some boys will talk of how pleasant it is to be satisfied with just necking with a girl and not to need to be more sexually aggressive: "Both of us are satisfied." On the other hand, some boys with homosexual conflicts report having been seduced by other males while they were turned on:

> Tom came to see a psychiatrist on his own because he was worried in case he was gay. He had been away camping with a friend of his who was two years older than he. They had both smoked marijuana, and after going to bed he had let the other boy sodomize him. "The terrible thing was that I think I enjoyed it, although I am not sure."

Some boys with sexual conflicts typically take large amounts of amphetamines on the weekend. In American and European culture, this is the typical time for dating, so boys with sexual anxieties can use the chemical impotence of amphetamines both to save face with their peers and to avoid the anxiety they might experience because of sexual incompetence or disinterest. Some adolescents who are consciously aware of sexual anxieties, which the processes of psychological maturation might have resolved without drugs, may deliberately use amphetamines and methedrine to inhibit potency. It therefore becomes possible for these young people to say that they use drugs and therefore do not need sex. In small amounts, amphetamines are said to enhance a boy's capacity to maintain an erection; in large amounts, no erection is possible. The association between the use of stimulants and sexual anxieties in girls is also evident.

> Jane, a seventeen-year-old, was suffering from a personality disorder with many histrionic features. Initially, she took many drugs and was also sexually promiscuous. When she caught syphilis, she took seriously the injunction that she should not have intercourse. Then she began to inject drugs, saying that the feeling she obtained from the injection was like the feeling of having intercourse. Jane was hospitalized for a short time and then absconded. She went to live with a boy who, when she angered him, would punish her by refusing to have intercourse. Whenever he did this, she would go and buy some speed and take it by mouth.

The price paid by the individual is almost certain inhibition of psychological maturation, but not necessarily permanent impairment. Without other treatment than intermittent supportive psychotherapy, Jane had given up drugs by the age of nineteen, finished her high school education, and established a semi-permanent relationship with a stable young man of twenty-five.

Heroin and cocaine are often associated with homosexual fantasies in both sexes. Heroin may produce prolonged erection during intercourse for the male with an inability to ejaculate. Women may behave with less inhibition on heroin. Although there is an apparent relationship between mainlining and sexual activity, to a girl with a histrionic or an infantile personality the "phallic" injection has the same meaning as the use of a penis; what is really being sought is the omnipotent oneness that is obtained with infantile sucking.

Among the hallucinogens, LSD is sometimes described as giving special erotic parameters to sexual intercourse; more often it appears to be associated with masturbatory activity. Psilocybin and phencyclidine obliterate erotic experiences and so psychologically have a similar effect to the chemical blocking of large doses of amphetamines.

RELIEF OF INTRAPSYCHIC PAIN WITH DRUGS

Drugs are commonly used by adolescents to avoid the experience of anxiety. With this type of behavior, young people are very directly imitating the behavior of the adult population. Drug-taking, in adolescence, may often occur following traumatic loss of parents by death or divorce, loved adults, or peer-group members. Since the awareness of death is a threat to an adolescent's necessary feeling of immortality, the effect of the drug defends against this by allowing a return to omipotent infantile feelings. Since excessive drug usage is dangerous to life, adolescents may also use drugs self-destructively, playing a game of Russian roulette with their bodily and psychic health. The injection of morphine derivatives was used in this way by one seventeen-year-old patient, both of whose parents died when he was ten. He said, "When I shoot up, I feel at first as if I am going to die. Then I feel sleepy and warm and comfortable." Thus drug-taking can be an attempt to work through a mourning process.

Those adolescents who suffer from a severe, chronic sense of personality disintegration or who suffer from a variety of borderline states may use drugs as tranquilizers. If they use hallucinogens or stimulants, their overt clinical condition worsens, although they are apparently less aware of psychic tension. Those adolescents who take large doses of marijuana, for example, three or four pipes of hashish daily, and who continue to function with a high degree of competence in academic or other work, clinically often appear to be suffering from either schizophrenia or borderline states. Although it can produce psychosis, the marijuana may also provide a defense against such disintegration.

Drugs can also be used as a defense against severe chronic feelings of deprivation. In adolescents suffering from an anaclitic type of depression, in which they cannot form relationships because of early trauma, drug toxicity may become a substitute for a loving mother or act as a transitional object. A patient's description of his LSD trip clearly symbolized his omnipotent wish to be mothered.

> I feel as if I am in a room manufactured by the government given to all its citizens, which will take care of all my survival functions: eating, breathing, living. It will prevent me from hurting myself, and it can even hold my hand. In the room I have nothing to worry about, everything is done for me. I have no fear of bodily harm; it is a great place to trip.

A seventeen-year-old boy who came into treatment because of heroin addiction was "cured" by the use of methadone. He then became highly dependent on hashish, which he smoked each evening. The following interchange occurred in his therapy, as he described having taken heroin:

> He said, "I feel when I take smack as though I am hugging a teddy bear." While making this statement, he was playing with his mouth and the therapist said, "I guess you really want to feel loved." The reply was, "I cannot bear to be pushed around." The therapist said, "No, I did not mean that, I meant loved as your mother might love you as a small child." The boy answered that he wanted nothing more than to be able to curl up into a small ball and be looked after.

COMPLICATION OF DRUG ABUSE TREATMENT

Treatment for drug abuse is complicated because adolescents find it so difficult to give up the easy solution to a feeling of frustration. The social and educational organizations to which young people belong can be very helpful. Youth centers that have managed to produce a setting in which there is no drug-taking provide a haven for the adolescent. This environment can be maintained if such organizations refuse to admit regular drug-users or pushers. Schools can create the same environment by sending away those young people they know take drugs. With schools, however, the situation is more complex. If schools expel adolescents who use drugs, they may not be further educated. The logic of the individual school's position is clear: If they do nothing when they discover adolescents are taking drugs, they will be seen by other boys and girls as colluding in such actions. It would be better to see that young people got adequate treatment, if this were available. The realistic thing would be to create a social environment in schools that enhanced, rather than impeded, environmental growth.

If adolescents trust adults with whom they have a relationship, it is worthwhile to try to show the unreality of generational conflict. Young people might then see that their use of drugs may make them victims of adult greed; they can also be helped to understand the addictive needs of mankind, in general. When a man cannot tolerate pain and frustration, he is likely to become addicted. The first addiction all humanity experiences is for the magical relief from pain that a loving mother gives an infant. Those people who retain an infantile need for relief may become addicted to food, drugs, or sex; these can all be used in an unthinking, impulsive way. The people who are vulnerable may be of any age.

In an editorial, the *British Medical Journal* (1967, p. 692) wrote that to "a large extent the solution to drug abuse lies in the hands of local health authorities and hospital general practitioners and voluntary bodies: Imagination, energy and good organization are needed in the many local communities where drug addiction is established or beginning to be seen." The clinical evidence is that the drug-taking problem among the young will not be solved while their other difficulties remain. It cannot be dealt with simply by the provision of treatment services. The answer must lie in more effective organization of society so that the needs of the young are met.

REFERENCES

Bowlby, J. (1969), *Attachment,* Vol. 1 of *Attachment and Loss.* London: Hogarth Press.

British Medical Journal (1967), Editorial. 3: 692.

Chein, I. et al. (1964), *Narcotics, Delinquency and Social Policy.* London: Tavistock.

Connell, P. H. (1958), *Amphetamine Psychosis.* London: Chapman and Hall.

Emery, F. E. et al. (1967), *Affect Control and the Use of Drugs.* London: Tavistock Institute of Human Relations.

Erikson, E. H. (1968), *Identity, Youth and Crisis.* New York: Norton.

Gibbens, T. (1968), *The Psychiatric Offender.* London: Routledge, Kegan and Paul.

Grunspoon, A. (1969), Marijuana. *Sci. Am.,* 221: 17–25.

Hartmann, D. (1969), A study of drug taking adolescents. In *Psychoanalytic Study of the Child,* 26: 348–399. New York: International Universities Press.

Hoffer, A., and Osmond, H. (1967), *The Hallucinogens.* New York: Academic Press.

Hollister, L. E. (1968), *Chemical Psychosis—LSD and Related Drugs.* Springfield, Ill.: Charles C Thomas.

Mahler, M. S. (1968), On human symbiosis and the vicissitudes of individuation. In *Infantile Psychosis.* New York: International Universities Press.

Miller, D. (1969), *The Age Between.* London: Hutchinson.

———, (1983), *Behavior Disorders: Etiology and Treatment.* In Press.

New York State (1977), Report from Office of Drug Abuse Services.

Robins, L. N., and Murphy, E. G. (1967), Drug use in a normal population in Negro men. *Am. J. Public Health,* 57: 9.

Weider, H., and Kaplan, E. H. (1969), Drug use in adolescents. In *Psychoanalytic Study of the Child,* 26: 399–432. New York: International Universities Press.

Winnicott, D. W. (1953), Transitional objects and transitional phenomena. *Int. J. Psycho-Anal.,* 31: 89–97.

Chapter 19

The Treatment of Drug Abuse

Adolescents need to assert themselves, to form judgments, to prove bodily competence, and to demonstrate adulthood. The adolescent must also find a place for himself or herself in relationship to the opposite sex and society-at-large (Zachary, 1945). Drug abuse has added a complex parameter to adolescent therapy; it has made many otherwise reachable needy adolescents apparently unreachable. Because of its danger to young people, society naturally seeks the simplest, least expensive, and most magical solutions to the problem. Drug education is the politician's dream of omnipotence: it allows people to think that something useful is being done, although there is no evidence that it is of value. Education about cigarette smoking has been pervasive since the 1950s, yet cigarette smoking among adolescents is still excessive. Education as a vehicle for continuous relationships with a valued adult may be useful; content alone is never enough.

PARENTAL AND SOCIETAL ROLE IN DRUG ABUSE

Chronic drug abuse, regular or progressive, is a symptom, not a disease in itself. This is often ignored by society, in general, and by many who wish to help youth. Legal intervention has made the treatment of drug-abusing adolescents who are not consciously motivated to seek assistance impossible, over a certain age, in many states. Parents may no longer have the right to insist that their children have treatment after the age of fourteen to sixteen, depending on the state. In Illinois, for example, nothing can be done to insist that a youth who surfaces at seventeen as a chronic drug-user obtain treatment, if there is no evidence that he will be physically assaultive to himself or others.

Parents may have to insist that their children leave home to face the real consequences of their abuse. This is dangerous to the youngster and, as a recent attack on the U.S. President demonstrated, may be of little value to society. The evidence is that the law, in an attempt to ensure the rights of children, has, as is so often the case, provoked multiple tragedies. Attacking parental rights does not ensure adequate psychiatric care (Burt and Miller, 1977).

Significant emotional or developmental disturbance is present in all drug-abusing adolescents, although familial and societal pathology may be highly significant. A particular problem is the collusion and unconscious provocation by parents and society in drug abuse by adolescents, which is very like that found in sexual perversions and in symptomatic aggression (Eissler, 1958).

Many parents do not understand that drug experimentation is an unnecessary way of defiantly and secretively attempting to prove autonomy. They destroy this attempt with permissiveness, producing either a swing to increasing drug use or, if all attempts at externalization of aggression are blocked, some degree of personality disintegration:

> Peter was the fourteen-year-old son of parents who highly valued understanding the norms of modern youth. When he experimented with marijuana at twelve, they gave him permission to do this, providing he did not smoke excessively. Peter became a regular user, becoming high two or three times weekly. He then externalized his aggression by seeing his role as making peace between the black and white factions in his local high school. He began to feel less and less able to relax and became increasingly tense with a press of ideas and some hallucinations. He called his parents from a friend's home one night and said he was insane. They immediately called a drug-help organization, thinking he was on a bad trip. He was acutely schizophrenic.

This is a dramatic example; more usually, parental and societal failure to offer control of abuse leads to increasing toxicity with all its complications.

PREVENTION OF DRUG ABUSE

The appropriate way to prevent drug abuse is to build social networks for adolescents, providing them with anchor points for development. This, however, implies making difficult social changes in schools and other settings that are of service to youth. Organizations by which parents of adolescents form social networks around their children's needs are enormously helpful. Inferentially, they rebuild a human network that is developmentally necessary, and they give young people a good sense of psychological place. The negativism of adolescence has led some to continue to believe that if the sale of marijuana were legalized, abuse would decrease. Inadequate controls perhaps provoke some adolescents to use pot, but the absence of controls because of inadequate law enforcement has produced a pandemic among adolescents, as has permission to use the drug by allowing parades and meetings which proselytize its use. Yearly there is a "hash bash" on the University 'Diag' in Ann Arbor, Michigan. In 1983, the City of New York issued a permit to allow a parade up Fifth Avenue to propose the legalization of marijuana.

Adolescence is an action-oriented age and significant communication is often nonverbal. Being caught smoking may be a request for control, help with emotional difficulties, or a test of whether the individual is cared for by the adult world. If neither help nor control is offered—and there is no response other than words or an automatic sense of responses which are more or less punitive—an increase in symptomatic disturbance is likely. Adolescents need to feel adults care about what they do; they may also need to produce in others the experience of helplessness that they themselves experience. The constant repetition of symptomatic behavior, when its causes are understood and an appropriate response given, means that drug abuse is masking a severe characterological difficulty.

Rarely do adolescents ask for help in words; this implies a loss of independence and is a threat to autonomy (Miller, 1968). Antisocial activity, from academic underachievement to theft, running away, promiscuous behavior, taking drugs, leaving joints of marijuana, pills, or letters describing drugs or sex left around for adults to see, and becoming intoxicated in front of authority adults are ways of asking for help. Similarly, smoking marijuana in school parking lots and returning to classes high is a desperate, if unconscious, request for assistance. Many such adolescents are not helped because the meaning of this behavior is not recognized, or it is ignored. A drug-toxic adolescent may be taken home and nothing else may be done. Alternatively, punitive control may be attempted. When adolescents misbehave as part of an unconscious request for help, the agency used often depends on both what the symptom of the disturbance happens to be and who catches them. Disturbed adolescents may thus see a member of a family service agency, a psychiatrist, or a juvenile court official. Pediatricians and family practitioners other than those who become known for their interest in adolescents are usually involved by parents not by the adolescents.

Some people misperceive adolescent drug abuse as symptomatic of the norms of a disturbed society and adopt the attitude of many adolescents that it is normal or part of growing up. Adolescents involved in drug experimentation or occasional or even regular use, as part of an identity crisis and an ensuing acute conflict with parents, may grow out of it. If they have never really reached psychosocial adolescence, either because of the drug abuse or other basic characterological defects, the situation is more serious. Parents, in particular, want to believe that their children are no different than others or that episodes of drug use are at worst part of a transient adolescent crisis. A pertinent issue in early and middle adolescence is whether the drug use is associated with the individual's being out of the parents' control. Young people may secretly misbehave, but when confronted with a parental demand or request, adhere to it; failure to do so means that an adolescent with few inner controls lacks the support of control from outside. There is then an escalation of disturbance:

> Patricia, age fifteen, defied her parents successfully on three separate occasions. She refused to stay home when told and ran away from home. On the first occasion, she stayed at a friend's house; on the second, she arrived at a local runaway center for youth who played the game of being on her side against her parents. After a third runaway, she was overheard talking to a friend on the telephone; she indicated that she had intercourse several times, might be pregnant, and had snorted cocaine.

This indirect request for help gives some indication of what might be done. If the adolescent is able to form relationships with extra-parental adults, outpatient therapy is possible. Some agencies can provide the adults to offer controls on the basis of a human contact. This will help contain self-destructive behavior; it is unlikely to resolve personality difficulties that have roots in childhood conflicts. If Patricia perceived the whole adult world as persecuting, evaluation of the difficulties in a setting that provided a controlling network of human relationships, often a hospital, would be necessary. She could not be contained in an outpatient situation. The success of these approaches depends on the quality of the services offered; poorly staffed adolescent units in inadequately equipped state hospitals may be as pathological as certain aspects of the correctional system.

If drug education is attempted, apart from the fact that it must provide continuity of relationships, it needs to be factual about drugs; in particular, about their here-and-now effects. Overstressing danger may lead to denial. It may be useful to tell adolescents how they are being used by certain segments of society when they take drugs. If drug education is offered by an individual who is boring, the information will not be heard. If offered by a young and "with it" speaker, the youngsters may be turned on to try drugs. Reported follow-ups show drug education in schools to be unsatisfactory: the information about alcohol abuse did not affect the accident rate of young alcoholic drivers, nor did it reduce the reported incidence of alcohol abuse. If a drug educator has a long-term relationship with students it is possible that a number will seek assistance earlier than they otherwise might.

The evidence about the effects of various drugs comes from clinical reports. Although a drug-dependent youth may appear superficially very sick, it is difficult to know whether he or she would have been less disturbed without it, although accessibility to therapy is certainly lessened. Moreover, only those who are disturbed are likely to be seen by a psychiatrist; we know less about those drug-takers who are not disturbed enough to be seen, although they are heard about in clinical practice.

The best prevention is in control of drug availability. Parents need to be educated both about drugs and their own role in perpetuating drug abuse. They need to be assisted not to be collusive in covering the drug abuse of their children's friends because it is "none of their business." They also need to ensure that they not collude in alcohol abuse. Liquor stores that provide alcohol to minors and those who deal alcohol and drugs to the young should face much stiffer penalties. The State of Singapore, with the accurate assumption that dealers are businessmen who assess the odds, has effectively dealt with its drug problem by having the death penalty as the maximum punishment for drug dealers!

Most drug dealers are never caught, and no significant effort seems to have been made to catch the student pushers in high schools who prey on their peers. Apart from pressuring local law enforcement and being prepared to campaign for stiffer penalties for using and dealing, parents who communicate with each other, and plan appropriate consequences for their children who abuse drugs and alcohol, also create a network of supportive adults. Inferentially, if law enforcement is to be used, affluent parents may cease to tolerate the disgrace of juvenile correctional institutions, which often are a blot on a society that claims to be civilized.

Society fails to protect its young and thus may be colluding in its own ultimate destruction. This has occurred before in history. If youth is to be the victim of societies' malaise, civilization in the West cannot survive; the nuclear threat and the provision of pathological escape mechanisms is a lethal combination.

PARAMEDICAL TREATMENT

Acute drug toxicity has always been a problem in emergency medicine. The age of individuals who are alcohol- and drug-toxic and who require treatment has dropped. A change in medical care delivery has led to the widespread use of paramedical treatment settings—alcohol and drug help services and chemically dependent treatment services for the young have been created because orthodox medicine has either failed to deliver or has become excessively expensive. Their very presence offers disturbed adolescents a refuge, although the quality of care is often not the best and sometimes they may be a provocation to behave self-destructively. These centers are often based on the belief that adolescents mean what they say; for example, wishes to be separate from adults are believed. Alienation from adults is partly a result of the latter's refusal to listen. A seventeen-year-old who denies a wish to communicate across the generations is much like the early adolescent who, in the middle of a family fight, rushes to his room and slams the door.

If ancillary treatment centers are to be used, such services commonly need to be upgraded to provide both diagnostic and therapeutic care. Paramedical solutions are often looked upon by society as the magical answer to the problem of drug abuse, and the acceptance of symptomatic behavior as a diagnostic entity is, nowadays, with our increasing knowledge of the biopsychological etiology of such problems, unsatisfactory. This also is true for most social–psychiatric endeavors.

Compliance in the establishment of a relatively low level of care merely perpetuates the rejection of adolescents. The centers sometimes make it possible, however, for runaway adolescents to get in touch with their families, and adolescents who are being exploited sexually or otherwise by their more aggressive peers may find a haven. They often provide food, shelter, and immediate care for toxic youth. The centers may also provide the only nontoxic human contact that can demonstrate caring for nonmotivated drug- and alcohol-abusing youth.

Many alcohol and drug abuse treatment centers commonly depend upon one charismatic individual for their success. Their provision does not prevent the appearance of more medico-psychological sophisticated services for which society is increasingly unwilling to support. One-half a loaf of bread is better than no bread at all, and when non-medical services are competent, they clearly help a significant number of self-destructive young individuals.

MEDICAL MANAGEMENT OF HEROIN OVERDOSAGE

The management of acute heroin overdose requires that the syndrome be recognized. The patient may be in severe shock, and death may occur due to respiratory failure. Typically, a continuation of needle track marks, coma, pinpoint pupils, and respiration depressed to two to four breaths a minute, with consequent cyanosis confirm the diagnosis. Treatment, apart from measures to support circulation and respiration, consists of 0.4 to 0.8 milligram of Naloxone (Narcan) given intravenously. This should immediately lighten the coma, but if repeated doses fail to yield a response, heroin is not responsible. The patient may recover from the acute respiratory and circulatory distress and develop the acute withdrawal symptoms of abdominal pain, lachrymation, yawning, and painful muscle spasms. Furthermore, if the heroin is impure and contains sedatives, respiratory failure is a possible side effect. Physicians should be particularly prepared to deal with this. Naloxone, (Waldren et al., 1973) is the drug of choice for both heroin and methadone overdosage. One hundred milligrams blocks twenty milligrams of heroin for up to ten hours. Since Naloxone is short-acting, the patient must be continuously observed in case coma returns.

The acute phase is ended with the withdrawal of the adolescent from heroin by methadone substitution. An initial dose of thirty to fifty milligrams of methadone is given by mouth and then one milligram of methadone is substituted for one of heroin. Since the exact dose of the latter is rarely known, the initial dose of methadone probably is slightly larger than is really necessary. It should, however, be withdrawn at a 20 percent dose reduction daily. There is no indication that adolescents should be on a maintenance dose of methadone—it is the underlying pathology that requires treatment. Similarly, there is no evidence that group homes for drug-dependent adolescents or programs, such as Synanon, Lexington, and Daytop Village, help this age group once these centers have been left. The treatment of the young heroin addict is the treatment of their basic character problems and the social pathology that helped create this. Realistically, society has neither the resources or the will to undertake such a task. Testing the urine of the young is not the equivalent of undertaking adequate treatment for disorders of character (Aichorn, 1923).

THERAPY FOR ADOLESCENT ADDICTS

Heroin addiction poses a psychotherapeutic problem apart from the issue of drug withdrawal. If the adolescent is genuinely addicted and highly motivated, both relatively unusual in this age period, outpatient withdrawal is possible. If, as is usual, motivation is in some doubt or if there is a question about underlying characterological or other difficulties or the reality of heroin addiction, hospitalization is necessary. Preliminary observation of the patient if physicians or nurses do not suggest symptoms of drug withdrawal may indicate that little need to be done to alleviate these. Sometimes librium (chlordiazepoxide hydrochloride), in doses of twenty-five to fifty milligram tablets three to four times daily, effectively makes withdrawal a smooth process. Unless liver function tests can be given, it is probably unwise to give chlorpromazine to abate the reactions of a cold turkey withdrawal. Only if physical addiction is certain is methadone withdrawal justified. Psychological and social habilitation of heroin-abusing young people usually requires long-term treatment. For most this is not available, and it is not unusual for heroin abuse to be replaced with marijuana and alcohol abuse.

Some adolescents have so damaged a capacity to relate to other human beings that, even with every conceivable effort, little can be done. There is little point in keeping such young people in traditional psychiatric hospitals; often the only way to stop them from absconding is by the ethically questionable use of chemical restraint. However, methadone maintenance, with the justification that adequate psychiatric treatment is not available or would be refused, is offered adolescents without any real effort at serious rehabilitation having been made—the sequence of foster home, juvenile detention center, intermittent social work, and youth prison is not an adequate trial of therapy. Very often, if such adolescents are well diagnosed as to their basic difficulties and treated in an environment with positive implicit mores and in which a network of human relationships is available, improvement does take place (Miller, 1966). Treatment may be stormy. Some boarding schools for maladjusted children in Britain both contain and help adolescents with very severe personality damage (Shields, 1962), and the same is true for a few treatment centers in the United States. Despite legal requirements, provisions of funding for these is quite inadequate.

PSYCHOTHERAPEUTIC PROBLEMS IN DRUG ABUSE: INPATIENT CARE

Many drug-dependent adolescents are consciously satisfied with their ways of handling reality and forming interpersonal relationships. Adolescents who have learned to medicate themselves with drugs thus appear to prefer ego regression to facing the frustrations of existence. An initial goal of therapy is to help such young people become consciously motivated to change. One aim of the opening stages of therapy is to show the patients, affectively as well as intellectually, that their style of personality functioning is not helping them. This requires of the patient a capacity to form a positive relationship with a therapist and a preparedness to suspend destructive acting out.

However, drugs of abuse change the adolescent's capacity for self-observation in a complex way. This also varies with the extent of personality maturation. A boy or girl who has made many LSD trips or is constantly strung out on any drug may be quite incapable of forming such relationships for a long time, unless offered other emotional support, usually hospitalization. Those who have used such hallucinogens may take weeks or months to be really approachable.

These are adolescents who are only potentially able to form relationships, and they are not consciously motivated to abandon drug dependence. They remain psychotherapeutically inaccessible unless authority figures other than the therapist, either parents or representatives of society-at-large, are primarily responsible for entry into treatment. The conscience of such drug-dependent adolescents tends to be harsh and weak. It is rarely powerful enough to control impulse discharge. Neither is the individual capable of handling regression without personality functions being overwhelmed. If, early in therapy, the therapist becomes identified with this harsh, weak conscience by being realistically responsible for the patient's entry into treatment, then the patient will attempt to escape from the therapist as he does from his own conscience. Therapy then becomes impossible.

When parents have made arrangements for the treatment of their adolescent child, such a step threatens the intra-familial libidinal equilibrium (Spiegal, 1951). After the immediate crisis is over, it is often very difficult for a parent to support the continued treatment of a drug-dependent adolescent (Miller, 1958). The therapist needs to keep the responsibility with the parents and refuse to accept the role of forcing the adolescent to stay in the hospital. In any case, a hospital psychiatrist is likely to represent the early omnipotent mother in the patient's mind, and psychotherapeutic movement may not take place. Like the person who is drug toxic, the hospitalized adolescent may have no motivation to move from a state of idealized dependence. Probably, successful psychotherapy in that situation is possible only with a therapist who first works interpretively with the patient in his life-space and is prepared to continue administrative psychotherapy. If the therapist also has been responsible for the hospitalization, this is impossible. The idea that the therapist is responsible for everything cannot be given up, and the therapist cannot move from direct involvement with the patient's life-style. The transitional point, which has the same hazards as the abandonment of an idealized relationship in outpatient therapy, when the patient must agree to exercise his own controls without the therapist acting as an external control, will not take place. The patient may appear to become integrated in the hospital setting, but this does not carry over into the world outside the hospital.

Because of the chemical and psychological insults to the personality involved in drug abuse, not all drug-toxic, drug-dependent adolescents are able to form affectionate and meaningful object ties (Rado, 1926) even when drugs are removed and they dry out.

BARBITURATE, METHAQUALONE (QUAALUDE), AND ALCOHOL INTOXICATION

Quaaludes (Mandrax) have become popular among adolescents because they are said to give a special erotic quality to the "high" experienced on this sedative. Along with alcohol and/or barbiturates, they can produce lethal toxicity, since these drugs have an addictive effect. Death occurs from a profound depression of breathing. All these drugs produce sleep disturbances, and in adolescents, treatment is generally instituted because of chronic dependence and its side effects, or acute intoxication.

Adolescents dependent on barbiturates need to be withdrawn, in a hospital, at the rate of one-tenth of a gram daily. A number of young people die each year in status epilepticus from the result of the acute withdrawal of "downers." Sometimes in injecting themselves or their friends with barbiturates, adolescents inadvertently pierce an artery and cause severe arteriospasm. This occurs relatively frequently because the high of "downers" is, of course, the exact equivalent of alcohol intoxication, when judgment is not likely to be at its best. Liver disease due to syringe hepatitis is a complication of barbiturate injection, as with all other injectable substances, and it may also occur as a result of chronic alcohol abuse. It is not uncommon in the latter for blackouts to occur with acute toxicity although chronic brain syndromes are not reported in the adolescent age group as they are with adults, nor have cases of DTs been seen. Acute toxicity with alcohol is common in adolescents who "binge drink," and since there is increasing abuse of alcohol among adolescents, this is being seen with increasing frequency. The treatment of acute alcoholism in adolescents is the same as in adults and includes correction of vitamin deficiencies, attention to fluid balance, antibiotics and use of such cross-dependent drugs as pentobarbital (0.6 to 1.2 grams daily), paraldehyde (60 to 80 cubic centimeters daily), or librium (300 to 500 milligrams daily). The latter is the drug of choice. Adolescents who are admitted to hospitals intoxicated, but not in coma, may be allowed to dry out with no particular pharmacologically supportive measures.

The treatment of those syndromes after withdrawal is the treatment of the underlying condition. Alcoholism is seen in a significant number of adolescents with mood disorders, and these must be treated if any success with drinking is to be obtained.

> John, a fifteen-year-old boy, was picked up drunk in an alley and brought to the hospital emergency room. He had a two-year history of binge drinking. Alcohol abuse occurred throughout his family as did depressive illness. Apart from his alcohol abuse, which was clearly genetic in origin, he had a sleep disturbance that had lasted as long as he could remember; he never had an appetite before lunch; and he was irritable in the morning. The biological marker for depression was positive and he was treated with imipramine (Tofranil). Four weeks after the treatment began, he continued to think about alcohol, particularly under stress, but his mood was quite different and he said that he knew he was an alcoholic and that he could not drink.

Like many alcoholics who start to drink liquor in early adolescence, he had eroticized the use of alcohol and thought of it at night when boys more usually fantasize about sex. Unlike those whose alcoholism occurs before they have any sense of self as a major psychological issue, he was able to say quite quickly "I am an alcoholic" (and mean it). The problem with most such adolescents is that early alcohol abuse becomes an integral part of their personality, and they are unable to separate themselves from drinking and thus develop the concept that drinking is a problem for them. Treatment by abstinence, which is an essential formula for success, thus becomes very difficult and requires a long period in a setting in which alcohol cannot be obtained.

ACUTE HALLUCINOSIS

It used to be that in hospitals the most common form of drug intoxication seen among adolescents was due to LSD; this is no longer true, and other hallucinogens are in common use. Alcoholism and gross marijuana abuse are now more commonly seen. The incidence of toxicity due to hallucinogens varies cyclically in incidence, as their use varies.

It is generally agreed that tranquilizers should not be used for the acute hallucinosis of a bad trip, for they may hide the effects of other drugs, such as strychnine, that are commonly mixed with street drugs. Similarly, barbiturates, which are potentiated by the phenothiazines, may be mixed with acid.

The optimum treatment of acute hallucinosis is to talk down an adolescent. If this is to be done satisfactorily, it requires adequate handling of the patient in a safe, comfortable, nonthreatening environment. The more womblike the surroundings the better. The average emergency room, with its bustle, surgically oriented rooms full of instruments, and so on, is a frightening place for drug-toxic adolescents. Nevertheless, because of the toxicity of many street drugs, numbers of adolescents on bad trips end up in these areas as part of an adequate overall treatment. The street scene has, therefore, implications for hospital design, particularly emergency and walk-in areas. Adolescents on a bad trip should be under the care of physicians or paramedical personnel who can spot effects of drugs other than hallucinogens and who can monitor vital signs within the context of the acutely diagnosed intoxication.

Talking down is done by two primary techniques: accepting the attitudes, words, and feelings of the patient and moving to a generally supportive stance. It is helpful to make clear to the individual that he exists apart from the effect of the drug. A patient's attempt to hurt himself needs to be prevented by gentle, firm, physical control by other people, not by physical restrains. Often body-image boundaries become highly fluid and physical contact such as holding and stroking is needed. This may sexually threaten the patient and produce anxiety. Boys who are anxious about homosexuality may become frightened of either sexuality or aggression. One boy who became wildly anxious when his best friend tried to be physically reassuring said:

> I felt he was putting my arms and legs through a meat grinder. Then I thought he was going to do that to my cock and balls—it's funny I felt all that because he is my best friend.

Talking down and holding the patient should thus be done by men and women working together. It is a technique that is also valuable in the acute disturbances of schizophrenia and mania, and in both these situations it works well in calming the individual.

The acute hallucinosis may be over in about six hours, but, particularly after a bad trip, episodes of acute intermittent flashbacks are common for weeks or months. It is not unusual for perceptual distortion ("the world looks flat") to be present for some weeks. The anxiety produced by this may induce the individual to perpetuate the state of being strung out by taking small doses of hallucinogens. The adolescent's attempt to control the helplessness of a painful experience by deliberately re-experiencing it is obvious.

The duration of a trip varies, but when patients are high on a hallucinogen, these are always finite states. Because of the time it takes to talk a patient down from a bad drug experience, some are tempted, once they are sure other drugs aside from LSD have not been taken, to arrange for chemical intervention. An assurance of adequate liver function is needed, particularly if the patient has a history of heroin usage with the possibility that previous syringe hepatitis has caused liver damage. Valium (diazepam) in small doses of five milligrams by mouth relieves the tension associated with a trip, but does not oversedate the patient. Many patients in a toxic confusional state may be hyperanxious, if not paranoid, about any pills that may be offered them. They may refuse all medication by mouth. Furthermore, a physician has to decide the implicit message given to a patient when the individual who has set himself up to be helpful becomes the dispenser of "downers."

A chronic toxic psychosis may be impossible to differentiate clinically from a schizophrenic process because some who are vulnerable to that illness stimulate its appearance by the use of street hallucinogens. If the diagnosis of such a toxic psychosis is incontravertible, the use of tranquilizers may facilitate the inhibition of stress-induced acute episodes within the chronic process; recovery, however, can be complete without the use of transquilizers, which may prolong the illness. Treatment also involves the therapy of the underlying disorder of personality development, which may have been produced by the drug abuse or may have existed before it. The current fashion for brief intervention in drug-related and other psychiatric illnesses of adolescents is thus disastrous.

MOTIVATION AND TREATMENT

In all the emotional problems of adolescence that require treatment, the motivation of the adolescent and his family is always a crucial issue. Before drug use spread pervasively through society, the most difficult adolescent treatment problems were those connected with sexual perversions and promiscuous behavior. (These activities seemed to offer a magic solution to difficulties and, by infantile behavior, helped in the flight from the experience of psychological tension.) Now drugs provide a regressive solution to conflict, and motivation for therapy is adversely influenced. Furthermore, adolescents who were initially motivated to seek assistance and are in ongoing psychotherapy for another problem may discover drugs and become relatively inaccessible.

Alcohol and mood-changing drugs may be used by adolescents as a resistance in treatment. Providing there is no idiosyncratic or continuous response to the drugs, and the abuse can be controlled, the situation needs to be dealt with by interpretation, like any other resistance. However, drug toxicity may be the downfall of otherwise successful psychotherapy. Accurate and well-timed interpretations do not necessarily control acting-out behavior in adolescence, and the use of drugs may block therapy that would otherwise have been successful.

Before the present pandemic of drug abuse, conscious motivation for therapy became more likely early in mid-adolescence and was very likely a little later. As the complexity of society has increased, in particular, as social networks have deteriorated, individual adolescents have tended to isolate themselves more and more from adults. Without adult support, middle- and late-stage adolescents who are psychologically disturbed find it increasingly difficult to separate themselves from the regressive dependency needs of childhood. They are likely to see psychiatrists as the hostile representatives of an alienating world. These adolescents also tend to involve themselves in the drug culture and, particularly, if they are dependent on alcohol or marijuana or are regular users of hallucinogens, often resist therapy even into young adulthood.

There is thus justification for hospitalizing adolescents who are severely drug dependent for a brief period of four to six weeks to see whether, when they are detoxified, they are able to form meaningful emotional relationships with others. Some may be found to be sufficiently intact as personalities so that they can work at their difficulties either in groups or individual psychotherapeutic relationships. Others, without being able to use formal psychotherapy, may be able to utilize human contacts:

> Cathy, age fourteen, was hospitalized in an adolescent unit because of severely disturbed promiscuous and drug-abusing behavior. Her parents rejected her and wanted her permanently institutionalized. After four months of intensive therapy with a psychiatric resident and a full milieu program including school in the hospital, she absconded and fled to Toronto. After six months she was picked up by the police there and returned to her home. The court social worker wanted to arrange for further hospitalization, since she was intermittently delusional.
>
> In Toronto she had lived in a commune in which she earned her keep by washing dishes and living with one of the male members in a pseudo-marital situation. Each morning she would go to one free clinic to rap with the staff, in the afternoon she would go to another. She was picked up by the police only because she asked her way and accidentally gave her correct name. When she returned she had gonorrhea, which was appropriately treated.
>
> Instead of hospitalizing her, she was allowed to live in a group home and each day went to a day hospital where she attended school for two to three hours daily. Occasionally, she would fail to turn up and then would go to the local free clinic to talk to the staff. She reduced her

> drug-taking and her promiscuity and had a flirtatious relationship with a
> psychiatrist who saw her for five to ten minutes daily.

With this type of regime other similar adolescents appear to be able over the years to slowly mature and gradually decrease drug intake.

As adolescents progress into maturity, they may be able to ask for help, depending on the way of life in their social environment, the availability of helping people, how they are perceived by others, and the quality of care available. If magical solutions are offered, adolescents are quick to perceive these as pretentious and no better than the solutions they themselves try. "All you want to do is get me strung out on your thing, rather than mine," said one angry late adolescent to a family practitioner who offered him tranquilizers for his drug dependence. The ability to ask for assistance in words also depends on an adolescent's perception of the value of helping adults as people. To assess this, adolescent drug-takers, like delinquents, attempt to corrupt helping adults. One technique is to manipulate them so that they appear to collude with drug-taking activities.

> A juvenile court probation officer was approached by a drug-taking, heroin-dealing boy of sixteen who requested admission to the juvenile detention home. The boy was on probation for being a previous runaway. He handed the worker four packets of heroin worth about $200 in order to be admitted on the basis of breach of probation. Apparently, he was seeking refuge from the vengeance of some larger dealers whom he had crossed. The court worker admitted him to the detention home. When the boy told a sad story of deprivation to the juvenile court judge, the latter was prepared to have him placed in a foster home, providing he agreed to come in for a daily urine test for heroin. The boy was reported to have had a $75-a-day habit.

The boy succeeded in his manipulative efforts. Nothing was done about his illegal possession of heroin, as the court worker "forgot" to turn it in to the police. The message to the youth, and his peers in the local drug scene, was that the juvenile court authorities did not take dealing in drugs very seriously.

The severity of the symptoms in drug dependence, however, generally does not necessarily indicate the degree of underlying personality disturbance. In particular, adolescents may become heavily involved with drugs as part of a developmental crisis or genuine painful experiences. Providing drug abstention is possible, those suffering from problems of identity may be significantly helped by a whole variety of community interventions: group homes, outpatient psychotherapy and psychiatric intervention, boarding schools, special education. Which is chosen depends on the severity of the youngster's personality difficulties, the presence of underlying brain pathology, especially neuroendocrine processes, and what is available.

OUTPATIENT CARE

Although outpatient pyschotherapy is particularly difficult for those individuals who find it hard to form object relationships, in any case, significant drug abuse may be suspended because of an initial idealization of a therapist. To make ongoing therapy possible, however, the adolescent must begin to understand that his projection of an idealized mother onto the therapist is unreal; it represents the patient's wish to retain his own omnipotence. The frustration involved in this recognition is the point at which efforts at outpatient psychotherapy break down and destructive acting out of the wish for omnipotence restarts. On the one hand, the therapist must use the omnipotence given him by the patient as part of this idealization; on the other, he must carefully titrate the ending of this phase of treatment. Otherwise, the patient is exposed to an intolerable level of psychic frustration, as the therapist becomes the representative of a frustrating world that denies him satisfaction. The patient needs to be able to abandon the use of drugs because of his infantile, loving feelings for the therapist; he needs to feel self-love, not just self-preoccupation, which is no bar to self-destruction.

In the initial stages of individual therapy, drug-dependent adolescents may have to be seen daily if they are able to give up drug abuse. At the same time, it is necessary to interpret both the patient's wish to have an omnipotent therapist and the patient's hostility to the therapist because he is not omnipotent. The goal is therapy valued at a more mature level, therapy that will be worth keeping and not lost in a fog of drug toxicity. The nonmotivated delinquent adolescent with a character disorder similarly has to abandon the gratification of his impulse-ridden behavior to avoid the risk of a jail sentence and so preserve therapy. Once the problem of idealization has been worked through, the frequency of psychotherapy can be reduced to more manageable proportions. Depending on the extent of the patient's characterological difficulties, this may vary from supportive therapy once a week either as an individual, in a group, or with the family, to three times a week intensive psychotherapy to psychoanalysis. The particular difficulty is interpreting the patient's feelings of rejection at the time he perceives a rejection. A therapist's vacation will almost certainly be catastrophic in these patients, since they are likely to return to drugs.

> John came to see a psychiatrist at the age of seventeen at the instigation of his parents. He had a long history of LSD use and was a heavy smoker of marijuana. He was confused, circumlocutory, and relatively affectless. In the first three weeks of therapy, when he was seen four times weekly, his drug use effectively ceased. He became more coherent, and his emotions were more appropriate. He then insisted on going on a

previously arranged visit with his girlfriend and during this reverted to his previous drug-taking habits. His opening words when he saw his psychiatrist after the return home were, "Why weren't you there when I needed you?"

ACTING OUT WITH DRUGS

Drug toxicity is a problem for those already in individual or group psychotherapy. An adolescent may appear for a session intoxicated on one of a variety of drugs. The therapist then must decide whether specific medical intervention is necessary. The type of drug taken may not be known, either to the therapist or to the adolescent. Young people may not know what drug they have taken because, just as many adolescents have an irrational distrust of adults, they may also have an equivalent irrational trust in their peers. Many seem as trusting toward the latter as infants with their mothers. Others have apparently such low self-esteem that they do not care what drug they buy; they tend to try anything they are offered. Honesty is not usual among drug dealers.

The mix of social and personal pathology means that when a patient appears toxic for a psychotherapy session, a therapist must have doubts about the safety of the patient. For nonmedical therapists, particularly, the possible complications produced in a transference neurosis do not justify a failure to take an individual to the nearest hospital emergency room, if there is any doubt as to what might have been taken or its possible effects. For the patient who has taken a large number of "downers," hospitalization is necessary because withdrawal in a nonmedical setting is dangerous.

Apart from complications associated with dangerous toxicity, since the capacity to feel involved with others, to observe oneself, and personal controls are interfered with by drugs, a therapist has to decide whether or not to continue such a session. The drug may have been used in an attempt to relieve anxiety, but appearing toxic also shows contempt for the therapy and the therapist. To continue the session may be to collude with an attack on a process designed to be helpful. This, in turn, may lead the patient to conclude that the therapist does not really value what he believes to be a worthwhile effort. Because an LSD trip requires someone to be with the patient and to be generally supportive until the episode is over, and since therapists are time-bound because of their commitment to other patients, the implications for manipulation of the therapist if patients have a bad trip in psychotherapy are obvious. If the therapist tries to talk the patient down himself, there may be an active change of role, with all its implications. The need, in drug intoxication, to have one's body touched and stroked is equivalent to cuddling a frightened child; patients who regress in psychotherapy may act out their infantile wishes in the therapeutic situation. A psychotherapist may become involved in a counteraction that may turn out to be unhelpful. He may also seem to be playing favorites; time spent talking down an adolescent on a bad trip may force mass cancellation of other patients' appointments. On the other hand, the therapist's finding someone else to talk the adolescent down may be felt as a rejection. In psychotherapy, a patient who becomes high on acid is acting out a regressive fantasy in which the therapist is cast in a maternal role that becomes either accepting or rejecting but is not interpretable at the time.

There are other specific complications of drug abuse that are particularly relevant. Drug withdrawal is necessary before the underlying psychopathology can be treated; paradoxically, the causes of drug dependence often cannot be treated until drug withdrawal has occurred. The symptom must be contained before its underlying cause can be treated.

PEER COUNSELING

A fashionable belief is that only people with similar problems can help each other. Thus, black people alone can assist black people; only youth can really understand youth. Adolescents, therefore, often use informal, so-called peer-group networks for assistance. These rarely are able to offer highly technical help; they are supportive and useful for some, but the helping peer often acts out his own internal conflicts with his "client." The desire to relate only to one's own age group is an aberration produced by social pathology, but it is easier and perhaps less expensive for adult authority figures to sponsor peer-group counseling than to arrange for well-trained workers to be available. A particular belief is that individuals who have had a bad drug experience will really understand this and thus be able to be helpful to others. The problem is that such an individual may constantly relive his own anxieties through the pain of others, and perhaps gain vicarious satisfaction. Furthermore, there is little evidence that an episode of acute toxic confusion necessarily leads to an attempt to stop drug use in those people who are regular or progressive drug-users. Many of those who are involved in drug help organizations are themselves still users. By apparently assisting others, some adolescents prove to themselves how invulnerable they are. Far from being a deterrent to further drug use, fear may actually precipitate it. Some adolescents may change the type of drug used; others do not even react this way. Particularly with hallucinogens, chronic use may lead to such an impairment of judgment that even repeated flashbacks do not lead to a cessation of the habit.

NETWORK THERAPY

Character disorder in adolescents, even if accessible to individual or group psychotherapy, needs many treatment parameters. Young people with such a disorder should be spending a large part of their day in a social system that provides a network of potentially caring adults and a stable, non-drug-taking peer group. For those who cannot use individual relationships because pre-existing personality damage is too great, a network of therapeutic relationships in a social system with a meaningful life-style is the treatment of choice. In modern society, this is inordinately difficult to find. Some good treatment centers, some small boarding schools, some small alternate schools within the larger public high school system are able to be helpful.

BRIEF THERAPY WITH DRUG-DEPENDENT YOUTH

Adolescents who become drug and alcohol dependent as a result of a psychic trauma late in childhood or early in adolescence may be significantly helped by brief focal intensive psychotherapy, once they are withdrawn from drugs.

> Sixteen-year-old John was referred for outpatient assistance from his local high school because of an acute falloff in his grades. He was a tall, gangly youth whose clothing had the typical sweet smell of grass. He, at first, denied drug-taking, and it was interpreted to him in the first session that maybe he wished it was that way, but, by the smell on his clothing, he was indicating otherwise. He then said he smoked seven joints daily, seven days a week. "You must deal, then," the therapist said. John then gave a two-year history of intense marijuana usage that followed a car crash in which his friend who was driving was killed. John had escaped with only minor injuries.

The therapist's ability to pick up the nonverbal communication of John's drug abuse and his "omnipotent" comment about drug dealing were both designed to have John perceive the therapist as a perceptive and valuable person. Arrangements were made to see John the next day, only on the condition that he himself wished to come. John was apparently sufficiently intrigued to do this; he arrived stoned. The therapist interpreted this as contempt and refused to spend time with John, offering him the chance to return the next day sober. "But I don't expect you can make it. You are, after all, a pothead." This made John furious, and he came back at 9:00 p.m. the next day, saying he had no dope since 11:00 a.m. The actions of the therapist were designed to show John that:

1. Like dope, the therapist required some effort to be used.

2. The therapist was sufficiently sure of his value to behave towards the patient like Tiffany's: He had valuable things to offer, but the patient had to wish to buy.

3. The therapist was as capable of the same arrogant omnipotence as the patient himself.

In subsequent sessions, the therapist focused on the death of John's friend and, in particular, John's use of marijuana to avoid getting involved with people. John's affective isolation, loveless sexuality, need to be criticized, and destruction of his own goals were all interpreted in relationship to John's guilt about the death. Fifteen sessions later, John was a very occasional dope smoker, had found himself a "straight" girlfriend, and the parting from the therapist was interpreted as yet another important separation. That John did not completely abandon marijuana use was, however, ominous and this "insurance policy" against further disaster should not have been accepted, even implicitly, by his therapist.

John represents the group of drug-taking adolescents who are the most treatable. Their drug-taking is a ticket of admission for help; their statement that they are "into dope" does not negate the fact that they are people. Initially, the therapist is used as a substitute for the drug. If there is an acute underlying conflict, particularly those associated with relatively recent loss, especially associated with death or divorce, the prognosis of such individuals is excellent. If the underlying pathology is a profound emotional deprivation, extra-hospital therapy is rarely useful. The psychotherapeutic relationship is insufficiently gratifying to prevent the patient from taking flight into the regressive solution of the world of drugs.

REFERENCES

Aichorn, A. (1923), Quoted by Eissler, R. S. (1955), Scapegoats of society. In *Searchlights on Delinquency,* ed. K. R. Eissler, 288–306. New York: International Universities Press.

Burt, R. A., and Miller, D. (1977), Children's rights on entering therapeutic institutions. *Am. Psychiatry,* 134(2): 153–156.

Eissler, K. R. (1958), Notes on the problems of techniques in the psychoanalytic treatment of adolescents, with some remarks on perversions. In *Psychoanalytic Study of the Child,* 13: 223–255. New York: International Universities Press.

Miller, D. (1958), Family interaction in the therapy of adolescent patients. *Psychiatry,* 31: 277–284.

————, (1966), A model of an institution for treating delinquent adolescent boys. In *Changing Concepts of Delinquency and Its Treatment,* ed. H. Klare, 97–117. Oxford: Pergamon.

————, (1968), Principles of psychotherapy in adolescence. *Wis. Leitschuft Univ. Rostock.*

Rado, S. (1926), The psychic effects of intoxicants. *Int. J. Psycho-Anal.,* 7: 396–413.

Shields, R. W. (1962), *A Cure of Delinquents.* London: Heinemann.

Spiegal, L. A. (1951), A review of contributions for a psychoanalytic theory of adolescence. In *Psychoanalytic Study of the Child,* 6: 375–395. New York: International Universities Press.

Waldren, V. D. et al. (1973), Methadone overdosage treated with Naloxone infusion. J.A.M.A. 255:53.

Zachary, C. B. (1945), A new tool in psychotherapy with adolescents. In *Modern Trends in Child Psychiatry,* ed. L. N. Pacella, 79–88. New York: International Universities Press.

Chapter 20

The Treatment of Delinquency

MEANING OF DELINQUENCY

Delinquent acts, in a socioeconomically underprivileged boy, are typically associated with the struggle for a secure masculine identity. On this basis, an experiment in model building showed that a penal setting with a social system designed to enhance a boy's feelings of masculine identity produced less recidivism after discharge than the usual more punitive setting (Miller, 1965). However, providing they are able to form meaningful emotional relationships with others, most disturbed adolescents with identity problems tend to consolidate some more or less secure feelings of self by young adulthood. There is apparently a built-in recovery process to antisocial behavior, although as adults, ex-delinquents may replay conflicts with their children.

Delinquent girls, being usually even more disturbed than boys, are less accessible to social system intervention alone. They are much more difficult to treat than boys even under optimum circumstances so their outlook in corrections is even less satisfactory.

Most adolescents have the urge from time to time to behave in a way that is sufficiently antisocial to get them into trouble if they are caught. Only when this happens is the label of deliquent behavior properly applied. Probably the most common form of antisocial activity in which adolescents engage nowadays is the illegal use of cigarettes, alcohol, and marijuana. These socially defined crimes are followed by theft. Offer (1969) reported that the middle-class teenagers he studied rated the control of antisocial tendencies as among the three most difficult problems faced by a teenager. During the psychosocial moratorium allowed by society (Erikson, 1959), the breaking of some rules is common, but theft, whether from parents, peers, or society-at-large, is not accepted, although petty pilfering may not be taken too seriously. The fact that many stores put up notices indicating to adolescents that if they are caught stealing, the police will be called, indicates that there is an assumption that this will not happen.

Delinquent behavior is socially defined, and what is classified as an offense in one culture may not be one in another. Even within social class and ethnic groups in one country, definitions of the word delinquent vary (Jersild, 1957). Nevertheless, the individual delinquent can be understood as an individual who is trying to obtain relief from tension, actual or potential, by gratifying his own wishes at the expense of others. An attack on family standards or the self is not generally looked upon as delinquent, and legally it is not so defined, although its etiology may be the same as the behavior that carries this definition. The attack is designed to reduce the tension produced by the stimulation of an internal conflict by external frustration. However, the individual, in addition, is gratified either by acquiring objects, as in a robbery, or by the excitement of avoiding capture or directing aggression at others.

Antisocial behavior may be abandoned because adolescents like the adult who is trying to be helpful. Sometimes adolescents behave appropriately because of fear of punishment, although this is rarer than is commonly supposed.

It is a judicial fantasy that deterrence is a significant aspect of crime prevention for those individuals who, either in general or while they are committing a crime, are full of their own omnipotence. Since adolescents, even those who are healthy, experience both excessive omnipotence and excessive helplessness, neither of which cancels out the other, most delinquents do not consider the serious possibility of being caught. An adolescent who has been a highly successful thief, and who finds that crime does pay, is satisfied by delinquent behavior and can only give it up when appropriate control is available. The problem is quite different from that of an individual with basically similar emotional difficulties who has not discovered that antisocial behavior can be gratifying. The delinquent has discovered that relieving intrapsychic tension can be pleasurable; the nondelinquent's symptomatology may, in and of itself, be troubling. The delinquent then needs more environmental control than the nondelinquent. Alternately, special parameters are needed in any possible psychotherapy, so that such a relationship will maintain intrapsychic equilibrium without the necessity for antisocial behavior.

The use of the judicial process to assess whether or not a crime has been committed is entirely justified.

The essential problem is that society, having refused to support a competent rehabilitative and correctional system for the young, thrashes around, being more and more neglectful and punitive in a sterile and unsatisfactory manner. The scandals of juvenile corrections are legion and nowadays are rarely reported. Most "cruel and unusual punishment" occurs in correctional settings. This tends to mean that well-meaning people, to avoid exposing young people to these places, become collusive with juvenile crime.

Judicial process, when an adolescent is found guilty, is an important technique of indicating to adolescents who have behaved in a way of which society disapproves, that what they did was not acceptable. Disapproval of an action should not mean being punitive or arbitrary, nor should it vitiate against empathy with the child's underlying difficulties. As with other symptom pictures, delinquents who are unsure of their identity may use a court appearance, and its consequences, as a label in an attempt to define a sense of self. The answer to "Who am I?" may be "I am a delinquent."

Delinquent behavior has biopsychosocial determinants and can be understood as being largely situational, intra-familial, or biopsychological within the personality. Whichever of these provides the principal source of stress for the individual provides a basis for a diagnostic classification of delinquency. This can make for a more rational treatment approach in that the weight of efforts to be helpful can be appropriately placed (Miller, 1965). Antisocial behavior must have consequences, and society is entitled to be protected from those who prey upon it. The processes of correction should not, however, teach adolescents to further dehumanize others, nor should it increase the technical skills of antisocial behavior.

SITUATIONAL DELINQUENCY

Situational delinquency has its major determining factors in the environment (Sutherland and Cressey, 1955). There are a number of these:

1. *In high delinquency subcultures in the larger cities, delinquent behavior conforms to the mores of the social system. This is not unlike the system that used to exist, as historically in certain tribes in India, the Dacoits*

for example, where antisocial behavior was accepted as a way of life. A state of cultural and social conflict, when old values are no longer wholly accepted and adolescents no longer get support from the implicit and explicit norms of society, produces this type of subculture. Theft may become part of the way of life of a social system; it is not rare in the average high school or in university dormitories; it is very common in army units with poor morale and in penal settings.

2. *The breakdown of the extended family and consequent alienation from adults and authority figures.*

3. *Rapid social change, for example, in newly developing countries, and the abandonment of emotional prejudices in older societies. This may mean that one way of dealing with aggression, the projection of hostility onto an out-group, is no longer possible. The attack is then made on individuals who technically belong to the same social group. Prejudicial behavior is in some societies labeled delinquent.*

4. *The most common cause of adolescent crime in the cities at the present time is probably drug dependence. A decade ago it was not unusual for a psychiatrist to see an early adolescent who was dependent on cigarette smoking steal in order to buy an increasing quantity of tobacco. The frequency of theft in association with the use of other drugs of abuse has considerably increased. Clinical evidence indicates that there is a correlation between drug dependence and the necessity to deal in drugs to finance the habit. This is as common with marijuana as with other drugs.*

Sometimes situational delinquency is related to society's promising objects and gratification, but failing to deliver; the implication of television advertising that goods are easy to obtain is an example of this.

Not all individuals who are exposed to situational pressures become delinquents, so it is unusual for these to be the sole cause of the behavior. The behavior of an individual adolescent is a function of a group process insofar as it affects the individual personality, but the strength of nuclear and extended family ties may protect young people from this. If the neighborhood adolescent code generally requires theft, it is not only the well adjusted who stay home; the most severely disturbed may also fail to join in the activity. Isolated, withdrawn adolescent boys may not take part in gang thefts because they cannot make contact with their peers.

Group contagion (Redl, 1955), when numbers of adolescents, impelled by a common conflict and similar situational pressures, act in an acutely antisocial way, is another determinant of situational delinquency. A riot arising during a political demonstration may involve otherwise law-abiding people who are affected by the situational pressure under which they find themselves.

For most situational delinquents, no special treatment is required, but individuals brought up in a delinquent subculture may have a personality structure society finds intolerable. If this happens, society applies pressure on these people to get them to accept the general view. Whether a subculture's way of life is labeled "delinquent" depends on the attitude of society-at-large. In some societies, notably the USSR, political deviants are considered delinquent and may be incarcerated as "mentally ill." But even in family units of people whom society would label "delinquent," some behavior is antisocial and perceived as psychologically disturbed.

> The nineteen-year-old daughter of a gangster was given a mink coat by her father for successfully lying to a Congressional Committee aout his whereabouts. He later referred her to a psychiatrist because she lied in an inveterate manner to him and her whole family. Although he controlled the local prostitutes, he could not tolerate his daughter's promiscuity.

Situational delinquency may occur in small social systems, especially boarding schools, correctional centers, and psychiatric hospitals. The sole responsibility for the behavior is often projected onto the adolescent group, and perjoratively labeled as delinquent because the authorities in the system cannot accept their role in the etiology of the behavior. A group of six patients on an adolescent psychiatric ward in a general hospital were noted one evening to have wantonly destroyed most of the furniture. The etiology of the episode was as follows:

> None of the physicians concerned with the group had interpreted to them their hostility. By confronting them only with their reality situation, they had reinforced the youngsters' anger with environmental staff. The furniture episode began because the staff stopped a sixteen-year-old boy from leaving the ward to obtain some stashed marijuana. He stirred up a group with conflicts similar to his own, and one of the male staff became frightened, and thus provocative. Another retreated to play checkers with some quiet patients. The boys began to throw books around, and the doctor on call came to the ward, stood, watched the episode, and said he didn't think it mattered, as no individual was being hurt.

With no external controls, more and more furniture was destroyed until the shift changed; the new shift stopped the episode with firm behavior. Some angry staff members tried to find a leader to scapegoat. The episode was, however, primarily a function of poor staff morale; the ward had been going through much social change. Thus, it was situational, although some of its etiology was related to the internal conflicts of individual members of the group. The episode would not have occurred in a more stable environment.

In most situational delinquency, scapegoats tend to be sought. A serious attempt is made to resolve these social system tensions which are significant determinants of the occurrence. To do this might perhaps mean that the power structure of the organization would have to accept its responsibilities and be ready to change.

INTRAFAMILIAL DELINQUENCY

Intrafamilial delinquency occurs when the significant determinant of an individual's antisocial behavior is conflict within the family. Its appearance depends on the balance between the psychosocial resilience of the individual and the emotional pressure that is experienced. The pressure may be applied in a variety of ways. An adolescent's antisocial behavior may be reinforced by his parents because it satisfies their unconscious needs (Szurek, 1942) and the behavior is then unconsciously provoked.

> A boy of fifteen was referred to a psychiatric hospital because he had destroyed a new housing development with a bulldozer. In discussing his son, the father got evident, if unconscious satisfaction out of the behavior. He then described how he, as a boy, used to enjoy putting sleepers across railway lines.

Sometimes parents are collusive, and a more direct reinforcement of delinquent behavior occurs when adolescents steal clothes, stereo equipment, and other goods, and their parents fail to notice the new acquisitions. A middle-stage adolescent boy may tell his parents that a collection of stolen goods have been acquired as the result of a successful gamble. Willingness to believe such a story is taken as permission to continue stealing. Parental collusion is commonly reinforced by society; it is very rare for a juvenile court magistrate to order stolen clothes returned, or the financial rewards of drug dealing and theft taken. Court social workers may be aware of expensive drug habits and never inquire seriously as to where the money is obtained.

Certain families are traditionally antisocial and have occupied this community role for generations.

> A fifteen-year-old boy was seen by a psychiatrist at a school for delinquent boys because the principal was concerned about the amount of illegality in which the boy had been involved prior to his admission. The boy was apparently well adjusted for his age and rather proudly indicated that he was doing what his father and brothers did. He gave a family history of antisocial behavior that went back for three generations.

Some families are so rigid that the structural organization of the family may be such that the individual is unable to play out at home the aggressive impulses that are aroused by family tensions. The children are forbidden to act out their conflicts when they are put under stress. Those families that do not allow young people to show their anger and despair fail to meet the developmental needs of their young. Thus, aggressive impulses will spill out into the larger community; if they are internalized, they produce a variety of individual stress responses. Help for an antisocial early adolescent who lives with his family is unlikely to be successful unless the family conflict is resolved. In the middle and late stage of adolescence, autonomy from the family is a reasonable goal, and once the adolescent has reached this maturational position, it must be accepted that the family is unlikely to change. The therapeutic issue for such young people is why they are so influenced by the behavior of their parents:

> A seventeen-year-old boy described how he had begun to break and enter houses when he was fourteen. He then stole electronic equipment from radio stores, became a dealer in drugs, and eventually developed a racket in which he persuaded his friends to steal Volkswagen cars that they then dismantled and sold. He was charming and a perpetual liar.
>
> He rationalized his behavior because he had to get away from his controlling and domineering mother who used tears as a weapon whenever he was untidy, late, verbally aggressive, or did poorly at school. It never occurred to him that he could have defied her in many socially acceptable ways, nor was he aware that his contempt for all girls was related to his maternal relationship.

This boy's passive-aggression was further justified by him because he was angry with his powerful intellectual father. This type of response is common in young people who have not attained emotional independence from their families. They are so dependent on their parents that to attempt to prove autonomy they become rebellious and defiant at best, at worst grossly antisocial.

PERSONALITY DELINQUENCY

Personality delinquency should be diagnosed when an individual, by reason of his personality structure, attempts to relieve or abort the psychic tension, produced by conscious and unconscious conflicts, by acting out his anxiety and rage on society. The personality may be so weak that the pain of frustration and anxiety cannot be tolerated. Impulse release and gratification are then sought, irrespective of the pain inflicted on others. This can occur in people who suffer from mental deficiency, a variety of neuroendo-crine and characterological illnesses. In these syndromes, the demands of reality produce greater tension than the personality can tolerate. Sometimes the resulting antisocial behavior is an attempt to gain environmental mastery when, because of growth, the family can no longer support and contain their child's tensions and no other outlets are available. This situation is typical of those with learning difficulties. Schools are often inadequate, and cannot assist such children, who deal with the helplessness of being unable to learn, prior to puberty, by having the excessive tension relieved by dependence on their parents and the consequent support they receive. After puberty, this is no longer tolerable and antisocial behavior becomes an available pseudo-solution.

In another type of personality delinquency, organic brain damage due to chemical toxicity or intercurrent physical illness is the cause; in another group, growth problems may produce transient misbehavior. Typically, in early adolescence, the personality may not be sufficiently mature to deal with the psychological upsurge of aggressive and sexual impulses; in angry or inappropriately sexual ways these spill over into the community (Winnicott, 1971).

Mood disorders are a common cause of delinquent behavior and this is particularly relevant in those who suffer from excessive rage as a response to frustration. Youngsters who suffer from a genetic vulnerability to manic-depressive illness, or depression, commonly have antisocial behavior as the presenting difficulty. The failure of the juvenile justice system to provide personnel to provide adequate diagnosis and treatment for these conditions means that a disproportionately large number of such youngsters are in correctional institutions, and then in adult prisons.

Acute emotional trauma is a common cause of personality delinquency. Typically, such a response may occur in a prepubertal child or an early adolescent following parental death or divorce. If mourning is not possible, owing either to the age or the emotional situation of the child, the anger at parental loss may appear as antisocial behavior. The request for punishment implicit in this may be an attempt to expiate guilt.

Personality delinquency falls into three main psychological syndromes any one of which may be present with biological vulnerability in the central nervous system.

1. *There may be a failure to develop an adequate conscience. The adolescent may feel entitled to behave in an antisocial way and temporarily abstains only for fear of the consequences. When the opportunity presents itself, the behavior occurs. Such an adolescent requires a prolonged and intensive period of help, which may have to be in some type of therapeutic setting.*

2. *There may be a transient psychological disturbance associated with an imbalance between the strength of the personality and the pressures put upon it by society or the conflicts of puberty. Auto theft is a typical example. Often boys who steal cars are unsure of their own masculinity and need to prove to others how powerful they are. If the lack of certainty is developmental, the chances of a boy becoming honest, whatever is done, clinically appear excellent.*

3. *Finally, personality delinquency may be due to feelings of profound deprivation of love and affection (Aichorn, 1935). This type of delinquency appears common among girls and is often associated with sexual promiscuity. These are symptoms of a failure of personality development, and recovery is unlikely without highly competent assistance.*

Whatever the cause of the behavior, what is actually done depends on the social system as well as psychological factors. Crimes can be understood as being committed against people and property and an understanding of the reason for the type of crime is as important as understanding the person who committed it.

THEFT

In Western countries, a common delinquent occurrence is theft. The preoccupation of society with property and the sense of the importance of material goods is great. In many such countries, the penalties for offenses against the person are often less than for those against property.

From an early age, children are taught that only some objects belong to them. The boundaries of acceptability are, however, blurred. Many consciences, both for children and their parents, are elastic. "Finders keepers, losers weepers," chant children in some parts of England, and stealing by finding is common. Many people are surprised if lost valuables are returned, implicitly recognizing that honesty is rare. Children deny that they have stolen some object by insisting that the article is borrowed and will be returned. The concept of diluting the significance of theft begins in childhood to avoid parental punishment. In adolescence, boys who steal scooters and automobiles to joy-ride, insist that their taking the vehicle was not really stealing, as they intended to return it.

> A sixteen-year-old boy who had hitchhiked to a resort area with some friends realized that they were short of some camping equipment that could only be obtained from a town thirty miles away. He stole an automobile that had no plates from a used-car lot; later he was picked up by the highway patrol. He said that he had every intention of returning the automobile. Although he understood that he had broken the law, he did not really feel that he had stolen anything.

Automobiles taken in this way are often returned to a place near their original location.

When a group, usually boys, steal small objects from a department store as part of a gang activity, it usually indicates an attempt to prove masculinity to one's peers. Dare-devil activity, which is defiant of adult standards, especially that which is relatively safe, is difficult in cities and small towns. Usually this type of theft will stop with a response that clearly demonstrates disapproval. There are two exceptions to this assumption: if the individual within a group that steals in this way has previously stolen from a mother's purse, the theft usually represents anger at emotional deprivation. Early-adolescent gang theft reinforces this solution to deprivation, so symptomatic treatment is usually of little help in itself. When a theft is highly successful and becomes one of a series, this convinces the youngster that crime does pay. In such situations, the youngster has little motivation for change and parental and societal disapproval will generally be ignored.

Theft that is solitary and occurs toward the end of early adolescence has different implications from that which has been present throughout childhood. A boy or girl at the end of early adolescence may be found to be stealing at school. If the staff register disapproval by reacting to the theft in their usual way, and the stealing persists, this may indicate more serious personality difficulties. Adolescent stealing from other children in school, or from teachers, is evidence of difficulty in developing a sense of self. This is particularly likely when the adolescent is always caught. The theft appears to be an attempt to establish a relationship with a stable extra-parental adult. These young people do very well, providing they are given the opportunity to gain such a relationship without theft as an intermediary. Such a relationship must often last for up to three years. When it is with a psychotherapist, the latter will often comment that his role is only to be interested. If such a relationship is terminated too soon, the adolescent will almost certainly return to theft. These adolescents, when treated by court social workers, are then seen regularly during episodes of stealing; as soon as these stop, the frequency of contact is reduced. If thefts are an attempt to obtain an adult relationship, such behavior reinforces antisocial rather than social behavior.

The often inadequate approach on the part of society to the treatment of theft is possible because most adolescents who engage in such activity spontaneously desist. Probably, of all caught delinquent acts, for every action taken by society, half the children will never reappear, at any rate, until the stage of institutionalization is reached. This applies to everything from warnings by policemen to probation with a court social worker. Good therapeutic settings for delinquent adolescents should have an 80 percent recovery rate; most have an 80 percent recidivist rate. This is more a measure of institutional inadequacy than of initial psychological disturbance in most of the adolescents.

The juvenile correctional system, depending on the severity of the problem behavior, is implicitly using the fashionable concept of "the least restrictive alternative" as a substitute for adequate diagnosis as to the cause of the difficulty. The problem is that very disturbed behavior does not necessarily indicate an equally disturbed personality, although this is not true when serious assaults are made on others. Relatively minor conflicts may be acted out with episodes which society takes very seriously, for example, repeated auto theft. On the other hand, quite trivial antisocial behavior may be the way a profound personality difficulty shows itself:

> Paul was seen by a psychiatrist because his teachers felt that his inability to hand in homework on time, although he came from an apparently happy home, might indicate some hidden difficulty. The boy told his psychiatrist that he spent a lot of time around the neighborhood stealing bicycles, joy-riding, and then abandoning them. It emerged that he was carrying a knife on these trips. Finally, it became clear that he was hunting a boy about two years younger than himself in order to stab him. Paul despised himself and he felt that if he found someone who represented that badness inside him, and his forbidden homosexual wishes, he would thus destroy his own bad self.

By the time adolescents are institutionalized, the failure to make an adequate diagnosis as to what the cause of the difficulty might be, along with rational recommendation as to what the institution ought to do, makes rehabilitation impossible. Correctional institutions thus become the entry to the adult penal system. The failure on the part of society to use up-to-date rehabilitative techniques is used to justify a clumsy punitive and coercive approach. Rehabilitation has not failed; it has never been properly tried.

Family attitudes have much to do with the development of a sense of possession. However, to appear comfortable about objects borrowed without permission is not just an adolescent attitude. Many people have little intra-familial sense of the importance to others within the group of their own property or of the hostility that is produced by taking objects without permission. In families in which the concept of personal ownership is well developed, the person whose possessions are taken without permission becomes enraged. Sometimes family groups, in particular, middle-class families, act inconsistently; at one time, it is acceptable to borrow without permission, at others, it is not. Those social-class groups whose poverty makes them live in great intimacy with each other may have either an intense sense of personal property or none at all. The concept of personal property is related to a need for privacy; people whose houses have been robbed often feel as if they had been personally violated.

Victims of offenses against property often have a role in its loss. The ambivalence of individuals toward personal possessions is shown by their failure to protect them. Automobiles are left unlocked with the key in the ignition; people go on vacation and forget to cancel newspapers; windows are left open in empty houses. This carelessness has multiple meanings: It may be associated with a disinclination to be envied by others or with guilt about possessing things in a poverty-stricken world. A disregard for the importance of objects may be present either because they have never been owned or because the individual has had so much that things mean nothing. Sometimes careless behavior is rationalized by alleging that objects are insured anyway. Adolescents who steal often offer the same justification: no individual will be hurt, since the organization is large and can afford it or the insurance company will pay.

PERSONALITY DEVELOPMENT AND THEFT

Children develop the concept of objects apart from themselves initially as they perceive themselves as separate from their mothers and then as they begin to recognize parts of their own body. Very early babies recognize the change in their mother's expression and imitate it. When mother is first perceived as a separate person, she is clearly felt as always available. Under stress, the howl of a six-month-old baby shows how enraged it feels at not having immediate succor and solace. The routine of living in a world in which mothers do not wait with bottle or breast poised to provide immediate satisfaction makes it possible for children to begin to learn to tolerate frustration. The awareness that the world is not automatically their oyster precedes the ability to recognize that some objects belong to others and that greed must be automatically contained.

Overanxious mothers, who cannot bear to hear their infants cry, paradoxically, in the need to contain their own anxieties, ignore the emotional needs of their children. The children are, in a sense, depersonalized and a situation is created in which they are not recognized as separate. Such children find it hard to learn to handle frustration, and difficult to accept that everything does not belong to them by right. They feel entitled to swallow the world. They may become compulsive thieves.

Human beings use objects both to comfort themselves and to meet essential needs. The pangs of frustration are appeased by infants using parts of their own bodies; early spontaneous thumb sucking, which may occur while babies are in the womb, becomes a learned response that occurs with a need for comfort. Children then amuse themselves by playing with their own toes and other parts of their bodies: boys discover their penis; girls may find the vaginal entrance. Some children suck the end of their blankets under stress; others are given soothers or pacifiers. All these are the first transitional objects (Winnicott, 1971) used as a substitute for mothering. Bright objects are visually offered infants as a distraction; mobiles are attached to baby carriages and cribs. Teddy bears are hugged when mother is not available. Food is used in some cultures to comfort children. In the north of England, when a child is hurt, it is commonly comforted with a "sweet" (candy).

From early infancy onward, an association develops in the child's mind between comfort, bright objects, cuddly toys, or food. Toys are also used to gain a feeling of mastery over the world. Children throw them out of their cribs to have them picked up and returned; thus, they take the first steps to dominate their environment, using objects that can disappear, be lost, and then magically return. The genesis of "theft" becomes clear.

The two-year-old with a strong sense of possession clings to toys, however they are acquired. When toys that belong to others are taken, adults take these away, reinforcing the child's concept that some things belong to him and others do not. It may also reinforce the idea in the vulnerable that the issue is not theft, but to be bigger, and better at it.

Children who are emotionally deprived may take money or food without permission, and one or both of these actions may be considered stealing by adults. Family feelings about this tend to be mixed. Some parents have no concern about children taking food from the refrigerator; others insist that the child always ask. Many parents make no fuss about the child picking up a dime that has been left lying about; some regard both of these actions very seriously and see them as wrong. The first object commonly stolen by children are other children's toys and food; money left lying about is picked up, initially because it is bright and shiny, later because parents spend money and children use it to identify with father and mother.

Stealing money that is left lying around may be an identification with parents; girls put it in their purse; boys wish to rattle it in their pockets. Money is then picked up to spend, which is different from money acquired as a squirrel takes nuts.

Money taken from a mother's purse or a father's wallet has a still different meaning. This is not just a theft, it is also messing about in the private possessions of a parent. The need to investigate mother's property, which may also include going into drawers and looking through closets, indicates both a preoccupation with mother's person and an aggressive involvement with her possessions. The comfortable development of a sense of property depends, in a child who is not otherwise deprived, on the parental reaction to theft. Amusement may imply that there is nothing wrong with the action. Punitive overanxiety may make a child overanxious. If money is taken to shop "just like Daddy," punishment may also mean that it is forbidden to want to be like father. If a theft is an angry act designed to spite parents and if the latter react with spite, the message is that the fault is to be weak.

The feelings of chronic deprivation associated with chronic illness may be relieved by objects.

> *When I was sick and lay abed,*
> *I had two pillows at my head,*
> *And all my toys around me lay,*
> *To keep me happy through the day.*
> (*R. L. Stevenson*)

The same applies to those who suffer from emotional deprivation due to isolation from other children or parental absence or loss. The collection of small items is a reaction to such deprivation: a "squirreling" or "thieving magpie" syndrome. Children from underprivileged families may steal many small items from other children in school. In deprived neighborhoods, children of eight or nine are principal shoplifters from stores and supermarkets.

An outbreak of shoplifting may be a reaction to an acute stress. Its success may ultimately reinforce the infantile longings that led to the outbreak; if it continues over a long period of time, it becomes difficult to convince adolescents that crime does not pay, because they feel that it does.

The difference between stealing at home on one or two occasions and chronic, long-term theft has greater significance than simply that they are socially different acts. It would be simple if the former could be looked on as more normative, the latter more disturbed. But an adolescent who becomes a chronic thief is not necessarily severely psychologically disturbed, but rather a distortion of personality development is ultimately created. This is likely to be reinforced if chronic drug abuse is also present, nowadays a common combination.

> Larry was a big seventeen-year-old boy who was charged with homicide after he and another boy had beaten up a youngster who later died. Larry had continued to hit the boy after he was clearly not able to defend himself and he justified this with the very concrete statement that the dead boy had insulted him. His attitude toward insults from others was that if the person did not stop, they should be hit, an attitude typical of his father who had beaten Larry as a child for exactly that reason. Larry never appeared to worry over the consequences of his own behavior. He was social only insofar as he believed that one should not behave in an antisocial way if one was likely to be caught and punished. He had little or no sense of the future and little or no capacity for empathy under stress. Yet, on psychological tests, his I.Q. was 110; he was able from time to time to be caring for others.

At the age of twelve, he had become a chronic abuser of marijuana, using at least five joints daily by the time he was sixteen. He was a successful thief and made, he said, about $20,000 a year stealing from apartments. He spent the money buying drugs and plastic models and refurbishing his beat-up automobile. Insofar as his failure to develop formal thinking, his inability to perceive the consequences of his own impulsive actions, his limited capacity for empathy, and his poor sense of the future were concerned, Larry, maturationally, was an early adolescent. He was of course being tried in an adult court.

The severity of the symptom is not necessarily an arbiter of the severity of the emotional maladjustment. Theft, apart from the quality of the actual act, may have many meanings and is the final common path of a variety of internal conflicts. Sometimes it occurs because it has become acceptable to the personality as a way of acquiring goods; it is then "ego-syntonic." Sometimes it may be the result of a conflict with authority in which the latter is felt as persecutory. Antisocial behavior is then thought to be justified.

A fifteen-year-old high school boy was very fond of his math teacher, a woman of about twenty-eight. She had collected funds for a school outing and had left the money in her desk. John felt that she had marked him unfairly in a test and had been overly critical of him. He stole a large part of the money, did not spend it, but took it home and put it in a drawer. One week later, he confessed to the school social worker.

Just as with other adolescent misbehavior, the act of stealing may carry an implied request for help. Theft in school often represents a seeking of help with a conflict at home. Guilt-ridden adolescents may steal in such a way that they will be caught; their goal is to be punished and perhaps rescued.

Kenneth, age fourteen, began to steal from other children at school following the death of his father in a car accident. He obviously made no real effort not to be caught, and only the ineptitude of the system allowed him to get away with so much for so long. When he was apprehended, his immediate question was whether he could be tried as an adult, and if he would be sent to the state prison.

Until the advent of the drug scene, such stealing was very evident. Today, adolescents may replace contact with adults with the regressive experience of drugs. There are three main psychological causes for theft: a failure to develop an adequate conscience; a transient psychological disturbance because of societal or pubertal conflicts; and feelings of profound deprivation of love and affection. These are discussed, as psychological syndromes, on p. 416.

THE ADOLESCENT RUNAWAY

A typical symptom of adolescent and sometimes child disturbance in the United States is running away from home, but this type of behavior is less common among adolescents in other countries. The etiology of this symptom, which is clearly culturally determined, is the conflict between dependence and emancipation, and it is socially reinforced in a variety of ways; novels and movies glorify runaways, houses that are set up to shelter runaway adolescents often may unwittingly encourage the activity. Historically, running away seems to be related to the concept of the open frontier, but the mobility of the nuclear family in which all special roots are left behind is, to an extent, mimicked by adolescents. The fact that parents are often the only available adults to adolescents arouses intense conflict over dependent feelings that have to be denied. Physical withdrawal is a common way of trying to prove that parenting is not needed. Drug-related and promiscuous behavior is common among runaway adolescents. Thus they deal with conflicts about dependence that are enhanced by the stress of isolation of the nuclear family by a regressive dependent experience.

Often when adolescents have run away they leave a trail that clearly indicates where they have gone. Unfortunately, adults are not as perceptive and omnipotent as the runaway unconsciously wishes them to be. Sometimes young adults or other adolescents sexually exploit the runaway. Because of the intense wish for dependence of runaway adolescents, they are particularly vulnerable to this type of exploitation, as they seek the reassurance of physical contact.

Like all other syndromes of adolescence, there are a multiplicity of personality difficulties behind an episode of running away. Furthermore, some adolescents who are legally described as runaways have gone to stay at the house of a friend; they run to extra-familial support rather than away from the parental home. As with many other delinquent symptoms (Johnson, 1955), running away is often unconsciously encouraged by parents. So, some run away because their angry parents tell them to "get out of the house" or, in more subtle ways, may convey to their offspring that they are a nuisance and not wanted. The threat to run away may be a request to parents to be reassured that the child is loved. This is common among small children who then may be provocatively told by father or mother "to pack-up and go." There is little sadder than the sight of the seven-year-old who trudges up the street waiting for father or mother to call him or her back. Worse, the child may be humiliated enough to return without this. This parental behavior can be the genesis of serious emotional withdrawal from the family in adolescence, if not actual run away behavior.

The more disturbed the adolescent, the further he or she is likely to go. Some move thousands of miles from home. In the late summer, certain towns and areas of the country seem to act as magnets for runaway adolescents, and numerous centers have properly been created to help these young people. The usual goal is to provide help in the crisis and return the adolescents to their home base for further help.

In dealing with runaway adolescents, the maturational age of the individual is always significant. Early adolescents need to understand that their behavior is inappropriate and a failure to take them to task for this self-destructive and antisocial behavior is an insult to a developing sense of autonomy. To be only empathic may be to infantilize them.

At the beginning of the middle stage of adolescence, running away may be related to anxiety about testing out new biological roles. A failure of identity formation is associated with a feeling of bored emptiness, and the excitement of running away at this stage provides a special feeling of being alive. In middle-stage adolescents, who may appear with a pseudomaturity due, in particular, to early sexuality, the temptation is often to agree that these young people should live away from home.

As a general rule there should not be an agreement on the part of therapeutic or legal authorities that the child has bad parents, and bargaining about a return home is not helpful. The implication of reinforcing poor contact with parents may be to destroy the possibility of a good adult relationship with parents when the adolescents are older. Such reinforcement should only be done if, after an adequate assessment, it is clear that family relationships are damaged beyond a reasonable chance of repair. Parents who sexually or physically abuse their child are a clear example of this.

TREATMENT TECHNIQUES—PUNISHMENT AND CONTROL

The problem with any type of antisocial activity is to reject the behavior without rejecting the individual. Apart from the importance of an adolescent not enjoying the fruits of ill-gotten gains, a treatment principle that is often ignored is the necessity to make reparation. All antisocial behavior should have consequences that are rational and aimed to protect the youngster from the developmental distortions that occur because of such behavior; at the same time, society needs to be protected. The latter is quite consonant with the former, and positive societal needs should not be considered as antithetical to the growth and development of the young. When behavior is controlled, the adolescent may feel punished, but this is not the same as the non-parental adult deliberately inflicting punishment.

Punishment, however, is valuable in family situations because it is a way in which parents demonstrate to their child that they can love and hate at the same time. It is rarely necessary to control intra-familial antisocial behavior. It allows parents to relieve feelings of anger and frustration; it is an important way of showing a boy or girl that they are not emotionally helpless and can influence their parents' feelings. Parental punishment may convey to an adolescent boy that he is seen as manly and tough.

The reasons for parental punishment may become blurred; sometimes in punishing their children, parents punish the bad part of themselves. Antisocial behavior is more often a request for external control than for punishment. An adolescent may have made no real effort not to be caught, yet when confronted he tells a series of blatant lies. A boy may steal because he feels his parents are giving him more responsibility than he can handle.

Punishment applied by loving parents has a deterrant as well as a controlling function. This certainly seems to be the case in emotionally healthy people, although if parental responses do not control the unacceptable behavior of their children, the punitive repetition of inadequate actions by parents is likely to produce emotionally immature adults. Children identify with such parental attitudes; they either become self-punitive or punish others, beating themselves as their parents did or behaving toward others as their parents behaved.

Punishment that may be reasonable within a family has no value when applied by society in the treatment of delinquents as a technique of revenge (Menninger, 1969). It is sometimes used instead of necessary external controls; it may be a substitute for reparation, and is related to a fantasy of deterrence. Punishment applied to adolescents by adults who do not love them is valueless. Such behavior deters only those people whose reality testing is good, and these individuals rarely appear in the courts of law. Reparation and control are adequate manifestations of society's disapproval.

The treatment of adolescents who engage in antisocial behavior requires the containment of symptoms. Adolescents need not be institutionalized in the service of rehabilitation or diagnosis unless the adolescent is a danger to himself or others, cannot be adequately contained while the diagnostic and therapeutic process is under way, or is getting so much emotional or reality gain from antisocial behavior that no motivation to change is possible. Drug and alcohol abuse that cannot be abandoned is a further indication for institutional placement, as it interferes, at best, with the adolescent capacity to form relationships. If this cannot be done, control of behavior is almost impossible, as is diagnosis. Large institutions are almost always unable to meet the cognitive, imaginative, creative, physical, and vocational needs of the young people in their charge. Inevitably they institutionalize and create an "emotional deficiency disease," on the one hand, and a string of institutional reactions, on the other. Small institutions can, of course, be similarly destructive. In 1982 in Idaho, up to eight adolescents waiting court appearance were kept perhaps for weeks in an isolated area of a county jail without education, adult supervision, privacy, adequate reading materials, and exercise facilities other than a small yard. The last meal of the day was at 4:00 P.M. and no canteen was available. In the State of New York, in 1978, adolescents in remand on Rikers Island were watched by guards, floated food on the toilet to keep it cool, had no underclothes, and were not allowed outside for exercise from 4:00 P.M. on Friday until 9:00 A.M. on Monday. Highly disturbed personalities with a distorted capacity for giving and receiving affection and with a tenuous control of aggressive impulses are thus created. Such individuals, unable to adjust in the community-at-large, enter a vicious cycle of antisocial behavior, repression, and further antisocial behavior.

Adolescents who are dangerous require treatment in sophisticated settings that are aware of emotional needs and that do not institutionalize. Those who are not dangerous, if they cannot live at home, require either good boarding school placement, group homes, or excellent vocational training centers. Psychotherapy may be a necessary adjunct to treatment in either situation, but its type and quality need to be properly prescribed; therapy prescribed in any other way is likely to be valueless. Vocational training is essential. Without the capacity to be productive in a socially valued way, the development of identity is not possible (Miller, 1966).

When young people lack imaginative and creative outlets and when they are alienated from their own productive capacity, they are likely to become more destructive and rebellious. The angry frustration that is so commonly created with underprivileged youth may lead to delinquent activity. This situation is so chronic that it is now hardly a subject for comment, except where there is a variation in its incidence. The help offered such youngsters in penal settings parodies their earlier experience. A constant shifting of human relationships, activities that offer them hardly any outlet for their imaginative and creative abilities, and dull, ugly, sterile surroundings means that there is little chance that efforts can be made to help them get in touch with themselves and become more responsive, responsible citizens. After attempting to be understanding, but not sufficiently imaginative to offer such young people appropriate help, society becomes repressive. The foundation for rebellious antisocial activity is laid down long before the act takes place. Repressive inhibition, without a change in the causes of the discontent, merely means that the next bout is likely to be more destructive.

More than any other syndrome, delinquency demonstrates the particular problems for the adults who are trying to help adolescents. Attempts to be useful, because they often arouse the primitive emotional greed of disturbed and delinquent adolescents, are likely to be met with manipulative compliance, sullen hostility, or withdrawal. The helping adult must not only bear the frustration his client may inflict upon him, he must tolerate, as has the adolescent, the frustration of living in a world in which individual integrity is often not respected. Sometimes parents cannot see a problem, but little can be done for younger adolescents without their parents' cooperation. Sometimes adolescents do not appear for help until their parents have lost all control over the situation.

It is difficult for the therapist to compete with the short-term gratification that adolescents who are "into sex, drugs, or delinquency," can obtain. Such adolescents are tempted to fly from the treatment situation because therapy does not offer magic and no one contains them in the therapeutic situation.

In the therapy of delinquent adolescents, after a competent diagnostic assessment of the biopsychosociological etiology of the behavior, a certain basic initial stance is necessary to make psychotherapy possible, especially with those who have serious personality difficulties.

1. *The therapist must not allow himself to be corrupted in the eyes of the patient. The patient attempts to do this by getting the therapist to collude in an unwilling way in antisocial behavior.*

   An eighteen-year-old boy, in a burst of honesty, told his doctor that he had on him many packs of cigarettes that he had stolen from a local supermarket. He told his doctor that he intended to sell them at 25¢ each to some of the doctor's other patients. The psychiatrist made interpretations about the patient's aggression, but did not insist that the stolen goods be returned. Thus, in his behavior, the therapist became an accessory after the fact.

2. *Delinquent, problem-adolescents tell a therapist part of the truth to fob off investigation into the depth of their antisocial activity. If the therapist accepts a part truth, the patient feels only contempt and acting up increases because of enhanced anxiety.*

   A group of adolescent boys on a psychiatric ward were about to go on a camping trip. They were tense and restless and the staff felt there was something wrong. However, nothing was done and the boys left for camp. The first day there they were obviously smoking marijuana and the staff confiscated a "hit" of marijuana. They accepted the boys' statement that there was no more. The staff called one of the ward therapists who accepted this statement. The boys continued to behave in a disturbed way, and two days later a large cache of the drug was discovered.

3. *Communication with the therapist about delinquent activity commonly takes place with action rather than words. A failure to perceive the significance of the communication means that therapy flounders. The reverse, with appropriate counter action, may assist growth.*

A seventeen-year-old English boy, on parole from a school for delinquent boys on condition he had psychotherapy, appeared for his third session dressed in a magnificent red velvet-lined black cloak. He was known to be jobless. After a short time, the therapist asked him when the "rip off" had taken place. The boy reddened and described how he had robbed a well-known department store. There was a long discussion about what a poor crook the boy was. The therapist regretted that he could not agree to join the boy in his actions because he had too much to lose and the boy was not a good enough criminal. At this, the boy boasted of his numerous delinquencies about which the therapist was scornful. Finally, he told the boy that if the therapy was to continue the boy would have to return the cloak to the local police station.

The boy continued to come for his therapy, in many ways he acted out his conflicts but he remained out of trouble and ultimately abandoned his delinquent stance.

4. *The therapist has to reinforce the patient's narcissism and to some extent the instinctual gratification obtained by the delinquent act has to be possible in the therapeutic session. The therapist should not be judgmental in a stereotyped way and should accept the communications of his patient and understand them. The therapist, thus, has to be interested, involved, non-judgmental, but not collusive.*

5. *Providing the patient is not acting destructively, the therapist should look on all communications as significant and need not be preoccupied with whether the patient is telling the truth or not; a lie is an interpretable communication.*

6. *Non-medical therapists need to be aware of the patterns of behavior that are typical of brain dysfunction, whether neuroendocrine or organic. Without adequate psychopharmacological treatment, when it is indicated, other therapy is almost possible.*

7. *The stage of personality development of the adolescent needs to be recognized and understood. Early adolescents are not the same as late adolescents; the issue is maturational as well as chronological age.*

8. *The educational ability and cognitive capacity of the youngster must be recognized, along with the developmental capacity to have a sense of time and to be empathic. Learning disabilities need adequate diagnosis and treatment. Adequate physical care is important, including physical assessment.*

These approaches make adequate diagnosis and treatment possible. The adolescent feels cared about and can then begin to perceive the therapist as an extension of himself. Personality strengths are reinforced and sometimes therapeutic work with the underlying conflicts is possible. On other occasions, the adolescent makes a firm identification with his therapist and either sustains himself thereafter, or returns to therapy as a young adult.

Society rarely provides helpful resources for the adequate treatment of disturbed delinquents. So, too, there is a temptation for helping adults to give up in despair. Many start to treat delinquents, but give up because they feel the adolescent will not use the therapist's knowledge or skill. The treatment of these young people requires that therapists should be able to tolerate their own helplessness and be sufficiently in touch with their own inner delinquency so that they can see that which exists in their patient.

With all the difficulties of this period of life, adolescence provides the optimum time for therapeutic intervention. When the social systems of society value the integrity of the youth, the prognosis for the resolution of disturbances and the enhancement of maturation becomes excellent.

REFERENCES

Aichorn, A. (1935), *Wayward Youth*. New York: Vantage Press.

Erikson, E. H. (1959), Identity and the Life Cycle. *Biol. Issues,* 1: 1–171.

Jersild, A. T. (1957), *The Psychology of Adolescence*. New York: Macmillan.

Johnson, A. M. (1955), Sanctions for super-ego lacunae in adolescents. In *Searchlights on Delinquency,* ed. K. R. Eissler, 225–245. New York: International Universities Press.

Menninger, K. A. (1969), *The Crime of Punishment*. New York: Viking.

Miller, D. (1965), *Growth to Freedom, The Psycho-Social Treatment of Delinquent Youth*. Bloomington: Indiana University Press.

——, (1966), A model of an institution for treating delinquent adolescent boys. In *Changing Concepts of Crime and Its Treatment,* ed. H. Klare, 97–117. Oxford: Pergamon Press.

Offer, D. (1969), *The Psychological World of the Teenager*. New York: Basic Books.

Redl, F. (1955), The phenomena of contagion and shock effect in group therapy. In *Searchlights on Delinquency,* ed. K. R. Eissler, 315–329, New York: International Universities Press.

Sutherland, E. H., and Cressey, R. (1955), *Principles of Criminology*. Philadelphia: Lippincott.

Szurek, S. (1942), Genesis of psychopathic personality traits. *Psychiatry,* 5: 1–15.

Winnicott, D. W. (1971), Adolescence, struggling through the doldrums. In *Adolescent Psychiatry*, eds. S. C. Feinstein, A. Miller, and P. Giovacchini, 48–59. New York: Basic Books.

Index